THE CLASS OF '74

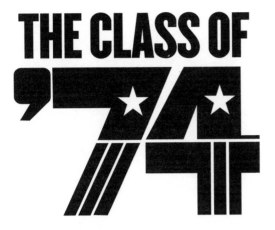

THE CLASS OF '74

CONGRESS AFTER WATERGATE AND THE ROOTS OF PARTISANSHIP

JOHN A. LAWRENCE

JOHNS HOPKINS

UNIVERSITY PRESS

Baltimore

Johns Hopkins University Press

2715 North Charles Street

Baltimore, Maryland 21218-4363

www.press.jhu.edu

Library of Congress Cataloging-in-Publication Data

Names: Lawrence, John A., 1949– author.

Title: The class of '74 : Congress after Watergate and the roots of partisanship / John A. Lawrence.

Description: Baltimore : Johns Hopkins University Press, 2018. | Includes bibliographical references and index.

Identifiers: LCCN 2017022924| ISBN 9781421424699 (hardcover : alk. paper) | ISBN 9781421424705 (electronic) | ISBN 142142469X (hardcover : alk. paper) | ISBN 1421424703 (electronic)

Subjects: LCSH: United States. Congress (94th : 1977-1979) | United States—Politics and government—1977–1981.

Classification: LCC JK1059 94th .L39 2018 | DDC 328.7309/047—dc23

LC record available at https://lccn.loc.gov/2017022924

A catalog record for this book is available from the British Library.

Special discounts are available for bulk purchases of this book. For more information, please contact Special Sales at 410-516-6936 or specialsales@press.jhu.edu.

Johns Hopkins University Press uses environmentally friendly book materials, including recycled text paper that is composed of at least 30 percent post-consumer waste, whenever possible.

*To the members of the
House Class of 1974, whose
service provided the story line of
this book and whose generous
participation enabled me to
write it. I am grateful to them
and to the congressional staff,
journalists, and others who have
trusted me with their recollections
of campaigns and service in the
House of Representatives.*

CONTENTS

Illustrations appear following page 146

PREFACE

his book is the outgrowth not only of extensive research but also nearly four decades of service on the staffs of two extraordinary members of the US House of Representatives: Rep. George Miller of California, for whom I worked for 30 years as chief of staff and staff director of two committees, and Speaker Nancy Pelosi, whom I served as chief of staff for eight years. After leaving Capitol Hill, I entered an academic track that had been interrupted following graduate school in the mid-1970s, teaching at the University of California's Washington Center with the goal of providing students with a pragmatic understanding of the history and operations of the Congress.

I also was interested in combining my Hill experience and perspective as a history PhD to write about what often seems an unwieldy and chaotic institution (as it sometimes is). The Class of 1974 presented an unusually rich topic for study. Although this large cohort of freshmen legislators was much scrutinized and analyzed upon its arrival on Capitol Hill, inadequate scholarly attention has been paid to its contribution to the democratization of the House and the promotion of critical legislation. Too often, the members of the Class have been collectively labeled the "Watergate Babies," a moniker that both trivializes their significance and overlooks the remarkable diversity of their backgrounds, outlooks, and actions. One trait, however, largely unified them: this was a group of politicians who came to Washington not simply to occupy seats in Congress but to change the world, and they believed they could.

I began the four-year-long process that led to this book by immersing myself in the scholarly literature on Congress in the mid-1970s, including important work by Burdett Loomis, Julian Zelizer, Norman Ornstein, and David Rohde, among others. I examined contemporaneous accounts of journalists who tracked the successes and failures of the 94th Congress, and I studied the debates on the key issues that consumed the floor.

Most uniquely, I was able to conduct extensive interviews with nearly 40 members of the Class—Democrats and Republicans—concerning their congressional careers, as well as with other members, staff, reporters, and other Washington insiders. Because I arrived as a House staff member contemporaneously with the Class, I had known many of them over the years and had formed working relationships characterized by trust and mutual respect. Although in some cases decades had passed since we had been in touch, these long-standing relationships afforded me the unique opportunity to elicit their recollections and analyses of the experience of running for and serving in Congress at so crucial a time in the history of both the nation and that institution. Few Class members had written about their time in Washington; many professed incredulity that anyone would still be interested in their recollections, which were invaluable in enriching the story of those turbulent years and how they helped shape our contemporary political environment.

Most statements attributed to interviewees have appropriate citations. However, in some cases, frank statements were made with the understanding of anonymity, and, in those cases, no reference is provided. Audio files and handwritten notes of these interviews have been deposited in my papers in the Library of Congress and will be available to researchers in the future.

Lastly, this book focuses almost exclusively on the House of Representatives. This singular focus is not due to my bias toward the house in which I worked, but rather because most of the significant change during the 94th Congress occurred in the House. The biennial revision of House rules, as opposed to the continuing rules of the Senate, provided far greater opportunity for a sizeable incoming class, along with veteran reformers, to effectuate significant modernization and democratization. There were important reforms in the Senate as well, in particular modifications to the filibuster rules—but, for that account, readers must look to other sources.

ACKNOWLEDGMENTS

I deeply appreciate the unwavering intellectual and personal encouragement of my wife, Professor Deborah Phillips of Georgetown University, who has been an enthusiastic supporter of this project, of my own long service as a House staff person, and of my belated admission to the ranks of productive historians.

In addition, I wish to thank members of the community of congressional scholars, which has welcomed me into its ranks and has encouraged my efforts, including this book. In particular, Professors Julian Zelizer of Princeton University and Frances Lee of the University of Maryland have provided invaluable assistance, as have Matt Dallek of George Washington University, James Grossman of the American Historical Association, and Helen Shapiro of the University of California.

I also want to thank my agent, Lauren Sharp of Aevitas Creative, who was an invaluable source of guidance and advice along the way, and my editor at Johns Hopkins University Press, Elizabeth Demers, and her staff. In addition, I appreciate the careful attention to editing provided by Carrie Watterson, as well as the assistance of the Office of the House Archivist and the Prints and Photographs Division of the Library of Congress. Thanks also to the librarians at the Library who assisted me at desk 221 of the magnificent Main Reading Room.

For their invaluable early guidance of me as a scholar, I want to thank my dissertation advisor, Leon Litwack of Berkeley, and posthumously, my undergraduate mentor who remarkably saw promise in my potential as an historian, Geoffrey Blodgett of Oberlin College.

THE CLASS OF '74

INTRODUCTION
WE CAME HERE TO TAKE THE BASTILLE

> Don't try to go too fast. Learn your job. Don't ever talk until you know what you're talking about. If you want to get along, go along. Any jackass can kick a barn down, but it takes a carpenter to build it.—Speaker Sam Rayburn (D-TX)

> We were a conquering army. We came here to take the Bastille. We destroyed the institution by turning the lights on.—Rep. George Miller (D-CA)

It was January 1975, and in the chamber of the US House of Representatives Congressman William A. Barrett's world was about to rudely change. As he sat reading memos on the upcoming vote on the Rules package and staff drafts of responses to constituent inquiries, Barrett was beginning his 15th term in the House. The newly elected Democratic members—76 in all—had provided the key votes to effectuate a slew of significant changes to caucus rules reducing the power of autocratic, conservative chairmen who for years had thwarted the efforts of reformers. Like most of the more senior members, Barrett likely could not recognize the faces of most of those who had just taken their oaths as members of Congress.

As was usual, few members were on the floor as the House prepared for its daily session that January day. They were outnumbered by House pages, high school juniors selected for six-month placements to run errands, deliver papers, and cater to the whims of the legislators. The pages had been a ubiquitous presence in the chamber for nearly two centuries.

Barrett was used to being treated with considerable deference. At 78 years old, he was beginning his 29th year as a member of the House, occupying a seat he had first won in 1944 but had lost in the Republican resurgence of 1946 that gave the GOP control of the chamber for the first time in 14 years. Two years later, he regained his seat and had successfully held it through 12 subsequent elections. Gathering up some of his papers, Barrett hailed one of the boyish-faced youngsters with a mop of long brown hair, clad in the unmistakable uniform—dark blue suit, white shirt and tie—of a House page.

"Here," Barrett instructed, as he had hundreds of times to pages, barely looking up from the work before him. "Take these papers to my office."

"Go fuck yourself!" the young man replied flippantly. "Take them yourself!"

Barrett was dumbfounded, unable even to ask the young man to repeat himself. In his three decades in Congress, *no one* had spoken to him in such a manner, and certainly not a 17-year-old page! He thought he must have misunderstood the young man's response. Reaching under the leather seat, he pressed the buzzer that rang in the Democratic cloakroom behind the chamber, an L-shaped room filled with wooden phone booths, chairs and couches, and a small lunch counter. Members socialized in the cloakroom between votes, reading newspapers, catching a quick nap, or watching television amid the strong odor of grilling hot dogs.

Barrett's buzzing summoned the cloakroom superintendent, Donn Anderson, an instantly recognizable Hill denizen with his old-fashioned handlebar mustache and gold watch chain drooped across his belly. He rushed to the astonished congressman's chair in the chamber. The young man stood by, unperturbed.

"This *page* just told me to go *fuck* myself!" Barrett sputtered indignantly.

Anderson stared aghast back and forth between the young man and the senior congressman, and chose his words carefully. "Mr. Barrett," he stammered, "this 'page' is your new colleague, Thomas Downey, from New York."

Downey, who had not even been born until Barrett's second term in Congress, later admitted that he had entered the House only a few weeks earlier with "a certain amount of arrogance," so he wasn't entirely surprised it had gotten him into an uncomfortable situation so soon.[1] He quickly apologized to the still-stunned Barrett and offered to take the papers across the street to the senior member's office. Regaining his composure, Barrett declined, but the incident symbolized the divide between senior legislators and the new generation of legislators who had just arrived in Washington: assertively independent, skeptical of governmental institutions and their leaders, and determined to modernize, democratize, and energize the House of Representatives.

The November 1974 congressional election resulted in one of the largest infusions of new faces into the House of Representatives in modern political history, a far greater sweep of seats for Democrats than many pundits had anticipated. On January 3, 1975, 93 men and women became new members of the 94th Congress, 76 of them Democrats, of whom 49 replaced Republican incumbents who, in several cases, had defeated the very same Democrat only two years earlier.[2]

The 94th was the first Congress since the Watergate scandal had overwhelmed American politics, the House and Senate investigations of White House wrongdoing, the resignation of President Richard Nixon, and his controversial pardon by the unelected new president, Gerald Ford, a longtime House veteran. It was also the first election that fully reflected the impact of the recent redrawing of congressional districts mandated by the Constitution after each decennial census. Many of the redesigned House districts reflected the impact of the 1965 Voting Rights Act, adding millions of African Americans who previously had been excluded from voting and changing the demographics of dozens of districts, particularly in the South. The unanticipated victories boosted the Democratic domination of the chamber to postwar highs, fueling expectations of sweeping legislative successes and the ability to regularly override the frequent vetoes of President Ford.

The interchange between William Barrett and Tom Downey captured in a microcosm the awkward adjustment required of many officeholders in a new post-Watergate era. It was, as political scientist Burdett Loomis has said, a "break point in American politics."[3] For as long as anyone could remember, junior members were expected to accede to the accumulated wisdom and experience of more senior members. "Don't try to go too fast," legendary Speaker Sam Rayburn cautioned incoming members anxious to promote their personal agendas. "Learn your job. Don't ever talk until you know what you're talking about." The key to a long and successful career in the House, the Speaker advised, was deference to your seniors. "If you want to get along," he famously counseled, "go along."

"Getting along" and "going along" meant rarely speaking in caucus or committee meetings or during debate on the House floor, and even less rarely offering amendments. It was the rare newcomer who had the opportunity to see a bill he had authored taken up for consideration, and even more extraordinary for a novice to manage a bill on the House floor.

While this pre-reform House is often recalled as an efficient, productive body, in fact, the House had long been a secretive, hierarchical, conservative, tradition-bound institution that gave little regard to newcomers until they had been reelected once. Power was concentrated so assiduously in the handful of committee chairs that even the elected leadership hesitated to challenge one of the old men with a gavel in his hand. When Rules Committee Chairman Howard Smith of Virginia refused to consider civil rights legislation reported from the Judiciary Committee, neither the chairman nor the Speaker could force their bill past the crusty old segregationist for years.

From the early years of flight to the dawning of the space age, through two world wars, Korea, and a host of more minor military excursions, through the Roaring Twenties, the Great Depression and the summer of love in 1967, through the eras of flappers, auto fins, and acidheads, from the dour Woodrow Wilson through the charismatic John Kennedy—the House lumbered along in its top-heavy, anachronistic style, incapable of competing with an executive branch that was increasingly agile and expansive, well suited to modern mass communications, and aggregating power by virtue of its ability to act decisively.

That model changed in the 1970s, along with many core aspects of American society. "We were the first class" that demanded broad reform and empowered more junior members, Phil Sharp of Pennsylvania later reflected, "and now the whole place" does. The story, however, is more complex. In actuality, the Class of 1974 was not the only group of freshmen to chaff at the hidebound nature of the House, which was dominated by southern Democratic conservatives. Nor was it the first to demand substantial internal reforms. But the 1974 Class may have been the first to include such a large proportion of non-deferential freshmen from virtually every region of the country. The reform movement they represented changed the Congress and the country permanently, and it could not have happened without them.

Overwhelmingly, the newcomers were progressive, male, white, and ambitious. Many, with their youthful appearance, long hair, and informal attire, drew "blank stares from usually knowing guards." One mortified Capitol Hill policeman sheepishly admitted he had ordered a freshman off a "members' only" elevator.[4] From the moment they arrived in Washington, they were collectively labeled the "Watergate Babies," a sobriquet suggesting immaturity and self-centeredness that few appreciated (and that I will avoid using in this account).

Indeed, many accounts have portrayed the Class of 1974 as uniformly brash, politically inexperienced, and filled with a "determination to re-form government," which they perceived as "ossified, beholden to power-ful interests, unresponsive to the people and ripe for the taking."[5] And it is true that many of the 93 freshmen represented a new breed of politician: born of an age of political turbulence, hardened by political struggles, willing—even eager—to challenge authority, and devoted to pursuing new policy objectives.

This was not, however, just another group of the post–World War II House liberal reformers who had struggled against a stultifying, obdu-rate institutional structure. Members of the Class believed that if they were able to make the institution and its procedures more transparent to the public, the House and American politics would change forever. "We were a conquering army," recalled George Miller of California, who had been elected at the age of 29 after serving for five years as a staff aide for the California Senate majority leader. "We came here to take the Bastille. We destroyed the institution by turning the lights on."[6]

Unlike earlier reformers who had entered the House fresh from fight-ing World War II, many members of the Class of 1974 had been forged by battles on campuses and in the streets of their districts, enlisting as sol-diers in the civil rights and student movements, the struggle for women's equality, Vietnam war protests, and the growing consumer and environ-mental movements. The new Class contained dozens of intelligent, tacti-cal, and in some cases obnoxious politicians who altered the institution in which they served and reformed the politics of the nation it governed, sometimes with unpredicted and unintended consequences. They neither thought nor acted like those whose seats they now occupied or even the more senior reformers who now called them colleague. "We were young. We looked weird," Connecticut's Toby Moffett, a 30-year-old community activist, recalled. "I can't even believe we got elected!"[7]

While the story of their Class would become the story of congressional reform, few had focused on that issue during their campaigns. With rare exceptions, neither they nor the public understood or cared about the complex organizational structure of the House or the provincial tradi-tions, like seniority, that concentrated disproportionate power in the hands of elderly conservatives. The bitter battles within the House during the 94th Congress were not simple antecedents of the partisan strife between Democrats and Republicans that pervades our contemporary politics but largely a struggle *within* the parties in the House.

The aggravations confronting reform Democrats—the majority party from 1933–1994 with only four interrupted years (1947–1949 and 1953–1955)—were imposed not by their Republican colleagues but rather by the caucus rules that enabled senior members of their *own* party to occupy key committee and subcommittee perches, defy the elected leadership, and obstruct legislative objectives favored by a majority of the caucus. That struggle within the Democratic Party had been building since the infusion of liberals in the election of 1948 and was marked by fitful starts and stops and ineffective results. With the elections of 1972 and 1974, however, the ratios of liberals to conservatives in the Democratic Caucus changed decisively, and the progressives' prospects for unprecedented change markedly brightened.

A sometimes mystified Washington press corps described the newcomers as "thoroughly iconoclastic" and "tradition-shattering."[8] Future Speaker Jim Wright remembered the "zealous" class teeming with "fervent indignation" and a "sense of outrage" toward the "scandalously unethical and illegal deeds of some in the Nixon Administration . . . and the seeming failure of the Congress" to respond.[9] They arrived, as one scholar noted, with a "sense of mission . . . [a] mandate . . . to have an impact on the legislative process . . . impatient . . . [, with] no habit of being deferential to the established and the powerful . . . either in Committee or on the floor."[10]

And yet, many aspects of the Class stereotype do not hold up to detailed analysis. While many of the more outspoken and heavily reported freshmen, such as Toby Moffett, Andrew Maguire, or Tim Wirth were uncompromising liberals, the ideological leanings of Class members overall were more varied, their views more nuanced, their seriousness and sophistication often underestimated. On key issues like abortion, busing, and deficit control, which increasingly and frustratingly came before the House, Class members embraced a variety of positions reflecting their personal outlook and their political calculations.

Moreover, while most freshmen enthusiastically joined the reform effort to democratize the House, they were not the originators of the reform plans, and few had campaigned on the need for internal congressional reform beyond the need to "clean up Washington." The goal of this book is to place the Class of 1974 in the proper historical context while ensuring that the work of earlier reformers is accurately understood and appreciated. The misunderstanding of the freshmen class led many congressional observers, including scholars and leading journalists of the time, to become quickly disenchanted with its performance. For decades, the popular perception of the Class has been that of the "Watergate Babies" who merely sought to disrupt the political establishment rather than act as thoughtful policymakers or skilled politicians. The Class's achievements are often seen as limited to the replacement of three committee chairs during the 1975 organizational caucus, a gross oversimplification of the goals and accomplishments of the reform movement in the House. Within just six months of its arrival, critics were remonstrating the Class for failing to achieve far more sweeping change than anyone had promised or anticipated. In a "sad epitaph" written only a few months into the first session in 1975, the *Washington Post*'s David Broder prematurely bemoaned the "fading promise" of the freshmen class that "began so boldly . . . to make this 94th Congress something different from its predecessors and more worthy of public esteem."[11]

As this book documents, such criticism of the Class is largely unwarranted. Few members of the Class of 1974 ran for, or entered, Congress with a detailed agenda for institutional reform or even specific policy objectives; their immediate goals were far more limited and were largely achieved; as freshmen, they had limited capability to dramatically impact the design or speed of reform. Responsibility for the failure to override most of President Ford's numerous vetoes, a chronic source of Class displeasure with the leadership, lay far more with the enduring power of the bipartisan Conservative Coalition, which still could prevent the securing of the two-thirds margin needed to overturn vetoes. Nor is it reasonable to blame junior freshmen legislators for the inability of Congress to expeditiously address complex and divisive issues like energy policy, particularly when confounded with the nation's continuing economic weakness, which was a higher priority to many Class members and their constituents.

Class members often were criticized for overemphasizing personal goals, including the desire to be reelected, at the expense of loyalty to the party. "The day they hit here," Rep. Neal Smith of Iowa charged, "they started campaigning for the next election instead of helping us legislate," an observation that described many incumbents. Members of the Class may well have been more attuned to emerging campaign techniques and communications strategies than older members in more secure districts, but they were hardly the only incumbents focused on retaining their seats. Given the nature of the districts many occupied—having displaced incumbent Republicans or conservative Democrats—a substantial number of the freshmen were compelled to pay close attention to constituent satisfaction.

A central argument of this book is that the large Democratic majorities won in the aftermath of Vietnam and Watergate, including those seats vulnerable to a Republican challenge, created an unwarranted confidence in the sustainability of Democratic hegemony, which contributed to the failure to recognize the growing GOP threat. Few adequately appreciated the enormity of the political, ideological, cultural, and demographic changes that were reformulating the electoral dynamics in dozens of districts, especially in those suburban and southern seats that Class members had unexpectedly won in 1974. When volatile political, religious, and cultural issues combined with procedural reforms that enabled frequent votes on highly contentious and divisive subjects, the changes set in motion unanticipated transformations that would endanger the Democratic majority, promote the realignment of the political parties along ideological lines, and help to institutionalize a hyper-partisan environment that permeates contemporary American politics.

The initial chapters of the book provide a retrospective of reform efforts in the House dating back to the late 1940s and continuing through the liberalizations of the 93rd Congress during the Watergate crisis. In these introductory chapters, the durability of the hierarchical seniority system is described, as well as the numerous efforts to persuade the powerful chairmen to be more responsive to the increasingly liberal Democratic Caucus. The story shifts in chapter 3 to an introduction to many of the members of the Class of 1974 as they describe their motivations for running, their diverse levels of political sophistication, their sometimes surprising election in November 1974, and their early introductions to their colleagues and challenges as they arrive in Washington.

Even before they were sworn into office, the large cohort of "reinforcements," as they are dubbed in chapter 4 by a veteran reformer, was enlisted into efforts to effectuate reforms that had languished for years. By January

1975, as described in chapters 5 and 6, they provided the crucial votes needed to achieve historic alterations in the organization and operation of the House, not only toppling chairmen but expanding the base of power, which allowed the elevation of new players and long-suppressed legislative agendas. The members themselves, as well as much of the press corps that had bestowed enormous expectations on the freshmen legislators, were heady with the prospects for the ensuing two years of the 94th Congress. Much of the optimism was chilled when the early success achieved within the liberal-dominated Democratic caucus confronted the durable remnants of the Conservative Coalition of southern Democrats and Republicans who retained substantial power on the House floor. Those disappointments, which fueled resentment at the party leadership, were especially acute when, despite a two-thirds Democratic supermajority, the House frequently failed to override President Gerald Ford's aggressive use of the veto on priority legislation.

Although Democrats constituted the large majority of members of the Class, many Republican freshmen shared reformist objectives, an often-overlooked feature of the period, which is described in chapter 8. The challenges they faced in building alliances with Democrats were compounded by a growing estrangement from increasingly conservative forces inside and outside Congress. This emerging New Right challenged the presumption of an unassailable Democratic majority and proved increasingly skilled at employing the reforms intended to benefit liberals for its own strategic purposes. But Republican hopes for regaining many of the seats lost in 1974 were dashed in the 1976 campaign as incumbent freshmen employed a variety of innovative techniques and emerging technologies to foster close relationships with their constituencies, as detailed in chapter 10.

In the next chapter, most of the Class members returned to Washington to meet the new group of freshmen in December 1976, whom they joined in choosing a new Democratic leadership. The leading candidates included several of the most creative proponents of House organizational reform, and the surprising outcome of the election would appear to mark the apogee in the efforts of reformers to sweep away the traditionalism that had constrained their role and blunted their legislative goals.

Lastly, in chapter 12, the book considers the long-term impacts of the reforms of the mid-1970s, both the intentional achievements of opening participation in, and expanding the transparency of, the legislative process, but also the unanticipated consequences that are the inevitable by-product of the imperfect art of politics and lawmaking. Those developments inadvertently helped to shape the far more conflicted and less productive political environment of our current era.

1 TOOTHLESS, SAPLESS, AND SECRETIVE

This Congress is too resistant to change. I'd like to be in a position to do more than shout "aye" and "no." I don't want to feel like a ghoul waiting around for people to die.—Rep. Charles S. Joelson (D-NJ)

The failure of the House is a failure of the Democratic party, of which I am a member.—Rep. Richard Bolling (D-MO)

The Democratic Party controlled the US House of Representatives for most of the mid-twentieth century, but the organization and operation of the House was anything but democratic. Through the years of the New Deal, World War II, and the Eisenhower administration, and into the New Frontier and Great Society, real power was largely in the grip of a bipartisan "Conservative Coalition" composed of Republicans and southern Democrats who tightly controlled the legislative process from subcommittee to the House floor. Although the immediate post–World War II period would see an influx of young veterans dedicated to reducing the dominance of this conservative alliance, these efforts proved largely ineffective for more than two decades.

This was the era of the "committee system," when the chairmen of the various House panels exercised more power than the elected leadership—the Speaker and the majority and minority leaders. The committee system had emerged early in the century as a result of bipartisan efforts in 1910 to rein in the autocratic power of Speakers like Thomas Reed (1889–1891, 1895–1899) and Joseph Cannon (1903–1911), who had wielded such sweeping authority that the fractious House was able to address the complexities of modern economics, commerce, and international military policy.

Fed up with Cannon's unilateral dictates, the bipartisan reformers in 1910 rescinded the Speaker's power to designate (or remove) committee chairs, substituting a system that awarded chairmanships—and thus enormous power—to majority members using the ideologically and politically neutral criterion of one's duration of service in the House. The resulting "seniority system" would last nearly three-quarters of a century with rare exceptions. While this innovation effectively checked the ability of a powerful Speaker to handpick loyalists as chairmen, it disproportionately empowered southern Democrats, who rarely faced Republican opponents and therefore enjoyed long tenures in office.

As a result, throughout the heyday of progressive Democratic policy-making under Woodrow Wilson and Franklin Roosevelt, Congress's key committees were in the hands of Democrats, who often were as suspicious of the president's programs as were many Republicans. Their loyalty to the New Deal's expansion of governmental activity and spending was often secured by the president's acquiescence to Jim Crow laws and in limiting the access of black Americans to employment and relief programs. Little wonder that those few blacks who were able to cast ballots in this era often remained loyal to the party of Lincoln well into the 1950s. But while congressional conservatives passed legislation showering their impoverished districts with vast public works spending and grants, they also remained skeptical of empowering a federal government that might use its expanded authority to challenge conservative tenets like racial segregation.

The Postwar Influx

With the end of World War II and the election of scores of younger representatives, it became clear that many of these elderly southern conservatives were out of step with a liberalizing Democratic Caucus. This new generation included veterans whose war exploits "profoundly influenced their lives and shaped their public service"—searing experiences that left them less "frightened by the need to cast a hard vote now and then."[1] The freshmen of the 1946 and 1948 elections included men who would reshape American politics and the Congress and play significant roles in the nation's politics for decades: Democrats John F. Kennedy, Eugene J. McCarthy, Abraham Ribicoff, Sidney Yates, Richard Bolling, Peter Rodino, and Lloyd Bentsen, as well as Republicans Richard Nixon and Gerald Ford.

Within a few years, many of these young officeholders began to chafe at the secrecy, autocracy, and rigidity of the House organization. The core of the problem, many believed, was the disproportionate power concentrated in the hands of the chairmen, who controlled all aspects of the legislative process. The closed nature of deliberations both in committee and on the House floor—most committee hearings were closed and most floor votes went unrecorded—left both the press and the public without essential information concerning members' opinions and votes, and it freed members from accountability.

Information and expertise were firmly concentrated in the hands of the committee elite. Congressional staffs consisted of only a few people, both in Washington and in district offices. Committee staff was hired exclusively by the chairman, and subcommittees, where the chairman chose to create them, used staff of the full committee. Subcommittee chairs were generally designated by the full committee chairman and could hold hearings only when authorized to do so on subjects approved by the chairman. Most legislation originated in the full committee or was modified in full committee drafting sessions (or "markups") to reflect the will of the chairman. As a result, the average member was heavily dependent on the chairman and his staff for any detailed information about legislation. One member of the Appropriations Committee recalled a staff person refusing to show him the report on which the committee was about to vote. "The clerk said—the clerk, mind you and *I'm* the Member—the clerk said, 'You can't see it, chairman's orders,'" recalled Charles Joelson of New Jersey.[2]

Even when legislation passed out of committee, it often faced a formidable obstacle before reaching the House floor: the House Rules Committee, which governed the timetable and parameters by which virtually all legislation moved to the floor. Unlike the modern Rules Committee, whose members are appointed by and function as a virtual extension of the Speaker, the Rules panel was appointed by the Ways and Means Committee, which served as the "Committee on Committees," and functioned largely autonomously of the leadership. The chairman of Rules from 1955 to 1967, according to the rules of seniority, was Howard Smith, a staunch segregationist who would refuse to convene the committee and instead retire to his Virginia farm when he wished to block legislation. When the African American diva Marian Anderson rose to sing the national anthem at the inauguration of President John F. Kennedy in January 1961, Smith walked out of the event.[3] As a result, the Rules Committee remained the "graveyard of liberal legislation," including civil rights and health care bills, well into the early 1960s.[4]

The House floor operated under a cloak of near secrecy. Most legislative activity occurred (as it does today) in the "Committee of the Whole House," a parliamentary contrivance that permits the House to operate under committee rules rather than as the formal full body. A large proportion of the votes on amendments in the Committee of the Whole was conducted secretly under House rules dating from 1840. Rather than publicly declaring their positions, individuals would "walk the gauntlet of the tellers," or designated clerks, to record their votes. While waiting in line, members often would be accosted by a chairman or other influential member of the committee whose bill was being considered. "You want that bridge in your district?" the member would be asked. "You're not voting for this [amendment]."[5] The press, constituents, and lobbyists often huddled in the spectators gallery trying to read members' lips as they indicated their vote to the teller. Only rarely did a member suffer any retribution for this process, as when reformer Jonathan Bingham successfully ousted longtime Bronx boss Charles Buckley in 1964 after alerting constituents to the congressman's secret votes against progressive legislation.[6]

This clandestine procedure not only protected members from accountability for the votes but also prevented many issues from being debated by the full House. Under the rules, an amendment that had been defeated in the Committee of the Whole could not be offered when the House considered the underlying bill, and the rules governing the debate prevented any similar amendment from being offered. For decades, members had chafed at the sheer difficulty of breaking through this tight-fisted control of the legislative process. "I am overwhelmed, discouraged, disheartened by uselessness and the terrible frustration of it all," Sidney Anderson of Minnesota had bemoaned as early as 1913![7]

Surprisingly little had changed in the subsequent decades as aged conservatives continued to control the rules governing legislation. During his freshman term during the so-called Do-Nothing Congress in 1947, John Blatnik of Minnesota recalled watching a stooped, elderly man walking slowly across the House floor.[8] The senior member was Carl Vinson of Georgia, who had begun his House service in 1914. As chairman of the Armed Services Committee, he had imposed the so-called Vinson Rule, which allowed Committee members to ask one question in a hearing per year of service, and he insisted that he approve all questions in advance. Freshmen like Blatnik might be kept waiting for days to be recognized. "Well," Blatnik comforted himself, "this guy can't last. I'll be important some day."[9] When Vinson finally retired, 18 years later, he had served for 51 years, longer than anyone else in history to that point, and Blatnik was still years away from his own chairmanship.

The Rise of the Liberal Reformers

Resistance to this calcified system arose in the mid-1950s, partly spear-headed by California's James Roosevelt, son of the late president. His ad hoc group of liberals, known as the "Light Brigade" or "Jimmie's Crazies," launched numerous—usually unsuccessful—offensives against sacrosanct programs protected by the conservative alliance, like farm subsidies. Another mid-1950s reform group—"McCarthy's Mavericks" or "McCarthy's Marauders"—led by Eugene McCarthy of Minnesota, included liberal stalwarts who would gather in McCarthy's office or at a Chinatown bar to concoct challenges like the dismantling of the House Un-American Activities Committee (HUAC), an effort that was blocked by Speaker Sam Rayburn. In January 1957, the Mavericks released the "Liberal Manifesto," demanding action on long-delayed progressive legislation including civil rights, health care, and education. The document was a response to the "Southern Manifesto," issued a year earlier by 77 House conservatives and 19 senators denouncing the US Supreme Court's *Brown v. Board of Education* ruling barring segregation in public schools as a judicial effort "to legislate, in derogation of the authority of Congress."

The McCarthy group actively supported liberal candidates in the 1958 off-year congressional election, impressively helping to pick up 49 seats and swelling the Mavericks to more than 80 members from 21 states.[10] Early in the new Congress, the frustrated liberals focused on checking the power of Rules Chairman Howard Smith, who had obstructed passage of the 1957 civil rights legislation. Shortly after the 1960 election, the leadership responded. Concerned that Smith would thwart the legislative program of the newly inaugurated president, John F. Kennedy, Speaker Rayburn finally took action against Smith. On January 31, 1961, the Speaker took the unusual step of addressing the House from the podium, in front of the dais where he typically presided, and urged members to vote to expand the Rules Committee by three seats. Even with that extraordinary gesture by the Speaker and Kennedy's vigorous support, the proposal passed by a mere five votes, 217–212.[11] Essential support came from 22 moderate and liberal Republicans from the Northeast and Midwest who ignored their own party leaders and supported the expansion, which most southern Democrats strongly opposed.[12] The sanctity of the seniority system, however, was not challenged by this action, as Rayburn made no effort to remove Smith from his chairmanship.

The addition of moderate members to Rules enabled action on a number of Kennedy and Johnson initiatives that otherwise might well have remained bottled up, but it also raised hackles among southerners whose "disaffection with northern policy positions" was steadily growing.[13] Still, the victory marked a major coup for the reformers and may well have encouraged reform proponent Missouri's Richard Bolling to run for the position of majority leader in 1962 when John McCormack vacated the position to move up to the Speaker's chair. But the effort was premature, and unlike the Rules expansion, where Republicans could provide votes to offset conservative Democratic opposition, GOP members could not vote on a leadership race within the Democrats' caucus. Bolling was defeated by the whip, Carl Albert of Oklahoma.

The closeness of the vote on expanding the Rules Committee highlighted the continuing floor influence of the Conservative Coalition, which controlled 311 of 433 votes in the House and 71 of 98 in the Senate as late as 1958. A substantial portion of coalition members were drawn from the southern Democrats, who continued to dominate the region into the early 1960s. As late as 1950, there were only two Republicans out of 105 members from the former Confederacy, and the numbers grew slowly for the next decade and a half. The long seniority enjoyed by these infrequently contested southern Democrats allowed them to play a significant contradictory dual role: ensuring that the Democratic Party retain majority control of the House but simultaneously frustrating that majority's ability to enact the legislation the national party, and its president, embraced.

While the percentage of southern Democrats in the House dropped from 43 percent of the caucus in 1955 to just 24 percent a dozen years later, the devotion to the seniority system meant that the region's disproportionate hold on powerful chairmanships remained consistent, even as southerners' unity with the party in voting plummeted from 62 percent in 1955–1957 to just 40 percent a dozen years later. On the eve of Kennedy's inauguration, more than half of House committees, including the most powerful—Appropriations, Ways and Means, and Rules—were chaired by conservative southern Democrats who voted with the majority of Republicans an astonishing 86 percent of the time.[14] By the late 1960s, one-fifth of House Democrats—largely from the South—were voting against the party's position on legislation, a tenfold increase from a decade earlier.[15] Yet the importance of these seats to maintaining the Democratic majority was undeniable; so dominant were conservative Democrats in the solid South that the party needed to win only one-third of the seats in the remainder of the country to ensure its majority, the chairmanship of many committees, and the enduring power of the alliance with Republicans in the Conservative Coalition.[16]

The Seniority System

More than any other anachronism, the seniority system infuriated the newer House members, whose priorities were obstructed, and whose level of participation in committee and floor activity was squelched, by unresponsive chairmen who had little fear of retribution for their voting apostasy or for their dismissive attitude toward junior legislators. "If you live longer and get elected oftener than anybody else on your committee, you, by God, will become chairman of it when your party is in the majority," wrote Bolling, who authored several books during the mid-1960s arguing for far-reaching reform of House organization and rules. The absoluteness of the seniority system, Bolling wrote, gave a chairman "license to cavalierly defy the majority on his own committee, the Congress, the President, the courts, and most Americans except his ever-loving constituents." He heaped disdain on chairmen like Agriculture's Harold Cooley of North Carolina, who had "brazenly manipulated sugar quotas in defiance of everyone else," and Rules' Smith, whom he labeled the "king of obstructionists."[17] Nor was the leadership, which was elected by the caucus, able or willing to confront most of the chairs. Even the formidable Speaker Rayburn "had to bargain, cajole, and persuade" powerful chairs to accept leadership guidance.[18]

Only on the rarest of occasions did defiance of the party provoke retribution. When John Bell Williams of Mississippi, the chairman of the Commerce Committee, and Albert Watson of South Carolina endorsed Barry Goldwater for president in 1964, the caucus had enough. "I don't want to put up with these traitorous bastards anymore," declared Hale Boggs of Louisiana, the Democratic whip.[19] The leadership rescinded Williams's seniority, which deprived him of his chairmanship. Watson, who declared he would "not sit around and be bullied by northern liberals," renounced his status as a Democrat, quit the House, and was promptly reelected as a Republican, the first in South Carolina in the twentieth century.[20] Some

17

southerners claimed their region was being punished by liberals, pointing to the failure of the caucus to rescind the seniority of Adam Clayton Powell of New York, a black representative who had endorsed President Dwight D. Eisenhower for reelection in 1956.[21]

A significant number of liberal Democrats were carried to victory in Lyndon Johnson's landslide election in 1964, which saw Democrats pick up 40 seats to win a margin of 295–140, but the jubilation proved short lived. Only two years later, after the passage of a historic trove of progressive legislation Johnson termed the "Great Society," House Democrats suffered a harsh setback, losing 50 seats. Many of the liberals elected in the 1964 rout proved to be "one-term wonders," and their swift departure ended any immediate hope of adjusting the balance of power for liberals in the caucus. Indeed, conservatives quickly moved to repeal an on-again-off-again reform, first established when Democrats regained the House in 1948, which empowered any committee member to call up a bill for floor consideration if the Rules Committee had refused to act on it for 21 days. With the loss of so many liberals, this "21-day rule" was repealed in January 1967 by a vote of 233–185, securing the support of 79 percent of southern Democrats and 86 percent of Republicans, which restored enormous discretion to the Rules chairman on scheduling legislation for the floor.

Still, all was not secure for the conservative Democrats, especially as the impact of the Civil Rights and Voting Rights Acts passed in 1964 and 1965 was increasingly felt in their districts. As millions of black voters registered for the first time, and longtime white conservatives began shifting to a reviving southern Republican Party, the security of many Democratic incumbents became less certain. Few tears were shed in the caucus in 1966 when a more liberal Democrat defeated Chairman Smith, whom fellow Rules member Thomas O'Neill of Massachusetts dismissed as "an arrogant son of a bitch who was no more a Democrat than the man in the moon." However, the emerging trend lines of southern elections were illustrated by the victory of the Republican in the 1966 general election. The losses were a harbinger of a trend in which southern seats shifted to Republicans following the departure of an entrenched Democrat, a trend foreseen by President Johnson and by Majority Whip Carl Albert, who asserted that the party's support for civil rights meant that other southern Democrats would soon join Smith "in the graveyard of the white man's democracy."[22]

The Democratic Study Group

The electoral setbacks of 1966 did not diminish the demands of reformers for substantial changes in caucus and House rules. Pennsylvania senator Joseph S. Clark lamented that Congress had deteriorated into a "sapless branch" of government, hamstrung by archaic rules and traditions, hopelessly deadlocked and unproductive, incapable of challenging the powers of an "imperial presidency." Bolling authored *House Out of Order*, detailing a litany of needed reforms to improve congressional efficiency, and Williams College professor James MacGregor Burns criticized Congress's unproductivity in his *Deadlock of Democracy*. The successor to McCarthy's Marauders, the Democratic Study Group (DSG) had been organized in 1959 "out of a liberal frustration and dissatisfaction with the information and initiatives provided by the formal party structure" and drew inspiration from such treatises. In particular, members objected to dependence on manipulative and secretive chairmen and their staff, who maintained "a virtual monopoly of the most visible communication channels," disseminating only material supportive of their bills and often doing so only at the beginning of floor debate.[23] In addition, DSG demanded that chairmen act on liberal legislation, advocated for more prestigious committee assignments for liberals, and coordinated liberals to serve as a counterbalance to the Conservative Coalition.[24]

In a sign of increasing sophistication, DSG was the first liberal group to hire a staff person to scrutinize legislative proposals and advise members on issues coming before the House, providing an important source of analysis independent of the committee leadership. DSG's objective analyses of pending bills and amendments quickly became valued not only by liberal Democrats but by conservatives and Republicans who were just as cut off from objective information from the committees. Indeed, for years, the names of those who subscribed to the DSG were kept confidential to shield members from being associated with the progressive organization.[25]

DSG was immeasurably strengthened by the decision in 1966 to hire a young journalist and American Political Science Association fellow, Dick Conlon, as its chief staff person. Smart, creative, and often acerbic even with members, Conlon would play a vital role in developing DSG's agenda and strategic planning for more than a decade, earning a reputation as the 436th member of the House. Under his leadership, DSG's membership swelled beyond 200, constituting nearly a majority of the House. Its growing staff of researchers, analysts, and writers produced legislative reports, weekly reports, staff bulletins, and other mimeographed publications that served as essential reading for members, staff, and journalists alike.[26]

In the years before a distinct separation of political and official business was required, DSG also became involved in electoral activities in support of Democratic candidates. While they disagreed on policy matters, DSG members were united on the need for information, the desirability of electing Democrats, and the urgency of internal reforms to democratize House operations. The dichotomy—united on reform, diverse on policy—would also characterize the large group of reformers who joined the House in 1974. DSG members particularly took a strong stand against those who defied the party's institutional interests. When Williams and Watson broke with the party to endorse Goldwater in 1964, it was DSG chairman John Blatnik who pressured Speaker McCormack to strip them of their seniority. Williams facetiously called Blatnik after his election as governor of Mississippi to thank him for the punishment, which proved to constituents that he was no loyal Democrat.

One area of policy disagreement within DSG concerned the deepening debate over the Vietnam War. A strong anti-war subset, named the "Group," was composed of hard-line progressives like Phillip Burton and Don Edwards of California, Bob Kastenmeier of Wisconsin, and Ben Rosenthal of New York. In 1967, the Group issued a report entitled *The Liberal Papers* outlining its positions on the Vietnam War and highlighting the need for seniority reform. Members regularly sought out new liberal talent like Abner Mikva, a reformer elected in 1968 by defeating an 86-year-old incumbent Democrat. Although some in the Chicago machine would never forgive Mikva for bucking the local organization, shortly after arriving on Capitol Hill in 1969, Mikva remembered the Group's titular leader, Burton, putting an arm around him and inviting him to join.[27]

As the policy divisions between DSG and the Group illustrated, House liberals desperately needed improved discipline. For years, insufficient numbers and notoriously slipshod strategic execution had beset them. McCarthy had been regarded as an idealist and an intellectual, but neither operational nor practical.[28] "The failure of the House," an exasperated Bolling wrote, "is a failure of the Democratic party, of which I am a member."[29] An acerbic, analytical critic who was frustrated by the liberal ideologues, Bolling rarely minced words about his colleagues. "The liberal is always spreading himself too thin," wrote Bolling in the mid-1960s. Liberals' platform, he said, was "a holy tablet," and they displayed an incessant "tendency to tinker." If there were three liberals in a room, Bolling noted disparagingly, they would "produce four violently advanced viewpoints" ricocheting from "totalitarian[ism to] voodooism." Their unwillingness to confront opponents made Bolling consider whether liberals possessed a " 'will-to-lose,' a sort of death-wish" that left them "not so effective a legislator as is the conservative."[30]

Bolling's frustration was echoed within the House leadership, including majority leader (and future Speaker) Carl Albert, who complained that liberals "want to own your minds," whereas he preferred to examine issues "in terms of conditions and not in terms of someone's inborn political philosophy." Such high-ranking criticism by the formal leadership convinced DSG to develop its own whip network to ensure that its members were present on the floor for crucial votes, combatting a chronic complaint that liberals lacked organizational skills.

A shrewd tactician, Bolling advocated promoting procedural reforms within the Democratic Caucus, where liberals were increasingly powerful and from which Republicans—the allies of Democratic conservatives on the floor—were obviously excluded. "The place to reform the procedures of the House," wrote Bolling, "is not in study commissions or on the floor of the House," where the bipartisan Conservative Coalition would defeat such initiatives.[31] The caucus could modify the seniority rules, undercutting the accumulation of power in a few, conservative hands and increasing the influence of progressives. Moreover, Bolling suggested that the caucus consider mandating that all Democrats be required, at the risk of losing seniority and chairmanships, to vote for positions adopted by a majority of the caucus. Such a recommendation might well have been prompted by a DSG report that disclosed that non-DSG Democrats voted more like Republicans and that one-third of all subcommittee chairmen voted more frequently against party proposals than for them.[32]

Shortly after the 1968 election, a poll conducted by DSG chairman James O'Hara of Michigan indicated strong support for monthly meetings of the caucus, which often met only at the outset of each Congress to adopt rules and approve committee assignments.[33] Reformers speculated that the leadership purposely avoided calling caucus meetings, fearful they might open "bloody regional wounds" over issues like civil rights and

Vietnam.[34] Speaker John W. McCormack's skepticism about frequent caucus meetings was shaped by his own confrontations with young reformers whom the aging Speaker barely recognized; for years after his election, McCormack would refer to Bob Kastenmeier of Wisconsin as Bill.[35] McCormack finally relented on scheduling additional caucus meetings, reportedly after Majority Leader Carl Albert intervened on behalf of the reformers.[36]

Still, McCormack urged patience, reminding the reformers of Rayburn's advice to new members to "go along [and] learn your job" before making demands of the caucus.[37] Dave Obey, who won his seat in a 1969 special election, recalled being told to "learn, learn, learn, wait, wait, wait, listen, listen, listen" and "spend my time learning how to operate in the House [while] focusing on strengthening my position back home."[38] Meeting with liberals on the Education and Labor Committee in December 1969, McCormack was pressed to challenge the new Nixon administration over Vietnam and other issues. The younger members were unimpressed with his admonition to respect tradition. "I'm not interested in what you did before I was born," the 37-year-old freshman Bill Clay of Missouri told the startled Speaker, who responded, "I think some of you want to run the House." Frank Thompson of New Jersey cheerfully replied, "That's perfectly true. Some of us do!"[39]

McCormack could respond to the reformers' demands and schedule caucus meetings, but he couldn't require attendance, and fewer than half of the first 27 meetings achieved the quorum needed to transact business. Still, DSG leader Don Fraser believed that these early caucus discussions constituted "the turning point . . . the beginning of the incremental approach to reform." Conlon agreed, declaring the revival of the caucus the "key to the reform movement because empowering individuals to bring items before the Caucus for discussion circumvented the ability of chairs to silence those with whom they disagreed on key issues like the Vietnam War."[40]

Early Reform Efforts

Still, merely forcing a concession like additional caucus meetings was no guarantee that reform would proceed. Earlier efforts to promote the modernization of House operations had met with limited success at best. A perennial goal was reduction in the number of committees that had proliferated over the years in response to member demands for influence.

A reform effort in 1927 had eliminated 16 House committees, but 46 remained, more than twice today's number. (A Senate reorganization effort in 1921 had shrunk the standing committees from 74 to 34.) Shortly after the end of World War II, Congress passed the Legislative Reorganization Act of 1946, an effort to streamline Congress's organization and operating procedures based on the 1941 nonpartisan recommendations of the American Political Science Association. Academics hailed the law, which reduced the number of House committees to 19 and Senate panels from 33 to 15 and increased their staffs, as the "most sweeping changes in the machinery and facilities of Congress ever adopted."[41] But recommendations to eliminate overlapping jurisdictions foundered, as did proposals to end the seniority system, limit the power of chairmen, and reduce the number of senators needed to end filibusters. The following year, to promote efficiency, the proliferating subcommittees were reduced from 126 to 59 in the Senate and from 142 to 89 in the House.

There was little interest in additional structural reform that tampered with procedure or personal fiefdoms for another two decades. In the mid-1960s, Congress created a House-Senate Committee on the Organization of Congress cochaired by Rep. Ray Madden of Indiana and Sen. Mike Monroney, an Oklahoman who had chaired the 1946 reform committee as a House member. One goal of the committee was to modernize Congress to enable the institution to compete more effectively with the growing power of the executive branch. Reformers also demanded curtailments on the powers of chairmen, greater transparency in committee and floor operations, and greater opportunities for participation by more junior legislators. Appropriations Committee member Charles Joelson complained, for example, that the panel "operates under rules which are as archaic as they are undemocratic," empowering the chairman to "shape the Committee and predestine its determinations" through his power to appoint members to subcommittees.

The resulting report recommended opening proceedings to public review, publishing roll call votes, increasing resources and staff for the minority, and expanding staff resources overall, but again it avoided changing the seniority system or altering floor procedures.[42] Nevertheless, the recommendations still encountered stiff institutional resistance, including from Speaker John McCormack. After seven weeks of rancorous floor debate, the recommendations were approved in the Senate in 1967, but the package died in the House. Bolling was not surprised, castigating McCormack as "the greatest defender of the *status quo* because it made him Speaker." Joelson, the frustrated New Jersey reformer, was so disgusted that he quit Congress to become a state judge. "Don't get me wrong," Joelson said, "I've enjoyed Congress, but I'd like to be in a position to do more than shout 'aye' and 'no.' I don't want to feel like a ghoul waiting around for people to die" in order to advance to a more substantive role.[43]

Republicans chastised the majority for resisting reform. Thomas Curtis of Missouri bemoaned the "wheeling and dealing" that had replaced "honest study and honest debate" in the House. Like Democratic reformers, he denounced both the "narrow-mindedness on the part of the chairmen and senior members" and the "groups outside the Congress who wish to manipulate the decision-making process" that had promoted "successful resistance to reform" for most of the 1960s.

With the infusion of additional reformers, major bipartisan legislation finally was enacted by the following Congress. The Legislative Reform Act of 1970 included provisions to open committees to the public and press, permit a committee's majority to expand the agenda prepared by the chairman, mandate recorded votes in committee markups, and set regular meeting times for each committee.[44] To check the power of chairs to bottle up legislation they disliked, a majority of committee members was empowered to schedule a hearing on a topic or bill if the chairman refused to do so. Significantly, minority members were granted the right to call their own witnesses during hearings to ensure balanced testimony, and the independent General Accounting Office was expanded to provide independent oversight of government spending.

A bipartisan floor amendment by O'Neill and Charles Gubser, a California Republican, took aim at the secret teller voting in the Committee of the Whole. The amendment required a recorded vote if just 20 members (a quorum of the Committee of the Whole) requested one.[45] Few features of the Legislative Reorganization Act would have greater institutional or public consequence. Members would now face greater accountability for voting to kill amendments to keep them from being offered before the full House, where a recorded vote could easily be demanded. In years to come, the ability of so small a number of members to demand on-the-record votes in the Committee of the Whole would serve as an unintended means for forcing votes on divisive, party-defining issues and compelling marginal members to cast votes on controversial topics that exposed them to political retribution. Conversely, requiring recorded votes complicated the traditional ability to pass amendments anonymously in order to improve chances for a bill to pass the full House.

The House also authorized electronic voting in 1973.[46] Before the installation of the push-button machines that display how each member has voted on huge screens above the chamber, recorded votes required clerks to call the names of all 435 members. While time consuming, those delays afforded chairmen and leadership the opportunity to buttonhole wavering members to twist arms and plead cases. With the reduction of voting time to just 15 minutes or less, members could surreptitiously slip in and out of the chamber before a senior member or whip could corral them to change their mind. Moreover, electronic voting, by speeding the process, would also facilitate a substantial expansion in the number of votes, which, when combined with more open rules permitting more amendments to be offered, would have multiple unforeseen consequences that lent a partisan atmosphere to floor deliberations.

In mid-March 1970, the caucus discussed initiating a renewed effort to review the seniority system. Speaker McCormack remained wary of authorizing such a review panel, but caucus chairman Dan Rostenkowski spoke out for institutionalizing the process rather than blocking it and encouraging members to concoct revisions at caucus meetings. The chairmanship of the special Committee on Organization, Study, and Review (OSR) went to Julia Butler Hansen, a 10-year House veteran who also had served for two decades in the Washington state legislature. Hansen was "tough as nails," one staffer recalled, and could more than hold her own in the male-dominated House. A committee staff member recalled her frequently downing several martinis before lunch and employing decidedly unladylike language, which won respect from her male colleagues but inspired fear among staff people. "She doesn't pull that 'woman' bullshit," one observer bluntly observed. "She really knows her stuff and doesn't pull any punches."[47] She was highly sensitive to the senior role she had been given, and if people forgot that she was the "powerful" chairman, she brusquely reminded them.[48]

The 11-member panel represented the diversity of the caucus and focused on issues of chairmanships and subcommittee reform—what Frank Thompson of New Jersey called creating an opportunity to "give younger members a chance [to] spread the action." Illustrating the reluctance with which many viewed its mission, the committee got off to a slow start. After its creation in March, a second meeting was not held until mid-May, and no additional meetings were scheduled until after the 1970 election. Shortly after convening the following year, the caucus quickly considered Hansen's recommendations, including an unprecedented challenge to the seniority system that would permit 10 members to demand a vote on anyone nominated for a chairmanship by the Committee on Committees.[49] In a move that many considered even more significant, the caucus limited members to the chairmanship of only one legislative subcommittee, even if their seniority entitled them to multiple chairmanships (which many already held). The reform was warranted, advocates argued, because their accumulated service on numerous committees had entitled senior members to as many as four subcommittee chairmanships, which allowed a small group to exercise its influence across committee lines while blocking younger members from rising within the committee structure.[50]

To increase their autonomy, subcommittee chairs were authorized to hire one staffer independent from the chairman's full committee staff. Although unevenly enforced (the Science and Astronautics Committee voted 22–3 *against* allowing its subcommittee chairs to hire a staff person), the change was of enormous significance because it freed members from dependence on staff wholly controlled by the chairs. Subcommittees were also given power to hold hearings on their own and mark up legislation before sending it to the full committee, where it often encountered a more diverse and resistant response than it had received in the specialized subcommittee.

These changes reflected acceptance of Bolling's strategy of empowering the caucus, where the liberals carried growing weight, as the vehicle for reform rather than the House itself, where the Conservative Coalition remained a formidable obstacle. Yet these early reform efforts also won support from many Republicans who were pleased to be granted additional staffing and legislative autonomy. Democrats gave little thought to the implications of granting these additional resources to the minority because few believed the concessions could in any way jeopardize the long-dominant role of House Democrats. As long as the South kept electing Democrats who bolstered the size of the caucus, even if they were conservatives who often voted on policy matters with Republicans, little thought was given to the possibility that Republicans could successfully compete for House control. Virtually no one—certainly not House

Democrats—could anticipate that the days of bipartisanship on reform and legislation were on the wane because of a reviving southern Republican Party that was attracting conservative white voters, electing a growing number of House members, and plotting a challenge to the Democratic majority.

2 SEEDS OF REBELLION

Sit down, you smart-ass young punk. What do you know?
—Rep. John Rooney (D-NY)

Kiss my fanny, you senile old goat! What do *you* know?—Rep. Dave Obey (D-WI)

With the passage of the 1970 Legislative Reorganization Act, the House took a major step toward sweeping "away the dark procedural corners in Congress in which members could hide their actions from the public and press," inching Congress instead toward becoming a more transparent and efficient institution.[1] But the hard work of modernization was far from complete.

Four developments would soon shake the institution to its core, culminating in a tainted election that left Congress, and the nation, vulnerable to even greater change: the escalation of the war in Vietnam, the bombing of Cambodia, and the massacre of students at Kent State University in 1970; the Watergate inquiry and the resignation of President Nixon; the increasing assertiveness of Congress as a coequal branch of government in response to the imperial presidency; and the continuing infusion of reformers willing to challenge the pillars of House orthodoxy. These volatile developments combined into a roiling brew that exploded mid-decade, leaving impacts on Capitol Hill unlike anything seen during the preceding 60 years.

Many liberals had bristled under the domination of Congress by Lyndon Johnson, particularly with respect to Vietnam, while conservatives in both parties distrusted the rapidly expanding federal role that resulted from passage of the Great Society legislation when liberals enjoyed a brief, inflated majority on Capitol Hill after the 1964 election. The bipartisan determination of many to reassert Congress as a coequal branch of the federal government expanded significantly with the election of Richard Nixon in 1968. The deference liberal Democrats had grudgingly given the Johnson White House evaporated, especially once Nixon's promise of a "secret plan" to end the Vietnam War turned out to be little more than an escalation of the controversial conflict into Cambodia and Laos. But a lethargic, seniority-bound Congress remained unable to respond to presidential initiatives with agility. Increasingly, the drive to modernize Congress was closely linked to liberals' determination to challenge Nixon's conservative agenda as well as to protect Great Society initiatives.

Reformers blamed the House's hesitant response on its calcified leadership, especially that of the aged, pro-war Speaker, John McCormack. In February 1970, Jerome Waldie of California had forced a caucus vote of no confidence against McCormack in response to his practice of limiting the floor speeches of anti-war Democrats to as little as 10 seconds. Two years earlier, Morris Udall of Arizona had suggested that the frail Speaker consider retirement, but Waldie unwisely forced the issue to a caucus vote, an impulsive move that garnered only 27 votes. It was the sort of undisciplined initiative by a liberal reformer that drew criticism from more skillful reform tacticians like Richard Bolling and Phillip Burton of San Francisco, who both opposed Waldie's motion.

Challenges to Seniority

But the repeated attacks had an impact, and, in May 1970, the 78-year-old McCormack, who appeared to sometimes doze off when presiding over the House, announced he would retire in 1972. His departure raised hopes among reformers that one of their own might secure a place on the leadership ladder that routinely promoted only moderate and conservative members to top slots in the caucus. Next in line to the speakership was the diminutive majority leader, Carl Albert of Oklahoma, an institutional pragmatist who declared a preference "to face issues in terms of conditions and not in terms of someone's inborn political philosophy."[2]

The traditional peristaltic movement of the leadership ladder meant that the whip, Hale Boggs of Louisiana, would likely become majority leader, but two reformers opposed his automatic elevation, Mo Udall of Arizona and Jim O'Hara of Michigan, a Democratic Study Group founder, as did Wayne Hays of Ohio. As Bolling and Burton lamented, the reformers' vote counting skills did not match their passion for change. "Do you know how to tell the difference between a cactus and a caucus?" Udall ruefully asked after a crushing defeat that revealed that many colleagues had lied to him about their support. "With a cactus, the pricks are on the *outside*."[3]

All official Washington was stunned in October 1972 when Boggs (along with Alaska Rep. Nick Begich) disappeared in an airplane crash in remote Alaska. The tragedy elevated the new whip, Thomas "Tip" O'Neill, to the majority leader role, leaving vacant the whip slot, a position typically appointed by the Speaker. However, Phil Burton, a master liberal strategist with deep friendships within conservative circles, proposed making the whip's position elective, like the other two leadership posts. A vote by the caucus, he reasoned, might provide liberals with an opportunity to break into the upper echelons of the House management and propel Burton, eventually, to the Speaker's chair.

Burton had been an early supporter of Albert, whom he thought would favor an elective whip, but O'Neill disliked the calculating and often coarse Burton. Hearing that Albert was considering the Californian's idea, O'Neil confronted the Speaker. "You can't do that," O'Neill remonstrated. "He's a revolutionary. He's crazy. We can't work with him on a leadership team."[4] Burton's plan was defeated narrowly, 123–114, and the position of whip went to John McFall, a moderate and quiescent Californian.[5] Still, liberals took note of the fact that, despite the opposition of the new leadership, they had fallen only 5 votes short.

The other object of liberal concern remained the seniority system, which a DSG staff report blamed for having "fragmented and diffused power in the House, thereby crippling effective leadership and making it impossible to present and pursue a coherent legislative program."[6] New caucus policy declared that seniority need not be the only criterion used in recommending chairmen, a position similar to one already adopted by House Republicans. While this change did not directly challenge any specific chairman, its adoption was a concession to those who questioned an outdated criterion that largely rewarded conservatives for their longevity in non-contested districts.

Liberals did not wait to flex their new rights to challenge the sanctity of seniority. In January 1971, they confronted John McMillan of South Carolina, who for more than two decades had enraged unrepresented residents of the nation's capital with his arrogant chairmanship of the District of Columbia Committee. McMillan made little attempt to hide his contempt for the capital's African American majority or the weak local government. When appointed mayor Walter Washington sent the first city-developed budget to the Hill for the committee's review in 1967, McMillan responded by sending a truckload of watermelons to Washington's office. But McMillan's antagonistic opinions brought new challenges in his own district when rising numbers of black voters, a product of the Voting Rights Act, had forced him unexpectedly into a primary runoff in 1970 against a black physician. During the 1971 caucus organizing meetings, liberals proposed replacing McMillan with Charles Diggs, a black member from Detroit. The proposal alarmed Chairman Wilbur Mills of Arkansas, whose Ways and Means Committee was charged with recommending chairmen for caucus approval.[7] Removing McMillan, he warned, would inflame old passions and "risk the loss of Democratic votes in the South" in the 1972 elections. Like it or not, the younger members were reminded, the foundation of Democratic control of the House rested in large part on maintaining the seats of conservative southerners.

The debate in the caucus "got pretty hot," but, once again, the liberals revealed their weak vote-gathering skills, and McMillan retained his chair by a 126–96 vote. McMillian did not appear chastened by the rebuke. At a hearing the following month, he refused to recognize the District's newly elected representative, Walter Fauntroy, calling instead on archconservative John Rarick of Louisiana, who denounced the new delegate's district as a "sink-hole, rat-infested . . . laughingstock of the free and Communist world" and insulted his constituents as "transients and migrants." An outraged Diggs condemned Rarick as "a leading racist in Congress."[8]

The liberals' pent-up frustration reached the boiling point during the organizing caucus of the Appropriations Committee. A proposal by Sidney Yates of Illinois to open all Appropriations meetings to the press and public met with a stony silence. Finally, Dave Obey, a newcomer serving only his second term in the House, stood up to second Yates's proposal. "Sit down, you smart-ass young punk," growled John Rooney of New York, a subcommittee chair and 27-year veteran of the House. "What do you know?" Rooney had picked on the wrong liberal. Obey bristled, "Kiss my fanny, you senile old goat. What do *you* know?" The gasps of the committee members were audible. "I thought senior members . . . were going to go into cardiac arrest," Obey later recalled.[9] But Rooney laughed and slapped the table, and, remarkably, the Yates motion passed.

Despite such limited successes, the House largely remained "a closed, static, opaque and inefficient institution" that was incapable of successfully challenging the conservative bloc on the floor or the Nixon administration on issues from spending restraints to Vietnam expansion.[10] Chairmen retained enormous power, particularly those on the most influential committees like Texas's George Mahon, the conservative chair of Appropriations who used his power to ensure that conservatives held most of the key subcommittee chairmanships and the key slots on each panel.[11] Wilbur Mills of Arkansas did not even allow the creation of subcommittees on Ways and Means, ensuring that all decisions were made at the full committee level and subject to his will. Tom Harkin, working as a young staff member in the early 1970s, recalled that House committees remained "really insular, their own little world, . . . very closed, very secretive." Only three or four people in the entire House, according to Harkin, developed the enormously complex farm bill that impacted dozens of districts. "No one else had any input," he said. The House "was not on the up and up."[12]

The 1972 election was a presidential disaster for Democrats, with Richard Nixon winning more than 60 percent of the vote against George McGovern, but, surprisingly, the impact on the House was minimal. Democrats lost just 11 seats and retained a healthy majority of 241 votes. Among the freshmen were the first southern African Americans elected in nearly a century, Andrew Young of Georgia and Barbara Jordan of Texas, who benefitted from the expanded voting of the region's African Americans. Democrats even gained two seats in the Senate despite the Nixon landslide. The new Congress included many other new faces resulting from the retirement of 46 members, the largest number of voluntary departures in two decades, possibly prompted by a generous (but time-limited) pension package Congress had crafted to encourage voluntary departures.[13]

Many of the newcomers won their seats as opponents of the administration's Vietnam policies. California's Pete Stark defeated a pro-war incumbent Democrat in a primary after gaining wide publicity by hanging a gigantic peace sign on the exterior of the bank he owned. Emanuel Cellar of New York, the 25-term dean of the House and chairman of the Judiciary Committee, lost his primary to a young liberal, Elizabeth Holtzman, who criticized him for opposing legislation aimed at protecting the rights of women. Anti-war candidate Patricia Schroeder, who had been nominated to challenge a Republican incumbent after several men concluded 1972 was not a promising year for Democrats, was elected in Colorado despite Nixon's carrying her district by 28 points.

Democrats' appetite for reform was undiluted by the loss of seats or the presidential debacle. The unfolding revelations tying White House officials to the burglary of the Democratic National Headquarters in the Watergate complex fueled reformers' demands for transparency in government and the restoration of congressional power. Within only six months of the Nixon landslide, the largest electoral mandate in history was obscured by cascading revelations of scandal involving administration officials and possibly the president himself. By March 1973, the Senate had created a select committee to investigate Watergate, chaired by North Carolina's Sam Ervin, whose hearings would be the first to be nationally televised gavel to gavel by the three television networks.

Challenges to Chairs

One of the most sweeping reforms as the caucus reorganized in January 1973 was a proposal to allow members to vote on candidates put forward by the Committee on Committees for chairmanships. Voting on the chairs, Frank Evans of Colorado argued, would serve as a "reminder to the chairmen that they are creatures of the Caucus," which should have "the final say on the standard of competency for committee chairmen."[14] The debate on the proposal revealed a chasm within the caucus. Not surprisingly, many of the defenders of the seniority system were themselves chairmen. Chet Holifield, chairman of Government Operations, declared, a chairman nominee "should be approved unless there are compelling considerations to the contrary." Julia Hansen, who chaired the special reform committee, warned that the voting would descend into a "popularity contest," and others counseled, "The press would have a field day [reporting] what chairman received the most votes." Wayne Hays, chairman of House Administration, warned that conservative southerners would likely receive substantially fewer votes, which would "cause discord and dissension" within the caucus and potentially jeopardize continued Democratic control of their seats and perhaps even the Democratic majority in the House.

Others speculated that abandoning the seniority system might have the unintended consequence of undermining the chances for minority members to achieve chairmanships. "You have a secret vote and bigotry will prevail," predicted Martha Griffiths of Michigan, a leading spokesperson for gender equity. "No black, Jew or any minority will ever be elected chairman. Seniority may not work well," Griffiths asserted, "but seniority protects you [and] works for everybody," wondering whether women could achieve chairmanships without it.

The new majority leader, Tip O'Neill, pleaded for unity, reminding members that an increasingly adversarial press would exploit any evidence of caucus division. "Let's have no splinter groups in this Caucus," he pleaded. "It is not the ideology of the Democratic Party to vote hatred, bigotry, sectionalism or factionalism. Let's not pit one section of the country against another." Dedicated reformers like Burton and Udall argued that the results of any vote be kept secret so that those voting against chairmen might avoid retribution. O'Neill agreed, and on January 23, 1973, the caucus by a vote of 117–58 agreed to a compromise that enabled 20 percent of those present at a caucus to vote openly in favor of a secret vote on any chair nominee.

Not all of the prospective chairs facing a challenge were southerners or conservatives. Reformers asserted that 15-term Chet Holifield, a DSG cofounder veteran, lacked the energy to chair the Government Operations Committee, the House's major investigatory panel. Chairs "should be held to a high level of performance," New York liberal Ben Rosenthal noted, particularly given the likely need to "engage the Executive Branch in what may be the most serious struggle over constitutional and legislative authority in our country's history." Under Holifield's chairmanship, Rosenthal asserted, the committee's investigative output had dropped by half, and its subcommittees had held no hearings on more than two dozen executive agencies. Especially damning, Holifield's own Subcommittee on Military Operations had held "not a single day of investigative hearings" despite widespread anger about war strategy in Vietnam. Nor had there been any oversight hearings on Nixon's controversial impoundment of $12 billion appropriated by the Congress.[15]

Holifield reminded his colleagues that he had served for 30 years and had secured enactment of 10 bills during the recently concluded 92nd Congress. Echoing O'Neill's warning, he complained about the "barrage of critical newspaper headlines" in the Los Angeles press resulting from the "derogatory attack on my reputation," angrily comparing the process to being "executed in secret following a 'star chamber proceeding.' If I'm going to be stabbed in the back," Holifield demanded, "then I want it to be done openly."[16]

Holifield avoided the embarrassment of being removed by a 172–46 vote, after Speaker Albert, Ways and Means Chairman Mills, and Majority Leader O'Neill rallied to the defense of their longtime colleague.[17] The rest of the voting was fairly anticlimactic, with no chairs displaced, although nearly a quarter of those voting opposed Agriculture Chairman W. R. Poage and one-fifth voted to oust Banking Chairman Wright Patman. Notwithstanding Griffiths's admonition, Charles Diggs, an African American, won the chairmanship of the District of Columbia Committee.[18] Still, the fight over so basic a reform as allowing the caucus to vote on chairs illustrated the tenuous nature of reform in the caucus as well as the anxiety that challenges could jeopardize conservative Democrats, enabling Republicans to win their seats and diminish the Democratic majority.

Reformers also granted expanded subcommittees greater autonomy from the full committee chairs.[19] Allowing subcommittees greater independence, they argued, would disseminate power more equitably and allow issues suppressed at the full committee level to receive greater attention. Approval of the so-called Subcommittee Bill of Rights, academic observers agreed, strengthened the liberals and the leadership, producing "a congressional power structure which will soon be virtually unrecognizable in contrast to . . . [that of] the 1950's and 1960's," one that circumscribed the disproportionate influence of conservative southerners built around seniority and the chairman's gavel.[20] By limiting the number of subcommittees any one member could chair, the new rules further assured that more junior members would not have to wait many years to chair their first subcommittee. Indeed, the prior rules so protected the seniority claims of veterans that although nearly half the House had been elected since 1966, only sixteen members elected since 1958 had been able to secure their first subcommittee chairs by 1971.[21]

Some like Bolling warned the proposed changes might redistribute power in unintended ways, creating "120 baronies" that would weaken the ability of the leadership as well as the chairmen to manage the often-fractious House. Others were concerned that elevating dozens of junior members to subcommittee chairmanships might dampen their reformist zeal. "My God," one member complained, "you'll bring another 30 or 40 guys into the *status quo* and we won't get *any* change in the future."[22] Among those critical of the expanded role of subcommittees was the Republican leader, Gerald Ford, who noted that the number of House subcommittees had grown from 83 in the mid-1950s to well over a hundred by the early 1970s despite efforts to pare back proliferating panels.[23]

A further effort to improve the assignments of junior members required that legislators select the subcommittees on which they wished to serve according to their seniority on the full committee. This reform stymied the capability of a chairman to appoint only his own supporters to a subcommittee, shutting out alternative viewpoints. The "Bill of Rights" also required that bills be referred to a subcommittee within two weeks if not referred by the chairman, unless the members voted to retain the bill at the full committee level.

While granting more legislative power to the subcommittees, these changes inadvertently facilitated the work of lobbyists, who were able to target a small group of key subcommittee players to shape a bill to their liking. Such targeting facilitated junior members' solicitation of contributions from special interest groups whose issues came before their subcommittees. With the expansion of political action committees allowed by election law reforms, members would gain greater independence from party organizations in their fundraising, further weakening the ability of leaders to keep the membership in line on crucial votes.

Not all reforms undercut the leadership, however. Hansen had proposed creation of a "policy or steering committee" to make committee assignments at the beginning of each Congress, removing this power from the Ways and Means Committee, which had long functioned as the Committee on Committees.[24] Shifting the assignment power to a committee dominated by the elected leadership marked an important return of power taken from the Speaker in 1910. The change enhanced Albert's role not only in making committee assignments but also in developing the party's legislative priorities, coordinating strategy with Senate Democratic leaders, and arranging the scheduling of legislation on the floor. The Speaker gained the power to name the majority members of the Rules Committee, vastly enhancing his ability to prevent the obstructionism that had been practiced by Howard Smith and other Rules chairs. "For the first time since 1911," Speaker Albert wrote, "the elected House leadership controlled . . . the flow of bills through the Rules Committee."[25]

With these changes, many believed, "the groundwork for the [chairmanship] upsets of 1975 was laid."[26] Chairmanships were no longer granted solely by seniority but by votes of the caucus. Chairmen no longer exercised exclusive power over the policies in their jurisdiction but had to contend with empowered subcommittees and their chairs, who no longer owed their positions to the whim of the full committee head. Subcommittees had their own staffs, and even the minority had independent staff assistants, providing information and analysis independent of the full committee chair. And the power to appoint members to committees and the Rules Committee had passed from a single committee—Ways and Means (which selected its own members)—to the elected leadership of the party.

The reform groups were cheered by the decision to restrict the ability of the Rules Committee to block "any germane amendment to any bill." If 50 members gave written notice of a germane amendment they wanted to offer, the full caucus—not the Rules Committee or the leadership— would decide whether it could be offered on the floor. Although the leadership and Rules members must have seethed at this constriction of their authority, the proposal, authored by Phil Burton, was approved by a voice vote, demonstrating that the aggrieved leadership had little interest in an on-the-record confrontation with the aggressive caucus. A further bow to transparency occurred with the decision on February 21 to open committee hearings and legislative drafting sessions to the press and public unless an affirmative vote were taken to close them.

Adoption of these transparency rules was aggressively promoted by bipartisan reformers outside the Congress. Veterans of the civil rights and anti-war movement joined with new organizations like Common Cause, a nonpartisan organization formed in 1970. Common Cause was led by LBJ's secretary of health, education, and welfare, John Gardner, a Republican, and included labor leaders like Jack Conway of the United Auto Workers and grassroots activists like Fred Wertheimer. David Cohen, who became the organization's director for field operations, explained that Common Cause was not the successor to earlier good government, or "goo goo," progressive reform idealists. "It was not about abstract reform," Cohen explained. "It was about power, correcting the imbalances of power within the Congress."[27] Such objectives met with the bitter opposition of congressional power brokers like Wayne Hays. "Do any of you think that John Gardner of Common Cause has any respect for the Congress?" Hays asked at a caucus. "He has the utmost contempt for all of the Congress."[28]

Not all reform proposals met with caucus approval, however. Charles Bennett of Florida dismissed the option of voting down the nomination of a chairman as "no real reform at all" because everyone would understand the implication for a defeated chair. A no vote would be interpreted as "tantamount to impeachment," according to Bennett, carrying a "heavy implication of wrong doing or incompetence" that would undermine reelection.[29] Instead, Bennett proposed imposing term limits on future chairmen, which he believed would correct the "worst defect of the present system" while ensuring "fresh and new leadership needed to produce constructive changes in changing times," encouraging the retirement of older members. The proposal won support from Jim Wright, who stood to inherit a chairmanship if term limits were imposed. "I don't expect it will endear me to some Chairmen," Wright said, in a gross understatement, but "6 years is an adequate time for anyone to serve." Southerners, who stood to lose the most by any restriction on seniority, recoiled from the suggestion, and Joe Waggoner of Louisiana proposed a poison pill to extend the same limitation to all subcommittee chairs. But the caucus was not ready to impose such a rigid restriction, and the Bennett reform failed 46-107, as did a Udall proposal to limit chairmanship of the Democratic Campaign Committee and the whip position to two terms.[30] It was clear that if further challenges were to be made successfully to check seniority, a different strategy—or a different caucus composition—would be required.

The impact of the altered rules was felt swiftly. In March, the House voted to cut off funding for the supersonic transport aircraft, a costly and environmentally controversial proposal. The victory, which was attributed to the difficulty members newly faced in concealing positions on a controversial issue, marked a breakthrough for environmentalists whose earlier attacks on the aircraft had been notably ineffective. Now that members' votes were more easily made a matter of public record, more liberals showed up to cast votes and to successfully lobby their colleagues.

Assertion of Congressional Authority

Senior members agreed that many of the internal reforms were required if Congress was to reassert itself with respect to the more agile executive branch and to check presidential wrongdoing. "If you were trying to be a coequal branch, you couldn't [match] the Rayburn House versus Nixon White House," recalled Joel Jankowsky, an aide to Albert, who became the first Speaker to hire a press secretary.[31] "According to Jim Wright, the changes were a direct outgrowth of the Watergate scandal, "motivated at least in part by a sense of outrage at the scandalously unethical and illegal deeds of some in the Nixon Administration."[32] One staff person recalled that the aggressive use of power by the White House "drove the Speaker crazy," leading him to quietly support internal changes. Albert and other House leaders also bristled at less weighty slights by the Nixon White House, including long delays in responding to phone calls.

But Albert was less convinced of the wisdom of more widely distributing power inside Congress, which he feared would add to his management headaches. In August 1971 he had complained that "no fewer than 113 Congressmen hold subcommittee chairmanships, an unprecedented distribution of legislative responsibility to more than 25% of the entire House of Representatives."[33] Such a dissemination of power appealed to Burton, who favored dissipating the power of conservatives, but anguished other reformers like Bolling who worried about the ability of the leadership to corral so many independent operators.

Albert was innately cautious, a product of Little Dixie, Oklahoma, but he was not without political courage. He reflected the era of weak House leaders, a somnambulant caucus, and dominant chairmen. While lacking a distinctly ideological record, he vigorously protected the rules of the House, including the rights of members, a crucial trait in any leader. When Adam Clayton Powell, a controversial African American, was stripped of his chairmanship of the Education and Labor Committee and refused seating by the House because of ethical problems, Albert himself occupied Powell's seat on the committee until he was reelected, after which he yielded the seat—though not the chairmanship—back to Powell. He also demonstrated increasing interest in the growing feminism that was affecting both the House and broader society. In 1973, he initiated a policy of granting maternity leave when Yvonne Burke of California became the first member to give birth while in office, and he also appointed the first female page in 1973. Albert also welcomed the passage of the Twenty-Sixth Amendment to the Constitution in 1971 granting 18-year-olds the right to vote, which he viewed as "akin to the abolition of slavery and the removal of property, racial, and gender qualifications for voting: it was another step in 'perfecting our democracy.'"

But Albert was under constant pressure to respond to a caucus that he realized was very much in the throes of change and unaware and unconcerned with respecting long-standing House traditions. Half of the membership had been elected since 1966, an unusually high level of turnover, and these new members offered different perspectives than had those with whom he had arrived a generation earlier. "For many of them, the defining global experience of their own political orientation was Vietnam, not Munich," Albert wrote. "The domestic concerns that moved them included inflation and the environment, not unemployment and civil rights." The slowly rising number of African Americans and other minorities, as well as women, improved the House, he acknowledged, even as they "flew right in the face of the prevailing stereotype of Congress."[34]

Albert's sensitivity to the changing nature of the House led key aides to view him as a "transitional" Speaker rather than the vigorous defender of the status quo as he was often portrayed, willing to reach out to new members and reformers while hesitant to publicly embrace their demands. Jim Wright recalled Albert, who was cautious about addressing the new members in 1972, soliciting him to speak with the incoming freshmen "who wanted to stimulate a broad-based change in House rules."[35] Despite his own misgivings, he also allowed liberals to push through the caucus a 1972 resolution instructing Democratic members of the Foreign Affairs Committee to approve a resolution calling for an end to the Vietnam War.

Other senior members were less openly tolerant of the innovations pushed by the caucus, and confrontations soon erupted between the crusty chairs and the restless younger members. As the House began organizing, Pat Schroeder, a 32-year-old Denver lawyer and registered pilot, requested a seat on the Armed Services Committee, which had never had a female member. Also requesting a committee seat was second-term Ron Dellums, a charismatic anti-war orator from Berkeley who reasoned that, given the high proportion of blacks dying in Vietnam, Armed Service needed a black member.

The chairman, F. Edward Hébert of Louisiana, a 71-year-old segregationist, had begun his House career in 1941 when Schroeder was 1 year old. Although he insisted, "This is a non-partisan committee," his view of nonpartisanship did not extend to those critical of the Southeast Asia war. Hébert rejected both requests, but Wilbur Mills, whose Ways and Means Committee still determined assignments, was influenced by his wife to consider the expanding number of black voters in his own Arkansas district. Many saw the decision to override the chairman's objections as a "slap in the face to Hébert," which the chairman repaid during the committee's first meeting in January 1973. Glaring down at the committee's two newest members, he ordered Dellums and Schroeder to share a single chair because he considered each "only worth half a member." Schroeder recalled, "Ron and I gulped and sat on one chair."[36] Rep. Barney Frank of Massachusetts later remarked that sharing a chair with Dellums was "the only half-assed thing Pat ever did in Congress!"

Vietnam: The "All-Consuming Issue"

Opposition to the war in Vietnam was quickly becoming what Dave Obey termed "an all-consuming issue" as well as one dividing House Democrats. In mid-1970, Jeffrey Cohelan, who represented the strongly anti-war Berkeley-Oakland area, had been defeated in a primary by Dellums; across the continent, insurgent Democrat Bella Abzug unseated another pro-war incumbent, Leonard Farbstein of New York. Senior party leaders who remained pro-war, including the chairmen of major committees like Appropriations, Armed Services, and Foreign Affairs, drew increasing criticism from Democratic colleagues for barring anti-war amendments from consideration on the floor. Between 1966 and 1972, although there were 94 floor votes pertaining to Vietnam, rarely was one allowed that would reduce funding.[37] "I'm not going to be a party to the appeasement of communism," Speaker Albert had once declared, and, indeed, Albert was a "consistent supporter" of the war and was accused of using "his leadership prerogatives" to block amendments restricting funding or ordering changes in military strategy. When the House finally voted in opposition to the war in 1973, after the signing of the Paris Accords, Albert "stayed on the sidelines."[38] His neutrality led anti-war members to propose a caucus rule barring members of the leadership from speaking on the floor in contradiction to positions taken by the caucus.[39]

The divisions that wracked Democrats over Vietnam even affected DSG, whose membership included many veteran liberals who continued to embrace a Cold War anti-communism. The anti-war faction, which had formed the Group in the late 1960s, published a book analyzing the recently disclosed Pentagon Papers whose leak had undermined the official rationale for the war. But internal tension even undercut the Group, reportedly after the sharp-elbowed Abzug pressed for admission. "If we let her in," warned Burton, who thought she lacked pragmatism, "you might as well just forget about 'The Group.' Even our institution will be too straight for her, too close to the leadership. There won't be any other reason for us to exist. She'll pull it apart." As predicted, Abzug proved a confrontational addition, and the members decided to disband rather than continue with her presence.[40] Nevertheless, the number of antiwar members continued to grow steadily, reaching into more senior ranks, including John Brademas, Frank Thompson, and Jim O'Hara.

Energized by their growing numbers, liberals increasingly pressed the caucus to embrace positions ignored or opposed by committee chairs, especially regarding the Vietnam War. In the spring, the caucus approved a resolution barring commitment of US forces to foreign hostilities unless authorized by Congress. In May, furious that the Defense Appropriations subcommittee had defeated an amendment barring funds for the bombing of Cambodia by a 14–31 vote, Connecticut's Robert Giaimo, along with Georgia's John Flynt and New York's Joseph Addabbo, proposed a caucus resolution directing that a floor amendment be permitted to prohibit funding the air campaign.[41] The tactic drew complaints from conservatives like Sam Stratton of New York, who warned the caucus was interfering with ongoing peace negotiations and legislating "without detailed study of the issues."[42] But in the face of Armed Services' unwillingness to hold hearings on such controversial topics, Giaimo's resolution was agreed to by an overwhelming caucus vote of 144–22, and the next day the House gave its assent 219–188. "*We* were the leadership on that issue," crowed DSG's Dick Conlon.[43]

Congress "Finding Its Voice"

Congress also was growing more determined to confront Nixon, increasingly weakened by the Watergate scandal, over the use of "impoundment," a 70-year-old practice by which presidents refused to expend money included in appropriations laws. Having been maneuvered into signing spending bills in excess of his desires, Nixon retaliated by refusing to expend the additional $12 billion he had not requested. By the spring of 1973, the disagreement had escalated into "a red hot issue" between the branches of government.[44] During a lively caucus meeting in April, the conservative Appropriations Chairman George Mahon proposed a new law to require the president to present to Congress his rationale for impoundment and to give Congress the ability to constrain him by passing a Joint Resolution not subject to a veto, an idea embraced by the caucus.

The 1972 freshmen supported the impoundment proposal but wanted the leadership to confront Nixon more directly. "All of us came out of the grass roots," declared Iowa's Ed Mezvinsky, one of the leading malcontents, "where we found a strong feeling that Congress should be a dynamic branch," as opposed to the "sapless branch" described by Sen. Joseph Clark. "This institution has not been able to respond."[45] Another freshman leader, Barbara Jordan of Texas, chastised the Democratic majority for its "inability . . . to decide a course of action and to move on it." The impotence of the caucus, she asserted, "has caused a deep sense of depression not only among the freshmen but among some of the most senior members of Congress."[46]

In April, several members took to the floor for a four-hour special order speaking marathon to demand leadership action on impoundment.[47] Some construed the speeches as criticism of Albert, an impression one participant quickly sought to dispel. "Nothing could be further from the truth!!" freshman Bill Gunther of Florida wrote to the Speaker. "Had that been the case, not only would I not have participated in this effort—I would have actively opposed it," as would "an overwhelming majority of my freshmen Democratic colleagues."[48] Albert was grateful for Gunther's assurances but exasperated since he and O'Neill had joined freshmen in their floor discussion.[49]

A meeting between the Speaker and the disgruntled freshmen did little to assuage the criticism. In a note to his staff, Albert wrote that he was puzzled by the continuing disapproval "because we had a very friendly meeting and I encouraged them."[50] Albert may have misread the tone of the meeting, which followed an override attempt that failed because 28 Democrats had defied the leadership and joined with Republicans. To each point raised by the freshmen, Albert had cordially responded, "Fine." Finally, Barbara Jordan "explode[d]" at the Speaker. "In the 90 days that I've been here, I find that Congress is having difficulty finding its back and its voice," she lectured him. For his part, Albert was "equally frustrated" with members who were reluctant to challenge Nixon's actions. "I've never seen a President who had so many people tamed like puppies on a chain when he cracks his whip," the Speaker observed.[51]

Even within the GOP Conference, Bill Archer, a Texas conservative, recalled a similar feeling that "the president has too much power" and "is abusing his power." As Archer saw it, all members, notwithstanding party or ideology, had a constitutional responsibility "to take power away from the president and constitute it within the Congress."[52] Republican leader John Rhodes complained that meetings with the president were "a one way street" because Nixon "did all the talking. We could never convince him that we needed input in the process before legislation was sent down to us."[53]

A grimmer challenge to the presidency arose in early 1973 as the courts, prosecutors, and Congress extended their probe into the 1972 Watergate burglary and possible connections between the perpetrators and the White House. Taken together with the congressional anger over Vietnam and impoundment, the unraveling Watergate story provided renewed opportunities for legislative challenges to the imperial presidency. "The reforms have reduced friction among House Democrats. We have gained power and strength," Tip O'Neill gloated, "and downtown, the Executive is on the ropes.[54]

Democrats seized on Nixon's falling public approval to pass legislation reining in the executive branch's autonomy. The preceding year, in response to press stories about secret negotiations that had kept Hill leaders in the dark, Congress passed the Case-Zablocki Act requiring that all international pacts receive legislative review.[55] Late in 1973, Congress passed the War Powers Resolution requiring that Congress be notified within 48 hours of any decision to deploy US forces into combat and restricting deployments to 60 days absent congressional approval. Nixon vetoed the resolution, asserting an unconstitutional infringement on his executive powers, but Congress overrode the veto by a bipartisan 284–135 vote in the House and a 75–18 vote in the Senate.[56] Within a year, the Nelson-Bingham Amendment also gave Congress authority to block any presidentially negotiated arms sale through passage of a resolution of disapproval.

Congress also approved the Budget and Impoundment Control Act to check Nixon's refusal to spend approved funds and to create a formal congressional budget process to free Congress from dependence on the administration's budget experts. The law created new budget committees in each house to develop a congressional resolution setting out spending and revenue goals, and a nonpartisan Congressional Budget Office to develop independent budget estimates. The law was not without controversy within Congress itself, because it imposed time constraints and spending limitations on the freewheeling Appropriations and Ways and Means Committees. Even some reform advocates were wary, with DSG warning the new committee could become a conservative vehicle for forcing spending cuts.[57] "The proposal would negate any of the reforms enacted by the House over the past 2 years," junior appropriator Dave Obey cautioned, by limiting Congress's ability to spend on its own priorities. House leaders placated the committees by guaranteeing the two committees membership on the Budget panel.[58]

A Formal Effort at Reform

Hopes for additional internal reforms before the end of the 93rd Congress increased when Albert appointed Richard Bolling to chair a special committee to review House organization and operations, including the restructuring of committee jurisdiction that had proven so elusive in 1946 and 1970.[59] Some reformers were immediately suspicious, particularly Burton, who dismissed Bolling as a "white collar liberal" with whom he had long clashed over the question of consolidating power in the leadership, as the Missourian advocated, or disseminating it more widely, as Burton envisioned.[60] Burton endorsed shifting greater power to the increasingly liberal caucus, which he hoped to chair, to undercut the disproportionate power of the conservative chairs. While Bolling agreed the committee structure was in "disarray," he favored empowering the Speaker, a historic shift in congressional power of greater significance than the jurisdictional modifications, thought Bill Cable, a veteran House staffer who monitored the Bolling panel's work.[61]

Bolling's final report did not shy from boldness. He proposed moving all health policy to Commerce, which liberals believed would be more hospitable to national health insurance. The recommendation represented an enormous loss of power for Ways and Means, whose chairman, Wilbur Mills, had opposed much of the Great Society legislation. Another proposal to split the Education and Labor Committee along its policy lines drew sharp objections from organized labor, which feared anti-union conservatives would flood onto a labor-only panel to weaken the nation's labor laws.[62] A recommendation to consolidate energy and environmental legislation into a single new committee drew vigorous opposition from both pro-energy conservatives who feared environmental influence and from environmentalists who warned the committee would be dominated by the oil and gas industry. Bolling also proposed restricting all members to one committee and eliminating the referral of legislation to multiple committees.

The debate over the Bolling panel's recommendations reflected deep divisions and mistrust as members quickly prioritized self-interest over institutional reform. Bolling despaired this "herd of elephants" was preparing to trample his plan when it came before the Democratic Caucus in May 1974, and he had good reason for pessimism. The proposal was quickly ridiculed as a "kooky report prepared by kooky professors."[63]

45

Although some reformers supported Bolling's sweeping changes, liberals like Frank Thompson, Jim O'Hara, Bill Ford of Michigan, John Brademas, and Burton all declared their opposition to the dismantling of Education and Labor. Similarly, senior members like John Dingell, whose Commerce Committee stood to lose energy jurisdiction, rejected the plan, warning it would enable special interests to target their lobbying.[64] Those with the most at risk, the chairmen, were especially unamused. Leonor Sullivan of the Merchant Marine and Fisheries Committee declared her "outright opposition," dismissing the "proponents [who] are attempting to wrap themselves in the flag of reform and dare opposition to such a noble goal." It was a provocation Sullivan, one of the few women chairs, did not hesitate to challenge. "Well, *I* dare, because I don't consider it true reform at all [but rather] a mere restructuring, a reshuffling that will create more problems and conflicts."[65]

Others opposed the plan's proposal to end proxy voting in committees, which allowed the chairman (or ranking minority member) to cast ballots for absent members. The large number of subcommittees on which they served often prevented members from attending simultaneously scheduled markups, and without proxies a panel's work could come to a standstill. Such a change, Chet Holifield warned, represented "a weakening of Democratic control" that would give Republicans "more power as a party, but not more responsibility. They will have more power to harass and hinder, to obstruct and delay." For the same reason, he opposed the plan to give the minority one-third of a committee's staff, which seemed disproportionate to actual Republican membership.

Bolling pleaded for positive action on his plan, asserting, "If we fail to adopt organizational structure now, it would be hopeless in a new Congress." Speaker Albert praised the panel's "excellent recommendations" but urged the caucus to send the plan to the full House under an open rule that would allow unlimited amendments to be offered. "I do not want the Democratic Party in this House to become labeled the anti-reform party," the Speaker declared. But Bolling's changes trampled on too many powerful feet, including those of his archrival, Burton, who succeeded in having the caucus divert the plan to the Hansen Committee "for further study" by a 95–81 caucus vote. Observers concluded the action was the death sentence for jurisdictional reform. "We could have beaten everyone else" but the labor leaders, Bolling bitterly complained, "who are so far out of touch with what Congress needs."

When the Hansen panel met to review the complicated Bolling plan, Burton sought to exclude staff, allegedly to ensure secrecy but likely to enhance his own domination of the process. Other panel members were naturally suspicious of the wily Burton. "Do you have any idea what is in this fucking book?" asked Phil Landrum, a 20-year veteran. Burton readily admitted he did not. "Well, don't you think that *somebody* in the room ought to know what the fuck is in it?" Landrum inquired. Staff members took weeks to go through the entire document, meeting privately with each committee member. Bill Cable recalled conferring with Burton, who reclined on a couch, a glass of vodka in hand, methodically explaining his opposition to Bolling's overall design, although he welcomed eliminating Ways and Means' jurisdiction over health policy, which would enhance the influence of the Californian's own committee.

The Republican Conference, which stood to gain additional staffing and financial resources under the Bolling plan, gave its swift approval, but Democrats dragged the review into the summer of 1974. To Bolling's dismay, the revised bill that finally passed the House 203–165 in July contained none of the major jurisdictional changes he had recommended nor the additional staff resources for the minority.[66] Republicans denounced the majority for abandoning reform, but many Democrats rejoiced. Staff members on the Education and Labor Committee brought flowers for Chairman Carl Perkins, who had fought the plan, and Perkins gave a raise to Cable, who had monitored the deliberations for him.

Climax of the Watergate Scandal

The dominating public issue in mid-1974 was not reformulation of the House's complex jurisdictional structure but the profound crisis over Watergate. Vice President Spiro Agnew had already resigned in 1973 over corruption charges linked to his days as Maryland's governor, and Nixon, employing the Twenty-Fifth Amendment for the first time, had appointed the popular House Republican leader Gerald Ford as vice president. On February 6, 1974, just 14 months after Nixon's historic landslide reelection, the House voted 410–4 to direct the Judiciary Committee "to investigate fully and completely whether sufficient grounds exist for the House of Representatives to exercise its constitutional power to impeach" the president for only the second time in history. Within the House, the Judiciary Committee's Watergate hearings were a pivotal moment in the reassertion of Congress's role as a coequal branch of government. Congress now seemed to have the upper hand, calling in administration officials for grilling before the television cameras, issuing subpoenas to the president, and considering whether to remove him from office. Public estimation of the Congress rose as tens of millions of Americans had their first opportunity to witness a televised House hearing. Obscure House members suddenly gained celebrity status as skilled questioners.[67]

House Democratic strategists fully appreciated that the unfolding of the Watergate melodrama provided them with a rare electoral opportunity, and they were quick to seize it. Burton pushed DSG to aggressively recruit liberal candidates for the fall election and directed his veteran election pollster Mark Gersh to identify districts where Democrats might be competitive. Democrats became increasingly giddy as the year wore on. "If Mr. Nixon keeps destroying the programs that help the people of this country and advocates more spending in Vietnam," Campaign Committee Chairman Wayne Hays gloated, "I predict . . . there will not be enough seats on the Democratic side of the aisle to seat all the newly elected Democrats." As in 1972, Burton raised money to support the candidates, largely irrespective of their ideology: as long as they were Democrats and stood a reasonable chance of winning, Burton and DSG provided assistance.[68]

In addition to DSG, affluent and savvy political activists including Maurice Rosenblatt and Russ Hemingway bolstered the work of the National Committee for an Effective Congress (NCEC), whose board included such liberal luminaries as Amherst professor Henry Steele Commanger, *Washington Post* publisher Eugene Meyer, Hans Morganthau of the University of Chicago, Dean Francis Sayre of the National Cathedral, and Nobel laureate and Harvard professor George Wald. During the summer of 1974, the small NCEC staff helped identify attractive reform candidates, eventually selecting 49 for strategic targeting and media assistance.[69]

Events moved swiftly during the summer. On July 24, a unanimous Supreme Court ordered the president to yield tape recordings of Oval Office conversations with conspirators that revealed Nixon's illegal personal involvement in obstructing the Watergate investigation. Two weeks later, the nation was simultaneously stunned and relieved by Nixon's resignation, which elevated Ford—only eight months earlier the virtually powerless House minority leader—to the presidency. The nation, and the political outlook for the fall, were then immeasurably impacted by one last, unanticipated development: Ford's unconditional pardon of Nixon just after Labor Day at the beginning of the fall campaign.

For many of the young men and women seeking seats in the House, the game-changing impact was almost impossible to believe. Not only were the White House and the Republican Party in shambles, but suddenly campaigns that seemed destined to defeat appeared eminently winnable. Candidates who were running on a lark, or to "get it out of my blood" like Oklahoma's Glenn English, suddenly found themselves headed for victory. "We thought, 'Whoa, better find a place to live,'" said George Miller, "because we were coming to Washington."

By the time Congress recessed for the election campaign in September, the members of the 93rd Congress could look back on two sessions of significant legislative and organizational modernization, but the work was unfinished. Speaker Albert credited the caucus with having "affected more reforms of its own procedures then had any Congress since the Cannon revolt" of 1910. Even before the large infusion of new members and challenge to the seniority system that would soon come, fully half of those chairing House committees had held their gavel for less than four years.[70] The Democratic Caucus had limited the powers of chairmen, expanded the authority and independence of subcommittees, reformed campaign finance, overridden vetoes in areas including war-making powers and budget and spending that circumscribed the formerly unchallenged powers of the executive, and tinkered just enough with committee structure and jurisdiction to have "adopted the House's committee structure to the nation's modern needs."[71]

The record extended to the legislative productivity of the House as well. Analysts noted the "impressive array of legislation" enacted by the Congress, sometimes over the president's objections, which "signaled its determination to recapture its constitutional powers."[72] Nevertheless, despite a "sharp swing to the left among the moderate Republicans," the Conservative Coalition remained powerful, winning 63 percent of its battles on the House floor.[73]

It had been a challenging Congress and a difficult time for the nation. "We had been through hell and back," Pat Schroeder recalled. Washington "was a war zone," with National Guardsmen patrolling the streets, demonstrators filling the Mall with angry protests, and tear gas occasionally wafting across the Capitol's manicured grounds. But after years of frustration, procedures were now in place to challenge those who opposed the growing liberal base of the caucus; all that was needed were additional liberals to enforce the discipline. The reformers did not have long to wait.

3 **THE CLASS** DIVERSE AND DETERMINED

I'd knock on doors and tell people, "I'm running for Congress," and they'd ask, "Are you a Republican or a Democrat?" I'd say, "Democrat, but . . ." and the person would say, "Good, I'll vote for you." Almost every house. People were ready for a change, even the Republicans.—Rep. Jerry Patterson (D-CA)

Yes! Yes! Yes! Yes. We're going to win!!—Rep. Jim Blanchard (D-MI)

President Gerald Ford's unanticipated pardon of Richard Nixon on September 8, 1974, changed everything. "Yes! Yes! Yes! Yes!" cheered Jim Blanchard, a youthful candidate in Michigan, as he heard the bulletin on his car radio. "We're going to win!"

The hostile public reaction to Ford's action extinguished Republicans' already thin hopes of gaining momentum toward a House majority that had stalled two years earlier. Nixon's landslide victory had bolstered the expectations of Republican strategists that the end of two decades of Democratic dominance of Congress might be imminent. Their carefully crafted appeals to spending restraints, patriotism, law and order, and, more subtly, to white racial anxieties stoked by years of urban and antiwar unrest had lured millions of conservative Democrats to Nixon. But while Nixon swept 49 states, his party gained just 14 House seats nationally and remained 26 seats short of a House majority. GOP leaders felt "stung by [the] failure to cash in on Nixon's landslide."[1]

Republicans had remained confident that 1974 would reignite the trend toward a GOP majority. Even before Inauguration Day 1973, the Republican campaign committee launched a 1974 "talent search" for candidates to run for as many as 80 seats occupied by Democrats. They focused on states that had voted for Nixon and GOP senators, such as Texas, where Sen. John Tower had carried 10 districts that nevertheless continued to elect Democrats to the House.

Republicans also anticipated that the reform pressures roiling the Democratic Caucus might encourage embattled conservatives to retire, forcing Democrats to complete in swing districts without the benefits of incumbency. "Some of 'em feel a bit emasculated by the reforms that have taken away some of their power," Ohio Republican Clarence Brown counseled, and "aren't very comfortable with the direction their national party or the direction a majority of the Democrats on their committees want to go." Faced with an aggressive, young Republican opponent, he speculated, a conservative Democrat might choose to "pick up his retirement benefits and play golf at Burning Tree full time instead of part-time."[2]

But as the scandals, resignations, and indictments related to Watergate continued to grow during the spring, Republican optimism withered. Nixon's embarrassments extended beyond the break-in and cover-up: in April, he paid more than $430,000 in back taxes the Internal Revenue Service had concluded he owed. In July, seven Republicans on the Judiciary Committee joined the Democrats in voting for one or more articles of impeachment against the president. As panic began to spread, Nixon invited House Republicans to a meeting to assure them no crimes had been committed. Soon afterward, Charles Sandman, a New Jersey conservative who had faithfully voted against all of the impeachment charges in the Judiciary Committee, approached Lou Frey of Florida with an ashen face. "There *is* a smoking gun," confided a crestfallen Sandman. A newly released Oval Office tape recording revealed Nixon's undeniable complicity in the Watergate cover-up. "I couldn't believe it!" said Frey.[3] Three days later, Nixon resigned the presidency.

Then, implausibly, the outlook for Republicans *worsened*. Only one month into his term, President Gerald Ford informed a small number of his former Republican House colleagues of his decision to grant Nixon "a full, free, and absolute pardon" for any crimes related to Watergate. Without the pardon, Ford concluded, Nixon "would have been indicted [and] the probability is he would . . . have gone to jail." The "long, torturous appeal" process likely would have dragged through the 1976 election season with potentially disastrous results for Ford.[4] The horrified Republicans were significantly more concerned about the imminent *1974* election, when every House member would be on the ballot. They urged their former colleague to defer any action until after the approaching midterm election, but Ford was resolute. "The country is more important than re-election," he told his incredulous visitors, days before announcing the pardon on national television.[5] The pardon was "a big damage item," in Frey's understated words. Ford's negatives in public opinion polls soared by 36 percent as speculation erupted that the president was delivering on an illegal quid pro quo that had eased Nixon out of the Oval Office.[6]

Members of Congress were further stunned to learn that Ford had agreed to allow Nixon to share joint custody of his White House papers with the federal government, which many believed would allow the former president to tamper with the official archives. A close friend, former Justice Department lawyer Benton Becker, advised Ford to rethink the agreement. "You will be writing the history of your presidency in the first weeks," Becker warned, "and history is going to say Jerry Ford participated in the final act of the Watergate cover-up."[7] Ford's popularity went into a dizzying tailspin, plunging from 71 percent to 49 percent in one week. His longtime press secretary, Jerry terHorst, resigned in protest. Nationally, 57 percent of voters thought that Ford was wrong to issue a pardon or to yield Nixon's presidential papers to the former chief executive.[8] An election already trending poorly for Republicans took a decisive lurch toward the Democrats.

Surprisingly, few members of the Class of 1974 credit Watergate as a central motivation in their decision to run for Congress, since many had made the decision before the full dimensions of the scandal were known; nor did many believe it was a decisive issue in their campaigns. Nevertheless, election victors were instantly labeled "the Watergate Babies," a caricature meant to attribute their victories to the crisis and to accentuate their youth, inexperience, self-aggrandizement, impetuousness, and disdain for the formal traditions of the House, their senior colleagues, and the leadership. "The 'Watergate babies' who entered the Congress in 1975 included many amateurs," one critic generalized.[9] No less a figure than House Majority Leader Tip O'Neill chastised them for their alleged political inexperience, asserting many in the Class "had never rung doorbells, or driven people to the polls, or stayed late stuffing envelopes at campaign headquarters."

These portrayals have persisted for decades, the result of actions and comments by some Class members. But these broad generalizations distort the backgrounds and seriousness of the men and women who entered Congress in 1975. While the Class has long been portrayed as composed of young zealots who swarmed Capitol Hill intent on destroying the seniority system and reforming archaic House procedures, few identified congressional reform as a major objective. Indeed, interviews with more than 40 Class members revealed it was the rare candidate who was even aware of the battles waged by McCarthy's Marauders, the Democratic Study Group, or the Hansen and Bolling Committees.

So, who were these Class members? To understand the backgrounds, motivations and goals of the Class of 1974, we must first tease apart the individuals from the collective group into which they have been conveniently, but inaccurately, lumped for four decades. Its members included novices and experienced legislators, businesspeople and consumer activists, educators and legislative staff. There were liberals and conservatives, and a few whose political philosophy was indeterminate, even to themselves. Some would have brief congressional careers while others would remain for decades, occupying the chairmanships they began their careers challenging. In one respect, the characterizations were accurate: they were young, the majority in their 30s and 40s, and some were barely above the constitutional requirement of 25. Their addition to the ranks of Congress dropped the average age of House members below 50 for the first time in decades. Many were angry, especially about the war in Vietnam. And, clearly, they were impatient for change.[10]

Candidate Profiles of Class Members

Tom Harkin, a Vietnam-era veteran, had been fired from his congressional job. Dave Evans and Floyd Fithian were teachers, Bob Edgar a minister. Leo Zeferetti headed a New York police union. Tim Wirth, Phil Sharp, and Andy Maguire had earned doctorates in government. Helen Meyner had been First Lady of New Jersey, where Millicent Fenwick was a patrician, pipe-smoking state legislator. Larry Pressler, a South Dakota Republican, was a Foreign Service officer awarded a Rhodes Scholarship because of his knowledge of pig husbandry. Toby Moffett, who worked both for Nixon's administration *and* for consumer advocate Ralph Nader, was a registered Independent just two weeks before filing as a candidate. Berkley Bedell and Fred Richmond made millions in business before turning to politics. Marilyn Lloyd replaced her husband on the ballot after he died in a plane crash en route to his primary victory party. Steve Neal published a newspaper in North Carolina, while Butler Derrick, John Jenrette, and Elliott Levitas were state legislators in South Carolina and Georgia. Larry McDonald was an Georgia urologist and John Birch Society member, while Tom Downey was a recent Cornell graduate who admired portions of the radical manifesto of the Students for a Democratic Society. Ed Beard was a housepainter from Rhode Island. Gary Myers worked in a steel plant. Bill Hefner was a North Carolina gospel singer.

Not all of the Class members were complete strangers to Capitol Hill. Some were already skilled at navigating the labyrinthine tunnels that snake among the congressional office buildings, the Capitol, and the Library of Congress. Negotiating these poorly marked subterranean pathways, past steam pipes, electric cables, and rooms of mechanical equipment and staff carryouts is one of the great challenges confronting any new legislator. One freshman who knew his way was Jim Oberstar, a top aide to longtime Minnesota representative John Blatnik, chairman of the Public Works and Transportation Committee.[11] Oberstar was well aware how Blatnik, as a younger legislator, had been regularly slighted by the Rules chairmen. "Young man," Rules Chairman Smith had once declared, dismissing Blatnik's signature water pollution control bill, "you want the federal government to build toilets, but we are not going to do that."[12] When Blatnik became ill, he endorsed Oberstar, and the young aide presented himself throughout the district as the natural successor.

Tom Harkin had been inspired by President Kennedy's call to public service and began volunteering in local Iowa campaigns at a young age. He attracted the attention of local congressman Neal Smith, who hired him for the staff of the House Select Committee on US Involvement in Southeast Asia. An Air Force veteran still mourning "lots of friends [who had] lost their lives" in Vietnam, Harkin leapt at the chance to work in Congress while also studying law at night and participating in demonstrations against the Vietnam War.[13]

Harkin's career path changed dramatically during a committee trip to Vietnam in 1970 during which former prisoners of the South Vietnamese government invited him to inspect prison facilities on Con Son Island, where they had been jailed. Harkin was horrified by the sight of hundreds of prisoners, including Buddhist monks, crammed into "tiger cages"—pits in the ground covered with bars. Ordered by committee members and Attorney General John Mitchell to turn over photographs he had taken at Con Son, Harkin refused, convinced the evidence would be destroyed. Instead, Harkin published the pictures in *Life* magazine and authored an article in the *Progressive* warning against "blind acceptance" of the official accounts of the US and Vietnamese governments.

Harkin quickly found himself transformed from "just a goddamn staffer" to the object of a major confrontation with the Justice Department and his own committee members, but he was not contrite. "I learned," Harkin wrote, "that you don't have to go along. One man can stand up and make a difference."[14] One "difference" was his termination from the committee; another congressional job offer was quickly rescinded, and a "high-ranking member" with influence over House hiring—likely Wayne Hays—vowed Harkin would never again work in Congress. Harkin listened in shock from the House gallery as legislators of both parties denounced him on the House floor. Only the anti-war activist Allard Lowenstein of New York rose to defend his actions. His treatment confirmed Harkin's distrust of Capitol Hill. "This place not on the up and up," he said. "It is very closed, very secretive. Everything was done behind closed doors. No press. Nothing." Chairmen made all the decisions, he complained.[15]

Capitalizing on his unanticipated celebrity, Harkin traveled across the country speaking at churches and campuses before returning to Iowa in 1972 to challenge incumbent William Scherle. It seemed an impossible task since the district had rarely elected a Democrat, but the recent reapportionment had made thousands of Iowa State anti-war students eligible to vote as 18-year-olds because of the Twenty-Sixth Amendment. Harkin received a respectable 45 percent, carrying all of the counties newly added to the district. "I figured it was worth another try," he concluded. Two years later, with public distaste for Vietnam and the Watergate scandal raging, he ran again. Like many Democrats running in traditionally Republican districts, Harkin avoided national controversies and hammered away on local issues like the impact of Agriculture Secretary Earl Butz's policies on family farmers. He also criticized Scherle's opposition to environmental legislation, a topic of increasing importance to younger voters. To the extent that he discussed Vietnam, he was careful to remind voters he was a veteran, not an agitator.

Some members of the Class, as scholars of American politics, were knowledgeable of recent reform efforts. Andrew Maguire had stuffed envelopes in Los Angeles during the early 1960s for Rep. James Roosevelt. Fifteen years later, with a PhD in government from Harvard and experience at the State Department under his belt, Maguire was working for the Ford Foundation when he decided to seek a seat on the Bergen County (NJ) Board of Chosen Freeholders. His narrow loss persuaded him in 1974 to challenge the Republican congressman, William Widnall, a local institution who was the senior Republican on the House Banking Committee, as well as a Nixon critic both on Vietnam and Watergate.

"I felt unusually qualified to enter the fray effectively and make a difference," Maguire recalled. "I wanted directly to be a maker of decisions and a shaper of policies."[16] Maguire avoided partisanship, praising both Republican senator Clifford Case and Harrison Williams, the state's Democrat. He framed his campaign as "a run against Congress from outside rather than inside," presenting himself as unwilling to follow "the traditional patterns of timing and hierarchical stepping stones," a route followed by other Class members who also refused to serve long apprenticeships before running for Congress.[17] Like others, he compensated for a severe fundraising disadvantage by building a grassroots network of volunteers who conducted "serious door to door work over many months as well as sophisticated targeting, fundraising, and advertising." After defeating several more-experienced primary opponents, he was tutored in the general election by experienced reformers like Lowenstein and former representative Abner Mikva, who was running to regain an Illinois seat in the House.

In Colorado, another candidate brimming with self-confidence was Timothy Wirth, who radiated the star quality of his friend Robert Redford's idealistic, photogenic character in the recent film *The Candidate*: prep school at Exeter, bachelor's from Stanford, PhD from Harvard (where he briefly served as the dean who approved the undergraduate admission of future president George W. Bush). In the words of one Capitol Hill staffer, the personable Coloradan "looks too good to be true." Others expressed admiration for Wirth as well. "Big, blond and beautiful," one profile noted gushingly, "he would have beaten Tarzan!"[18] Wirth was compelled to enter politics by the chaos of the late 1960s—the violence at home and abroad, the demonstrations and the assassinations that had shaken the idealism of his generation. "More than anything, [Robert] Kennedy's death had propelled us into politics," recalled a "profoundly saddened and changed" Wirth, who had watched Kennedy's funeral train roll past in June 1968.[19] By the time he was 30, Wirth had worked as a White House Fellow, at the Urban Coalition, and at the Department of Health, Education, and Welfare, where he formed a close relationship with Secretary John W. Gardner, who would soon organize the nonpartisan reform group Common Cause. But Wirth felt constrained and longed to jump into the action himself. "How could we be wasting our time like this when there was so much to do?" he asked his wife, Wren.

Returning to Colorado, he contemplated challenging first-term Rep. Mike McKevitt but hesitated, fearing 1972 would be unfavorable for Democrats. Patricia Schroeder, who seized the opportunity to run, recalled she was not the only woman elected in 1972 because male colleagues, sharing Wirth's hesitancy about his prospects, deferred until a more promising cycle. Two years later, when the hostility to Nixon, the war, and Republicans enabled candidates to "smell it, see the disgust," she noted, "women got pushed aside."[20]

In 1974, Wirth chose to run in a Republican-leaning district against incumbent Don Brotzman. For Wirth, Watergate was "a really big deal"; Vietnam, the impeachment hearings, Nixon's resignation, and Ford's pardon all congealed to create a sense that Washington was out of control.[21] Wirth dismissed the incumbent as an affable but ineffective legislator, a politician so reflexively personable that he "shook hands with fire plugs and tipped his hat to telephone poles."[22] At a time of national tumult, he pointed out, Brotzman's signature legislative achievement during a dozen years in Congress was a law creating a "National Salute to Eisenhower Week." Wirth highlighted the generational change he would bring to Congress. "We were products of computer politics not courthouse politics," Wirth declared. "We were the children of Vietnam, not children of World War II. We were products of television, not of print. We were the reflections of JFK as President, not FDR."[23] Still, the race was far from easy. For all his star quality, door knocking and high-mindedness, Wirth was running 40 points behind only months before the election. He became reluctant to solicit campaign contributions, leading a friend to offer a dose of hard-nosed reality. "If you don't have enough confidence in yourself to ask for money," he told Wirth, "you don't belong in politics."[24]

Another PhD running in a marginal district, Phil Sharp was similarly imbued with the Kennedy-inspired fervor of "government service as honorable." After studying at Georgetown and Oxford, Sharp was living in Indiana, one of the most inhospitable northern states for Democrats. Nevertheless, in 1970, at just 28, he had launched a quixotic race against three-term incumbent David Dennis. Sharp defeated several other Democrats for the nomination, including former representative Randall "Front Porch" Harmon, who earned his nickname during his single term in the House for using official funds to pay himself rent on his own porch, which he claimed as his official district office.[25] Undeterred by his loss to Dennis, Sharp ran again in 1972, losing by a larger margin. But Watergate altered the odds for 1974, particularly after Dennis emerged as a Nixon apologist whose loyalty remained untrammeled until the Oval Office tapes incontrovertibly established Nixon's culpability. Like others who stuck with Nixon to the end, Dennis saw his own career evaporate only weeks after Nixon's did.

Another Indiana educator, Dave Evans, had also run unsuccessfully in 1972 against a longtime incumbent. After methodically analyzing data from every precinct in the Republican district, Evans decided his only path to victory in 1974 lay in personal contact with constituents. Eventually, he estimated, he knocked on more than 55,000 doors, leaving a handwritten note when no one answered. Outspent three to one, Evans tried raffling off a Cadillac for $75 tickets, only to be accused of violating campaign laws. No one, except Indiana's Sen. Vance Hartke, gave him a chance of winning.

No candidate offered a more dramatic contrast to Maguire, Evans, Sharp, and Wirth than Edward Beard of Rhode Island. Growing up poor in the West End of Providence, Beard left school at 17 to work in a factory to support his widowed mother. His only exposure to higher education, he liked to say, was at the Rhode Island School of Design, where he painted dormitory rooms. An impassioned advocate for working people, Beard won a seat in the state legislature in 1972. Two years later, he asked his supervisor at the painting company whether he could have his job back if he lost a race for Congress. Assured his position was safe, he decided to challenge three-term Republican Robert Tiernan. Throughout his campaign and thereafter in Congress, Beard was instantly recognizable by the small paintbrush he carried in his suit pocket to remind himself of his working-class roots.[26] Decades after his brief congressional service had ended, he was asked how he would like to be remembered. "As working man who cared," he said.

Some in the Class virtually stumbled into their campaigns. Marty Russo had left the Illinois state attorney's office to open a small law firm when, in October 1973, he was approached by local party activists seeking a sacrificial opponent for 3rd District incumbent Robert Hanrahan. "I have no experience," protested the 30-year-old Russo, who had only managed some precincts in local elections. "I love politics, but I'm not sure I want to do it." The local committeeman assured Russo his lack of political sophistication was immaterial. "It doesn't matter," Larry Pettis counseled, "because you can't win." Perplexed, Russo asked why he would take time away from his new law practice to run a race he was certain to lose. "Look, you always told me you want to be a judge," Pettis explained. "Your dad came from Italy, worked 3 jobs. Wouldn't be nice if you were *Judge* Russo." That prospect appealed to Russo, but he questioned how a judgeship was related to a doomed race for Congress. "You need to sacrifice yourself for the party," Pettis explained. "You run for Congress; you lose. You run for state representative; you lose. Then we get the guys to appoint you judge because you put the time in, you took your beatings. You make your dad proud of you. And your new firm will get publicity [because] you're running for Congress."

Russo consulted his friend Bob Macari, who speculated the race might not be altogether hopeless; Adlai Stevenson III, he noted, had narrowly won the 3rd District in his 1970 Senate campaign. Besides, "when would a guy like you ever get a chance to ever run for Congress in the first place?" he asked Russo. "What's the worst that can happen? You lose? Well, everyone *thinks* you're going to lose anyway." Macari offered to manage the doomed campaign for $50 a week. "Where am *I* gonna get 50 bucks a week?" Russo complained.

A few days after being designated the nominee, Russo was "blown away" to find himself in "the inner sanctum," preparing for his first meeting with Chicago mayor Richard J. Daley. With his thick moustache and long black hair, Russo resembled the anti-war protestors Daley had angrily denounced in Chicago during the Democratic Convention of 1968. But the mayor enthusiastically shook his hand and, after a photograph was taken, advised, "Mr. Congressman, you just keep working hard!" As a suddenly confident Russo turned to leave, he overheard Daley ask an aide, "Is *this* the best we can do?"[27]

Russo campaigned on the "nuts and bolts issues" that Republicans had increasingly used to lure blue-collar voters to defect from the Democrats. "The machine didn't elect me," he later recalled. "I had to get there on my own. Nobody cared if I won or lost." He cited his experience as a prosecutor, opposed abortion, and emphasized law and order, all familiar themes in Nixon's realignment strategy. With the weak economy the major issue in many districts, including his own, Russo also linked Hanrahan to Ford, whom he blamed for a $1 trillion budget, the $25 billion deficit, and worsening inflation. Still, Russo was dismissed by many local Democrats who considered him "an insignificant bump on a log" and provided him with scant aid. One powerful Democrat sought to console Russo by assuring him that his doomed candidacy would make Hanrahan a better congressman. "I don't want to make him better," Russo asserted, warming to the challenge. "I want to beat this guy!" If he was serious, he was advised, he should cut his hair and shave his moustache. "Dewey lost because he had a skinny moustache," a local politician advised. "People don't trust people with moustaches. If you think you have a chance, shave and cut your hair." Russo followed the advice.

In Brooklyn, Leo Zeferetti was also initially ambivalent about running. At 47 years old and a veteran of World War II, he did not fit the profile of the typical Class member. By the early 1970s, he had risen to the presidency of the Patrolmen's Benevolent Association after winning praise for his handling of several prison riots. Republican governor Nelson Rockefeller and President Nixon both appointed him to criminal justice positions. Shortly after the district's Democratic congressman, Hugh Carey, announced he would vacate the seat to run for governor in 1974, Zeferetti was stunned to read an article in the *Daily News* by a local judge endorsing him for the House seat, and the idea was quickly endorsed by numerous Democratic and union leaders. The response of his wife to the suggestion that they disrupt their settled life for a race for Congress echoed those of the skeptical spouses of several other candidates: "Are you nuts?" Like Russo, Zeferetti focused on law and order issues, including prison reform, which he argued would prevent future riots. To his good fortune, a slew of liberals split the Democratic primary vote, allowing Zeferetti to win by a tiny plurality.

While not as liberal as many Class members, Russo and Zeferetti were far from representing the conservative extreme. That role was filled by Larry McDonald, a Georgia urologist and member of the ultra-right-wing John Birch Society. McDonald again challenged John Davis, the Democratic incumbent to whom he had narrowly lost in 1972. He denounced Davis's votes against restricting school busing and a school prayer amendment, as well as his support for an increase in the debt ceiling (which had passed by a single vote), charging that Davis "basically had lost touch with the district." The day before the primary election, every household in crucial Cobb County received a two-page letter from McDonald excoriating the incumbent for his busing vote. Even a messy dispute over alimony that briefly landed McDonald in jail could not derail his campaign, and he dispatched Davis by 2,600 votes.

Not all members of the Class from the former Confederacy shared McDonald's conservative philosophy. Indeed, several won primary races—tantamount to election in what were still effectively one-party districts—by specifically appealing to the increasing number of black voters enfranchised by the 1965 Voting Rights Act. Indeed, these southern Democratic victories would prove one of the most salient outcomes of the election of 1974, helping boost Democratic numbers in the House. While many of these victories proved unsustainable over time, as southern Republican organizations attracted white conservative voters, nevertheless, the 1974 victories were decisive in maintaining the Democratic majority for another two decades.[28]

Where the Republican Party was already organized, the rising black electorate helped moderates defeat old-line conservatives in the Democratic primary but could not prevent the Republicans from winning the conservative Democratic votes in the fall. In Louisiana's 6th District, for example, expanding black participation helped Jeff LaCaze oust segregationist John Rarick, who had beaten a fellow Democrat in 1966 by accusing him of sympathizing with Lyndon Johnson's civil rights agenda. But in LaCaze's case, white conservatives migrated in November to Republican Henson Moore, one of the early examples of a rising GOP luring white voters away from their traditional Democratic loyalty.

Black voters played a similarly crucial role in South Carolina's 6th District, which had been represented since 1938 by hard-line conservative John L. McMillan. For decades the large African American population in the district—more than 30 percent—had been electorally irrelevant, since few were permitted to vote until the 1965 federal voting law. By 1972, McMillan's segregationist record presented an opportunity for John Jenrette, a young, four-term state legislator. The son of a onetime member of the Ku Klux Klan, Jenrette aggressively courted African Americans, who constituted more than one-third of the registered voters, 10 times the percentage as when McMillan had initially won the seat. "I was part of the New South, not the old South," Jenrette recalled. "I felt more kinship with other new and progressive members from throughout the country than I felt for the old guard, which had been against me," Jenrette declared. "It took a while for the Voting Rights Act to take full effect, but when it did, it completely changed the political landscape of my district."[29]

With the overwhelming support of black voters, Jenrette defeated the 76-year-old McMillan in the 1972 Democratic primary, but many of the defeated lawmaker's backers took their revenge on Jenrette in the fall, electing the Republican, Edward Young. In the 1974 rematch, Jenrette was confident he could both "mobilize the black vote, and then get at least a third of the white vote, and that is what I did." Like other rural candidates, Jenrette tied the incumbent to Ford's unpopular farm policies and castigated Young for his votes against education and a cost of living increase for Social Security recipients, while offering vigorous support for local military bases, which were crucial employers.

Another progressive southerner, Elliott Levitas had been embroiled in controversy since his first election to the Georgia legislature in 1964. Only days into his first term, Democratic leaders refused to seat the newly elected representative Julian Bond, a black civil rights activist critical of the war in Vietnam. Levitas's office was besieged with constituent demands to exclude Bond; his mother even received death threats. The risks from bucking his leadership were significant for a new member, but Levitas, an attorney, concluded that excluding a duly elected representative for exercising his free speech rights was "something I knew to be constitutionally wrong." He voted to seat Bond, expecting his decision would result in a "glorious but brief political career."[30]

No sooner was he reelected than he faced another controversy. A three-way race for governor had ended with no one winning the majority of the votes as required by Georgia law, throwing the decision into the Democratic-controlled legislature. Levitas voted for the Republican, Howard "Bo" Callaway, Georgia's first GOP congressman since Reconstruction, instead of the Democrat, Lester Maddox, a controversial segregationist, or his former law partner, Ellis Arnall, a former governor who had lost the Democratic primary to Maddox but stood no chance of being selected by the legislature. Despite Levitas's appeals to 30 other Democrats to join him, none did, and Maddox easily won by a vote of 182–66.

Levitas cited that record of bipartisanship when he decided to challenge the conservative Republican Ben Blackburn in 1974. Both the lean of the district and Levitas's Jewish faith (in a strongly Christian region) left local party leaders skeptical of his chances. But like others in the evolving South, Levitas was careful to avoid sounding partisan and offset the incumbent's name recognition by building a large grassroots network and traveling throughout the district relentlessly. Blackburn remained an unwavering Nixon loyalist too long; Ford's pardon, Levitas believed, was the "reason I was able to prevail. Voters were ready to see something different."[31]

Norman Mineta knew something about being a minority. His father had emigrated from Japan as a 19-year-old, working in California's sugar beet fields until his health failed and then utilizing his bilingualism to sell insurance. "Life was pretty idyllic" in his childhood hometown of San Jose, Mineta recalled: college education for the children, family holidays at national parks, and only rare incidents of racial intolerance. Their lives changed six months after Japan's 1941 surprise attack on Pearl Harbor that launched the United States into World War II. Shortly after President Franklin Roosevelt signed Executive Order 9066 authorizing the forced incarceration of 120,000 Japanese Americans, the family was uprooted and sent to the remote Heart Mountain internment camp near Cody, Wyoming, one of several such facilities built by the federal government. "Some say the internment was for our own good" to protect them from angry Americans, said Mineta. "But even as a boy of 10, I could see that the machine guns and the barbed wire faced inward."[32]

Following his family's release from confinement, Mineta received a business degree and served in the US Army before being appointed to a vacancy on the San Jose City Council in 1967. Within a year, he was vice mayor, and in 1971 he was elected mayor of the fourth-largest city in California, winning every precinct. He was the first Asian American to govern a major American city. Early on a Sunday morning in January, 1974, a friend called to ask whether the mayor had read the morning paper announcing the unexpected retirement of Charles Gubser, the 20-year Republican incumbent. Mineta declared he was not interested and went back to bed. The entreaties continued, however, and by March, Mineta was a candidate.

Mineta was "cautious, not given to catchy phrases," an experienced politician who had learned the necessity of compromise.[33] He also knew his way around Washington, having testified before Congress on behalf of the US Conference of Mayors, and had developed useful connections in the capital. His sister's husband, a well-known activist for the Japanese Americans Citizens League and the Leadership Conference on Civil

Rights, introduced the candidate to key political players like Tip O'Neill, who was impressed with his "get along, go along" style.

Service in local government had also developed a pragmatic streak in several other Class members, including three California mayors—Jerry Patterson, Jim Lloyd, and Mark Hannaford. John Krebs, who was born in Germany and raised in Israel, had served in local and county government in the conservative Central Valley. In Illinois, Paul Simon had spent 20 years as a state representative, senator, and lieutenant governor before running for the House in 1974 as a moderate. In Oregon, Les AuCoin was majority leader of the state house in just his second term.

Others in the Class, however, had no connection to local political organizations or even to electoral politics. Bob Edgar was an apolitical Baptist minister in southeastern Pennsylvania outraged by the "Saturday Night Massacre," Nixon's decision on October 20, 1973, to fire Watergate special prosecutor Archibald Cox, and then Attorney General Elliot Richardson and Deputy Attorney General William Ruckelshaus, who both had refused to discharge Cox. The next day, the 31-year-old Reverend Edgar recalled, "I literally looked up the word 'Democrat' in the phone book to find the local headquarters. Prior to that, I had never attended a political meeting." The district had not elected a Democrat to the House in decades, but, even so, his offer to run met with indifference from local Democratic leaders who preferred a more credible candidate, perhaps "a lawyer who needed some publicity."[34] When the four-term incumbent congressman, Lawrence Williams, was surprisingly defeated in a Republican primary, several more-experienced Democratic candidates expressed new interest in becoming the party's candidate, but, despite pressure from the local organization, Edgar refused to withdraw from the race. "We were the sixties generation that didn't drop out," he defiantly recalled.

In Lowell, Massachusetts, Paul Tsongas, a former Peace Corps volunteer, deputy assistant state attorney general, and county commissioner irritated the local Democratic machine by opposing the traditional use of patronage in hiring. In an upstate New York swing district, Matt McHugh aggravated the local party organization by promising a nonpartisan effort "to give people some means of participating in the process."[35] In Indiana, college professor Floyd Fithian had not been the first choice of local leaders in 1972, when he had lost, or in 1974. "We didn't owe anything to any ward heelers," he said. "We were pretty brash, not scared."[36] The three-term incumbent, Earl Landgrebe, proved himself an imperfect judge of the political atmosphere when he pronounced his fealty to the embattled Nixon on August 7. "I'm going to stick with my president," he declared, "even if he and I have to be taken out of this building and shot." It was a poorly timed statement, since Nixon resigned the following day.

Some were surprised to find themselves not only candidates but even Democrats. The founder of a hugely successful Iowa fishing supply business, Berkley Bedell's anger over the Vietnam War propelled him to a political career. "I looked at my life and thought, 'I wanted to do something more rewarding than run a big fishing tackle factory,'" he decided. He was wealthy, outraged, and determined to become involved. He was also a Republican, but that was about to change. A trip to Washington with other business leaders included a briefing from high-ranking administration officials that "shocked" Bedell.[37] "I can't imagine *anyone* reading the platform of the Iowa Republican party and thinking that's what they believed in and stood for!" he exclaimed in 1972. Local GOP leaders proposed that he forgo a race for Congress and pay his political dues, perhaps by serving as a block captain. "That was not my idea," Bedell decided. "That's why I changed registration."

It was not a decision to be made lightly in his overwhelmingly Republican hometown, and he feared his elderly mother might be required "to move out of town rather than live in town with a Democratic son." But on his 50th birthday in March 1972, he filed as a Democrat to run for the House. "I wanted a platform to voice my opinions and beliefs whether I won or not," Bedell declared. "I wasn't a good speaker, I didn't know much about campaigning, I didn't have much going for me." He admitted, "You can imagine the lack of enthusiasm which followed my announcement." But the incumbent Wiley Mayne had irritated Bedell during a "very, very, very unsatisfactory meeting" on the subject of Vietnam, and, despite strong objections from his mother, brother, and closest friends, he jumped into the race.[38] To everyone's amazement (including his own), Bedell garnered 49 percent of the vote and kept running. Over the next two years, Mayne made himself a glaring target by voting against the articles of impeachment against President Nixon, heightening his vulnerability to the likable Bedell.

Like Bedell, Bob Carr had grown up a Republican but was repelled by Barry Goldwater's "pretty damned dangerous" threat to employ tactical nuclear weapons in Vietnam. Four years later, Carr was a volunteer for

Wisconsin's Democratic gubernatorial candidate Bronson LaFollete, who loaned him money to join the Young Democrats. Throughout college and law school at Michigan State, Carr continued working in Democratic campaigns, becoming a leader in the effort to allow students to vote in local elections.

As in Harkin's case, reapportionment brought thousands of newly enfranchised college students into Carr's congressional district. In 1972, Carr ran against the longtime incumbent Republican, Charles Chamberlain, whose retirement plans were postponed at the request of his Michigan colleague, Republican leader Ford. When Carr surprisingly won more than 49 percent of the vote despite being significantly outspent, Chamberlain decided not to tempt fate again. His decision to retire in 1974 made Carr a "giant-killer" in Democratic circles, and Carr immediately announced he would run again, although he was still viewed as an underdog in the Republican-leaning district.

Although some Class members became candidates reluctantly or unexpectedly, others had aspired to political careers since childhood. New York's 2nd District seemed inhospitable to a Democrat, particularly one who admired some "excellent" ideas propounded by the Students for a Democratic Society.[39] In 1972, Richard Nixon had won 72 percent of the vote in the 2nd, and Republican congressman James Grover had won his fifth consecutive election by a large margin. But Tom Downey had "always wanted to be a member of Congress," and just a few years after graduating from Cornell had already twice won election to the Suffolk County legislature. Not even 25 years old, the constitutional minimum for a member of the House, Downey had an epiphany during the 1973 oil embargo while waiting in a long line of angry motorists to fill his car with gasoline. "I'm going to blame this on the incumbent!" he resolved.[40] Downey's greatest vulnerability may have been his age and his adolescent appearance, but Grover inadvertently neutralized the issue by discussing his own role leading troops during World War II when he had been the same age. Downey courteously thanked Grover for his service to the country, grateful that the charge of immaturity had been negated by the incumbent. Like many others in the class who faced better-financed incumbents, Downey relied on an aggressive, grassroots network of volunteers. "Money mattered," he noted, "but organization mattered more."[41]

Like Downey, whom he rivaled in boyish appearance, Jim Blanchard had harbored thoughts of a seat in Congress since childhood. Taking his

Michigan State coach's advice that politics "will change your life" more than baseball, Blanchard was elected student body president, then attended law school and began working his way up in the Michigan Attorney General's Office.[42] In 1972, a bad year for Michigan Democrats, Blanchard's candidate for a newly configured House district was defeated. Hearing the news, he arrived home at 2 a.m., woke up his wife and announced the loss. "Well, you never liked him anyway," she groggily consoled him. "No, no," Blanchard explained, "*I'm* going to run for that seat."

"If I ever wanted to get elected to Congress," he recalled, 1974 provided the opportunity to "do [it] in one fell swoop . . . as opposed to running for state Representative, state Senate, [and] spending years working my way up," as Bedell had been advised to do. For months, the impatient attorney methodically studied the district's recent voting behavior, sharing his plans with no one lest party officials discourage him. He was so discreet that Carr, a colleague in the attorney general's office, invited Blanchard to serve as his campaign manager. Not until late 1973 did Blanchard confide his plans to a small group of Democratic activists, and the response was positive. Focusing on the need for sweeping reform in the aftermath of Watergate, Blanchard defeated a popular school superintendent in the primary on his 32nd birthday. A month later, driving to campaign events, Blanchard heard on the announcement that Ford had pardoned the disgraced former president, and he grew confident he would soon be heading to Congress.

Not surprisingly, in a large number of swing districts unused to electing Democrats, Class members avoided sounding partisan and downplayed party affiliation, choosing instead to emphasize more nebulous concepts like "change" and chastising incumbents who paint scant attention to constituents. "People don't trust politicians," Max Baucus asserted as he hiked the length of Montana. He condemned "gross mismanagement" in Washington and pledged "to help restore confidence [in government] and to make the system work." In the conservative bastion of Orange County, California, Jerry Patterson avoided mentioning his party in his campaign literature for fear of generating reflexive opposition. Then he noticed an unexpected response from voters. "I'd knock on doors and tell people, 'I'm running for Congress,'" Patterson recalled, "and they'd ask, 'Are you a Republican or a Democrat?' I'd say, 'Democrat, but . . .' and the person would say, 'Good, I'll vote for you.' Almost every house. People were ready for a change, even the Republicans."[43] Patterson hastily redesigned his nonpartisan campaign brochure to identify him as the *Democratic* candidate.

With public disdain for politicians at a high level, many in the Class went to great lengths to avoid the appearance of being a typical candidate, not part of the inside Washington elite. "I tried to make it a campaign of common people," Berkley Bedell recalled. "They saw me as a likeable guy, one of them. The question is, 'Does he really represent us. Do we like him, can we trust him?'" Rhode Islander Ed Beard, the housepainter, wanted people to remember "that he was like us." In Indiana, Phil Sharp "didn't talk about much of anything other than being a good representative [and] improving government." The public desire for new faces became evident when a man ran across the street in Representative Dennis's hometown to profess his high admiration for the incumbent. "But I'm going to vote for *you*," the man told an astonished Sharp. "Well," Sharp admitted, "it shows you how stupid we were" in underestimating the impact of Watergate in conservative Indiana.

Their slogans often reflected these desires to restore confidence in government rather than to draw partisan differentiation with Republicans. Running against a longtime incumbent in Indiana, Dave Evans used the slogan, "It's Time for a Change," as did Bill Hughes, a tough-on-crime New Jersey prosecutor. When incumbent Charles Sandman emphasized his influence in Washington with billboards proclaiming, "When Charlie Sandman speaks, the nation listens," Hughes countered with billboards reading, "When the people of South Jersey speak, Hughes will listen." In California, George Miller, facing a popular Hispanic city councilman, employed the inclusive slogans "It's Time for the People" and "It's Time for Honesty," and in Georgia Levitas's slogan pledged "A Declaration of Independence" from party politics. In North Carolina, unknown newspaper publisher Steve Neal challenged Congressman (and former baseball star) Wilmer "Vinegar Bend" Mizell with the gauzy slogan "Working together, we can make America great again."

Yet while antipathy toward politics placed a premium on sounding like a reformer, few candidates focused on the rules changes that had consumed congressional reformers for more than a decade or were aware of the need for additional reforms. Virtually no challengers ran campaigns promising to end the seniority system or alter caucus rules to empower junior members, changes that would preoccupy them immediately after their election. Indeed, the issue of congressional reform in 1974 was ill suited to the general election campaign since the obstructionists in Congress were not the Republicans against whom the reformers were running but the senior members of their own party and the leadership and rules that protected them.

A Diverse Class of Candidates

As these biographies have illustrated, the Class was filled with neophytes as well as with experienced men and women who had substantial political experience before they set ever foot on the House floor. True, some in the Class did not fit the traditional profile of freshmen; they had not held elective office, and some had little involvement in electoral politics. But many others had already served in leadership posts at the state and local level, in state government offices, and in Congress at the staff level. Others had gained experience in a newer form of popular politics involving veterans and anti-war protestors, businesspeople and consumer advocates, environmental and social justice advocates. This nontraditional, activist experience of some Class members did not register on the radar screen of traditional politicians like O'Neill but provided Class members with rhetorical, organizational, and press skills equivalent to those of many elected officials.

Understandably, many senior Democratic were mystified by this huge cohort of candidates running in the wake of Watergate and riding a tsunami of public skepticism about government. Veteran legislators, like many journalists and academicians, were quick to form a simplistic portrait of the Class—a caricature that would endure for decades. "The Watergate Babies" were eager supporters of efforts "that revolutionized the way the House ran," as one typical account asserted. But, as the earlier discussion of reform efforts before 1974 established, the Class did not "launch" the revolution against archaic rules and the conservative leadership.[44] Instead, it *joined* a well-organized and well-developed revolt that had been building for more than a decade and awaiting additional support to achieve broader victories.

During that decade, public esteem for the Congress had plummeted from 64 percent in 1964 to just 15 percent. Watergate played a key role in crystallizing public anger and altering the political temperament to allow unconventional candidates to succeed. A key factor in their success was that, unlike during earlier reform efforts, the public was in the mood to support political reform, a key factor absent in earlier efforts except among a narrow group of academicians. Watergate and Vietnam exposed the need for cleansing government and reducing its secrecy. "Nixon was a gift," Mike Blouin of Iowa concluded. "He got us elected."[45]

Criticized as "unbelievably uppity," marked by "unbelievable assertiveness," many in the Class were clearly impatient.[46] Stylistically, the Class proved an exasperating mystery to some older legislators, even those sharing its policy objectives. "Close to half had never campaigned for any office before running for Congress," O'Neill marveled.[47] The majority leader, a product of Boston organization politics, viewed members of the Class as "outsiders," unburdened by tradition or deference. "I was struck by how many told me they had no interest in politics until Robert Kennedy's presidential campaign in 1968," O'Neill wrote. "They were a 'new breed' of legislator: young, brash, independent of its elders and their system," another observed.[48]

True, some were less deferential, "not steeped in the old traditions of . . . by your grace and favor, Mr. Chairman," as Tom Foley of Washington State put it, but they were certainly not hostile to government itself.[49] "The need is not bigger government," Phil Sharp explained, "but *better* government," a distinctly different rhetoric from that of conservatives like former California governor Ronald Reagan—already in 1974 planning to challenge Ford for the presidential nomination—who would famously declare that "government is the problem." They viewed with suspicion a government that had fought secret wars, covered up crimes, spied on citizens, and formed cozy relationships with industries it was supposed to regulate. They were wary of the excessive concentration of power in the executive branch and viewed skeptically the assertions of "executive privilege" invoked in the name of national security to keep Congress and the public in the dark. Reformulating government, opening it to greater scrutiny, demanding greater accountability, securing the public trust were the objectives sought by most members of the Class. They sought to restore an effective government that could exercise significant (and even expanded) powers, not retreat from activism.

To the leadership, it seemed that many in the Class arrived with "a million grievances," as O'Neill recalled. "We *did* have a million grievances," George Miller affirmed. Class members challenged the desultory pace and anemic legislative output allowed by the chairmen and tolerated by the leaders. A poll of the Class concluded its members were "very, very sensitive to the unrest in the country, the turn off and the alienation from politics."[50] Veterans of the long struggles for civil rights, for women, for children, for the environment, for people with disabilities, these new legislators articulated their agenda not merely as representing policy objectives but as defending constitutional and ethical "rights" that included a profoundly moral dimension: a *right* to a public education for special needs children, a *right* to an abortion, a *right* to clean water and air, a *right* to consumer safety.

Elevating policy goals to the status of rights would prove to be a crucial step in the evolution of ideological partisanship in the United States. While the practice occurred among liberals in the class of 1974, it increasingly appeared among conservatives during the decade as well: a *right* to gun ownership, a *right* to protect unborn fetuses, a *right* to lower taxes, a *right* to less government, a *right* to freedom from government regulation. The application of such a moral dimension to the framing of public issues served to diminish the attractiveness of compromise in pursuit of a common objective. Negotiating a compromise on a disagreement about an appropriations levels or whether to construct wastewater treatment plants did not raise thorny issues of morality; legislators were comfortable with legislating solutions by "splitting the difference." But compromising on issues imbued with moral absoluteness was regarded as far less meritorious by members and by the interest groups that rated, financed, and provided grassroots supporters for their campaigns. In a legislative environment that compels compromise to function efficiently, the elevation of policy options to moral choices was an unforeseen step toward a more polarized political atmosphere.

Of course, in 1974, not all issues were defined in such ethical terms, and not all conservatives or liberals had yet migrated to one party or the other, and, indeed, bipartisan collaboration on many issues including congressional reform would continue for years. But, first, the candidates had to win their elections.

4   THE REINFORCEMENTS

I've been voting for Republicans the last few times, but every one of them has gone bad. I'll be damned if I ever vote for another one.
—Blue-collar worker, Memphis

I really don't know exactly why I won. I guess it's because people trusted me. If they had wanted the smartest, brightest, most energetic person in the 18th District, they wouldn't have chosen me.—Rep. Tim Lee Hall (D-IL)

The reinforcements have arrived!—Rep. Bella Abzug (D-NY)

The election returns on November 5, 1974, marked a watershed in American politics. Republican hopes of expanding their numbers in the House were obliterated. The much-heralded regional strategy—the "Republicanization of the South"—failed to materialize. The "emerging Republican majority" that GOP strategist Kevin Phillips had predicted suffered a setback so grievous it would take the party a decade to recover numerically. Rather than Nixonian conservatives, the incoming Class of 1974 was filled with an eclectic, energized, and eager group of Democratic activists, many of whom would prove to be skilled politicians difficult to dislodge from their hard-won seats. Their victories helped to reshape congressional politics for a generation.

The warning signs had emerged early in the year. On February 18, Democrat Richard Vander Veen won a symbolically significant special election to fill the unexpired term of Michigan's Gerald Ford, who had resigned to become vice president. Ford had held the seat since 1948, and no Democrat had won it since 1910. But Vander Veen promised to vote to remove Nixon, which would help make the district's local hero, Jerry Ford, the president of the United States. To near-universal surprise, he defeated the Republican leader of the state senate, who had never lost an election. The outcome sent Republicans "into a state of panic," leading Nixon to meet hastily to reassure a very anxious Michigan delegation.[1] One news analysis predicted confidently that "other Democrats will pick up on the Vander Veen strategy in November, tying their GOP opponents to the scandal-ridden Nixon administration." Two months later, Democrat Bob Traxler won another GOP seat in Michigan vacated by a Republican whom Nixon had appointed to the federal bench. The anxiety generated by the Vander Veen and Traxler victories was compounded when Democratic candidates won two more Republicans seats in special elections—Tom Luken in Ohio and John Murtha, the first Vietnam veteran elected to Congress, in Pennsylvania.

During the summer, as the House Judiciary Committee's impeachment hearings were broadcast around the clock, Republican polling numbers ominously deteriorated. While Nixon's resignation and the elevation of the genial Ford seemed to diminish Watergate as a significant factor in voters' minds, concerns about political corruption remained high. From a high of 38 percent when the impeachment hearings began in May, Watergate's importance to voters fell to just 19 percent in late October on the eve of the election. Similarly, with US involvement in Vietnam winding down, fewer than 2 percent of voters cited the war as their major reason for selecting a congressional candidate.

As Election Day neared, the issues putting voters in "a bleak and pessimistic mood" were the weak economy, inflation, and rising energy prices.[2] In May, two-thirds of Americans cited the economy and inflation as the primary issues that would determine their vote, and that number would rise to nearly 80 percent by Election Day. Twenty-eight percent of voters described themselves as being in financial trouble. Those fearing unemployment doubled from 15 percent in May to 27 percent in October. Anxiety over energy, provoked by the Organization of Oil Exporting Companies (OPEC) oil embargo and inflamed by long lines and supply shortages at gasoline stations, skyrocketed from 4 percent in the spring to nearly 30 percent as winter began to settle on much of the country. President Ford's anemic "Whip Inflation Now" plan inspired little confidence, and his proposal to levy a 5 percent oil surtax to dampen demand suggested a president seriously out of touch with the economic pain of millions of voters.

A few weeks before the election, Ford was playing golf with longtime House colleague Tip O'Neill. The president asked how he thought the election would play out. "It's going to be an avalanche," the majority leader predicted. *Congressional Quarterly*, combing through the last data available before the polls opened, similarly predicted a "certainty of substantial gains" for Democrats, estimating a 35-seat pickup "and at least the hint of a landslide." Independent polls showed voters favoring Democrats in a generic congressional race by enormous margins, including a 55 percent to 35 percent spread by Gallup and 55 percent to 31 percent by Harris.[3] Democrats led in 18 seats held by Republicans and were reportedly running even in another 32.

Watergate and the economy were not the only reasons for Democrats' optimism. Many districts had been redesigned following the 1970 census and gained significant numbers of Democratic voters. Million of students had been added to voter rolls in districts that were home to universities as the result of ratification of the Twenty-Sixth Amendment in 1971, which gave 18-year-olds the vote. Democratic registration among black citizens was also expanding because of the implementation of the Voting Rights Act, particularly in the states of the former Confederacy where their participation had long been suppressed.[4] In some cases, emerging cultural issues also prompted support for Democrats. Carr attributed his surprising victory, by a margin of just 647 votes, to women who supported his pro-choice position on the increasingly divisive issue of abortion.

Yet antipathy toward politics remained high, and just 38 percent of eligible voters went to the polls, the smallest turnout in three decades. Watergate's damage to the Republican brand was evident: only 27 percent of voters identified themselves as Republicans, fewer than those calling themselves Independents. Democrats actively solicited voters to switch parties and found willing converts. "I've been voting for Republicans the last few times, but every one of them has gone bad," a blue-collar worker in Memphis complained. "I'll be damned if I ever vote for another one."

The 1974 "Wave" Election

The outcome matched the avalanche pollsters had predicted. There would be 92 freshmen in the House, the largest incoming class since 1949.[5] Altogether, 76 Democratic freshmen were elected, including 49 who won seats that had been held by Republicans. Significantly, Democrats expanded their total number of seats to 291, not just a healthy majority but more than the 287 that would be needed to override anticipated Ford vetoes. It was the largest loss for a sitting president's party since 1948. Democrats also increased their share of overall votes for Congress from 53 percent in 1972 to 58 percent in 1974. Even in the Republican heartland, the Midwest, Democrats gained 15 seats.

The electoral tsunami spared Republican moderates like Gilbert Gude of Maryland, Ron Sarasin of Connecticut, and Pete McCloskey of California, who had quixotically challenged Nixon in the 1972 primaries over the Vietnam War.[6] But 36 other Republican incumbents went down to defeat, including half of the conservative Republican Study Group's (RSG) steering committee. Numerous Nixon defenders, particularly those on the Judiciary Committee who had defended his conduct through the impeachment hearings, were defeated. Reformers quickly claimed credit for having influenced the outcome. The National Committee for an Effective Congress, despite being outspent by a three to one margin, had funneled $125,000 into key races and provided expert consultants to nonincumbents. The reform organization claimed 36 wins "in historically conservative districts, some of which have not returned a progressive representative for a generation."[7]

The results may not have represented a mandate for Democratic policy initiatives as much as a repudiation of the party of Nixon. Just one week before the election, Republican Party Deputy Chairman Richard Obenshain had predicted the outcome would spell "no obstacle to long-range party-building in the South, [only] a dampening effect . . . not a real setback."[8] Although *Time* magazine inexplicably asserted, "Except for an impressive five-seat switch in once-Republican Indiana, the [Democratic] pickup was piecemeal," even its editors recognized the extent of the damage. The election, *Time* admitted, meant that the GOP was undeniably "slipping deeper into the minority status that is unlikely to end in the foreseeable future."[9] Kevin Phillips, who had predicted a new conservative coalition that would achieve a House majority for Republicans, bitterly characterized the 1974 results a "conservative de-alignment . . . a failed opportunity" for Republicans unable to capitalize on Nixon's landslide two years earlier.[10] But for the poisoning of the GOP's appeal in the aftermath of Watergate, Phillips argued, "the 1972 elections might . . . have become a watershed in American politics" for Republicans. Now, because of a "third rate burglary," in the words of a White House operative, "the larger regional opportunity had slipped away" altogether, leaving behind an "abnormal Democratic resurgence [that] camouflage[d] the fundamental erosion of its constituency."[11]

"Democrats could have danced all night," it was reported, "and some of them did, as the champagne corks popped and the band played on in hotels and headquarters across the nation."[12] Some of the winners were stunned by their unexpected good fortune. Toby Moffett attributed his victory in Connecticut to a public "thirst for more independent, more candid, more honest politicians who didn't look like the old stereotype," candidates who were not "hand-picked, party-controlled."[13] Many in the Class "got lucky to win, including myself," admitted Marty Russo. Another who clearly got lucky was Glenn English, who capitalized on a preelection flood to remind voters that his opponent had voted against an emergency flood control bill.[14] In Illinois, a stunned Tim Lee Hall admitted, "I really don't know exactly why I won." He had spent under $30,000 to win the seat of retiring GOP whip, Les Arends, whose constituents had not elected a Democrat in a century. "I guess it's because people trusted me," Hall concluded. "If they had wanted the smartest, brightest, most energetic person in the 18th District, they wouldn't have chosen me."

Across the country, in victory after victory, voters sent a message that they wanted to purge corrupt and unresponsive politicians. In California's conservative Orange County, Jerry Patterson assessed, "Watergate made it possible for me to win" with 56 percent of the vote, while Democrats like Paul Tsongas in Massachusetts and Les AuCoin in Oregon became the first Democrats to win their seats in a century or more. Other winners included Bob Krueger of Texas, a Duke professor and Shakespearean scholar with an Oxford PhD who had been absent from his district for a decade, and Rhode Island's Eddie Beard, a housepainter who had never left his hometown. "Congratulations, kid," an exultant O'Neill bellowed over the phone to Beard on election night. "You won the biggest victory in the country!"

Especially significant were Democratic victories in the former Confederacy, a region where the number of Republican House members had quintupled from just 7 in 1960 to 34 in 1972. This was the region Phillips had predicted would boost Republican fortunes, but Democrats won back 9 seats in the region, increasing the number of southerners in the caucus to 81. The tide was so formidable that in Georgia, the ultraconservative Larry McDonald, who had been briefly jailed just a few months before the election for failure to pay alimony, *still* won with 50.3 percent of the vote over a former Vietnam prisoner of war.

For the first time in a decade, Georgia's delegation would be all Democratic. Baseball legend "Vinegar Bend" Mizell of North Carolina, who held "one of the most secure Republican seats in the House," was defeated by the inexperienced, small-town newspaper publisher Steve Neal. In South

Carolina, John Jenrette, who had lost the 1972 general election after having ousted the segregationist incumbent in the primary, defeated the Republican incumbent thanks to solid support from newly registered black voters. Two additional South Carolina reformers—Butler Derrick and Ken Holland—won as well. In Memphis, the African American Harold Ford Sr. defeated an incumbent by 744 votes.

Some of the southern candidates may have been bolstered by the efforts of outgoing Georgia governor Jimmy Carter, who had been appointed by the national Democratic chairman, Robert Strauss, "to bring a close relationship between our Committee and the Hill."[15] Carter campaigned heavily for aspirants in the South and dispatched chief aide Hamilton Jordan (later Carter's 1976 campaign manager and then White House chief of staff) to Washington to serve as executive director of the Democratic National Committee (DNC) unit providing strategic assistance to candidates. Whatever the explanation, the 1974 election provided Democrats with welcome southern seats that, through the skill of the officeholders and the benefits of incumbency, helped them sustain a majority.

On election night, Jim Blanchard sarcastically posed the question asked by the victorious, but vacuous, Robert Redford in his recent film, *The Candidate*: "What do we do now?" But Blanchard was anything but overwhelmed; with his victory, he felt that "a ton of bricks [were] relieved from my shoulders. It was," he declared, "the most exciting moment in my life."

"We have a White House weakened by Watergate, occupied by a president who is not elected, who campaigned hard for his party at the polls and was overwhelmingly repudiated," declared senior Democrat John Brademas of Indiana. Yet a careful examination reveals there were signs that the Democratic victory was less sweeping than the totals might suggest. Of the Democratic freshmen, 39 had received less than 55 percent of the vote, generally considered a marginal victory that invited a rigorous challenge for a first termer. Another 20 received between 55 percent and 60 percent, which still signaled potential vulnerability in 1976 when Democrats would likely be challenging an incumbent president. No sitting president had been defeated in 42 years, and it was expected that Ford might be able to bring large numbers of loyal Republicans to the polls.

However, the Republicans also faced vulnerabilities in the election aftermath; 14 of their 18 freshmen received less than 55 percent and would have to be aggressively defended in 1976. The election also added a flock of moderates to the GOP Conference in place of hard-line conservatives who lost seats to Democrats. The shift would help create an ideological tension within the Republican ranks not unlike that which had been roiling the Democrats, with conservatives concerned about moderates exerting too much influence within the conference and moderates worried that the Republican leadership was dominated by "the same highly conservative persuasion."[16]

Profile of the Newly Elected Members

The new freshmen Democrats had several characteristics in common; they were generally young, they were mostly male, and they were almost exclusively white. Overall, 87 members of the Class were under the age of 40, shaving two decades off the average age of Democrats in the 93rd House. (The average age of senators remained at 55.) Many newcomers were in their early 30s or even 20s and resembled college students more than national legislators. Toby Moffett's long hair and nervous energy gave him the appearance of a community activist used to "dealing with street gangs," which he had recently been.[17]

While the Class reflected a wide variety of backgrounds, its victories did not substantially add to the gender or racial diversity of the House membership. Congress remained an overwhelmingly male institution, with women rarely exceeding 3 percent of the membership. Although the chairwoman of the National Women's Political Caucus, Sissy Farenthold, had proclaimed the 1974 elections a "breakthrough for women," the advances in reality were limited. Rep. Ella Grasso was elected governor of Connecticut, and Mary Anne Krupsak won the lieutenant governor's chair in New York. Janet Gray Hayes was elected to replace Norm Mineta (who won election to Congress) as mayor of San Jose, California, becoming the first woman to win the mayoralty of a city larger than 500,000. A record 587 women were elected to state legislatures, an increase of 117, but women still held less than 10 percent of all seats.

The new Class only modestly boosted the number of women in the House, from 16 to 19, although significantly only one, Marilyn Lloyd of Tennessee, could be said to occupy a traditional "widow's seat" that had been previously occupied by her husband, an incumbent who had died in a plane crash the evening of his victorious primary.[18] Large delegations from states including Pennsylvania, Florida, Indiana, Michigan, and Ohio remained devoid of women while others—California, Massachusetts,

Texas, and Illinois—included just one. The situation was little different from the 93rd Congress, when Speaker Carl Albert had encountered the incoming Pat Schroeder and her husband during her 1973 orientation. The Speaker had reflexively turned to Jim Schroeder and asked, "What committees are *you* trying for?"

Although the number of women was not rapidly changing, the newer female members projected a confidence characteristic of the growing women's movement. Many senior male members had seemed perplexed by the recent decision of women—particularly young women with children—to seek public office. Noting that the 32-year-old Pat Schroeder had two young children, one veteran asked her, "Why are you here?" An astonished Schroeder, a certified pilot and Harvard-trained attorney, responded, "I have a brain *and* a uterus, and I use both." Male members were not the only challenge confronting new congresswomen. Shortly after being sworn in, Schroeder had introduced herself to Leonor K. Sullivan, who had risen through seniority to become chairman of the Merchant Marine and Fisheries Committee. "Hi, I'm Pat Schroeder, I'm a freshman!" Schroeder said enthusiastically. "*You're* my [regional] dean" on the Steering Committee. Sullivan looked disapprovingly at the exuberant Schroeder. "*My* name is Mrs. John B. Sullivan," the chairwoman replied, invoking the name of her long-dead husband, a former congressman. "Yes! And you can call me 'Pat!'" Schroeder brightly offered. "What should I call *you*?" Leveling her eyes at the buoyant Schroeder, the only woman in the House to vote against the Equal Rights Amendment replied, "You can call me 'Mrs. John B. Sullivan.'" "Holy crap!" Schroeder thought, the House was going to be a real adjustment.[19]

Martha Griffiths, a 20-year House veteran, sympathized with the mood of the young women members who seemed less willing to play a secondary role than their predecessors were. "The error of most women [in prior decades] was they were trying to make the men who sat in Congress not disapprove of them," she advised. "I think they wanted to be liked, they didn't want to make enemies. So they didn't try to do things they thought the men would disapprove of [but] I didn't give a damn whether the men approved or not."[20] Such boldness did not endear the newer generation of outspoken women members to some of their male colleagues. "I hope you aren't going to be a skinny Bella Abzug," Armed Services Chairman Edward Hébert told Schroeder, referring the gruff New York congresswoman who was elected in 1972.[21]

79

Of the women in the 1974 Class, Helen Meyner had the clearest political pedigree, having been the First Lady of New Jersey during her husband's governorship and a distant relative of two-time presidential candidate Adlai Stevenson. She had run in 1972 and lost to Republican representative Joseph Maraziti, known for his "tongue-tied oratory" and unqualified loyalty to Richard Nixon.[22] As with Schroeder in Colorado, she had nearly been elbowed out of the nomination in the more favorable climate of 1974, as former Princeton and Knicks basketball star Bill Bradley contemplated challenging Meyner. However, New Jersey senator Harrison Williams had dispatched his staffer, Ben Palumbo, to urge Bradley to defer to Meyner.[23] Once elected, Meyner quickly proved willing to take on the bastions of male prerogatives. Donn Anderson, who managed the Democratic cloakroom, recalled her breaking an unwritten rule by lying down on one of the leather-covered sofas, draping a towel over her weary eyes and taking a nap, to the astonishment of her male colleagues, who regularly performed this ritual. "There was utter shock in the cloakroom," Anderson recalled. "A woman had invaded their locker room and thought nothing of it."[24]

Martha Keys had gained political experience in Kansas, one of the most heavily Republican states in the nation. She had worked in the successful 1970 campaign of William Roy for the 2nd District House seat and two years later served as presidential nominee Sen. George McGovern's director in Kansas, where the South Dakotan received a dismal 29 percent of the vote. Keys's sister, Lee, was married to McGovern's national campaign manager, Gary Hart, who in 1974 was running for a Colorado US Senate seat. Pat Schroeder urged Keys to use her fundraising and grassroots experience to run for the seat that Roy was vacating to challenge incumbent Sen. Bob Dole. Although the Dole-Roy race became ugly—with Dole labeling the physician-legislator Roy a "baby killer" for supporting abortion funding—Keys avoided controversy by emphasizing what she called "the needs of the time"—education, the economy, and jobs—and won while Roy was defeated.

The lone African American in the post-Watergate Class was Harold Ford of Tennessee, and he barely was elected. The Fords were a politically connected family that had risen from poverty to own a profitable mortuary business, in which Harold briefly worked. He had won a seat in 1970 in the Tennessee legislature, where he was elected majority whip during his first term. The 8th Congressional District in which Ford lived was represented by four-term Republican Dan Kuykendall, a Nixon loyalist who favored the "all out obliteration" of North Vietnam. Following the 1970 census, Republicans had gained 18,474 whites to the district to replace whites who had moved to the suburbs following a controversial school busing decision. Ford narrowly won anyway, but only because an anonymous phone call on election night directed him to thousands of uncounted ballots from black precincts hidden in the basement of the county building.[25]

Ford joined a coterie of black House members, 13 of whom in 1971 had formed the Congressional Black Caucus. Despite the enactment of both the Civil Rights and Voting Rights Acts, there were few opportunities for their numbers to grow. In northern urban areas with large minority populations, district lines ensured the election of a minority officeholder, but elsewhere in northern states delegations included no minorities. Most of these incumbents remained in the House for lengthy periods, unable to run for statewide office because of the reluctance of much of the majority white population to vote for a black candidate, building important seniority that would translate into chairmanships in years to come.[26] Southern congressional districts were gerrymandered to disperse minorities widely to ensure that no minority candidate could win election. Indeed, before Ford's narrow victory in 1974, only two seats out of dozens in the heavily black former Confederacy were held by African Americans: Andrew Young in Georgia and Barbara Jordan in Texas. States with sizeable black populations—South Carolina, Alabama, Mississippi, and Louisiana—had all-white delegations thanks to the "cracking" of black population centers.[27]

Six members recaptured seats they had recently lost, several of whom would play a significant mentorship role in helping the Class meet key party players and acclimate to the ways of Congress.[28] "I could be helpful," Richard Ottinger recalled, because "I understood what the problems were."[29] In particular, Abner Mikva, who had spent a half-million dollars to win a new Illinois seat, was a close ally of Democratic Study Group Chair Phillip Burton, an important strategist on behalf of the freshmen.[30] Ottinger, who had left the House for an unsuccessful New York Senate campaign, also credited Burton, who "wrote the script," for his victory. "I was just the actor," he modestly declared.[31] The centrality of Burton to the role of the freshmen would have major implications for the caucus throughout the 94th Congress.

A "New Breed" of Legislator

Their youth, their sometimes unconventional appearance, their emergence from nontraditional grassroots political movements, and their strong dedication to policy reforms made some Class members appear impetuous and impatient, qualities that did not endear the newcomers to some of their senior leaders. They were a "'new breed' of legislator," a commentator wrote, "young, brash, independent of its elders and their system, rejecting cronyism and parochialism, [imposing] a new order of ethics and independence."[32] "We had," noted Andy Maguire, "a keen desire for public service, for participating in important ways where it counted for our country, for making good things happen to the best of our ability within one of the most powerful institutions in the world."[33] Their goal, a *New York Times* reporter summarized, was to open up the legislative process, to "restore Congress to its proper constitutional rank as a co-equal branch of government [and] to staunch the systemic corruption that seemed to be the price of a bloated Presidency."[34]

Despite assertions about the Class's inexperience, many incoming freshmen had backgrounds quite similar to the veterans in terms of their level of education, their ideologies, and their career backgrounds. More than 60 percent of the newcomers had served in public office, compared to 55 percent of the veterans prior to their own election to the House; 42 percent were attorneys, similar to 46 percent of the remainder of the caucus. Among the freshmen from California, four were former mayors, as was Ohio Republican Bill Gradison. George Miller and Christopher Dodd, whose fathers had been influential politicians, had grown up steeped in the culture of politics. Significant numbers had experience in state and local government despite their youth, including Tom Downey, Les AuCoin, Henry Hyde, and Edward Beard. Others, like Millicent Fenwick, Harold Ford, and Paul Simon, a former lieutenant governor of Illinois, arrived with years of political deal making under their belts. The Class also included academics like Tim Wirth, Floyd Fithian, Phil Sharp, and Andy Maguire, who had studied and often served in non-elective government positions.

With few exceptions, like Wirth and Maguire, the "outsiders" of whom O'Neill spoke and on whom many in the press imposed great expectations for change, did not come to Congress intending to change it. They came to Washington, overwhelmingly and almost without exception, with a single major objective: to end the war in Vietnam. Only after their arrival did most freshmen discover that a very different agenda awaited them, even before they raised their hands in the ornate House Chamber to take the oath as members of the 94th Congress.

Under the tutelage of veteran legislators who had battled for reforms while many in the Class were still in college, the freshmen learned that achieving their policy goals was inextricably linked to changing the institution's operational rules. Reform meant not merely cleansing government of corruption but removing obstructions that prevented the House from addressing policy areas like health care, energy, and the environment. In contrast to later Republican insurgents of the 1990s and 2000s, virtually no one in the Class advocated a reduced role for government despite considerable skepticism about the misconduct of powerful institutions when in the wrong hands. "We believed government could be a force for good," declared Blanchard. "We were the products of the inspiration of JFK more than the Vietnam War."[35] And they were determined, John LaFalce of New York noted, to exercise their "extraordinary influence . . . even before being sworn in."[36]

Although the 94th Congress would not convene until early January, Class members began streaming into Washington for preliminary meetings with the leadership and to attend caucus orientation sessions shortly after the election. Returning members like Mikva and Ottinger cautioned their new colleagues to avoid focusing immediately on legislation. "The first thing you do," the veterans advised, "is organize Congress. Don't attack deficit spending or whatever. The first job is to organize Congress."[37] Ned Pattison of New York recalled being advised of the urgency to "organize everyone coming in here right away."[38] He, Wirth, and Gladys Noon Spellman of Maryland emerged as conveners of an ad hoc organization informally known as the Class of the 94th, and later the New Members Caucus (NMC). "I figured we should get together before [the leadership] got to us [and] organize everyone coming in here right away," Wirth recalled. Jerry Patterson agreed. "We all had sense of urgency that we would be absorbed by the big system," he noted, "if we didn't stand together as a class."[39]

The New Members Caucus provided Class members with an entity of their own that could marshal forces in support of legislative priorities and enhance their committee assignments. It also provided, in Les AuCoin's words, the "comfort of companionship in a big place." Some felt lost in the rush of congressional organization, thousands of miles from family, familiar political advisors, and campaign staff. For Californian George Miller, who had only been to Washington once before his election, "back East was Chicago."

The New Members' Caucus

Wirth raised $8,000 from affluent, pro-reform donors to buy a few IBM Selectric typewriters and support a staff of two, including Hill veteran Joe Crapa. Several of the DSG and NCEC leaders who had provided strategic and financial assistance during the campaign now offered advice in making the needed adjustment to Capitol Hill. Burton and his wife, Sala, served as Class parents, calling and meeting with the freshmen, particularly those from marginal districts. They were "the glue that held [freshmen] together," Burton's biographer wrote, but, as always with Burton, the solicitude had an ulterior motive. Shortly after the election, Burton announced his candidacy for the chairmanship of the Democratic Caucus. Almost all of the 76 freshmen would ultimately support Burton's candidacy, happy to sign up as the "bodies for the last major bombardment on House tradition . . . to finish the job" on reforms.[40]

But even as they maneuvered to integrate themselves into the caucus, the freshmen remained wary about being suffocated by the senior members, even friendly ones. They made a conscious decision not simply to be subsumed into the DSG, however much they admired its leaders and supported its objectives. The Class members "were clannish, self-supportive, and not dependent on anyone," recalled Crapa. "They had the sense that the people had elected a different kind of Congress."[41] Downey highlighted the need to maintain a distinct role. "The New Members Caucus made sure you didn't become immediately what you came to fight," Downey recalled. Despite a longtime family connection to Burton, Miller valued having a unique institution that served only the freshmen. "They were the establishment and we needed an identify," he noted. Equally important, the freshmen wanted to send a clear signal to voters back home that they had not simply become a part of the congressional muddle they had been elected to purify. "Your people voted for you because they thought you wanted to change the system," Miller said. "We were running against this system. Why join up with the established group? You needed separation. That's just Politics 101."[42] Sharp echoed the observation, recalling it was important to "distinguish you from what these [senior] pols are like," a view shared by Paul Tsongas. "You have to countervail pressures to become part of the system," the Massachusetts freshman said. "There's a danger that we will forget why we were elected."[43]

The freshmen were so mistrustful of hierarchy that they hesitated in granting long-term power to one person for any length of time. Rather than elect one freshman as president for the entire 94th Congress, the Class decided to rotate the position every six months. They were "suspicious of power, even their own," recalled Les Francis, chief of staff to Norm Mineta. Paul Simon proposed Carroll Hubbard, whose Kentucky district abutted Simon's own in southern Illinois, as the first Class president. Hubbard was an unusual choice, "more conservative and more of the old-fashioned, 'go-along-to-get-along' mold" than many of his freshmen colleagues.[44] A state senator, he had won attention by ousting Rep. Frank Stubblefield, an eight-term Democrat who had run afoul of labor leaders. Hubbard's victory, the first defeat of a sitting member in a primary, had been regarded by many as an omen of the impending change coming in the 1974 elections.

Speculation abounds 40 years later about why a group of largely liberal freshmen would choose Hubbard as the public face of the Class. Some have conjectured the decision was strategic, to present a moderate face that would prevent the easy categorization of the overall group. Others hypothesize the choice was meant to highlight Democratic resurgence in the South. Some suggested a desire to avoid selecting one of the self-promoters who were viewed as excessively ambitious, such as Wirth, who had been tagged the "pick of the litter" among freshmen by one wag. "We disliked the Washington establishment picking the winner," recalled Bob Carr. Some even saw the invisible hand of Burton, who engaged in strategic alliances with conservatives by embracing regionally important issues like tobacco support payments in return for southern support for food stamps.

Whatever the motivation, second thoughts about Hubbard quickly arose. One Class member recalls being shocked at seeing Hubbard cheerfully chatting with President Ford at a White House breakfast for new members. "What have we wrought?" he whispered to Ned Pattison. The wariness about allowing class officers to accrue excessive personal influence seemed to have been justified when Hubbard launched an abortive effort to extend his initial term as chairman in late May. Instead, he was succeeded by Mineta, who was viewed as more representative of the Class overall.[45]

The NMC also needed a secretary to keep minutes of its meetings, and Bedell reflexively nominated one of the women in the Class, Gladys Spellman. In an atmosphere of rising sensitivity about consigning women to traditional roles in the family, workplace, or House of Representatives, the proposal drew immediate reproaches. Bedell retreated quickly, only to be selected *himself* as the new secretary.

The NMC assisted freshmen by sharing information and pressing for "ambitious goals" like good committee assignments. By gathering together, it also was also beneficial in enlisting them in the unfinished business of reforming the House.[46] "Most freshmen didn't know who was who," Sharp noted. The newcomers' group allowed them to "enhance our strength and power and deal with the anxiety we felt." In their early meetings in the rat-infested, aging Congressional Hotel tucked behind the House office building, the novices sat together for hours, introducing themselves, explaining their motivations for running and their priorities as new members of the House. They were delighted, and surprised, to discover they had so much in common notwithstanding their regional and ideological disparities. As Class members explained their motivations for becoming candidates, Toby Moffett remembered thinking, "Holy shit, we ran on the same thing!"

"I didn't know what to expect," said North Carolina's Steve Neal. "I'd never been in politics before [and] had no vision of it at all." Neal was relieved to discover "guys saying almost exactly the same thing as me, and I thought, 'Oh God, great, we *can* make a difference here.'" New York's John LaFalce described the feeling of meeting his fellow Class members as "like talking with your own, no one knows more than you. [We had] equal problems and aspirations." Georgia's Elliot Levitas agreed that they "shared a common sense, [a desire to] make changes, not just talk." Most important, they found broad agreement on the key issues on which they ran, including Vietnam and economic initiatives on unemployment and jobs.

There was also an "emphasis on helping each other," Russo said, a "common interest, a unity in numbers. That is what the Class meant. If a Class guy needed help, something about it was innate, [there was a] loyalty to the group." The Class was "unique," Neal believed, composed of "really good guys, honest, not beholden to special interests, [interested in doing] what is good for whole country. That's what motivated nearly the whole class." Martha Keys, from Kansas, was excited to be meeting "wonderful people." The freshmen realized they held great power, "if we stuck together," Russo said. Even though the group had never met before, the atmosphere was heady enough that Massachusetts's Paul Tsongas later noted in his diary, "There's something going on here."

The freshmen were determined to send a message that they would not be rubber stamps. There would have to be respectful consultation with the large, new, cohesive bloc of members who had not even taken the oath of office yet. They rejected the notion of simply following the instructions of senior members and the leadership. A member of the whip organization often "just stood at the [House] door with his thumbs up or down" expecting acquiescence from members, Miller recalled. The freshmen would insist upon inclusion in the decision making. "You could say there are 20 of us," recalled Miller. "We demand a meeting!" The freshmen's "mutual deference, not party discipline," the *National Journal* suggested, "would become the rule."[47]

The Reformers Gather

A month after the election, the Democratic Caucus, including the members-elect for the incoming 94th Congress, was scheduled to convene. The agenda included another round of possible rules changes affecting chairmanships, floor procedures, and committee assignments. Reformers in DSG had spent the weeks since the election soliciting the freshmen and instructing them on the upcoming resumption of the reform battles. Thanks to the large number of progressive freshmen, at last the "stage was set," Dave Obey believed, "to put into motion the procedures we had designed two years earlier" when the caucus was given the power to elect the committee chairs.[48] In preparation for the caucus meetings, senior members were openly solicitous of the newcomers, inviting them to meetings, dinners, and to talk with leaders of the House and reform organizations. Lee Hamilton invited his five new Indiana Democrats to his home for an evening of political discussion. At a dinner at Ottinger's home to meet with reform advocates from outside Congress, one member-elect recalled "everyone drooling all over John Gardner" of Common Cause, although another guest, Texas veteran Jack Brooks, snarled that he would "like to shoot [Gardner's] ass" for pushing campaign finance reform, which disadvantaged Democrats. It would not be the only time that divisions appeared between the freshmen and the older reformers.

"DSG went into overdrive to invite us in to tell us about proposals," Sharp remembered. DSG Chairman Phil Burton had created a "buddy system," designating trusted friends in the freshman class like Henry Waxman, Miller, Mikva, and his brother, John Burton (elected in a 1974 special election), to serve as contacts with the new members, an important step in his campaign to chair the caucus that would determine the new rules. The freshmen needed the guidance to understand the complex rules and organizational structure of the House. Doug Dibbert, recruited from NCEC's Public Interest Consulting Project to help staff the New Members Caucus employees, recalls that no freshman had thought, "If I get elected and enough of us get elected, I can go to Washington and change rules of House and maybe the seniority system." One of the least politically savvy of the freshmen, fishing tackle entrepreneur Berkley Bedell agreed. "I didn't know what it was like before we got there," Bedell admitted. "Reform was not an issue when I was running. It arose when we arrived in Washington, DC." Even Wirth, who described "reform" as a major issue in his campaign, acknowledged he did not appreciate the recent level of activity by those already serving in the House. "I didn't know the older reformers existed!" he admitted. Meanwhile, Jim Oberstar, a House chief of staff before his election, found it perplexing to be both part of the caucus and conspiring to alter its longstanding procedures. "It was like plotting against the regime while being a part of the machine," he recalled, with some senior members confused as to whether he was still John Blatnik's staff or a member-elect himself.

The organizations that had invested heavily in the campaigns had high hopes for the Class. Ted Henshaw, the director of the Democratic National Congressional Committee (and soon to be named clerk of the House by Speaker Albert) found the freshmen the "most impressive group in years from the standpoint of previous legislative experience." NCEC activists Rosenblatt and Irwin Miller were convinced that the reforms that had proven elusive might now be in reach. The sense was, "Wow, let's bring democracy to the House," recalled Dibbert.[49]

It is important to remember that interparty conflict had no role in these reform initiatives. The targets were not Gerald Ford or House Republicans but the Democrats' *own* leadership and committee chairs. The fight to democratize the House was a fight among Democrats, between generations, among regions and ideologies that constituted the diverse mosaic of the party, with the added elixir of 76 newcomers who altered the balance of power within the caucus. As the freshmen streamed into an early caucus meeting, a delighted New York reformer Bella Abzug cheered, "The reinforcements have arrived!"

Certainly the near unanimity in support of reform among the freshmen gave the New Members Caucus a substantial amount of influence. But, in addition to the political and strategic advantage of freshman unity, there was something broader than procedural modernization that led the newcomers to coalesce, however opportunistically, into a cohesive group. James Reston of the *New York Times* surveyed the Class and concluded, "This transfusion of new blood will almost certainly produce a new and activist spirit on Capitol Hill." He predicted the Class would prove "more liberal, more spendthrift, more partisan, and increasingly critical of the Ford Administration."[50]

"They were a force to contend with arithmetically, an entity whether you formalized it or not," recalled Les Francis, Mineta's chief aide. "There was a spiritual, philosophical glue . . . [T]hey were unique, younger. These guys got here independent of institutional ties and in some cases in spite of them." Their willingness to challenge convention did not stem simply from naïveté or altruism but from a recognition that some had won their seats unexpectedly and might not enjoy long tenures in Congress. "We didn't expect to make lifetime careers in Congress" following their surprising victories, Bob Carr recalled, "so we weren't worried about the consequences of tomorrow. We weren't worried about offending people."[51] If they declined to challenge seniority and the closed operations of the House, they would not only cripple their own careers but would leave in place the institutional barriers that had blocked progressive policy initiatives for a decade and a half. Whether experienced or novice, Class members largely shared this sense of activism, of willingness to take on complex issues and to defy traditions.

Wariness toward "Rambunctious" Newcomers

It was not surprising, therefore, that the Democratic establishment viewed them warily. To a large degree, Majority Leader O'Neill believed, they considered themselves "independent, and they didn't hesitate to remind you that they were elected on their own, often without any help from the Democratic Party." Some like Beard, Hubbard, and McDonald had even defeated incumbent Democrats to win their seats.[52] "They were young, they were brash," an observer recalled a decade later. "They were independent and reform-minded. They shunned tradition and wanted to do things their way." They were, according to this account, "the most rambunctious freshmen Democrats the House had seen in years . . . born out of the national discontent." Some asserted they "stumble[d] into Congress," while others labeled them the "Red Guard of the revolution," referring to Mao Zedong's army of youthful zealots, who arrived "armed with a post-Watergate mandate, change things or answer to their constituencies."[53]

NCEC pushed back against the criticism that the new Class was composed of an "unmanageable rabble that will ride to defeat two years hence and insure [sic] a Republican White House," as occurred in 1966 following the LBJ landslide. Others noted that similar large incoming Democratic classes in 1930 and 1958 had not prevented big Democratic victories in the following presidential cycle. Still, NCEC acknowledged this group of freshmen was unique, "distinctly different from the traditional congressional office-seeker who had an eye on joining the establishment and silently rising on the seniority ladder."

The freshmen disputed their characterization as zealots whose unrestrained spending and freewheeling legislating could not only cost them their seats but put at risk the party's 1976 presidential nominee. Miller dismissed leadership criticism as "typical of what any incumbency would say when presented with this group of people on their doorsteps." While they had strong views and demanded the attention their numbers seemed to justify, they were not necessarily hostile to following responsible leadership. "None of it was intended to challenge the leadership or cause trouble," recalled Don Bonker of Washington State. And while it is true that they were freshmen, NCEC reminded critics that the 94th class would convene in 1976, "on the 200th anniversary of a body made up entirely of freshmen."[54]

At the end of the month, a number of gatherings blended social activity with preparation for the upcoming convening of the 94th Congress. DSG held an all-day orientation meeting on November 30 followed by a cocktail reception in the cavernous and ornate Cannon Caucus Room. The freshmen heard addresses by *Washington Post* columnists David Broder and George Will, as well as a performance by humorist Mark Russell. The following day, there was a Speaker's luncheon followed by a DSG pre-caucus meeting, a DSG reception, and a campaign committee reception.

As they prepared for the first meetings of the caucus, rumors swirled through Washington that DSG reformers were confident the freshmen would provide the crucial votes needed to successfully challenge several of the most objectionable chairs. Among those cited as facing possible ouster were Armed Services' F. Edward Hébert, Agriculture's Bob Poage, Rules' Ray Madden, and Education and Labor's Carl Perkins. Additional rumors raised the prospect of stripping Ways and Means of its long-standing power to assign members to committees. Many liberals disliked the committee's chairman since 1958, Wilbur Mills, who had obstructed progressive health care and tax reforms. Two years earlier, Mills had outraged liberals in 1973 by ignoring a caucus demand to report legislation repealing the oil depletion allowance, a huge tax break benefiting the oil and gas industry, and he personally had blocked action on numerous health care laws as far back as Medicare a decade earlier. There also was strong feeling that committee assignments should be made by a committee composed of the elected leadership and its designees, not by a permanent committee whose permanent members were unaccountable to the caucus.

The biggest threat to Mills came not as a result of freshman opposition but because of a scandal of his own making. On the morning of October 7, a car in which the powerful chairman was riding careened into the Tidal Basin a mile from Capitol Hill. Piling out of the car was not only a drunk and bleeding Mills but also a stripper from the Silver Slipper Lounge named Annabell Battistella, known professionally as "Fannie Fox, the Argentine Firecracker." The House leadership collegially rallied to Mills's defense, with Speaker Albert praising him as "an outstanding member of the House." O'Neill expressed mystification that "Wilbur would be involved in anything of that nature."[55] But the scandal provided reformers with fresh evidence of the compelling need to scrutinize the competence of committee leaders and the allocation of power in the House.

The postelection lame duck session of the 93rd Congress clearly understood the voters' Election Day message and decisively overrode Ford's veto of an education rehabilitation law by 398–7 (the 7 opponents were all defeated or retiring Republicans) in the House and 90–1 in the Senate, one of the most one-sided overrides on record. Even leading conservative Republicans like John Ehrlenborn and Frank Horton spoke against Ford's position in the House, and his old colleague, Wayne Hays, advised Ford to "get rid of some of those fellows who are giving you bum advice."[56]

With the new Congress much more heavily Democratic, it was generally agreed, Ford would need to make greater concessions, but his veto of the popular education bill suggested more confrontation was more likely.

As Democrats prepared to convene on December 2, excitement mixed with determination and optimism was coursing through the long-frustrated House reformers, who, for the first time in their careers, believed they constituted an unquestioned majority in the caucus. "There is a mood of reform in the air on Capitol Hill," Common Cause declared.[57] But what course that exuberance would take, how extensive the changes might be, and who would emerge with powers expanded or constrained was still very much an uncertainty. "There's change," mused the intellectual godfather of House reform, Richard Bolling, "but I don't know what it all means."[58]

5 THE REVOLUTION

We *were* a pain in the ass. We went to Congress to shake things up, and we shook things up.—Rep. Bob Carr (D-MI)

We were pretty brash, not scared. We didn't know that we shouldn't take on a chairman.—Rep. Floyd Fithian (D-IN)

The winds of change have arrived in the House of Representatives.
—Rep. Phillip Burton (D-CA)

Watch out, the revolution is going to get you!—Rep. Phil Landrum (D-GA)

ess than a week after the Democratic landslide, anticipation was soaring about changes that would affect the 94th Congress. "The new House is likely to see more frequent challenges to committee power coming from the newly resurgent Democratic caucus, and the decreased strength of the committees," predicted the *National Journal*, and *Time* anticipated that the "youthful, more active nature" of the reformers would significantly impact the operation of the House. Would the leadership be able to control its "unduly large majorities"?[1]

The incoming freshmen had few doubts about their ability to alter the House. Washington State's Don Bonker "sensed rebellion," he recalled. "These young upstarts were eager to take on something or someone, and it was contagious." They soon found their targets. The dramatic changes implemented by the Class, in league with older reformers, shifted the political balance in the caucus, redistributing the power of older and more cautious leaders to a new majority that was eager to alter the rules of the political game. "I'd say," mused Republican leader John Rhodes after hearing decisions made within the Democratic Caucus, "things are going to be pretty rough around here."

Targeting Seniority and Chairmen

F. Edward Hébert loved his job as chairman of the Committee on Armed Services. He relished sitting behind his imposing desk underneath an enormous painting of the World War II flag-raising on Iwo Jima. His committee was so stocked with thickly drawling, pro-war southerners that that panel member Pat Schroeder joked she "almost needed simultaneous translation" during hearings. He detested the opponents of the war in Southeast Asia, which he had enthusiastically supported. For 34 years, he had represented the 1st District of Louisiana, and, given the House's reverence to the seniority tradition, he believed he would retain his gavel until he chose to retire. He was mistaken.

Hébert had "grown old and autocratic in Congress, [while] savoring the trappings heaped by seniority," one account noted.[2] But he was not the only veteran who missed the emerging challenge to the chairmen who had long dominated the members and even the leadership. The addition of 49 new Democratic seats, noted a report by the National Committee for an Effective Congress, "establishes the party caucus as the *de facto* congressional force" and the likely place where the "progressive bloc," which now decisively outnumbered the conservatives, would implement reforms.

In the days leading up to the December caucus meeting, Phillip Burton, chairman of the Democratic Study Group, and likeminded reformers recounted to the Class their frustrated attempts to strengthen the caucus, hold chairs accountable for the management of their committees, reduce secrecy in hearings and voting, and expand the ability of junior members to participate fully.[3] All of these structural and personnel changes, they explained, were essential precursors to achieving policy objectives. Even an experienced politician like California's Norm Mineta admitted he "didn't know the rules and the ways of Congress" until the senior members educated him and his colleagues. Most, like Marty Russo, a political novice, "didn't know who these [chairmen] were." But after hearing the history of thwarted reform efforts, Toby Moffett remembered "smelling blood in the caucus" as it moved quickly to take up a long litany of liberal reform initiatives.

Returning freshmen like Abner Mikva and Richard Ottinger counseled their new colleagues to pay close attention to the rules debate. "Your first job is to organize Congress, have a caucus," they were told, "decide the chairs and how the party will operate."[4] Organizing Congress, however, was a mystery to most. "Burton and DSG never let the new guys out of their sight," George Miller recalled. "They adopted us." Some, like Russo, were skeptical about all the attention showered on the freshmen. "We didn't know a lot about what was going on," Russo told me. "We were well-manipulated by the older guys," including DSG's Machiavellian staff director, Dick Conlon. These experienced strategists "maneuvered the class" to understand the opportunities for effectuating the reforms that had proven so elusive. "I would just sit there and listen," said Russo, rarely daring to raise a question. "You didn't want to make yourself sound stupid."[5]

The formal leadership knew that it was viewed warily and took pains to reach out to the incoming Class. Speaker Albert pledged that each incoming member would be appointed to at least one major committee, which was an easy promise to keep since there was a multitude of vacancies resulting from the election.[6] He also invited the freshmen to select one of their own to serve on the leadership's Steering and Policy Committee. Only Bob Carr and Bill Brodhead of Michigan expressed interest, and the latter was ecstatic about being appointed. "I'm not even sworn in," he recalled, "and I'm sitting in the ultimate council of power, with all most powerful people. I was in awe of being able to be there."[7]

Lastly, Albert also added three "at-large" members to the whip organization that took the pulse of the caucus on votes in order to provide direct linkages to black, female, and freshmen members.[8] The appointment of John Jenrette of South Carolina to the latter position represented an early acknowledgment of importance of the progressive new southern freshmen who were expected to contrast dramatically with the hard-line conservatives they had replaced, altering alter the ideological tilt of the caucus.

The veteran reformers explained to the freshman that the most urgent step in modernizing the House was the removal of several problematic chairmen who had long been protected by the nearly sacrosanct seniority system. "You come here to do something," nine-year veteran Tom Rees of California told the Class, "not just [to] sit at a desk and wait for someone to die." He described how, two years earlier, the caucus had lacked the votes to depose any of the chairs, although several had received a few dozen negative votes.[9] Still, the expression of caucus concern had not seemed to affect the chairmen's attitude significantly in the intervening months.

Opposition to unconditional seniority was the reform that unified the freshmen. During the campaign, the bipartisan reform group Common Cause had circulated a questionnaire asking whether candidates would support an on-the-record vote on chairs, and the result was almost universally positive. "I remember being amazed [by] how many of us had campaigned against Congress, citing the seniority system as Exhibit A," recalled Oregon's Les AuCoin. "It doesn't take brains to be an all-powerful chairman in Congress. All you have to do is outlive or outlast everyone else on your committee, and you inherit the throne."[10] Henry Waxman, a veteran of reform battles in the California legislature, also sensed an "eagerness . . . to dismantle the antiquated seniority system" and limit the authority of all chairmen, whose "power was nearly absolute."[11]

The newcomers, encouraged by the veterans and unfazed by the power of the chairs, were not easily intimidated. "We were pretty brash," said Indiana's Floyd Fithian. "We didn't know that we shouldn't take on a [committee chairman]."[12] Their innocence about the structure of the House was a benefit, Elliott Levitas agreed. Had they known more about the formidable powers arrayed against them, he speculated, "they might have backed off, so it was good to be naïve."

Quickly, "DSG went into overdrive," Phil Sharp recalled. The freshmen were ready to serve as the "shock troops . . . all charged up for change," said Tim Wirth of Colorado.[13] Even southern freshmen whose region had disproportionately benefited from seniority "joined in enthusiastically" to challenge "the power structure [that] was doing dumb things," North Carolina's Steve Neal said.[14] Pat Schroeder advised that too many of the chairs were "not in tune with the country. They were all in their seventies, and their vim and vigor was long gone."[15] That was enough for many of the Class members. "We were going to knock some heads off," Iowa's Mike Blouin recalled. "There was a cockiness on both sides, some of chairs were pretty cocky back[, asserting,] 'You can't touch me.' "[16]

The evidence justifying the purges was contained in an exhaustive report by DSG and Common Cause enumerating the shortcomings of several of the chairs.[17] Overall, 14 of 22 were faulted for being "disrespectful to the Caucus," echoing the prejudice of the former longtime Agriculture Chairman Harold Cooley. "I hate and detest junior members interrupting a senior member asking a question," Cooley once had declared. "Senior members will ask all the important questions and conduct all the committee work."[18] The report targeted five chairs: W. R. Poage (Agriculture), Wright Patman (Banking), Wayne Hays (House Administration), George Mahon (Appropriations), and F. Edward Hébert. All but Hays were southerners.

In addition to Patman, Ray Madden, the 82-year-old Rules chairman, and Harley Staggers, 67, of the Commerce Committee, were accused of "significant shortcomings," while Poage, Mahon, and Hays "showed a pattern of more serious abuses." The report was especially critical of Hébert for having "flagrantly violated standards of fairness and compliance with House and Caucus rules" by stacking subcommittees with pro-war members and by "punishing" those with whom he disagreed.[19] Others cited his megalomania, as illustrated in his book inscription for another member: "The Lord giveth and the Lord taketh away; I am the Lord." Critics also told the freshmen members how Hébert had refused to sign a routine authorization for committee member Pat Schroeder to join an international delegation, declaring, "I'm not signing a voucher for a god-damned woman to go to Paris."[20] The freshmen were alarmed to learn that their efforts to end the war in Vietnam would face enormous roadblocks if Hébert maintained the Armed Services chair.[21]

The acerbic Wayne Hays was faulted for serving as chairman of the House Administration Committee, which dispensed rooms, budgets, and favors to members, while simultaneously serving as chairman of the Democrats' campaign committee that disbursed money to candidates. But Hays's real shortcoming was his incivility and lack of courtesy. Ambitious, imperious, and arrogant, Hays seemed content to make enemies gratuitously. Dave Obey recalled how, shortly after winning a special election in 1969, he had asked Hays to consider trading rooms in the Longworth Building so the freshman's annex might be closer to his main office. Hays walked over from the Capitol and unlocked the door to his annex. Peering inside, Obey was astonished; the room was filled from floor to ceiling with expensive French furniture gathered during Hays's frequent European junkets. "This furniture is for my retirement home in Ohio," Hays explained. "Now, you wouldn't want me scratching it just to do a favor for some chickenshit freshman, would you?" With that, Hays relocked the annex door and walked away.[22]

"Hays is almost as intelligent and able as Burton and even more abrasive," one reporter wrote. "Most members flinch from taking him on."[23] Hays employed his considerable power as chairman "with vindictiveness," noted the *Washington Post*, "punishing staffers and House employees who crossed him. His sarcasm often rips up his colleagues on the floor."[24] He was, the normally genial Ab Mikva declared, "a miserable guy." Yet Hays assiduously catered to the needs of members, especially freshmen facing challenging reelection races. He was careful, for example, to drop by informal dinners held by Italian American members. Such personal attention would prove crucial in the coming days.

Wright Patman, the 81-year-old chairman of the Banking Committee, had begun his congressional career in 1929, the same year that Herbert Hoover had entered the White House. Unlike many of his Texas colleagues, Patman was no hard-line conservative. He had built a career as a populist, castigating the Federal Reserve, championing small farmers and businesspeople, and earning respect for the initial 1972 inquiry into the origins of the money paid to the Watergate burglars. But committee members resented his growing tendency to delegate key decisions to his staff, resulting in "a chaotic atmosphere lacking dignity and decorum."[25] Still, reform leaders like the Consumer Federation of America and advocate Ralph Nader rushed to support the aging populist.

Only a small number of the freshmen were wary of disposing of people they barely knew and with whom they had never served. Russo was one, recalling the veterans "pumping up our class to get rid of chairs," and he "was very 'anti' the liberals in my class" because they "gunned down Patman," who had been "progressive in Texas when Texas was not progressive."[26] As a consolation prize, he proposed allowing the old chairman to retain the title "emeritus."

Despite decades of mischaracterization about the goal of the reformers, a wholesale abandonment of the seniority system was never advocated, nor even was the removal of every conservative, southern, underperforming, or aging chairman. Rules chairman Ray Madden, who was a year older than Patman, was known to whistle tunelessly through hearings, occasionally forgetting which bill was before the committee. He often lectured witnesses irrelevantly about conditions in his Indiana district. Class member Tom Downey, who was less than a third of Madden's age, encountered the chairman in the House gym's steam room, and Madden asked whom Downey had defeated. "Jim Grover," Downey reminded him. "Well, Grover, how do you like it here?" Madden asked. "No, I'm *Downey*," the freshman corrected. "Who beat Downey?" Madden asked. The conversation continued along these perplexing lines for several minutes before Downey left the steam room, exasperated. Madden called after him, "Okay, Grover, see you around!" The exchange left Downey stunned that such a "benign bumbler" could chair an important House committee. Yet Madden was spared the reformers' hook, likely because the caucus had given the Speaker the power of appointing members to Rules, ensuring the committee would function as an arm of the leadership and the caucus.

As the formal caucus meetings opened on December 2, the reformers quickly demonstrated their strength by voting down the longstanding doorkeeper, William M. "Fishbait" Miller, who was famous for officially intoning, "Mr. Speaker, the President of the United States," whenever the chief executive entered the House Chamber. Miller's informal Mississippi style—he was known to walk through the Capitol barefoot—belied his sweeping powers, staff of hundreds, and multimillion-dollar budget. He had held the doorkeeper position since 1949 despite a brusque manner that offended members, and his removal was widely regarded as a harbinger of the rising power of the reform forces. "We've got the votes," thought Michigan's Jim Blanchard when Miller lost.

New Caucus Leadership

The caucus then moved on to the crucial election of its own chair. The prohibitive favorite was Phillip Burton, the masterful legislative tactician who had provided the Class with strategic advice and steered hundreds of thousands of dollars to more than a hundred campaigns.[27] Burton had assiduously courted the freshmen, including congratulatory phone calls on election night, and had promised to help the Class members secure influential committee assignments. He envisioned a more active role for the long-somnambulant caucus, meeting more frequently and embracing policies that all Democrats would be expected to support.

Burton was respected but not beloved. His California colleague, Bob Leggett, predicted that, in Burton's hands, the caucus chair's job could "become the same as the Speaker's," an ominous observation not lost on the wary Carl Albert or Tip O'Neill, the Speaker and majority leader who feared Burton's skill, influence, and ambition. A *Wall Street Journal* article noted, "There was something almost scary about the sheer animal energy that Burton brings to any task." He was described variously as "one of the most astute political animals," "one of the more brilliant, tireless, and infuriating members of the House," "one of the most sagacious minds I've ever encountered," and "one of the weirdest people I have ever met." Often unkempt, his clothing wrinkled, hair askew, and eyes bulging, the remnants of a recent meal on his tie or lips, with a sizeable glass of vodka and smoldering cigarette in hand, Burton had "a disconcerting way of walking away from you in mid-sentence, generally yours," the *Washington Star-News* reported.[28]

Yet Burton had also developed a reputation for pragmatism, and his support crossed ideological lines. "I actively supported Phil Burton for Caucus Chair," explained Bill Hughes, a law and order New Jersey moderate, because his election "helped propel us in the effort to reform the process and to ultimately provide the tools for re-electing Members."[29] Oklahoma's Glenn English, whose voting record would be among the most conservative of the freshmen's, called Burton "a very practical politician [who] understood my situation in Oklahoma was precarious, that I needed to get reelected. He understood that better than [Speaker] Albert," who had declined to campaign for his own state colleague.[30]

His opponent was fellow Californian Bernie Sisk, a rough-hewn Texas native, one of those moderates Sam Rayburn had added to the Rules Committee in 1961 to dilute the power of the conservatives. Sisk was a leader of the anemic United Democrats of Congress, a moderate alternative to DSG, but he was ideologically estranged from the liberal majority, earning only a 56 percent approval from Americans for Democratic Action compared to Burton's 100 percent. No one expected the race to be close.

The relentlessness of Burton's campaign raised the hackles of some traditionalists who objected to what Deputy Whip Jim Wright described as its "unbecoming" lobbying. Foreshadowing a clash that would reverberate for the next two years, the moderate Wright sternly reminded Burton that the caucus chair was "an office that [should be] bestowed rather than sought" and that the "chairman of the Caucus is not an independent initiator of policy."[31]

Leadership races always reveal elemental issues and personal tensions, and the Burton-Sisk square-off displayed the thinly veiled friction between the old guard and the reformers. Within the Illinois delegation, Dan Rostenkowski argued forcefully for Sisk and was supported by Mel Price, the delegation's dean who stood to inherit the Armed Services chairmanship were Hébert removed. When Mikva, a Burton confidant, called on his fellow freshmen to ally themselves with the forces of change, the gruff veteran Frank Annunzio censured Mikva for "never [being] with the party," reminding the group that Mikva had originally won a House seat by challenging a sitting Democrat. Ralph Metcalfe, a former track star, spoke up in support of Mikva, who had declined to challenge Metcalfe in a 1972 primary after being redistricted into the same seat. Annunzio exploded, telling the former Olympian he was "out of line" and calling him a "black S.O.B."

In the end, Sisk later acknowledged in his memoir, the moderate United Democrats of Congress "simply did not have enough power to take [Burton] out."[32] Winning the votes of perhaps 90 percent of the freshmen, Burton prevailed easily, 162–111. His victory, he proclaimed, "sent a message that liberals wanted action . . . It's self-evident that the winds of change have arrived in the House of Representatives. My election is a product of the electorate's decision in November." As the most powerful liberal elected to the House leadership, Burton had reason to celebrate. The caucus, the new chairman declared, was "no longer a eunuch."[33] Burton had successfully planted his foot on the first rung of the leadership ladder that he fully expected would lead to the speakership.

He may well have overestimated the enthusiasm of some of his supporters. "A lot of freshmen backed him to send a message to the leadership," Class member Tim Lee Hall advised, but "a lot of them who voted for Burton for Caucus chairman wouldn't vote for him for speaker." Another freshman complained that while he "could not see Phil as a [future] leader" of the House, in a competition with Sisk, he had no hesitation in supporting him for chair.[34] *Washington Post* columnists Roland Evans and Robert Novak speculated that the real loser of the caucus chair battle was not Sisk but Tip O'Neill, who had always anticipated an uncontested succession to the Speaker's chair once Albert retired. With Burton's triumph, however, there was now a tactical and cold-blooded competitor operating inside the leadership tent and with one foot on the leadership ladder, one whom O'Neill neither liked nor trusted. He could not have been pleased when Burton was labeled the "uncrowned King of the House."[35]

Emboldened, the caucus moved on to the next item on the agenda, shifting the power to make committee assignments from Ways and Means to the leadership-dominated Steering and Policy Committee. Chairman Mills's influence continued to evaporate following the Tidal Basin incident with "the Argentine Firecracker," but he dutifully made the rounds of the members, including freshmen, pleading with them not to emasculate the committee. "I'll never forget that moment," Les AuCoin recalled. "One of the fabled leaders of the House . . . reduced to asking a totally unknown freshman for help. I felt the most awful sense of human wreckage. I was watching the destruction of a congressional giant."[36]

By a vote of 146–122, the job of assigning members went to Steering and Policy, an instrument of the leadership far better attuned to the demands of the caucus. A few days later, an intoxicated Mills joined Annabell Battistella onstage at Boston's Pilgrim Theater and then held a press conference in her dressing room during which he referred to the stripper (whose husband was also in attendance) as "my little old Argentine hillbilly." Speaker Albert quickly asked for and received his resignation as chairman. The elevation of Al Ullman of Oregon to the chairmanship of Ways and Means raised expectations of "significant changes in power and composition of the key tax-writing body," which, under new leadership, was "almost certain to be more responsive to pressures for tax reform now gathering in the House as a result of the election."[37]

Following the uncontested reelection of Albert and O'Neill to their leadership posts, Burton moved swiftly to consolidate power in the caucus.[38] Three generations earlier, Princeton professor Woodrow Wilson had written that "the Caucus is an antidote to the Committees," meaning that the broader diversity of the caucus could check the special interest tendencies of the legislative panels.[39] More recently, congressional scholars Norman Ornstein and David Rohde had championed proposals for ending a seniority system that "ranks senility ahead of competence" and for empowering subcommittees and younger House members.[40] Finally, the reformers had the votes.

Changes to Committee Organization

Determined to disseminate power more broadly, the caucus decided to limit members to one subcommittee chairmanship, ending the practice by which a small number of members exercised their seniority to claim the gavel on as many as four subcommittees. Moreover, chairs were barred from heading a subcommittee on their own panel if they held the gavel on another subcommittee. Additional independence was granted to subcommittee chairs including the hiring of a staff person and the right to manage their bills on the floor, a privilege usually reserved for full committee chairs. The caucus also limited all members to two legislative committee assignments, ensuring that more senior members could not deprive younger members of access to key panels.

In a decision that had major implications for junior members, each committee member was allowed to select one subcommittee before anyone chose a second one rather than permitting senior members to reclaim all the subcommittee slots they had occupied in the prior Congress. This change meant that freshmen were able to fill up the slots on powerful sub-committees as their top choices, freezing out more senior members. As a result, the membership of some subcommittees became distinctly more junior and more progressive than was the composition of the parent committee that had been fashioned by the leadership to reflect the diverse views within the caucus. Taken together, the impact of these changes was sweeping: even those chairmen who were not challenged found their power significantly circumscribed by the energized subcommittees.

One caucus decision gave unmitigated delight to the veteran reformers and the liberal community throughout the country: the liquidation of the detested, red-baiting House Internal Security Committee (HISC), formerly known as the House Un-American Activities Committee. A controversial relic of the Cold War, HUAC had conducted years of terrifying inquiries into dubious allegations of disloyalty. This was the panel on which a young Rep. Richard Nixon gained notoriety by investigating Alger Hiss in the 1940s, and it later held dramatic hearings into allegations of communist infiltration of the Hollywood film community, organized labor, religious organizations, and universities. Refusal to cooperate with the panel's aggressive investigations had ruined careers and even led to imprisonment for many in the entertainment industry like Dashiell Hammett, creator of detective Sam Spade. In recent years, the panel had probed universities, peace organizations, and militant groups like the Blank Panther Party and the anti-war Students for a Democratic Society. For years, liberals had condemned these far-flung investigations, but with little success. At the height of the Cold War in 1961, there were just 6 votes in the House for abolishing the committee and, in 1963, just 23. A decade later, on March 21, 1973, a motion by Don Edwards of California, a relentless civil libertarian and former FBI agent, proposed eliminating the committee, which was "especially divisive and embarrassing to the Democratic Party." As with earlier efforts, the motion fell short by a 92–67 vote.[41]

With the arrival of the Class, however, the caucus majority shifted. Indeed, there were so many appealing committee vacancies thanks to the election landslide that members had little interest in using up a committee assignment to investigate supposed communists. "At the end of the day," as one member explained the strategy, "no one wants to be on it." Indeed, none of the freshmen, except the anomalous Larry McDonald, expressed interest in serving on the hated panel. Maneuvered deftly by

liberal reformer Bob Kastenmeier, the caucus abolished HISC, trans-
ferred its jurisdiction to Judiciary, and then required that all of that
committee's members be lawyers, barring McDonald, a physician, from
eligibility. The elimination of HISC was an early, and particularly satisfy-
ing, victory for the new liberal majority of the caucus, described by one
overjoyed member as a "delightful experience."[42]

On December 3, Charles Vanik of Ohio moved to expand the membership of Ways and Means, explaining the action as "imperative [if] the committee is to respond to the mandate of the recent election for dynamic
economic programs." Vanik was merciless in his critique, accusing the
committee of opposing "any progressive legislation applicable to the
twentieth century or to the seventies."[43] Three days before the vote, a hum-
bled Mills told Burton he would agree to adding progressives to Ways
and Means, but it was too late. Burton already knew he had the votes.[44]
By the time of the vote, Mills had been hospitalized and was not even present to defend his record. Speaker Albert lauded him as "one of the greatest congressmen of my generation" but also acknowledged, "he is a sick
man."[45] An effort by the new chairman, Oregon's Al Ullman, to bar progressive freshman from joining the important tax subcommittee was
quashed when Burton demanded that O'Neill "unscramble it, or we'll
whack their asses." Ullman was outraged and denounced Burton's remarks as "disgusting," but, recognizing the mood of the caucus, he chose
to retreat, admitting, "We are not stupid."[46] It was exactly the kind of vul-
gar behavior by Burton that worried O'Neill and that would ricochet
against Burton the following year.

To improve the chances of appointing a member of a racial or ethnic
minority to Ways and Means for the first time, the caucus allowed five
members to nominate candidates instead of simply leaving all of the designations in the hands of the Steering Committee. Burton allowed Ron
Dellums to deliver a powerful speech decrying the "built-in handicaps"
that had excluded minorities. When Richard Bolling launched into a
typically esoteric lecture on the 1910 nominating reforms, an impatient
Burton cut him off by abruptly calling for a vote, and the measure passed
115–31.[47] Once again, Burton had prevailed, but in a manner that seemed
boorish to some observers. Overall, however, the major rules changes
altering Ways and Means, and Ullman's hasty retreat, confirmed the
influence of the caucus and its aggressive new chairman.

Even the reformers, however, were divided over a proposal to allow a caucus vote, rather than seniority, to select the Appropriations Committee's subcommittee chairs. Appropriations subcommittees enjoyed an "inordinate amount of power," committee member Robert Giaimo argued, because their work was rarely reversed in the full committee. This autonomy allowed subcommittee chairs to cut private deals with Republicans that did not "reflect the desires and will of this Caucus." Giaimo wanted to send a message that the subcommittee chairs "did not own their chairmanships by divine right but by the right of the Democratic majority."[48]

Again, there was a clash between reformers and senior members, and not only conservative veterans objected. Appropriations Chairman George Mahon, still a possible target of the reformers, spoke directly to the Class. "I know how it feels to be a new member," he said. "You like to have a voice in what goes on in the Congress—and you shall have." But Mahon had not been a new member since 1935, and such discordant comments made him sound out of touch, seeming to blame the freshmen for a motion offered by Giaimo, who had first been elected in 1958. But the conservative Mahon was joined by fellow senior appropriators, including liberal Sidney Yates of Illinois, in opposing Giaimo's motion.

A Prescient Warning

An important and prescient caution was raised by Sam Stratton, who warned that Giaimo's plan would "destroy the committee system [by] turning the operation of the House of Representatives over to the Democratic Caucus," where, as a conservative, he knew he was outnumbered. "We are moving, I am afraid, into a kind of attitude that only those Democrats who can achieve a certain stereotype form are the ones who are going to be approved by the House caucus for membership as chairman of subcommittees," Stratton warned. Such insistence on ideological conformity would jeopardize the electoral security of marginal Democrats, he argued, and the loss of those seats could endanger the Democratic majority itself. "It's a mistake," he cautioned. "I think that is going to destroy the Democratic Party." But, in the heady atmosphere, such warnings went unheeded, and the Giaimo reform was approved 147–116.

Another reform, one with particularly profound implications for the Republican minority, imposed a permanent 2:1 ratio favoring Democrats on every committee "in view of the mandate that we have got from the American people." O'Neill defended the change, playing to the reformers and calling the permanent ratio "an excellent precedent to set." But Republicans responded angrily to the new ratio, noting that the rule would grant Democrats an unfair advantage even when future elections shifted the ratio less favorably toward the Democrats, but to no avail.

A further diminution of the conservatives' influence came with the decision to restore to the Speaker the power to appoint Rules Committee members. The initiative was authored by Bolling, who viewed an empowered Speaker as essential in managing the House, in contrast to Burton's preference for more widely dispersed power. "The trouble with this place . . . is that the leadership, the Speaker, and the Majority Leader, have virtually no institutional powers," Bolling reminded the caucus. Too much power, he said, was held by "a bunch of barons" who used their "reactionary power" to obstruct "all Democratic programs that were worth a damn," as had been the case with Rules' long obstruction of civil rights legislation.[49] Bolling's proposal troubled those with long memories. James Burke, a Massachusetts member since 1959, warned, "When a Speaker gets too much power, he is able to do an awful lot of things." Rules chairman, Indiana's Ray Madden, who first ran for office only six years after the 1910 coup against Speaker Cannon, expressed concerns the caucus might be returning to Cannon's style, recalling the "Czar" as an "absolute tyrant [who] ran the House like you run a sewing machine." Even Speaker Albert weighed in against giving himself the appointment power. But O'Neill, a Rules member, again split the leadership and aligned himself with the reformers, and the caucus embraced the Bolling amendment by a 106–65 vote.

Additional proposals to check the chairs did not fare as well. An amendment to impose an age limit of 70 on all future chairmen was defeated, as was a proposed limit of three terms. If a chairman was unresponsive, advised John Dingell, a Michigan member since succeeding his father in 1955, "discipline him within the Committee Caucus. Take him out of the Caucus. Strip him at that point, but don't arbitrarily and capriciously remove him because you haven't got the courage to face him at the proper time for his failure."[50] Others warned that time limiting the chairs would empower the permanent staff that served as each panel's institutional memory, and the plan failed by a vote of 63–131.

The challenge that attracted the greatest amount of attention at the time, and by historians during the ensuing decades, was to the near-absolute obeisance to seniority in selecting committee chairs. Seniority had originated in 1910 as a reform to prevent a Speaker from naming only his own friends and allies as chairs. Seniority, it was believed, based selection solely on one neutral factor: the amount of time served in the House; neither friendships, alliances, nor ideology entered into the designation of chairmen. John Dingell recalled that, as a younger man, he had viewed seniority as "one of the great evils that afflicted our country," but, as he became more invested in the House, his views had changed. Abandoning seniority would mean increased influence for lobbyists "who have no term limits . . . no rules of seniority," Dingell said. Eventually, Dingell would serve as chairman of the Commerce Committee and end his career as the longest-serving House member in history, nearly 60 years.

But, on this point, the freshmen were unmovable, and they accepted the reformers' arguments that seniority had empowered those who obstructed progressive legislation, particularly those from secure, southern seats where they faced meager opposition and thus accrued long tenure. "We wanted to keep the chairmen from having as much power as they did," said freshman Henry Waxman, who would challenge the seniority system in battling Dingell for the Commerce Committee chairmanship more than 30 years later. "We wanted to make sure the seniority system wasn't absolute and that more power could be put in the hands of the Democratic Caucus and the leaders so important, progressive legislation could move."

The "Peasants" Summon the "Gods"

The Class did not just follow the recommendations of senior reformers, however, but launched an unprecedented innovation of their own. During a meeting of the New Members' Caucus, Indiana's Floyd Fithian proposed inviting all prospective chairmen to appear before the freshmen members to describe their agendas and their management style.[51] "We went ahead and did these things not knowing they were impossible," said Fithian.[52] Berkley Bedell described the invitation to his predecessor, John Culver, who had just been elected to the Senate. Culver, who had served on the Bolling reform committee but had become "pretty much disillusioned" with the prospects for House reform, was stunned by the freshmen's effrontery.[53] "That's the advantage of being naïve freshman," one new member said. "We can ask God to come talk to us peasants."[54] The *Washington Post*'s Mary Russell marveled at the newcomers, not even yet members, "brazenly inviting the chairmen to appear before them."[55] As one veteran reporter recalled, just a few years earlier "the freshman wouldn't have dared summon the committee chairman to a question-and-answer session. And if they had, the chairmen wouldn't have come. But times have changed."[56]

In fact, the chairmen, most of whom were still chafing over being subjected to a vote of the caucus, initially declined to meet. "We said, 'That's okay, we will just all vote against you then,'" recalled Bedell. Immediately, a staff member reported, the chairmen reconsidered the invitation because they had "all heard rumors that the freshmen wouldn't mind knocking off one of the old bulls."[57] Soon, the chairs sent word they would appear for the interviews. "There were some pretty hard feelings," recalled Tom Harkin. "But we had the votes.[58] It was "pretty astonishing," admitted Brodhead, to have "people you'd heard and read about, standing in front of a bunch of us who weren't even sworn in, supplicating us."[59] From that day forward, Bedell declared, "House chairmen knew they had to conduct committees in democratic way where everybody had an opportunity to be heard."[60]

On the appointed day, the chairs "came in obsequiously and sat down," Tom Harkin recalled. "They talked to the freshmen, asking for our votes. That was incredible. It was quite a thing to see that happen."[61] Henry Waxman recalled the interviews as "a very heady experience to have these old guys who had been ruling their committees with an iron hand coming to us with hat in hand."[62] Indiana's Phil Sharp remembered that "two or three [of the chairs] were extremely disappointing in terms of general competence." Some, Elliott Levitas said more emphatically, "didn't have a clue what the hell was going on." Jack Brooks, the gruff-talking Texan who chaired the Government Operations Committee, acknowledged the power of the newcomers. Chomping on his ever-present cigar, Brooks glared at the freshmen members as he sat down. "Okay, you son-of-bitches," Brooks told the startled Class members. "You've got the power. I recognize that. What do you want me to do?" The room erupted in laughter. "His honesty disarmed us," Tom Harkin recalled. "It broke the ice."[63]

Edward Hébert appeared before the freshmen on January 11, and his disdain for the young inquisitors became instant congressional legend. Leaning on his knuckles on the desk before him, his voice dripping with contempt, he advised the "boys and girls" to sit quietly and learn the ropes for a few years. He flushed deep red as Gladys Noon Spellman questioned his refusal to authorize Patricia Schroeder's travel to Paris. (There was no love lost between the two; the deeply conservative Hébert had recently campaigned for Spellman's Republican opponent.) The freshmen were infuriated by his haughtiness and by his refusal to allow opponents of the war in Vietnam to offer amendments in committee. "That was the end of him," said Toby Moffett of Connecticut.

Bob Poage of Texas also did "a poor job," according to Marty Russo, confessing to the Class members, "I don't know why I am talking to you freshmen."[64] He tried to regale the Class members with stories of his long service in the Congress. The vote he most regretted casting, he confessed, barred funding the anti-Fascist resistance during the Spanish Civil War in the late 1930s, which was both ancient history to the new members and offensive to the liberals for whom that conflict retained emotional appeal.

Ultimately, all of the chairs appeared except Interior and Insular Affairs Chairman James Haley, from Florida. Frail at 75, Haley was occasionally overwhelmed by coughing spasms and was known to absentmindedly spit on the floor while presiding. But his feebleness empowered committee member Phil Burton to exercise great influence, and Burton was delighted for the aged Floridian to remain in the chair. His replacement almost certainly would be the popular Mo Udall of Arizona, over whom Burton's influence would be diminished. As a result, Burton secured a pass for Haley from the freshmen, and he faced no opposition.

When Steering and Policy met on January 15, 1974, to designate chairmen for the caucus's approval, O'Neill recommended the current chairs be renominated by a voice vote. New York reformer Jonathan Bingham insisted on a secret ballot, and Bolling backed him up. As in 1973, several of the incumbent chairmen drew negative votes; on Hébert and Poage, the vote was 14–10 in favor of their retaining their chairs, and George Mahon of Appropriations was approved by an 18–6 vote. The aging populist Wright Patman, a member of the Steering Committee and the dean of the House, was voted down by an 11–13 margin. One member remembered thinking, "The winds of change had hit this committee."[65] When the next two ranking members on Banking also were defeated, economist Henry

Reuss, a 20-year veteran who had flirted with the possibility of challenging Patman, received the committee's support 15–9.

The biggest shock was the vote to remove Wayne Hays, a strong Burton ally whom the freshman representative on the Steering Committee, Bill Brodhead, considered "cantankerous, arrogant [and] an unprofessional asshole who reflected badly on Congress." After three 12–12 ties on secret ballots, Speaker Albert asked committee members to search their conscience and "do what you think is right." On the fourth ballot, one member changed his mind, Hays lost 11–13, and a Burton antagonist, New Jersey's Frank Thompson, was nominated in his place. Shortly thereafter, Brodhead encountered the defeated Hays who growled, "I understand *you* are the son of a bitch who changed his vote on me" on the fourth ballot. Taking a deep breath, Brodhead responded, "Mr. Chairman, that's not true! I voted against you all four times!" Hays, who had spent the day leveling the same charge against other Steering members, appeared stunned. "You are the first to be honest with me," he told Brodhead. "You're my kind of guy. Every one of those other sons of bitches lied to me. If I can do anything for you, come see me."[66]

The Steering Committee's votes against Patman and Hays quickly reverberated across Capitol Hill. "Reform fever had hit the establishment," wrote the *Post*'s Mary Russell. Jim O'Hara, who had helped write the rule change empowering Steering to nominate chairs, was flabbergasted. "When we put that in the rule," he admitted, "we thought it probably was just a gesture." Emerging from the meeting, Speaker Albert was asked how such a rebellion could have happened within the Speaker's own leadership committee. "I don't know," he said, seemingly mystified. "I don't know." O'Neill, who had tried to hot-wire automatic reappointments without individual votes, admitted he was "shocked by the outcome. I expected all the chairmen to be re-nominated."[67]

For conservatives, the message was particularly ominous. "Watch out," Georgia veteran Phil Landrum cautioned his colleagues. "The revolution's going to get you." John Jarman, an Oklahoman just narrowly reelected to his 12th term, decided against waiting to see where the caucus lurched next. He renounced his seat in the Democratic Caucus and joined the Republicans, blaming the "liberal takeover of the House Democratic Caucus and the nullifying of the seniority system."[68] Jarman's defection personified the warning issued by Stratton about making conservatives unwelcome in the Democratic Party; over two decades, 11 Democrats would switch to the Republican Party, 5 of them after the GOP won control of the House in 1994.

The Caucus Chooses the Chairs

Despite his "arbitrary and abusive [manner] with members," Bob Poage had survived the vote in the Steering Committee but faced a renewed revolt when the caucus met to take up the recommendations.[69] A congressman since 1937 and chairman since 1967, Poage had earned a zero rating from Americans for Democratic Action, reflecting his promotion of agribusiness legislation that left consumer groups feeling "ripped off."[70] Unforgivable to many, he had voted against the majority of House Democrats 63 percent of the time in the prior Congress. "The fact is," concluded the *Texas Monthly*, "that Poage's time has come and gone."[71] Even so, the caucus voted only narrowly to reject his reappointment as chairman by a 141–144 vote, an outcome undoubtedly influenced by the fact that next in line was Washington State's popular Tom Foley, a former DSG chairman 30 years Poage's junior. Most new members, including many of the 18 southerners who included "a vocal contingent of urban and consumer-minded legislators," voted to oust Poage, although Foley himself did not.[72]

Poage was stunned and angry, blaming the defeat on his unwillingness to "go as far in my concessions to socialism as a majority of this House does."[73] Republicans who were excluded from both the Democratic Steering Committee and the caucus discussions, were shocked when they heard the news. Paul Findley, an Illinois Republican, said that "75 [Democratic] freshmen came here with some preconceived notion that Bob Poage represented ideas out of date." But within the energized Democratic Caucus, Findley's views, like that of every Republican, were irrelevant, and the long campaign to check the absolute fealty to seniority had recorded its first success.[74]

Wright Patman was staunchly defended by the old guard like Merchant Marine Chairwoman Leonor Sullivan, who declared charges of "autocratic behavior against Wright Patman are demonstrably false." He was, she insisted, the "most liberal chairman in this House, most courageous in public interest."[75] Numerous freshmen harbored reservations about dechairing the legendary Patman, and, even decades later, many expressed mixed feelings about ousting him.[76] Elliott Levitas praised his "significant legislative achievements," and Jerry Patterson anguished about replacing a "great old guy." Texans predictably rallied behind Patman. Former Shakespearean English professor Bob Krueger compared the House dean to King Lear.[77] Jim Wright recalled Patman's long legacy of progressivism, battling the Ku Klux Klan in Texas in 1922 and being one of the few southerners to support the 1964 Civil Rights bill (something Wright himself did not do). Patman's only shortcoming, said Wright, was his advanced age. "Well, friends, must we commit patricide?" Wright asked. Echoing Stratton's earlier warning, the respected Gillis Long of Louisiana warned about the appearance of caucus retribution against a region of the country where Democrats increasingly were "on the politically unpopular side," occupying a growing number of strategically crucial marginal southern seats.

But the problem, others reasoned, was not with Patman's politics or even his age, but with his inability to function effectively as chairman. Martha Keys, from Kansas, "thought the world" of Patman. "[He was] wonderful," she said, "but he didn't belong in chair; he had been there forever and a day."[78] New York's Ned Pattison called Patman a hero but ultimately cast a "reluctant vote" against him. On the second ballot, Reuss prevailed 152–117 and, in an act of magnanimity, named the committee's hearing room for Patman.

Class members felt no similar compunctions about ousting Edward Hébert, whose many offenses included approving as conferees only those who supported his views, which ensured that in House-Senate conference committees he would always have a majority of House votes to recede to more conservative Senate positions. His maneuvers were so offensive that the caucus had voted to instruct the Speaker (who formally selects House conferees) to name only those majority members who supported the House's position on legislation. This and more egregious behavior had led Common Cause to condemn Hébert for having "flagrantly violated standards of fairness and compliance with House and Caucus rules."[79]

Hébert's recent ploys to court the freshmen—giving Downey a room for a reception, casting a sympathetic vote on a marginal issue—were ineffective. "We may be new kids on the block," Gladys Spellman declared, "but we're not stupid." The vote against Hébert was 152–133. In his place, the caucus installed Mel Price, a pro-Pentagon Illinoisan who had just turned 70. Hébert castigated the reformers as hypocrites for championing transparency while voting him out with a secret ballot. "I couldn't tell you the names of one who voted against me," he said bitterly. "Yet this is the very group that feels all our meetings should be open and everybody should know how everybody voted."[80]

The Steering Committee's proposal to remove Hays, which some speculated was intended to thwart his expected bid for a leadership slot in 1976, encountered widespread opposition. Despite his brusque manner, Hays enjoyed broad support thanks to his generous contributions from the Campaign Committee and for boosting members' official expense accounts. His defenders argued that he had been unfairly blindsided by the Steering vote. "Oh, you may not like him," said James Stanton of Ohio. "But he is an honest man, a Member's Member." Even New Yorker Ed Koch, who had been labeled an "emissary from Hanoi" by Hays (who later apologized), declared it would be "a travesty, a pettiness on the part of this House to reject him . . . because his personality irks you." The message to members was: Hays sticks up for you, and in Congress that is a powerful message, particularly to vulnerable freshmen. "He's tough and I'm tough," Phil Burton, a close ally, said of Hays. "We understand each other." The caucus rejected the Steering Committee's nomination of Frank Thompson by a 109–176 vote and then reelected Hays chairman by a 161–111 margin. The sharp-tongued chairman claimed to have learned his lesson. "I am a miserable SOB," he admitted, but "I will try to be a nicer SOB." Later that day, Hays reached out to a critic, Tim Wirth, inviting him to his office to "bury the hatchet." Wirth, not convinced of the genuineness of Hays' transformation, warily responded, "Where, Mr. Chairman, in the middle of my forehead?"[81]

The Burton-Hays alliance illustrates how collaborations and rivalries in the House often have more to do with personalities, ambition, and tactics than with policy agreement. Indeed, Burton agreed on policy more closely with Thompson, another prolabor member of the Education and Labor Committee, but the two distrusted each other. Press coverage of the unprecedented decisions confirmed that the work of the caucus was "full of charges of conspiracies, pettiness and passion, selfishness and opportunism." And, unquestionably, some of the maneuvers reflected deeper agendas and ambitions as veteran members arranged the pieces on the chessboard for possible leadership races two years down the road.

Still, the *Post*'s chief Hill reporter had to acknowledge it was "clear that a major shift in power had taken place."[82] The outcome of the January organizing caucus meetings riveted Washington and set the tone for the next two years, but the impacts have often been misunderstood. Far from an all-out war against the seniority system or acts of immature petu-lance by a group of easily manipulated neophytes, the votes reflected selective and strategic decisions. The Class members supported those who were committed to realizing their own ambitions and policy goals, and they removed those documented to be obstructionists.

The actions of the caucus did not emasculate the South, as some had charged, but rather brought the number of chairs from the region into closer alignment with its representation in the caucus, and the decisions met with the approval of many of the Class's southerners. "Neanderthalic southern congressmen had to be gotten rid of if the South was to emerge," recalled Georgia freshman Levitas.[83] Nevertheless, by the end of the January meetings, southerners still held 38 percent of chairmanships although their percentage in the caucus was just 28 percent; two decades earlier, they had held 63 percent of the chairmanships despite having just 45 percent of the caucus. The diminished ratio of southerners in the cau-cus was due to a rise in the number of non-southern Democratic mem-bership and the success of Republicans in winning seats in the South through appeals to southern whites. That latter change would have the most profound implication for the future of Democratic hegemony over the House.

The changes implemented in December and January were the culmi-nation of five years of sustained efforts to check the authority of the chairs and expand opportunities for younger, more liberal members to play in-fluential roles in committees and on the floor. Far more than the removal of three chairmen had occurred. The ability of a small cadre of senior members to dominate multiple chairmanships was now ended. A new generation of subcommittee chairs was given greater autonomy to hire staffs, to hold hearings, and to promote legislation independent of the full committee's leader, which permitted a slew of new policy issues long sup-pressed by the chairmen to gain attention. Yet there were also cautionary voices that warned the caucus's activism could have unintended conse-quences, imperiling Democratic seats in moderate to conservative areas and potentially risking Democratic control of the House itself. "Some moderates and conservatives [are] worried that the winds might be too strong," the moderate Bernie Sisk warned. "People don't want to see Con-gress flying off into the wild blue yonder with too many innovations and wild spending schemes."[84]

Role of the Class in Securing Reforms

Lastly, the role of the Class in the sweeping reforms of 1975 was exaggerated at the time and ever since, although few Class members themselves were under such illusions. In the crucial caucus meetings when the arguments were offered for reforms and against chairmen, freshmen were rarely among the speakers. Dave Obey acknowledged that the Class of 1974 "were our bullets" but credited the DGS reformers for having "pulled the trigger," and the Class agreed. As Phil Sharp noted, "We provided the votes in the final step and we helped harvest the crop," but it was the earlier reformers who had "plowed the land." Still, their role was essential. As Phil Burton observed, "These freshmen are not all liberals, but they are all reformers."

Indeed, some of the older reformers begrudged the recognition and praise lavished on the members of the Class. Jim O'Hara complained that the attention showered on the newcomers "was a little hard to take" since earlier reformers had been "shedding blood on those issues when those people were still in high school." Those comments illustrated a chasm that would periodically open over the next two years between some of the longstanding reformers and the less patient recent arrivals.

Not surprisingly, senior members were uneasy and skeptical about the changes made by the caucus in January 1975. Jim Oberstar recalled encountering veteran Clement Zablocki, who had no idea he was speaking to the freshman elected to replace his old friend, John Blatnik. Disparaging the incoming reformers and their demands for modernization of the House, Zablocki dismissively predicted, "None of it will last two years."[85] Even some freshmen retained doubts about how far reaching the changes they facilitated would prove. "Anybody that thinks the seniority system is dead is wrong," New York's Ned Pattison accurately observed. Nor did they necessarily believe that the unity displayed in the organizational meetings would be replicated in the coming debates over controversial policy issues. "Congress will never be the same, no question about it," said Toby Moffett. "You can't be an autocratic chairman. But translating to changes of policy, I'm skeptical about that."[86]

Still, the scope of the organizational carnage was stunning and in some ways more extensive than people recognized at the time. While most of the chairs had retained their gavels for the 94th Congress, Bob Carr observed "every chair got the message" that they owed their chairmanships to the caucus and would be reevaluated in the next Congress. Ken Alexander, a political cartoonist at the San Francisco *Chronicle*, sent Burton an original drawing depicting walruses labeled "House 'Old Bull' Committee chairmen" falling into ocean as the "Seniority system" ice shelf cracks beneath them. He inscribed it, "To Phil: Keep it up: there's still plenty of old blubber left to hunt."[87] Indeed, during the course of the new Congress, six additional senior chairs, including Hays, who had survived the reformers' gauntlet in 1975, decided not to return after the 1976 election, assuring that the majority of House chairmen for the 95th Congress would be new, if not necessarily young, faces. The three chairs deposed in 1975—Hébert, Mills, and Patman—were all gone from the House by 1977 because of death or retirement. "This was an old, southern, get along go along, inside baseball operation" when the Class arrived, California's George Miller later gloated. By the time the 94th went to work, however, it was a brand new game.

6 TIME TO PUT ON THE LONG PANTS

What the fuck is a good idea if you don't have the votes?
—Rep. John Burton (D-CA)

The problem with you guys is, you think it's on the level. It ain't!
—Rep. Ed Patten (D-NJ)

s the members filed into Washington to formally open the 94th Congress, analysts predicted that the Democratic leaders would face a "difficult year" controlling the "restless" and "bucking colts" who would bring a "new and activist spirit" to Capitol Hill.[1] For the young legislators who had run for office to shake things up, it was, in the words of a senior politician, "time to put on the long pants" and get to work.

Expectations for swift action were high given the expanded Democratic majority in the House. As National Committee for an Effective Congress Chairman Sidney Scheuer argued, unlike the unelected Ford administration, the newly elected Congress "has just been handed the mandate" for broad policy changes.[2] But many of the policy issues that excited the Class elicited cool responses from key players on Capitol Hill, particularly the Conservative Coalition that remained an intact and formidable obstacle on the House floor: skepticism about initiatives on jobs, environmental protection, consumer safeguards, campaign finance reform, health care, energy independence, and, especially, extrication from Vietnam. The optimism of the Class was about to encounter the reality of a Congress that was not as reformed as some wanted to believe.

On Tuesday, January 14, the 93 newly minted representatives faced Speaker Carl Albert along with the rest of the House and raised their right hands. With parents, spouses, and children looking down from the overcrowded galleries ringing the House Chamber, the members of the Class swore their oaths and, with "the highest expectations for what Congress could accomplish," became members of the US House of Representatives.[3] With the election behind them, Speaker Albert expressed hopes the members would set aside partisanship and embrace a "spirit of unity . . . to fulfill our purpose, which is to legislate effectively," he inveighed. "The majority and minority must unite whenever we can."[4]

Despite the "bipartisan promises of cooperation" many hoped would be fulfilled, the *New York Times'* columnist James Reston anticipated bitter clashes as Democrats "portray[ed] President Ford as another Herbert Hoover who will not fight a radical problem with radical measures."[5] The first signs of unhappiness were directed within two days not at Ford but at the House's Democratic leadership, which Class members found "defensive and reluctant to be forceful." Although activists like NCEC implored the leadership to "utilize the talent and energy offered by the incoming freshman class," many senior members disparaged the Class's top priorities. Welfare and regulatory reform, health care, and other issues, they argued, would have to await the election of a Democratic president who would not force Congress to override vetoes with supermajorities. Unresolved jurisdictional disputes also complicated the prospect for complex issues, the new whip John McFall advised, and Brock Adams, the chairman of the new Budget Committee, warned that freshmen priorities might have to wait as long as five years, until Congress "decide[d] what it wanted to cut, and how." Advice like that revealed a serious "generation and communication gap" between the Class and the veterans, it was noted. "The priorities of the two groups weren't meshing," a reporter noted, "and there is slim chance Congress will go in the direction the freshmen want."[6]

Freshmen were especially frustrated with Albert for "prevent[ing] anti-war proposals from coming to a vote," although not all opponents of the Vietnam policy shared their irritation.[7] Les Aspin of Wisconsin, an anti-war Armed Services member, credited Albert with facilitating the recent caucus rules changes, a view shared by Albert's own staff. For his part, Albert viewed the Class's criticism as "crazy" and "problematic," wildly out of tune with the predominant mood of the caucus and the nation, and he resolved to "break them apart."[8]

Many freshmen, on the contrary, believed their numbers would compel Albert to bow their demands. "We were such a large class," Henry Waxman recalled, "and so determined to be independent and to make a difference."[9] Norm Mineta told a colleague that freshmen pressure would force recalcitrant leaders to change their minds. "It's amazing how some peoples' attitude will change when they have a hot poker up their ass," Mineta observed.[10] Mineta learned an important lesson about

Washington that day; a reporter standing within earshot included the quote in his story.

Securing Committee Assignments

Albert offered concessions to freshmen, promising each would be assigned to a major committee, and adding first-termers to Ways and Means and Appropriations, as well as naming John Jenrette of South Carolina as the freshman whip and placing Bill Brodhead of Michigan on the Steering Committee. Phil Burton and Richard Bolling also worked diligently to place liberals in key committee slots where they could impact long-stalled legislation. Their motivations were not purely ideological: delivering desired assignments would enhance support from members for an anticipated run for a leadership position.

Fortunately, there were many opportunities for good assignments because of the large increase in the size of the Democratic Caucus and the new caucus rules that gave Democrats two-thirds of the seats on committees. "We want to open up the system by which the House operates, and let every member have some say," Burton said. "That is what all new members want, even the most conservative," Burton said. "That is what I aim to bring about."[11] But Burton's generosity did not extend to those who had sided with Bernie Sisk in the caucus contest. "All the California guys got good assignments," complained Marty Russo, who had asked for Interstate and Foreign Commerce and Government Reform, but was instead relegated to the less desired Small Business and Judiciary panels.

Burton made sure his freshman ally Martha Keys received one of the freshman seats on Ways and Means (where older members called her "dearie" and "honey"), arguing a woman should replace the recently retired Martha Griffiths.[12] Joe Fisher, a liberal economist from a swing district in northern Virginia, earned a seat on the tax-writing committee for having defeated an 11-term Republican. Commerce, with 14 Democratic vacancies and broad jurisdiction, was a highly desirable assignment because it oversaw diverse issues like health care, energy, and consumer protection. Aided by committee veterans like John Dingell and California's John Moss, Majority Leader Tip O'Neill "fought to get a lot of new blood on the Committee," including Waxman, Andy Maguire, Tim Wirth, Jim Florio, Brodhead, Phil Sharp, and Toby Moffett.[13] O'Neill's goal, in part, was to reduce the influence of Chairman Harley Staggers and other senior members who were rumored to have drinking problems and less than incisive minds. "They were not guys with a lot of fastballs," Wirth recalled.

Eighteen freshmen (13 Democrats) were appointed to the Agriculture Committee, where they could serve constituent needs. Tom Harkin was described as "wilder than a hoot owl" in advocating for high price supports for farmers, and he launched an early investigation of meat-packers in southwestern Iowa.[14] The lone committee newcomer from an urban area, Fred Richmond, became a forceful advocate for expanding the nutrition programs within the committee's jurisdiction. Agriculture Secretary Earl Butz, anticipating conflict with Class members who had condemned him during the campaign, dismissed the newcomers as "city slickers" who "wouldn't know the working end of a cow if you showed them one."[15]

Four Democrats, including Larry McDonald, the most conservative freshman, joined Armed Services. Thirteen Democrats (and 6 Republicans) filled seats on Banking, Currency, and Housing, 9 joined Education and Labor (as well as 4 Republicans), and 11 (9 Democrats) won assignment to Public Works and Transportation. Only a few freshmen secured positions on the exclusive committees including Appropriations (Max Baucus), Budget (Butler Derrick) and Ways and Means (which in addition to Keys and Fisher, added Andy Jacobs and Ab Mikva, two returning members). Senior members steered Class members away from problematic or boring assignments. Bob Krueger initially requested a seat on the Agriculture Committee, but Albert viewed the panel as "inappropriate for a Rhodes Scholar" like Krueger. Instead, Albert reminded gave Krueger a seat on Commerce, reminding him that Sam Rayburn had "put more jurisdiction on Commerce than any other committee."[16]

Several freshmen balked at the leaders' requests to accept a less desirable assignment. Having secured him a seat on Commerce, Burton asked Waxman to join Ethics, whose revolving membership meant the Los Angeles freshman might soon become a chairman. But Waxman, who had observed scandals in the state legislature, wanted no part of investigating his colleagues. Similarly Tom Downey, pleased with a seat on Armed Services that was valuable to his Long Island constituents, told Albert, "No, thanks," when asked to serve on the District of Columbia Committee.

Once on the full committees, Class members took advantage of the new bidding rules to fill subcommittees in their areas of interest. On

Agriculture, freshmen joined specialized subcommittees that reflected their district's economy: Livestock and Grains, Tobacco, Dairy and Poultry, Cotton, as well as Consumer Relations. On the Commerce Committee, 7 of the 10 seats on the Energy Subcommittee were filled with Class members highly critical of the energy industry.[17] Placement on subcommittees sometimes boosted freshman careers with unexpected speed. When Wright Patman suddenly died early in 1976, Steve Neal inherited his chairmanship of the Subcommittee on Domestic Monetary Policy overseeing the Federal Reserve. "That was something that hadn't happened for as long as anyone could remember," Neal noted, since, before the recent reforms, senior members would have occupied the subcommittee slots. "The old bulls . . . had chaired everything, had kept all power to themselves for many years, until our class accomplished the reforms." Neal's chairmanship of the subcommittee over the next two decades helped him enormously in his district. "I would go home and explain at Rotary Club meetings [that] I held many subcommittee hearings during which I argued with Fed officials and others," he recalled, quickly elevating him above the status of a novice lawmaker.

Freshmen declared their newfound roles exhilarating. Wirth had not "even know[n] what the Commerce Committee was" during his campaign, but within a few weeks of entering the House, he and his fellow freshmen were influential on issues from energy to telecommunications to health care. Similarly, Brodhead used his freshman position on Steering and Policy to secure himself a seat on Commerce and later Ways and Means when fellow Michigander Richard Vander Veen was defeated in 1976. The easygoing Brodhead became, in his own words, "a cold hearted politician [who] just wanted power. I'm in the [Steering] room, being nice and polite, and I didn't have any problem getting what I wanted. That was the way the game was played."

It was soon clear that the momentum of reform had extended into the organization of the committees. Although Staggers had been spared dethroning, committee Democrats limited his power to manage the panel's budget, set subcommittee ratios, or control travel. Commerce also became the first to elect subcommittee chairs by a secret ballot, and reformers denied Staggers the chairmanship of the Oversight and Investigations Subcommittee. His 1973 complaint with the Federal Communications Commission over former Beatle John Lennon's use of the word "fucking" in his song "Working Class Hero" did not reflect the vigorous investigations the aggressive Class members envisioned. Nor was he skilled at asking junior colleagues for support. "I want you to know," he told Henry Waxman, a devout Jew, "I'm a good Christian." Waxman found the appeal "peculiar," assuming that "if 'I'm a good Christian and good person, I want to do what's right for country.'" Staggers was defeated after seven ballots by John Moss, a 12-term Californian feared for his zealous investigative style.[18] Other returning chairs were also denied the gavel they had wielded on powerful subcommittees, including Leonor Sullivan, who lost her chair on the Subcommittee on Consumer Affairs on the Banking Committee.[19]

For some senior members, the press attention showered on the newcomers was irritating. When the 94th Congress jointly convened on January 15 to hear President Ford's first State of the Union, the new doorkeeper, James Malloy, announced the entry of senators, Supreme Court justices, members of the Joint Chiefs of Staff to great applause. House members, already in their chamber, received no such recognition. Kika de la Garza of Texas, a 10-year veteran, muttered to a nearby colleague, "I wonder when he's going to announce the freshman class!"[20]

For many of the freshmen, being on the House floor was "fabulous, a most wonderful event," Steve Neal recalled, leaving him feeling "awestruck."[21] It was also an emotional visit to Capitol Hill for Gerald Ford, returning for the first time to the chamber where he had served for a quarter century. Now, Ford arrived as president, to the cheers and applause of colleagues genuinely relieved not to be welcoming back Richard Nixon. In his nine years as minority leader, he had never addressed the House from the dais from which he would now speak, a role reserved for members of the majority. Behind him, on the top deck of the three-tiered podium, newly appointed vice president Nelson Rockefeller stood clapping next to Speaker Albert, who would gavel the session to order. The president mounted the podium, handed them copies of his speech, and then turned to face the warm applause of the new 94th Congress.

With a nod to the 92 new faces he was addressing, Ford recalled his own arrival in 1949 as "a freshman Congressman . . . with lots of idealism who was out to change the world." But unlike the upbeat assessment he had heard that day from President Harry S. Truman, Ford starkly declared, "The state of the Union is not good." Citing a toxic brew of high unemployment, a rising debt, deepening recession, growing inflation, lax economic growth, and a national debt rising above $500 billion, he laid the blame on a "self-indulgent" Congress. Such accusations, as well as Ford's call to slow spending and expand business tax cuts met with little applause from Democrats hoping to enact public service jobs, more aid for education, energy independence initiatives, and other priorities carrying hefty price tags, as well as increased taxes on corporations and the wealthy and mandatory energy rationing.[22]

As the head of the executive branch, Ford objected to Congress "rigidly restrict[ing] in legislation the ability of the President to . . . execute foreign policy and military decisions," as illustrated by the 1973 War Powers Resolution, which required congressional approval to commit troops overseas. As a House member, Ford had opposed that resolution, arguing the Congress "should not be able to tell the President, 'You cannot do it' by doing nothing." Instead, he demanded that members "have the guts and the will to stand up and vote" on troop deployments. Ford's insistence that hard-won restrictions on the imperial presidency be rescinded did not sit well with Class members. Les AuCoin wrote in his diary of feeling "pity for . . . a man who was in over his head . . . uncertain of himself and his job . . . stumbling along, unsure of himself, and trying manfully not to show it."[23]

Ford's controversial policy prescriptions pleased no one. Conservatives renounced the high deficits in Ford's plan while liberals rejected the proposals as "a sham . . . inadequate [and] regressive."[24] Initially, Ford backed away from a confrontation with Democrats, allowing a bill extending the food stamp program to become law without his signature and releasing $2 billion for highway construction he had initially impounded, money Democrats claimed would generate 107,000 jobs.[25] But Ford's decision to impound $26 billion caused "grief on Capitol Hill" and fueled anger with the administration.[26] While some conservative Democrats, like Appropriations chairman George Mahon, sympathized with the administration's parsimony, Class members demanded more stimulus spending and approved only 1.3 percent of the rescissions requested by Ford.

Most Class members attributed their election to the economy, and they were less concerned with rising deficits than with unemployment, which already stood at 6 percent and which Ford himself acknowledged might rise to 9 percent. The construction industry—whose socially conservative workers Nixon had courted—was reeling, with housing starts down by one-third and unemployment more than double the national rate. The middle class continued to be pounded by inflation that had raised the cost of food, transportation, and housing by more than 10 percent in 1974, capping three years of what the Congressional Joint Economic Committee described as a period of "spiraling inflation."

When unemployment claims filed in February rose to 540,000, Democrats passed a major jobs initiative by a 313–113 margin, winning the votes of 40 percent of House Republicans who defied Minority Whip Bob Michel's admonition that the new Congress was showing signs of "spend[ing] ourselves into another Great Depression."[27] The bipartisan defiance rankled Ford. While playing a round of golf with Jackie Gleason, the actor asked the president to describe his biggest problem, meaning in his golf game. Ford glumly answered, "Congress."[28]

Caucus Showdown on Vietnam

The other high priority issue for the Class remained Vietnam. Although the US combat role had been significantly diminished following the Paris Peace Accords in January 1973, Congress continued to approve requests for hundreds of millions of dollars to maintain US forces and to prop up the unpopular government in Saigon. Class members were skeptical of Speaker Albert's willingness to cut off funding, even though he professed that "even at the time of the Gulf of Tonkin Resolution [I had] no great enthusiasm for the Vietnam War."[29] By late January, rumors were swirling that Ford would request aid for those fleeing South Vietnam, as well as additional military aid to the beleaguered government. Soon, a request for $522 million to "prevent aggression in violation of the Paris peace accord" arrived on the Hill with a stern warning, "the odds are in favor of a disaster if we don't do anything." Assistant Secretary of State Philip Habib warned that the chances of the Saigon government surviving were 100–1. "Everyone agreed that if the money was not appropriated, that would be the end of our involvement in Vietnam," Mikva remembered.

Ford's proposal faced "overwhelming opposition" within the caucus, but Albert worried the freshmen were "pushing the envelope too far," falling into the "who lost Vietnam" trap the president was setting.[30] When Army chief of staff Gen. Fred Weyland acknowledged that US aid to Vietnam would be required for another decade, Robert Drinan, a Catholic priest, attorney, and vigorous war opponent joined 20 other Democrats in filing a lawsuit to end all US funding. Early in February, 82 members of the Members of Congress for Peace through Law caucus defiantly wrote to Ford, "We can see no humanitarian or national interest that justifies" additional aid to preserve the South Vietnamese or Cambodian govern-ments.[31] Ford fired back in a letter to the Speaker on February 28 asking whether Congress was prepared to "deliberately abandon a small coun-try in the midst of its life and death struggle."[32] Secretary of State Henry Kissinger warned that the collapse of the pro-American governments in South Vietnam and Cambodia would damage American prestige around the world and agreed to meet with small groups of freshmen, although he expressed consternation he was compelled to solicit their support rather than simply meet with supportive chairs, as in the past.[33]

The new Armed Services chairman, Mel Price, faced a divided commit-tee. Although Schroeder warned him, "If you don't have the votes, it would be very silly" to press a vote on a pro-war measure, in fact, all but five of the committee Democrats were dependable supporters of military spending. But Price was concerned about offending the larger caucus and promised to give "attention to any position" it would embrace. Employ-ing the caucus to establish party policy or direct committee action was a delicate proposition, although one favored by Burton and the growing lib-eral majority. In 1971, Bella Abzug had attempted to force a caucus vote on an anti-war resolution, but many members boycotted the meeting to prevent a quorum. In 1973, the caucus agreed that all Democrats would be required to support a position endorsed by a caucus majority, a tactic that was used to require that a vote be allowed on the oil depletion al-lowance, although it did not bind members on the final vote itself. The strategy carried heavy risks; caucus mandates were an affront to com-mittees, which believed that they, not the general membership, should originate policy matters within their jurisdiction. Progressives should be careful in flexing their caucus muscle to impose controversial positions, Obey warned, or risk embarrassing members or provoking them to switch parties.[34]

In February, the caucus adopted a "sense of the caucus" resolution op-posing further aid to South Vietnam. In early March, the anti-war faction struck again, using another reform procedure that allowed 50 members to convene a special caucus meeting. A resolution authored by Class mem-ber Bob Carr would put the caucus on record opposing Ford's request for military assistance, and the institutional response within the House was swift. Foreign Affairs Chairman Thomas "Doc" Morgan charged that Carr's initiative undermined the committee system by forcing a decision before hearings had been conducted. "If this is the way we are going to operate," Morgan indignantly asserted, "let's abolish the committee system, open up the caucus, and call witnesses." Other recently elected chairs, including Banking's Henry Reuss and Agriculture's Tom Foley—both liberals—advised that while chairs should be "responsive to the caucus on big issues," they sympathized with those wary about having the caucus go so far as "instructing committees on specifics [that] would destroy the committee system." Some of the legislatively experienced freshmen, like Paul Simon, also decried as "Mickey Mouse" using the caucus to compel members to embrace a party line.

Carr's proposal "forces members to think what the caucus role is," Obey agreed. Several senior members agreed with Democratic Study Group veteran Don Fraser that the caucus not be "over-used," supporting a proposal that would allow Steering and Policy to vet resolutions prior to caucus consideration. Such a procedure, Bolling agreed, would "slow down the mad rush to take up issues," but conservatives like Joe Waggoner pushed back harder, insisting, "We've got to stop this damn caucus from legislating."

But many Class members dismissed the cautionary institutionalism of their elders and were determined to lock in party members who might otherwise join with Republicans to doom progressive ideas. One anonymous congressional aide—quite probably DSG director Dick Conlon—predicted that the caucus would be used to "highlight divisive issues . . . over and over again [to] enunciate party positions." Demonstrating little concern for the sanctity of the "committee system," the aide explained that the caucus's role would be "telling our agents on committees what party policy is on an issue and pointing committees in particular directions or forcing legislation to the floor."[35]

The power of the liberals, bolstered by Class members, was demonstrated quickly, as Burton rallied the freshmen to defeat an effort to send Carr's motion to the Steering Committee by a 98–151 vote.[36] Then, the freshmen—including 13 of the 15 southern Class members—joined with three-quarters of the other members to pass Carr's motion resoundingly, 189–49. Carr was exultant at achieving such a victory on "my 57th day in Congress!" Only the reliably conservative Glenn English, Robert Duncan, and Larry McDonald among the Class members voted no. While the resolution did not attempt to bind members against supporting funding, it illustrated the troubled path any war funding legislation would encounter, not to mention raised the possibility of retribution within the caucus.

For Burton, the votes on Vietnam affirmed the expanded role of the caucus and his own growing influence. The reforms had worked: the caucus overpowered the ability of recalcitrant senior members and committee leaders to defy the majority. But he also recognized the new procedure could ignite polarizing issues that could damage caucus unity, let alone inflame partisanship within the House. "We have to lay off using the caucus for a while," he cautioned, advising Class members to exercise "self-restraint" on divisive issues, and as a result "some people were steamed."[37] Efforts by conservatives to allow the press to cover caucus deliberations, in hopes publicity would cool down the liberals' passion, were swiftly rejected by Burton, who typically supported transparency but who asserted that private discussions would be "fuller, freerer and franker" than in an open meeting where the emphasis would be on "mathematics and less political insulation of the minority."[38]

Recognizing that he faced widespread opposition in the Congress, Ford took the unusual step on April 10 of requesting another joint session of Congress at which he would seek nearly a billion dollars in military, economic, and humanitarian aid for Vietnam. As many as half of the members did not even bother to attend the unusual joint session, and some who did responded with jeers and hisses, a stunning breach of congressional etiquette.[39] Even more astonishing, George Miller and Toby Moffett attempted to walk out of the chamber during Ford's speech, stopped only by the doors that had been locked for security purposes. "I can't recall such disrespect for the President of the United States in any other era," said a White House official. In his memoirs, Ford recalled the slight as an "appallingly rude display."[40] But the speech did not stanch the hemorrhaging of support for further spending. A White House memo three days later reported on a bipartisan meeting at which Minnesota's Al Quie, a senior Republican and Ford loyalist, warned that Vietnam "was going down the drain." Vietnam had become "altogether a new ball game" in the wake of the domestic political chaos of 1974, and even Bob Michel welcomed "a clean break" with past policy. Democratic freshman class president Carroll Hubbard, a participant in the meeting, endorsed further spending only for humanitarian purposes.[41]

"The distrust of the Executive Branch runs so deep in this chamber that members are afraid that [allowing] any discretion . . . will open the door" to further involvement, warned Minnesota's Don Fraser, a longtime war critic.[42] As advancing North Vietnamese and Viet Cong troops provoked panic in Saigon, Congress developed a $150 million package of humanitarian aid. Class members Stephen Solarz, Bob Edgar, and Helen Meyner offered amendments targeting the assistance and limiting the presence of any US troops, all of which were defeated.[43] What is significant, however, is that freshmen were given the opportunity to offer so many amendments on a major issue, a sharp contrast with the typically limited role allowed novice legislators.

Some Class members from marginal seats were cautious about conditioning US aid and supported a substitute proposal by Republican conservative John Ashbrook that prohibited working with international agencies that might pass funds to the North Vietnamese or the Viet Cong, a proposal that passed 340–70 with the support of many overtly anti-war class members, including John Krebs, Christopher Dodd, and Moffett. Like Deputy Whip John Brademas, who "never gave a speech in his district against Vietnam," many moderates took a low profile role during the debate, fellow Hoosier Phil Sharp recalled. He knew, Sharp acknowledged, that joining Carr in a high-visibility role against the war meant it likely "I would lose." Many expressed surprise when their votes excited little reaction. "People had come around," Steve Neal concluded. Only a few days later, the Saigon government collapsed, and within a week Ford declared to a cheering college crowd in Louisiana, "The war is finished, as far as America is concerned."

The reaction of the Class members was one of joy and astonishment. Participation in nearly a decade of marches, demonstrations, and teach-ins to "end the war in Vietnam, bring the troops home," as the chant went, had long preceded any expectation they might become members of Congress. Ending US involvement in Southeast Asia had been the singular motivation for many who sought a seat in Congress. Now, just three months since their swearing-in, the war was finally over, at least for the Americans. Many derived particular satisfaction in using the House's constitutional power of the purse to rein in the presidency. "We couldn't persuade the president to withdraw the troops," Mikva exulted. "We voted [the funding] down and the troops withdrew."[44]

Yet only a few weeks later, the president demonstrated that he retained the upper hand in national security matters. On May 12, gunships of the militant new Cambodian government seized an American flagship, the *Mayaguez*, which was sailing in disputed waters in the Gulf of Thailand. Military rescue of the crew and ship over the next several days resulted in clashes with Cambodian forces, the loss of US helicopters, and the deaths of 20 American servicemen, some reportedly executed after capture by the Khmer Rouge. Ford perfunctorily complied with the terms of the War Powers Resolution by alerting select members of Congress, although a subsequent General Accounting Office assessment concluded that the "available evidence suggests less than full compliance" with the resolution because Ford "only informed [Congress] of decisions already made" despite there being "sufficient time to consult in a more meaningful manner."[45]

The juxtaposition of the successful effort to cut off funding for the Vietnam War to Ford's unilateral intervention against Cambodia was a sobering example of the limits of congressional power. The similarities between the *Mayaguez* incident and the supposed attack on a US patrol boat in the Gulf of Tonkin in August 1964, which provided Lyndon Johnson with the justification for expanding US involvement in Vietnam, illustrated how the unilateral decision making inherent in the presidency remained a strategic advantage over the slower-moving legislative branch during crises in national security.

Presidential Vetoes Provoke Anger

Democrats became "increasingly bitter" about Ford's use of executive power, particularly his rejection of legislation passed by large margins in the Congress. Throughout the 1974 campaign, Ford had implored voters not to elect a veto-proof "dictatorship" that could thwart his legislative goals and promote confrontation between the branches.[46] During the lame duck session of the 93rd Congress, after voters had selected a far more Democratic House, Ford continued to condemn Democratic spending and veto flood control, milk price supports, health revenue sharing, and other bills, often employing the "pocket veto," used after Congress had adjourned and could not override a veto. In response, O'Neill labeled him "King Veto," a play on the Republican criticism of the return of "King Caucus" earlier in the year.[47]

Class anger quickly was targeted not simply toward Ford but toward their own leaders who seemed outmaneuvered by the president and incapable of persuading members to vote to override the vetoes. Early in March, after Ford rejected legislation restricting his ability to raise petroleum prices, Republican whip Bob Michel told the president he was confident he could corral enough Democrats to join most Republicans to sustain the veto. Wary Democratic leaders did not even schedule an override vote. Burton was infuriated, and on March 19, at a bipartisan dinner at the new vice presidential estate on Massachusetts Avenue, he cautioned Rockefeller against "cheap shots" that could ignite "one of the fiercest, bloodiest veto battles in history."[48]

But Burton's bluster was difficult to back up outside the liberal base, and Ford successfully continued to veto with even greater frequency. On May 1, the veto of an agricultural price support bill enraged rural and southern members with whom Burton curried favor. "I say, 'Nuts to Butz,'" Burton quipped, referring to the unpopular, blunt-speaking secretary of agriculture. "Let's override!" On this issue, one member confidently declared, Ford's overreach meant "the old coalition of northern and southern Democrats has been effectively restored," but the effort proved a stunning failure, falling 40 votes short of the needed two-thirds.[49] Even the freshmen were divided on the legislation because of the bill's high cost, and many leaders like O'Neill, Bolling, and McFall, as well as Budget Chair Adams, opposed the override. Later in the month, Ford vetoed a key Democratic initiative, an emergency employment appropriation, citing the bill's cost, and once again the House sustained his decision, 277–145. The following month, the House, with the support of most Class members, sustained the veto of legislation to aid middle-class home purchasers 268–157, despite pressure from organized labor and housing groups and a personal request from O'Neill.

As the year disappointingly slid into summer, multiple vetoes went unchallenged because there was no prospect for securing the necessary two-thirds vote. Even when a bill had passed with significant bipartisan support, many Republican supporters reversed their position on an override, unwilling to challenge their own president. On the highly visible strip mine bill, which Ford had also vetoed the previous year, only 40 of the 77 Republicans who had originally voted for the bill voted to sustain the veto, and the effort failed by just two votes. In this case, heavy lobbying from the mining industry and organized labor, which feared job losses, led southern Class members, including Derrick, Hubbard, and English, to vote to sustain the veto, and John Jenrette, a deputy whip, "really caught hell" from Albert and O'Neill for bowing to industry pressures. The risks of supporting the override were driven home as one coal executive threatened a member, "Boy, I've got $100,000 in the bank in Dallas, and I'm going to beat you next year" if he dared vote to overturn the veto.[50] The quick string of override failures frustratingly confirmed the postelection observation that, despite large Democratic majorities in the House, a "significant bloc of Southern conservatives" would prevent the Congress from successfully confronting Ford's veto strategy.[51]

Despite the anger, not all override attempts failed. The veto of an expansion of public health nurse training hit a raw nerve in the House. Following the pocket veto of a similar bill in 1974, health costs had continued to skyrocket. This time, Republicans abandoned Ford, and the veto was overridden by an overwhelming 384–43 margin in the House and a 67–15 margin in the Senate. Other override successes included education and child nutrition bills, which briefly boosted Democrats' spirits, but by the fall reformers again had soured on their leadership's seeming incapacity to deliver crucial votes. Especially galling was the failure to override the veto of the party's flagship jobs bill, which had passed the House by a veto-proof margin of 293–109. Only two Democrats had voted against the bill, but conservative Democrats switched to support Ford on the override, which fell four votes short, 277–145.[52] A dismayed Les AuCoin felt the "deepest sense of futility," admitting, "That was the moment when it hit home that all the confident talk of 'Congressional Government' had been an empty hope. The times call for hard decisions, but Congress is unwilling to take the political risks that meaningful solutions require."[53]

Class members also turned against committee chairs who voted to sustain vetoes, and calls soon began for punitive action. The chairs held their positions because of the caucus, they were reminded, and the caucus strongly favored the overrides. Some went so far as to accuse the leadership of complicity, asserting that Albert and O'Neill had scheduled the strip mine vote knowing they lacked the two-thirds votes. Others alleged ineffectuality, asserting that the leadership had contacted more than 20 dissenting Democrats prior to the jobs bill override and failed to deliver a single vote.[54] The new Class president, Norm Mineta, was unusually outspoken, calling for a "more assertive leadership . . . [, a] party position on certain issues," and tougher monitoring by the leadership to ensure compliance. The leadership "should use the party caucus either to bind members or to punish the four committee chairmen who voted to sustain," one frustrated member complained.[55] But Burton dismissed calls to punish those who abandoned the bill. "On philosophical stuff, it's brutal to bind people," he counseled, offering to utilize the caucus to help "release whatever hostility [some] might feel towards party renegades."[56]

Senior members were just as exasperated with what they considered the freshmen's naïveté. Their argument that "compromise with the opposition at some point is essential if there is to be any legislation" sounded to many like capitulation to Ford, which Class members found inexcusable.[57] "Oh Lord," one frustrated senior Democrat told a reporter, "this is a group that's been indoctrinated with the idea that you can't trust anyone over 30."[58] They were "bright and aggressive," another acknowledged, but often were "too insular, talking mostly to each other and not willing to seek advice or listen to older members." One chairman anonymously complained that the freshmen were "too far out . . . a bunch of wooden-headed goddamn ideologues." Some senior legislators blamed the Legislative Reform Act of 1970 and the decisions of the caucus for having "decentralized power [and] weakened profoundly the ability of Democrats to rally behind an individual or a policy."[59] Having emasculated the authority of the leadership, they asked, was it surprising that discipline was harder to impose? "Do you throw the leadership out because it can't get 5 votes?" asked the whip, John McFall.[60]

Albert Comes under Attack

Albert again felt besieged by reformers he thought he had tried to accommodate. Three years earlier, he had reached out to critics after surviving a challenge from New Jersey's anti-war Henry Helstoski, who charged that Albert's "general popularity and inoffensiveness are not in themselves suitable qualification for the office of Speaker."[61] He had responded to the charges forcefully, pledging to help Congress "resist [the presidential] challenge to our constitutional authority."[62] Now, facing a larger group of dissatisfied freshmen, he was exhausted by their simultaneous demands for diffusion of power that weakened the leadership while still insisting that leadership enforce caucus unity. "They don't want a Speaker," he complained, "they want a bouncer" to punish Democrats who strayed from the party position. "I just cannot do it and survive," he said. "Do you think it's a sign of weakness to be nice to people?"[63]

However, most freshmen did not join in the criticism of the leadership, and many expressed sympathy for the challenges presented by a divided caucus. Some agreed that their classmates spent too much time "stewing about problems." Those with legislative experience at the state level, in particular, tended to be more understanding of the challenges facing Albert. "I get along well with party leaders," Jim Florio declared. "They don't bother me, and I don't bother them."[64] Les AuCoin, the former Oregon majority leader, also complained about some of his new colleagues "with the loudest voice [who were] carrying the day" in the caucus. "They don't realize they don't have absolute freedom." One of the most conservative of the freshmen, Glenn English, who had been on the receiving end of similar challenges while working for California Speaker Jess Unruh, said that the leadership was doing "as fine as job as you could." Paul Simon, who had spent 20 years in the Illinois legislature and as lieutenant governor, reminded his colleagues that Albert had "tolerated and encouraged a pretty major change in the structure of the House" during the rules fights in December and January.

Both the Class critics and the press who chastised them misread the 1974 election results in concluding the large Democratic Caucus constituted a veto-proof majority. Given the sizeable cohort of marginal and conservative Democrats whose constituents and personal views were sympathetic to Ford's arguments, it was inaccurate to believe overrides would be effortless, particularly since most Republicans were inclined to support their president.[65] It was, after all, the reformers who had undercut "the traditional ways of running the House[, which was] a careful apportioning of power to a few individuals," choosing instead to disperse power and complicate the imposition of discipline.[66] "Failure to override vetoes does not bother me at all," said Class president Carroll Hubbard. "I do not see that as a lack of leadership in the Democratic Party but mainly just an insufficient number of Democrats who on a particular issue believe the veto should be overridden." The fault, Hubbard argued, was not in Albert or the leadership team. "Any man would have a difficult time being a terrific speaker of the House during this complex period in our history," he declared.[67]

Indeed, Don Bonker suggested the freshmen might have brought on some of the problem themselves by weakening the capacity of the leadership to influence members. "The freshmen should realize, since many ran against the established party candidates and we are also the ones to press for reforms to democratize House procedures, [that] the 'veto-proof' Congress is a myth," Bonker explained. "The real blame belongs to the Republican President."[68] Even Fred Wertheimer of Common Cause found himself sympathizing with the beleaguered Speaker who had produced more than 90 percent of the Democrats for most veto overrides. "What more do they want?" Wertheimer asked of the freshmen.[69]

But among the most dissatisfied freshmen, sentiment arose to replace Albert with a more aggressive Speaker. "We feel there should have been some arm-twisting on that [jobs] vote," one member told the *New York Times*, since it was "one of the key measures in what was supposed to be the Democrats' program. It didn't seem as though our leadership was as well organized [as the Republicans']."[70] Another declared, "This is one Member who wants him to quit. There has been a lot of private talk—off the floor, in the cloakroom—about getting rid of Albert and now it's getting more and more out in the open." New Yorker Jerry Ambro charged the leadership still believed that "doing things in the old backroom way is a lot easier than working with a bunch of rookies."[71]

Critics also pointed to Albert's seeming difficulty in keeping up with the accelerated pace of a rapidly changing institution. While presiding over the chamber during a contentious debate on arms sales to Turkey, the Speaker seemed confused by the torrent of points of order raised by the battling members. "He's completely lost," Aspin observed. "It would be nice to have a real Speaker." Even the moderate Bob Krueger, for whom Albert had campaigned in 1974, confessed, "I don't know whether to laugh or cry" as the debate spun out of control. AuCoin watched the debate with disbelief. "After giving up ten months of one's life, working nearly 7 days a week to get [to Congress], you expect to work in a thoughtful, serious place," he wrote in his diary. "Watching this spectacle was enough to break a man's heart."[72]

Soon, one Washington paper reported, a group began circulating a petition calling for the Speaker's removal, leading several Class members to anxiously dissociate themselves from any proposed coup. "I oppose any discussion of 'challenge to the leadership,'" Floyd Fithian wrote to the leaders. If he was displeased, Fithian assured them, "I will tell you myself. I don't need the *Washington Star* to do my thinking for me."[73] Ron Mottl of Ohio told Albert, "The speculation about members of the freshman class moving to oust you as Speaker is extremely disappointing to me," adding that he was "unalterably opposed to any such attempt. I feel you have done an excellent job . . . In this freshman's eyes, you have been fair, honest and trustworthy . . . [and] I consider it an honor to serve under you."[74] Don Bonker also expressed his "disappointment and concern" with the reports of a "freshman revolt," which he assured the Speaker involved fewer than 50 Class members. "I share the frustration and dismay of my colleagues," Bonker admitted, "but I believe it is unfair and unnecessary to point the finger at you . . . You can be assured that the unfortunate public airing of this matter does not fairly represent all of the 94th class."[75]

In an attempt to repair relations, Albert agreed to a meeting with several dozen Class members who had sent a critical letter.[76] Statements by invitees indicated it was likely to be a challenging discussion. "When your team stops winning games you get a new coach," Bob Carr said two days before the meeting, disclosing an effort to force Albert's resignation. "You don't get mired down in arguments about whether the coach did all he could." Carr said he knew "about 10 to 15" of his colleagues who favored dumping the Speaker "right now," but that as much as one-third of the caucus might eventually sign a "no confidence" petition. His remarks went far beyond the comfort level of most of his colleagues, drawing immediate criticism. Forcing Albert out would be "a stupid tactical mistake," responded Toby Moffett. "It would just be a big Fourth of July present for Jerry Ford."[77] Nevertheless, during an appearance on the *Today* television program, Carr, in a fit of "exuberance," called for the Speaker's resignation, an outburst the young legislator quickly came to regret.[78]

On June 18, the freshmen were escorted into the Speaker's large office suite where the diminutive Albert sat in his large leather office chair, his dangling feet not quite reaching the floor. They presented him with a list of their legislative priorities and requested that he punish Democratic members who refused to back up the majority on key override votes. "The Speaker doesn't have to be either an arm breaker or a marshmallow," Carr instructed. "There are other alternatives" to enforce party discipline. Albert deeply resented the accusations and reminded the freshmen that he had delivered on his pledge to grant each a seat on a major committee, and that he had added freshmen to exclusive committees and to leadership posts. "What do they want that they haven't got?" he asked.[79]

A dejected Jim Blanchard appealed to Majority Leader O'Neill, who was likely to inherit the speakership should Albert quit. "We have an image problem," Blanchard told O'Neill. "I'm not here to cause trouble, I'm not a bomb-thrower. But you have to figure out how to move up. Have Carl step down. He isn't helping us. You need to maneuver him out." O'Neill was horrified by the suggestion. "Jimmy, Jimmy, Jimmy, Jimmy, what am I supposed to do?" he asked. "Politics is loyalty. Albert is a great man, a

Rhodes scholar. I owe him loyalty. He's not going to serve forever. I'm his majority leader!" Sounding a little more like Sam Rayburn than he likely intended, O'Neill continued, "Be patient. Don't be in such a hurry. You young guys! It's not that simple. You can't change things overnight. Who would trust me if I was disloyal?" He wrapped a burly arm around Blanchard and instructed the freshman, "Don't *ever* repeat this conversation!"[80]

Tensions Rise within the Caucus

Frustrated and impatient with the "slow, haphazard way Congress works," a group of freshmen met in July for a two-day retreat at the Airlie House, a conference facility outside Washington, to reassess their "experiment in democracy" and discuss why "Congress wasn't dealing with the issues they had raised in their campaigns." The concern was less the failed veto overrides than the need to "make the system work better," how best to combat criticism of congressional inaction and how to improve constituent services to enhance reelection chances.[81]

The new Class president was Norm Mineta, an experienced and respected player, even tempered but still combative. Mineta was concerned that "polarization [existed] between freshman and older members," who sometimes viewed the newcomers as "hasty reformers, big spenders and opponents of a strong defense establishment." A strong proponent of using the caucus to pressure Democrats to follow the caucus majority, he suggested that freshmen task forces conduct hearings around the country, outside the constraints of the formal jurisdictional lines of House committees. Such a process, Mineta explained, would "help create national solutions . . . to help make the place function" and address what one recent survey had identified as "the unrest in the country . . . the alienation from politics."[82] The freshmen also discussed creating their own whipping system to maximize freshmen votes because, too often, new members did not reach the floor in time to demand recorded votes they might have won.[83]

Another issue that highlighted tensions between the Class and senior members—including reformers—was the issue of a congressional pay raise, currently set at $42,500. Beleaguered by constituent hostility, Congress had been unable to raise its pay for five years while the cost of living had risen 48 percent. For most freshmen—many of whom were making the highest salaries they had ever earned—pay was not an issue. True, some were sharing rooms with staff or colleagues or even sleeping in their offices. But Don Bonker's salary, for example, had increased 400 percent over his county official pay, and he probably spoke for most Class members when he sensed "every political impulse is screaming 'no' to a pay hike." Steve Neal admitted his finances were strained to "maintain two houses, pay heavy taxes, and take care of personal expenses," but few wanted to face another vote on the issue.[84] However, many veteran members were older, had children in college, and were burdened by the costs of maintaining two residences, and they insisted an adjustment in pay was essential.[85]

Although Ford endorsed raising congressional salaries, the fight quickly descended into what one participant called "vicious, one of the ugliest, most disgusting things I've ever seen." The arguments became heated and personal, with "Members who rarely say a thing during floor debate shouting and screaming at each other, saying, 'Don't be a hero. You want this raise as much as we do.' It was ugly."[86] When the measure reached the floor, Bonker quickly cast a no vote but made a freshman's mistake of remaining on the floor, in view of the whip operatives. Suddenly, the senior member of his delegation, Tom Foley, slid into the adjacent seat. "This is weird," Bonker thought. After five minutes sitting in silence with the vote extremely close, Foley turned to Bonker and said, "We need your vote." Bonker sat still. A few moments later, Foley repeated his point, with greater emphasis: "*We need your vote!*" Bonker remained frozen. A few moments later, the usually soft-spoken Foley roared "like a drill sergeant, *Don, your vote is needed!*"[87]

As the 15-minute vote clock expired, the pay raise was behind by a single vote. Amid accusations that the electronic voting machines had malfunctioned, Speaker Albert, displaying the adroit leadership he often was faulted for lacking, waited until a member switched to yes to bang the gavel and announce that the raise had passed 214–213. An exasperated Les AuCoin, who watched the leadership pressure Class members to cast perilous yes votes, wrote in his diary, "Sometimes the establishment on the Hill reminds me of the court of Louis XVI."[88] After the raise was approved, many Class members decided they would not accept the supplemental amount. Butler Derrick, like several others, returned the raise to the Treasury, while others dedicated the money to charities.[89] Steve Neal used his raise to supplement his office account to pay for additional newsletters and other mailings. The expected political fallout may have been less than feared. When Derrick's opponent failed to even mention the issue in 1976, the courtly South Carolinian, who "lived pay check to paycheck, dog-cussed" the aide who had recommended returning the pay to the Treasury.[90]

Debate over Energy Policy

Few debates of 1975 revealed the challenge of molding the fractured Democrats into a governing majority as did the battle over energy policy.[91] The embargo on oil exports by OPEC on October 17, 1973, had wreaked havoc with the economy and the pocketbook of most Americans. The nation's self-confidence was shaken; in addition to the humiliating defeat in Vietnam, the world's most powerful country had seemingly been brought to its knees by anachronistic Middle Eastern sheikdoms. For members of the Class, many of whom had campaigned on energy, the issue was not only the impact of the escalating price of gasoline but also the rising profits of the oil companies, which served as a perfect villain: beholden to foreign powers, unconcerned with average Americans, and largely supportive of Republicans. Their profits, which had risen by 82 percent during the first six months of 1974, were termed "unconscionable" by leading congressional critics like Sen. Henry Jackson.[92]

Nixon had pledged to make American energy independent by 1980. Shortly after becoming president, Ford proposed a 13-point energy independence bill, including imposing a three dollar per barrel fee on imported oil and a windfall tax on oil profits, slashing imports by 1 million barrels a day by the end of 1975, and doubling that amount within three years. "I will not sit by and watch the nation continue to talk about an energy crisis and do nothing about it," Ford declared. He embraced other politically sensitive initiatives including expanded offshore development (a controversial subject since the massive Santa Barbara Channel spill in 1969), the accelerated licensing of nuclear plants, a weakening of strip mining regulations governing coal, and a delay of scheduled auto emission and air quality standards. His goal, he asserted, was to make the country "invulnerable to cut-offs of foreign oil by 1985."[93]

At the outset, there seemed a possibility of bipartisan support for higher prices to encourage conservation. Lou Frey, a Florida Republican, declared that Americans would pay higher fuel prices "because we are stupid as a nation, we have not done what we should have." Both conservatives at the *National Review* and liberals at the Sierra Club embraced a gasoline tax to dampen demand. John Gardner of Common Cause endorsed a tax on gas-guzzling cars and an oil import fee, and lambasted labor and consumer groups that opposed such initiatives.[94] But many House Democrats recoiled from such proposals, citing the hardship to constituents whose gasoline bills had already tripled. Moreover, they warned, higher costs for consumers would translate in greater profits for the oil companies unless legislation also imposed a significant windfall profits tax, which they doubted would be included. Moffett, echoing his old mentor Ralph Nader, argued that decontrolled oil would skyrocket to $89 a barrel by 1980, with oil companies "holding us hostage [in a] government-sponsored, industry-backed rip-off." Maguire endorsed improved efficiency rather than higher prices. "It is totally unfair to make consumers pay more for food, clothing, health and transportation," he reasoned, "while doing nothing to promote conservation through non-price strategies." Instead, Ford should pressure Detroit's auto industry to scale down engine sizes to become more efficient.[95] Their argument was corroborated in a new report by the House-Senate Joint Economic Committee, which concluded a 30-cent per gallon tax would result in a "massive across-the-board subsidy for large energy producers . . . producing huge windfall profits . . . at the expense of the consumer."[96]

Class members were especially sensitive to such predictions of gas prices approaching a dollar a gallon since rising energy costs had helped propel many of them into office. Reflecting the reformers' faith in large government solutions and suspicion of corporate interests, three-quarters of House liberals endorsed creation of a federal energy corporation to develop and manage new forms of energy; nearly half of the liberals favored a government takeover of private utilities, and one-third favored federal seizure of the major oil companies.[97]

The public was understandably confused about the appropriate response to the energy crisis. Given the suddenness of the crisis and its impact on so many complex areas of the economy—technology, trade, national security, and regulation—there was little consensus on the most effective approach. As Class members asserted, consumers were not ready to make personal sacrifices, believing the problem lay more in the manipulation by foreign governments and multinational companies than in their own profligate habits. A mid-1975 poll concluded that while most Americans supported the idea of comprehensive energy legislation, they did not favor policies that would force sweeping changes in consumption.

What seemed most likely was a "fractious debate over energy policy.[98] And that is what they got.

The energy debate reignited Class dissatisfaction with Speaker Albert. When Ways and Means sent an energy tax proposal to the floor, the Class voted no with just 14 of the 76 freshmen supporting the committee recommendation. Many Class members reminded the Speaker they had campaigned against such a tax and expressed anger that he allowed the vote to occur in the first place.[99] Albert in turn chastised freshmen as unwilling to deliver tough news to their constituents, and some Class members agreed with him. "Where were the freshmen when the leadership desperately needed them on this important issue?" Bonker wrote to Albert. The failure of the tax bill, Bonker told Albert, was "probably the greatest setback this Congress will experience because we failed to seriously confront the energy problem."[100]

Efforts to find a consensus on energy proved futile. Ford made an overture to new members, inviting them to the Oval Office to discuss his energy proposals, and several dramatically carpooled from the Capitol to the White House to highlight their concerns about gasoline consumption. Ford's request for sweeping authority to impose an oil import fee reignited concerns about granting excessive power to the White House. Unable to reach an accord, Ford unilaterally established a fee and decontrolled the price of regulated oil. Even moderate Republicans like Sen. Lowell Weicker of Connecticut chastised the president, and the third branch jumped into the fray with a federal court ruling that Ford had exceeded his authority.[101] The confrontation did little to smooth relations between the branches or cool congressional concerns about an overly assertive presidency.

Liberals did secure one energy victory when, after years of abortive efforts, the Class helped pare back the oil depletion allowance, a half-century-old tax break for the oil industry. Under assault in Congress since the presidency of Harry Truman, conservatives, including oil state Democrats, had warded off repeated attempts to close the costly loophole.[102] Ways and Means Chairman Wilbur Mills had ignored the caucus's demand in 1974 to allow a vote on an amendment to a pending tax bill that would repeal the allowance. His departure, however, together with the newly "assertive liberal bloc" on Ways and Means, shifted power in the committee.[103] Anti-depletion forces quickly gathered 50 signatures to compel the caucus to debate adding a depletion amendment to a $21 billion tax bill. Mills's successor, Al Ullman, was no more pleased than the

Arkansan had been, warning Class members they "were playing Russian roulette with our careers," but the caucus voted to allow a depletion amendment to be offered, Ullman did not press the case, and the House passed it decisively, 248–163.

The victory was an early and substantive demonstration of the Class's power, and it left observers stunned.[104] Mills accused Ullman of being "scared to death of the Democratic Caucus," fearful the young activists will "dump him as they have so many others."[105] Mills was right; Class members had warned the chairs that they were vulnerable and the Class would not countenance defiance of the caucus majority. Past presidents and House leaders might have been able to cut deals in private discussions with the Ways and Means chairman, but now, as one analyst pointed out, Chairman Ullman "spoke only for himself."[106]

Beyond the depletion allowance, however, the Democratic Caucus remained "in disarray," riven with the inevitable majority factions that included oil state representatives, consumer advocates, proponents of renewable energy, and others. The conflicts ignited after Albert directed the Commerce Committee to write an oil pricing bill, a task that fell to the Energy Subcommittee chaired by John Dingell, whose subcommittee had been crammed with Class reformers. But it was not a reformer from the Class but an industry supporter who emerged as the star of the energy debate in the subcommittee.

Like Downey, Bob Krueger traced his passion on energy policy back to the angry drivers he had seen in lines at gas stations. An Oxford-trained English professor and dean at Duke University before returning to Texas to run for Congress, Krueger arrived in Washington in 1974 claiming no knowledge of or allegiance to the leading industry in his state. Tall, curly haired, his frequent Shakespearean quotes devoid of any Texas drawl, he brimmed with self-confidence, certain that an act of "divine synchronicity" had placed him on the Commerce Committee to effectuate the decontrol of oil prices. When a number of freshmen expressed admiration for the Harvard training program they attended shortly after the election, Krueger noted, "I had been vice provost at a big university, so it was no big deal for me."[107] Four decades later, he could still quote from articles describing him as the "startling new man from Texas," "the bard of oil," and "the most effective" freshman. He was barely into his first term when he began eyeing the Senate seat of John Tower, and his actions and voting record reflected a strategy of building statewide appeal.[108]

Yet Krueger denied being a shill for his home state's energy industry. "I wanted to be a *national* legislator," he declared. Critics noted, however, that shortly after emerging as a leading proponent of decontrol, Krueger's fundraising from the energy industry, like that of the appropriately named Frank Pool, significantly mushroomed, quickly retiring his huge $200,000 debt. "I have nothing to hide or be ashamed of," he indignantly responded to criticism. "There's nothing unusual for a Texan to see contributions from these kinds of people," his staff added.[109] He dismissed colleagues who questioned his motives as "cowardly [and] just looking to the results of the next election."[110] Such effrontery offended fellow Class members like Andy Maguire, who recalled asking Krueger to explain his support for decontrol. "He told me he was in no mood to be patronized," Maguire reported.[111]

The pro-consumer freshmen faction was determined to drive the subcommittee discussion, annoying the short-tempered Dingell. One evening, the chairman used the tardiness of freshman Phil Sharp to call a vote that defeated a decontrol proposal. When Sharp entered the room moments later, Dingell refused to allow a revote he knew would alter the outcome. "What does one do in a situation like this?" an incensed Maguire whispered to Dick Ottinger. "You appeal the ruling of the chair," the New Yorker replied, adding, ". . . but you never do it!" The admonition came too late as Maguire's hand shot up to raise an impolitic challenge to the chair. Maguire quickly withdrew his motion, but an enraged Dingell brought down his gavel and bellowed, "The gentleman will *not* withdraw his motion." He compelled each member to cast a vote for the chairman's ruling or for the freshman's challenge. Not surprisingly, Maguire received no votes, not even his own.

In the full committee, an amendment from Texas iconoclast Bob Eckhardt slowed the removal of price controls thanks to the votes of Class members, and, on the House floor in May, the freshmen again "were instrumental" in defending the restrained approach. The debate was intense. Indiana's Philip Hayes spoke for many freshmen when he discussed the absence of a public consensus. "Let the price of oil get up to buck a gallon," Hayes predicted, "and I will tell the Members that the American people *have* got a consensus, and they will let you know about it."[112] The dispute was the opening battle in a war over energy, auto efficiency, and clean air legislation between Dingell and the 1974 freshmen that would continue for decades, culminating in Waxman's successful challenge to Dingell's full committee chairmanship in 2009.

The bill enacted in December, the Energy Policy and Conservation Act (EPCA), was far from the sweeping energy policy some had hoped would pass, but it included innovations such as creation of the Strategic Petroleum Reserve, efficiency mandates for consumer products, and a Corporate Average Fuel Efficiency (CAFE) standard for automobile fleets. Less presciently, three decades before sensitivity to climate change, the law actually encouraged production of coal and incentivized power plants to convert from oil to coal. In signing the bill on December 22, Ford characterized the bill as being "in the national interest" but "only the beginning," advocating additional legislation "to put ourselves solidly on the road to energy independence." Many subsequent presidents and Congresses would confront that same elusive, expensive, and divisive goal.

Yet another issue that divided the freshman involved the looming default of New York City, which led city leaders to seek federal assistance to avert insolvency. Even some progressive freshmen were wary of casting a vote for a costly bill that seemingly bore so little relationship to the voters they would soon face. Late in 1975, Ford rejected a plan to supply direct federal loans to New York, leading the city's largest newspaper to run the devastating headline, "Ford to City: 'Drop Dead.'" Years later, Ford would bitterly insist that "those two words . . . in the immortal headline"—words he never actually uttered—narrowly cost him New York and the presidency in 1976.[113]

While Ford held out the prospect of offering an alternative relief assistance plan, the crisis in the nation's financial capital was too severe to wait. On November 24, he supported a scaled back plan that won the backing of leading House Republicans. But for many Class Democrats, even this limited approach was too risky, and reliable liberals like AuCoin, Keys, Baucus, Robert Cornell, and Wirth voted no. They were joined by southerners including Derrick, Jenrette, Ken Holland, Elliott Levitas, and moderates like Jim Santini, Mottl, and Ted Risenhoover, as well as most freshmen Republicans. Although 103 Democrats and 100 Republicans voted against the bill, it passed 213–203, and, following Senate approval, Ford quietly signed it with no ceremony.[114]

Disappointment as the Session Ends

By the end of 1975, despite passage of such legislation, the sweeping expectations for change resulting from the election of so many Class reformers seemed unfulfilled. "Where is the great leadership Congress once boasted?" John Gardner asked. "After Watergate, the Congress talked briefly of taking leadership. Where is that leadership now?" He heaped blame on the "divided and paralyzed" Democratic hierarchy and on special interests for promoting "a paralysis of leadership."[115]

Members of the Class shared a sense of frustration, a recognition that the unity they brought to the internal reforms of the House had not been replicated in addressing the legislative agenda. Several important points are worth remembering in evaluating this first session. The unified Class support that achieved reforms in seniority, floor procedures, subcommittee operation, and transparency occurred within the Democratic Caucus, where progressive forces, bolstered by the addition of 75 freshmen, finally overwhelmed more conservative elements. Expanding the rights and roles of junior members served the interests of all newcomers, even those whose region had typically benefited from the concentration of power in more senior leaders. But once policy questions moved to the House floor or required a two-thirds vote to overcome a presidential veto, even a largely unified Class often could not overwhelm the residual strength of the Conservative Coalition, which included most Republicans. When critics like the *Washington Post*'s David Broder castigated the Class for not remaining unified, the freshmen reminded critics they had never promised unanimity on policy matters. "Anyone who thought we would be doing anything together beyond the first month was mistaken," Dave Evans said. AuCoin questioned why the author of a critical *New York Times Magazine* article had presumed the freshmen would be united in "anything more than hostility to the seniority system." For the author to blame the Class for dividing into typical political factions, AuCoin charged, demonstrated he "was engaged in hyperbole."[116]

Class members came to understand the difficulty of matching "435 highly independent prima donnas who all have to be satisfied" against the single voice and the veto pen of the president. Michigan's James O'Hara mused that "the press may have overplayed the reassertion of Congress."[117] Nor should the fault lie with liberals for the failure of Democrats to vote en bloc. Republican-turned-Democrat, Rep. Don Riegle angrily accused conservatives of empowering Republicans to create a "tyranny of the minority" in sustaining presidential vetoes of bills that had won broad Democratic support.

But it also must be noted that the votes to sustain vetoes came from more than the conservatives in the caucus. Nearly half of the House's Democrats voted against overriding at least one of Ford's first three vetoes, and more than half of those were DSG members. Even one-third of the freshmen had voted to sustain at least one of the vetoes, sometimes because they shared Ford's argument that legislation was simply too costly. While many freshmen blamed their leaders, especially Speaker Albert, for not imposing greater voting discipline on House Democrats, Class member Chris Dodd, a deputy whip, admitted it was often a challenge to deliver the votes of his classmates. Many of the freshmen, he complained, "don't want to feel as though they have to be responsible to the leadership [because they] see *themselves* as the leadership."[118]

Unquestionably, the first session was a time of sorting out new roles for the Class and the veteran members. "We're looking like a bunch of idiots," Dick Bolling wailed.[119] "We've had a manic-depressive six months," acknowledged Paul Tsongas. The freshmen had harbored "unrealistic expectations" about the ease of changing the direction of politics, and now many were suffering from low morale following the repeated failure to override vetoes.[120] Progressive policy initiatives seemed stalled, leading California's John Burton (Phillip's younger brother, who had been elected in a 1974 special election) to ask, "What the fuck is a good idea if you don't have the votes?" New Jersey's rotund, white-haired, irascible Edward Patten, was amused at the freshmen's frustration. "The problem with you guys," Patten told Rick Nolan, "is, *you* think it is on the level. It ain't!"[121]

Indeed, rather than the Class modernizing the institution, one observer noted, "the House is changing them as much as they are changing the House."[122] In September, most freshmen agreed to fine-tune several recent reforms, in particular reducing the instances in which the caucus instructed members how to vote. Many tweaks were approved at the behest of moderate members who appealed to the liberal caucus majority not to force positions that would endanger their survival. As was often the case, the realistic Phil Burton smoothed the way to the adoption of the rule modifications.[123]

Despite the self-flagellation, there were undeniable achievements beyond the early caucus reforms. The "new members have already played an unusually significant role for first year Representatives," the *National Journal* noted, "both in their votes . . . and in their efforts to shape legislation."[124] In November, Congress passed legislation guaranteeing an appropriate public education to children with disabilities despite objections from Ford about the program's cost.[125] Overall, Tim Wirth asserted, the reforms effectuated by the Class improve the "efficiency and effectiveness of the Congress" and will "keep Congress in tune with the country and not as insulated as it has been in the past."[126] But despite their bold aspirations, many freshmen remained skeptical about the durability of the Class's impact. "We made our mark on procedural questions," Mineta agreed, "but we haven't had an impact on the substantive process." Instead, Mineta admitted, "the system has swallowed us up."

Speaker Carl Albert with Rep. Julia Hansen of Washington who led efforts to implement House reforms prior to the arrival of the Class. Photographer: Dev O'Neill, December 1976, Collection of the US House of Representatives, Gift of David K. Hansen.

Candidate Marty Russo (*right*) meets Chicago Mayor Richard Daley, who incredulously asks an aide, "Is this the best we can do?" Photograph courtesy of Rep. Marty Russo.

Sen. Edward M. Kennedy campaigns for George Miller (*right*) in 1974, promising his election will result in a national health care law. Photograph in John A. Lawrence Papers, Library of Congress, Manuscript Division.

Dave Evans campaigns for his Indiana seat in 1974.
Photograph courtesy of Rep. Dave Evans.

Tom Downey, at 25 the youngest Class member, was mistaken for
being a House page in January 1975. Library of Congress, Prints and
Photographs Division, LC-U9-30748-36/36A.

Edward Beard displaying the brush he always carried in his breast pocket to remind him of his humble roots as a house painter. Library of Congress, Prints and Photographs Division, LC-U9-30750-11A.

After Armed Service Chairman F. Edward Hébert unwisely greeted Class members as "boys and girls," Toby Moffett recalled, "That was the end of him." Library of Congress, Prints and Photographs Division, LC-U9-15907-11.

The Class is sworn in as Members of the 94th Congress in the House chamber in January 1975. Library of Congress, Prints and Photographs Division, LC-U9-30644-27A.

Class member Bob Carr (*left*) is congratulated by Democratic Caucus Chairman Phillip Burton on passage of the freshman's resolution curtailing funding for the war in Vietnam in March 1975. Photograph courtesy of Rep. Bob Carr.

Paul Tsongas displaying the Class's informal style of holding a constituent town hall. Library of Congress, Prints and Photographs Division, LC-U9-31550-24A.

Class members at the Airlie House retreat in July 1975 to discuss legislative and electoral strategies. *From left:* Dick Ottinger, Paul Tsongas, Butler Derrick, Tim Wirth, Norm Mineta, Toby Moffett, Gladys Spellman, Steve Solarz, Herb Harris, Andy Maguire, Dave Evans (partly obscured). Library of Congress, Prints and Photographs Division, LC-U9-31395-31A.

Millicent Fenwick was increasingly at odds with the rising conservatism in the GOP conference. Library of Congress, Prints and Photographs Division, LC-U9-30747-10.

George Miller (*left*) and the author during a hearing of the Interior and Insular Affairs Committee, 94th Congress. Author's personal collection.

Bill Hughes, a moderate Class member, greets President Gerald Ford, who angered Class members with his vetoes of priority legislation the House could not override. Photograph courtesy of Rep. William Hughes.

Class member Matt McHugh confers with New York governor Hugh Carey during the 94th Congress on efforts to provide emergency financial assistance to New York City. Photograph courtesy of Rep. Matt McHugh.

Les AuCoin was frustrated that some Class colleagues "with the loudest voices ... don't realize they don't have absolute freedom. It's anarchy." But he also complained the sclerotic leadership "reminds me of the court of Louis XVI." Photograph courtesy of Rep. Les AuCoin.

Rep. Richard Bolling (*left*), the brilliant but acerbic reformer, presiding as chairman of the Rules Committee. Class member Butler Derrick is in the center, hand on chin. Collection of the US House of Representatives.

The newly elected Speaker Tip O'Neill (*left*) was relieved by the surprise victory of Jim Wright in the majority leader's race in December 1976. Library of Congress, Prints and Photographs Division, LC-U9-33619-29.

A bipartisan group of Class members joins President Jimmy Carter, including Jim Jeffords (behind Carter), Abner Mikva (to Jeffords's left), Jim Blanchard, (two to Carter's left), and Tim Wirth, George Miller, Bob Edgar, Butler Derrick, and Berkley Bedell (opposite Carter). Author's personal collection.

Class members who as chairmen wrote the health care law, with President Barack Obama at the White House signing in March 2010. *From left:* Sen. Max Baucus, Sen. Christopher Dodd, Rep. Henry Waxman, President Obama, Rep. George Miller, and Sen. Tom Harkin. Photograph courtesy of Rep. George Miller.

7 THERMIDOR

We have more democracy, and less of a good work product.
—Rep. Jim Jones (D-OK)

Sooner or later, this place gets the best of you. You get tired. You get cynical.
I think even the best of us get worn down, sidetracked, compromised to
death.—Rep. Toby Moffett (D-CT)

hortly after the New Year, members of the Class and other legislators returned to Washington to begin the second and final
session of the 94th Congress. Many had spent the holidays disappointed that the first session had not been more productive. In
addition, Jerry Ambro admitted, many freshmen were concerned about
facing voters in 1976. It was crucial, Marty Russo noted, that they be able
to demonstrate to constituents that Congress was "still sensitive to their
problems."

Despite the frustration that they had not achieved more, most Class
members were pleased with the changes they had effectuated, and the
Harris Poll reported that three-fifths of all freshmen thought that House
reform needed to go even further. "Progressive new majorities now control most committees," according to Tim Wirth.[1] "The reform movement
is having a significant impact."

It was clear that 1976 would test the ability of the Class and Democrats in general. Would they have greater success in passing their priority legislation? Would Democrats be able to reassert congressional power
as so many relished, especially by improving on their record overturning
President Ford's vetoes? Would Democrats retain the marginal seats won
so narrowly in the aftermath of Watergate? And would their party secure
the presidency, removing the threat of the veto whose frequent use required two-thirds of each chamber to overturn?

The promises by some Class members to scale back attacks on their
own leadership did not last for long. Frustrated that their "highest expectations for what Congress could accomplish" had been unmet, some began "lashing out at the leadership" over the failed override attempts.[2] Carl

Albert, Tip O'Neill, and even Phil Burton came in for criticism for "perform[ing] below expectations" with respect to the overrides.[3] New chairs like Henry Reuss at Banking and Al Ullman at Ways and Means were chastised for "fail[ing] to fulfill their promise" by refusing to act on legislation the freshmen wanted reported from their committees.[4]

Even with the reforms they had approved, some feared the structure of the House remained "fundamentally irrational and badly in need of overhaul," particularly the overlapping committee jurisdictions that had defied reform in 1946, 1970, and 1974.[5] But ideas for additional reforms, like bringing all spending bills to the floor simultaneously rather than one by one, were dismissed by veterans as a practical nightmare. "I didn't come down here expecting it was going to be easy," Andy Maguire responded. "I came down here expecting it would be tough."[6] Indifferent to the disruptive effect they might be having on House traditions, Class members expressed satisfaction with their efforts to improve the operations of the House. As a result of the recent reforms, Wirth noted, Congress was becoming "an exciting and vibrant institution . . . with some real hope of fulfilling its mission."[7]

The leadership was anxious to work with the newcomers and praised their contributions. Meeting with the freshmen, Deputy Whip John Brademas pronounced himself "extraordinarily impressed with their energy and intelligence."[8] In mid-January, Albert spoke with the New Members' Caucus and acknowledged the role the freshmen had played in the success of the first session. "Not since the 89th Congress has any group of new House Members shown the dedication to the work of the Congress . . . that your membership has," he gushed. "Virtually all of you have had a greater impact on your constituents as individuals than any previous first termers." Commending the "diligence with which you have carried out your duties in Washington and the extent to which you have maintained contact with your constituents at home," Albert hailed the Class's "considerable influence [and] continued cohesiveness."[9] Playing to their most gratifying achievement, he recalled that, but for the Class's vigorous opposition to Ford's request, "we might still be involved in a war in Southeast Asia." He hailed passage of the 1975 tax cut, the preliminary steps on energy policy, and the "singular importance" of the "oversight function of our committees."

The blame for the Congress's inability to legislate more successfully, Albert posited, rested not with the Class or with his leadership but with

President Ford, whose vetoes of vital legislation like the Emergency Unemployment Act had left the economy sputtering. As a result of Ford's indifference, priority issues like health care and welfare reform "may not be resolved in the 94th Congress," but, he pledged, "we are going to try." (In fact, no action was taken on either plan.) In particular, Albert consoled Class members not to despair of the negative press that accused them of ineffectuality. "Many of you are chagrined to find yourselves, as Members of Congress subjected to unwarranted criticism and even ridicule," he noted. "As one who has lived with this for almost 30 years, I assure you it is something you learn to accept. It does have a somewhat beneficial effect in keeping one humble."

Other leaders addressed the freshmen as well, sometimes drawing chilly responses. Wayne Hays again warned them against supporting public financing that would effectively underwrite their opponents' races and result in "the most chaotic campaign in the history of the republic."[10] Al Ullman of Ways and Means floated the idea of an increase in Social Security taxes to address a shortfall in the trust fund, a proposal that most freshmen greeted coolly. Jack Brooks of Government Operations rejected revenue sharing, a Nixon-Ford proposal favored by some Class members to send funding to states and local communities with few federal strings attached. The freshmen listened carefully but expressed concern about leadership "foot dragging" and restated their support for using the leverage of a caucus vote "to pry the legislation out" when supported by the majority of Democrats.[11]

Divisive Issues Emerge: Abortion and Busing

Both the leadership and the Class sought to minimize votes on divisive and emotionally charged issues as they geared up for their reelection campaigns, but a number of these issues arose in the House throughout 1976. None was more problematic than the issue of abortion, whose volatility had grown exponentially since the *Roe v. Wade* ruling of the US Supreme Court in 1973, which had declared that women had a right to seek an abortion under specific circumstances.

The issue was certain to become explosive during the second session of the 94th Congress. In 1974, Rep. Angelo Roncallo of New York offered the first floor amendment seeking to end federal funding for abortion procedures. During the 1975 debate on the appropriations bill for the Department of Health, Education, and Welfare, conservative Republican Bob

Bauman of Maryland had offered an amendment barring the use of federal funds to provide abortions, mainly through Medicaid health service for low-income Americans, which failed on a voice vote. The following year, freshman Republican Henry Hyde offered a similar amendment that allowed no exceptions to the restriction on federal funding even for special circumstances like rape or incest or if the continued pregnancy endangered the life of the mother. This time, to Hyde's amazement, the restriction was approved 199–165, although nearly one-sixth of the House avoided casting a vote. A majority of Democrats (133) voted against the Hyde amendment, although a sizeable minority (107) voted for it; among Republicans, the vote for the amendment was 93–34 in favor.

The vote revealed not only the bipartisan nature of the abortion debate in 1976 but also the deep divisions within each party. Like other members, the Class split along the lines of religion, region, and electoral vulnerability. Many who had proven themselves reliable Democratic votes, including Russo, Leo Zeferetti, Ambro, Jim Oberstar, John LaFalce, and Robert Cornell (a Catholic priest) all voted for Hyde's restrictive amendment.[12] Freshmen in marginal and southern districts including Paul Simon, Bill Hughes, Floyd Fithian, Carroll Hubbard, Jim Blanchard, Bob Krueger, Glenn English, and Ron Mottl also voted yes. But those opposing Hyde included southerners like John Jenrette, Ken Holland, Joe Fisher, and Herb Harris. A host of freshmen avoided voting on the issue altogether, including Jim Florio, Bill Brodhead, Maguire, Ned Pattison, Ted Risenhoover, Les AuCoin, and Butler Derrick, although they were in Washington and voted on other matters on the same day. Two months later, after a protracted battle with the Senate, the conference report included a provision permitting an exception to the ban if the abortion was needed to protect the life of the mother. A number of those who had voted against an unconditional ban shifted to yes including Elliott Levitas, Rick Nolan, Max Baucus, and Henry Nowak. Some who had been absent for the initial vote also supported the compromise including AuCoin, Florio, and Derrick. Interestingly, Henry Hyde, the freshman Republican author of the amendment, voted against the final version because it had been watered down in negotiations with the Senate. The abortion debate would prove the most recurring of the cultural flashpoints that emerged during the mid-1970s, one of a series of issues that conservatives effectively raised to highlight the votes of Democrats in marginal districts and generate grassroots support for conservative initiatives.

Mandatory busing of schoolchildren to facilitate the integration of public schools also emerged as a polarizing issue within and between the parties. As with abortion, Class members who had been united around organizational reform objectives divided sharply, with opposition to busing coming not only in southern states where the brunt of civil rights agitation had been felt but in many northern cities where the de facto segregation of many communities had yielded segregated neighborhood schools that would be affected by the busing plans.[13] Southerners leapt at the opportunity to note that more than 45 percent of the South's students attended integrated schools compared to just 27.5 percent in Northeastern states and 29.7 percent in the Midwest, although they did not discuss the growing number of church-sponsored "seg academies" that subsidized the attendance of poor white children to avoid the public schools. Opposition to busing was especially fierce in Michigan, where neighborhood patterns and the rise in private schooling among whites meant that Detroit's public schools were nearly 70 percent black compared to just 19 percent of the broader metropolitan area's population. House liberals like Martha Griffiths and Jim O'Hara of Michigan bowed to constituent pressure and voiced strong opposition to busing while in Boston, liberal icons like Sen. Ted Kennedy were pilloried for supporting busing.[14]

Busing was a divisive issue even for those who had unquestioningly embraced earlier efforts to desegregate public accommodations. Forcing young children to take long bus rides early in the morning and late at night, often to neighborhoods where their presence was unwelcome or unsafe, upset not only whites but many in the black community, who viewed the practice as destroying community schools and neighborhoods. Polling indicated that black Americans opposed busing by a 47 percent to 40 percent margin; among whites, nearly three in four opposed the transporting of children. Overall, more than 70 percent of Americans favored banning the practice, even if it required a constitutional amendment.

During the 93rd Congress, an amendment by conservative Republican John Ashbrook of Ohio to bar the use of federal funds for busing had passed the House 231–137 with strong GOP support, 126–40, while Democrats were split almost equally, 105–97. Among southern Democrats, however, the vote was 5–1 in favor of restricting busing. Skirmishes over the issues continued into the 94th Congress when restrictive busing language ultimately was included in the appropriation bill for the Health, Education, and Labor Department in 1975. Although the bill was vetoed by Ford because of its high cost, Ford's veto was the eighth to be overridden and provided a "morale booster for the Democratic leadership" despite the inclusion of the controversial restriction.[15]

The issue was revived in 1976 when busing opponents sought to use the reform mechanism devised by liberals—a caucus mandate—to direct the Judiciary Committee to approve a constitutional amendment banning the practice. For many, it was a bitter, unintended irony that the mechanism designed to keep conservative Democrats in line was employed to pressure liberal Judiciary Chairman Peter Rodino. Albert weighed in against the proposal, which he feared would divide and weaken the caucus. "I don't think an amendment like that belongs in the Constitution," the Speaker commented. While many representing cities where busing violence had flared indicated support for a public declaration of opposition, others anguished over the proposal. Although unsympathetic to busing, Tom Downey (who was studying law at night) blanched at the idea of a constitutional solution. "I can't be for this," he informed the Speaker, a position shared by an ideologically diverse group of freshmen including Derrick, Harris, Jenrette, Risenhoover, and Krueger, as well as Wirth, Berkley Bedell, and Martha Keys. Even many Class members in states where busing was a potent issue—including Carr, Florio, LaFalce, Matt McHugh, Maguire, Helen Meyner, Simon, and Stephen Solarz—voted against directing the Judiciary Committee on the constitutional amendment.

In October 1976, on the eve on their crucial reelection, the House ultimately agreed to an antibusing amendment championed by freshman Delaware senator (and future vice president) Joe Biden. In the 260–146 vote, House Democrats remained split, 148 for and 122 against; many Class members engaged in difficult reelection races nevertheless voted against busing, including Wirth, Bob Edgar, John Krebs, Simon, Russo, and all five Indiana freshmen. In New Jersey, Florio and Hughes and Meyner all voted against busing. But many progressive southerners like Levitas, Jenrette, Derrick, and Holland could not risk a no vote so close to an election. Overall, southern Democrats split 73–13 in favor of the restrictive amendment.

Rancor over the Panama Canal

Yet another contentious issue with profound political implications involved ceding sovereignty of the Panama Canal and the 10-mile-wide Canal Zone that bifurcated that country from the Atlantic to the Pacific. With nationalism rising throughout Central and South America, continued US control of the Canal Zone as well as the navigationally crucial canal itself was an offensive artifact of the colonial era. Within the Congress, and throughout much of the country, however, ceding the canal connoted a humiliating American diplomatic and military reversal, especially coming on the heels of the ignominious retreat from Vietnam.

Discussions with Panama about handing over the canal had been secretly initiated in June 1970 when President Nixon had authorized Secretary of State Henry Kissinger to begin "exploratory" talks on a new agreement.[16] As was common in the pre–War Powers Act era, Nixon made only a cursory effort to consult with Congress about the discussions. Five years later, President Ford was fearful that the continued talks could explode as an issue in the political debate with Democrats and with his challenger for the presidential nomination, the conservative former governor of California Ronald Reagan.[17] A memo in the Ford Library warned, "The Canal is too important to become a subject of partisan political debate or to be discussed lightly with sweeping generalities and oversimplifications." Ford's advisors recommended highlighting prominent conservatives and military leaders, including the vigorously hawkish Barry Goldwater, who had agreed, "There is peril in refusing to look ahead to eventual relinquishment."

But many others were willing to fan the flames of strident US nationalism, erroneously asserting the canal was owned by the United States and welcoming armed conflict rather than relinquishment. The canal issue, one foreign policy expert warned, evoked "unique popular appeal," and Mississippi House Democrat David Bowen argued taking a hard line on the issue could bolster Democrats. "When I am home in my district, there is only one thing I can say that invariably makes them cheer," Bowen said. "I say that if we can keep the striped-pants boys out of it and leave the Canal to the Corps of Engineers, then things will work out fine." Other senior southern Democrats weighed in against a new treaty including L. H. Fountain of North Carolina, who declared he was "sick and tired of seeing America continue to yield and yield," and Bill Alexander of Arkansas, who predicted that if the canal were given back to Panama, "the next thing we know the Soviet Union is going to want Alaska back."[18] Nor were the fervent canal defenders only southerners. Another leading opponent of any reduction of US dominance in the Canal Zone was the waxed-mustachioed, cape-flowing, top-hat-wearing, former thespian Dan Flood of Pennsylvania, a powerful Appropriations subcommittee chair.

In June 1975, Rep. Gene Snyder had forced a House vote prohibiting the use of funds to "negotiate the surrender or the relinquishment of any United States rights in the Panama Canal Zone," which passed 246–164. Snyder, an activist conservative also prominent in the abortion and busing debates, relished throwing a congressional monkey wrench into the largely secretive negotiations. Class members supporting Snyder's restrictive language included moderates across a large swath of the North as well as many progressive southerners happy to use the issue to bolster their patriotic credentials.[19]

The vote on the Snyder amendment shook the White House. Many of Ford's chief advisors viewed the amendment as the equivalent to the earlier House votes to terminate funding for Vietnam operations. After the Miami *Herald* suggested the negotiations might be curtailed, Kissinger called on Ford to make "a clear statement" that the discussions would continue lest there be "a deterioration in our relations leading to possible abandonment of negotiations in favor of confrontation by the Panamanians."[20] Moreover, Kissinger warned that Snyder's amendment could unconstitutionally interfere with the president's "constitutional responsibility to negotiate treaties with foreign governments." The Senate backed away from the confrontation, approving a much milder directive that negotiators ensure that US "vital interests" be protected but avoiding insistence on continued US control. In late September 1975, the House narrowly defeated a motion to accept the weaker Senate language, with most moderate and southern freshmen opposing the milder Senate language.[21]

The canal issue would continue to serve as a touchstone for anxiety and anger about America's alleged diminished influence, and it would become a singular point of attack in Reagan's nearly successful challenge to Ford's nomination in 1976. At Ford's behest, on June 18, 1976, the House embraced an ambiguous restriction by a 229–130 margin—with a large number of members avoiding the vote—requiring that the negotiators "preserve the vital interests" of the United States rather than the tougher "control" language used earlier to signify opposition to the accord.

The battle over the Panama Canal was not the only issue on which Congress challenged the president's command of foreign affairs. Growing concern about the violent policies of the Chilean junta, which had overthrown the country's elected president, Salvador Allende, in 1973 with the assistance of the US Central Intelligence Agency, led Congress to vote to bar military assistance or weapons sales to Chile. Congress also restricted aid to Uruguay because of human rights concerns and barred funding of any party in the ongoing civil war in Angola. Having been deeply affected by the US involvement in Southeast Asia, many Class members played high-profile roles in arguing for restrictions on US aid including Carr (on Indonesia), George Miller and Tom Harkin (on Chile), and Don Bonker, Moffett, and Mineta (on Angola, to which aid was terminated in January 1976). The enhanced congressional role was regarded as unwelcome interference at the White House, and Ford vetoed an early version of the Chile restrictions. But the trend toward greater congressional involvement in foreign policy was unmistakable, and a significant historic development in the 94th Congress.

Another form of intervention also drew congressional scrutiny and created divisions among Democrats: the imposition of workplace safety standards. Upon signing the bill creating the Occupational Safety and Health Administration (OSHA) in 1970, President Nixon had termed the new agency "an example of the American system at its best." But Republicans quickly soured on OSHA, viewing proposed workplace safety rules as unwarranted intrusions into the management of the private workplace. Over the subsequent four years, more than 100 bills were introduced to reduce OSHA's scope or eliminate the agency entirely. Under both Nixon and Ford, restrictive amendments to cut its funding were frequently offered to appropriations bills by Paul Findley, an Illinois conservative Republican who argued that OSHA regulations were too complex and confusing for small employers.

Defending OSHA presented a serious dilemma for Democrats with small business constituencies who nevertheless relied on organized labor for critical election support. Republican Bob Bauman, who had led the early antiabortion battle, was one of a small but growing number of conservative rhetoricians adept at casting an issue in edgy and explosive imagery, and he turned his skills to the OSHA debate. "The question is whether you are on the side of a Gestapo, which can knock on your door at any time and tell you how to run your business," Bauman menacingly warned, "whether they will put you out of business, or whether under the free enterprise system we will provide jobs."

Facts mattered less than the framing of the issue. Critics like Bauman greatly exaggerated the intrusiveness of OSHA. By 1974, not a single firm had been put out of business by the agency, and the average fine was just $26.[22] But the accusations capitalized on lingering suspicions of the federal government's overreach both on the Right (over issues like environmental regulations and labor law) and the Left (over issues like military intervention and CIA spying) and benefitted conservatives who supported a less active government.

In a series of votes in 1976, the freshmen split on the OSHA issue, often reflecting their district leanings. Findley and other conservatives argued for exemptions for small employers, even though, as William Hungate of Missouri countered, "There is nothing inherently safe in being small." In fact, studies indicated that small businesses had a higher incidence of injuries. A vote to exempt firms employing fewer than 10 people from OSHA coverage passed easily, 273–124, and won support from liberal northerners from states with strong labor organizations.[23] When OSHA opponents proposed an even larger carve-out, to raise the exemption to 25 in order to exclude more employers, many Class members who had supported the initial exemption switched and voted no.[24] Nevertheless, Republicans had succeeded in exploiting the looser floor rules to press an amendment that exposed vulnerable Democrats to retribution. Even though studies showed that OSHA enforcement failed "to have a perceptible effect on either enterprise decisions or health and safety outcomes," Democrats were made to seem indifferent to small employers struggling through the recession.[25]

The Battle over Situs Picketing

Class members faced another difficult labor policy question on the issue of common situs picketing, which pitted construction unions against construction companies, an important source of jobs in the recession-affected economy. The percentage of US workers belonging to unions had plunged in the preceding two decades from 35 percent to barely 25 percent of the workforce, a grim decline both for the unions and for Democrats who depended on their funding and organizational capacity at election time.

Situs picketing, like OSHA, had begun as a bipartisan initiative. The question was whether unions could picket a construction site, demanding that not just some but all workers at the location be union members, a requirement that would greatly strengthen the negotiating hand of the unions. A 1951 decision by the National Labor Relations Board, later ratified by the Supreme Court, had forbidden such picketing activities, and building trades unions had sought to reverse the decision ever since with the support of Republican and Democratic labor secretaries. Even Sen. Robert Taft Jr., the unsympathetic coauthor of the Taft-Hartley Act, agreed the situs picketing court decision "had been too far-reaching."[26]

Aware that Republicans had made inroads under Nixon in appealing to the conservative building trades, President Ford had endorsed legislation developed with his secretary of labor, John Dunlop, to create a joint union-industry council to manage labor and wage issues in the construction industry. The legislation became the top priority of the AFL-CIO for the 94th Congress, and both Dunlop and the chief AFL-CIO lobbyist (and former Wisconsin congressman) Andrew Biemiller urged the Republican Conference to support the bill. With such strong, bipartisan backing, both the bill's sponsor, Frank Thompson of New Jersey, and organized labor were confident. "There was no need for us to make any changes" to earlier versions of the bill, AFL lobbyist Ken Young boasted after the huge Democratic gains in 1974. But labor had mistakenly assumed that Democrats would automatically support the situs bill.

Organized labor, while a crucial source of Election Day get-out-the-vote and financial support, had maintained a minimal presence during the caucus reform battles in late 1974 and 1975, missing an important opportunity to solidify relations with many members of the Class. Many labor leaders believed they had been damaged by siding with Jim O'Hara in his unsuccessful 1971 fight against Hale Boggs for majority leader. "That taught us that it's politically a mistake to get involved in internal [caucus] matters, and we haven't since," said Arnold Mayer, the longtime lobbyist for the United Food and Commercial Workers Union. "When all the chairmanships came up, we didn't get involved. It's painful to be embarrassed like that."[27]

Opponents had denounced the situs bill as a "union power grab" when it appeared on the House floor in late July 1975, despite the support of many Republican conservatives and southern Democrats. "Only ignorance of the issue or a passion for economic self-flagellation," the loquacious Bauman asserted, "would induce this Congress to vote for" a bill he determined would injure the construction industry.[28] Republicans offered a number of amendments to cripple the legislation, including one by John Anderson to bar situs picketing at construction sites of residential structures under four stories high and without an elevator, which was narrowly defeated 200–202. Republicans overwhelmingly supported the Anderson amendment 120–14, as did southern Democrats by a two to one margin, including Derrick, Holland, Steve Neal, Hubbard, Krueger, joined atypically by Harris and Fisher, whose Virginia districts were experiencing a high level of home construction. Freshmen in the big labor states generally opposed the home construction exemption, but several including Krebs, Phil Sharp, Florio, and Ambro voted with the anti-labor position.

Anderson also proposed exempting minority contractors because of the racial discrimination he asserted was rampant in the construction industry. That proposal prompted a bitter reaction from Bill Clay, a black member from St. Louis who scolded Anderson and his party for pretending minorities could secure jobs in construction. "A black man's chances of getting a job in the construction industry," Clay retorted, "are . . . 200 times as great as of getting a job with the minority staff of this House."

The House passed H.R. 5900 by a vote of 230–178, more than sufficient for a bill that enjoyed the support of the president. Most of the votes needed to win came from northern Democrats and Republicans who enjoyed labor support; 95 percent of northern Democrats voted in favor, three times the percentage of southern Democrats. Numerous Democrats who had voted for weakening amendments swung back to support the final version of the bill even without the amendments.[29] Indeed, it was the ability to demonstrate moderation to constituent interests by voting for those amendments that allowed these members to then support the bill's final passage. Once the broad opportunities for offering and voting for such amendments was curtailed in the late 1980s, members were left only with the more stark and more partisan choice of voting for or against a bill.

The key Republican staff strategist, Bill Pitts, saw the situs picketing debate as a crucial indicator of where the GOP could foment divisions within the Democrats' expanded majority. "We saw the [bipartisan] southern conservatism emerging on that bill, and took advantage of it," Pitts recalled. As for House Republicans, one-fifth of conference members voted for the pro-union measure, but freshmen Republicans like Millicent

Fenwick, Bill Gradison, Charles Grassley, Hyde, and Bill Goodling were all opposed; so, too, was Pennsylvania's Gary Myers, who often was sympathetic to labor. Larry Pressler, who had voted for the bill in the Education and Labor Committee, recalled that GOP members descended on him for supporting the rule to bring the bill to the House floor and persuaded him to oppose its final passage. "I wasn't invited to Sioux Falls labor temple again for a long time," he said.[30]

Assurances from Labor Secretary John Dunlop that President Ford remained committed to the bill persuaded many moderate Democrats to defy their local business interests and vote for passage. But by the time the conference report was sent to Ford on a 229–189 House vote, the political climate in the Republican Party had shifted along the lines Pitts had foreseen. Under Reagan's conservative challenge for the Republican nomination, Ford came under heavy pressure to reverse his position. Republican senator John Tower, the Texas chairman of the Ford campaign, threatened to rescind his support if the president signed the bill. An "irate and threatening" Bill Dickenson of Alabama warned the White House staff that if the president "sells out on this, I'm not going to help at the convention," where the battle with Reagan was likely to be decided.[31] Indeed, Reagan cited the president's support for situs picketing as illustrative of his insufficiently conservative credentials. The virulently anti-union Right to Work Committee issued strong press releases, and many construction companies phoned the White House to reject the bill. Even the *New York Times* called for a veto, criticizing the bill as a "meek capitulation to Washington's labor lobby."[32] Only two Republican members of the House, Hamilton Fish and Peter Peyser, both from New York, called the White House to support the president's stated intention of signing the bill.

Situs picketing, an obscure labor measure, had become emblematic of the deepening divisions within American politics, of the capability of special interests to marshal votes for and against legislation, and of the rising power of the Right to influence strategy against both the Democratic majority and moderate Republicans. Within the GOP, the strong opposition of conservative freshmen highlighted the emerging divide from veterans who supported the bill. For Democrats, the vote demonstrated how, on yet another a key policy issue, freshmen could not be counted on to stay with the leadership when legislation impacted their districts and their political futures, even when it was vigorously supported by organized labor, a crucial source of campaign funding and grassroots support.

Early in January 1976 a stunned Congress received Ford's unexpected veto of the bill. In a reversal of his long-standing position, Ford declared its provisions would "cause greater, not lesser, conflict in the construction industry" that could "lead to loss of jobs and work hours for the construction trades, higher costs for the public, and further slowdown in a basic industry." Having passed the conference report with only 229 of the 270 votes needed for a successful override, the Democratic leadership was outraged but did not dare attempt an override vote.

The conservatives' victory had immediate ramifications in the White House. The labor members of the Collective Bargaining Committee in Construction resigned, as did Labor Secretary Dunlop, his credibility with unions and the Congress shredded. Indeed, Phil Sharp declared that Ford's surprise action had ruined the reputation of his entire congressional relations team.

Class members who had voted against situs picketing came in for criticism as well. "Labor lobbyists are concerned that some first-term Democrats in both chambers aren't as responsive to working class concerns as liberal Democrats of years past," *Congressional Quarterly* reported. The AFL-CIO's head lobbyist, Ken Young, asserted, "The freshman Democrat today is likely to be an upper-income type," overly concerned about inflation and insufficiently "emotionally involved" in unemployment. Another labor lobbyist, Arnold Mayer, mused that "the party hack may be closer to the local union guys than the young independent lawyer" of the sort who populated the freshman Class.[33] The unanticipated defeat of situs picketing marked a turning point in labor's influence on the Hill, a development with profound implications for Democrats, who derived much of their campaign support from union members. Situs picketing was among the last labor bills to enjoy significant backing from Republicans as the Ford veto helped signal that assisting labor, whose electoral support skewed heavily to Democrats, was inimical to conservatives' self-interest.

A renewed effort to pass situs picketing was launched in 1977 with the vigorous support of the building trades, whose backing had been crucial to Jimmy Carter's election as president. But labor's legislative maneuvering again proved insufficient. Assuming easy congressional passage given the large Democratic margins, one key staff member thought the building trades "sleepwalked through" the floor debate.[34] A well-funded assault by a new coalition of conservative business groups, the National Action

Committee on Secondary Boycotts, targeted 68 new Democratic members.[35] Despite labor's confidence, the bill failed 205–217, largely because half of the earlier Republican supporters abandoned the bill under heavy pressure from business interests. In addition, 37 of the Democrats targeted by the business coalition voted no, including 13 Democrats who had been endorsed by labor's national organization, the Committee on Political Education. Support from southern Democrats plummeted from 31 to 24. For some sympathetic to labor's agenda, "it was really the beginning of the end" of labor's long-standing influence.

If labor was frustrated with Democrats, many in the party were exasperated with labor's myopic understanding of the new Democratic members who had demonstrated their unwillingness to walk in lockstep behind their leadership or other financial backers. Majority Leader O'Neill concluded that labor "had not learned how to deal with the new kind of Congress[, which was] . . . younger, more widely educated and independent." The new members, he explained, "were different from the past Congresses. You can't stand outside the door [onto the House floor] and tell them how to vote as they come in anymore." Labor needed to bring pressure to bear on members in their districts; unfortunately, grassroots organizing was a weak spot for many unions because of recruitment woes, one reason the AFL-CIO wanted to promote labor law reform rather than situs picketing in 1977.[36] More personally, Richard Bolling expressed satisfaction at labor's comeuppance, blaming the failure of his reorganization plan in 1974 on its vigorous opposition to splitting the Education and Labor Committee's jurisdiction.

Within the Class of 1974, the situs vote exacerbated tensions between reliable supporters of labor and their colleagues. Russo, who was strongly prolabor, complained to O'Neill about southerners who had abandoned the unions. "What's wrong with these guys?" he asked. O'Neill counseled caution, reminding Russo that, without the votes of the southerners, the Democrats' majority would be markedly narrowed. "They make one important vote, for the Speaker," when the majority organized at the opening of each new Congress, O'Neill admonished. "Get to know their districts." A similar plea to empathize with southern moderates was advocated by Carter's legislative liaison, Frank Moore. Too many northern Democrats, he argued, seemed indifferent to the local political pressures on their southern colleagues.[37]

New Energy Battles

The battle on energy policy, briefly resolved with the enactment of the Energy Policy and Conservation Act in December 1975, resumed with vigor early in 1976, further dividing Democrats and kindling greater friction with the president. EPCA had denied Ford the power he sought to adjust the price controls on domestic oil and gas production, restrictions that the industry asserted impaired domestic production while creating administrative and regulatory havoc. Far from helping alleviate the crisis, Ford argued, the recently enacted law maintained "distortions and inefficiencies" that would preserve the "illusion of cheap energy."

Early in 1976, Class member Bob Krueger launched a renewed assault on what he termed a 40-year-old "absurd . . . crazy system" that restricted interstate gas prices to a fraction of the price for which gas sold within a single state.[38] Once again dismissing concerns about consumer impacts, as he had in the earlier oil deregulation battle, Krueger castigated northeastern liberals for their bias against the energy industry. "You didn't need an Oxford Ph.D.," which he conveniently possessed, "to figure out that [continued price controls] was a kind of madness," Krueger declared."[39]

In January, the Commerce Committee sent the Dingell-Eckhardt natural gas bill to the floor, and Krueger saw an opportunity. He asked Speaker Albert, who paid special attention to Krueger, to allow him to offer a decontrol amendment, something the committee leadership had discouraged. "Bob, you have a bright future [but] we need you to go along with us," Chairman Harley Staggers had advised Krueger. "We can help you with the future."[40] When Albert, a "bright, bright man [although] not a giant in strength," in Krueger's opinion, uncharacteristically overrode the chairman, committee leaders were furious that he had allowed a freshman to offer an objectionable amendment. At a caucus meeting, Dingell rose to criticize the leadership for "flouting the committee system." Class members were put in an inconvenient position: the Speaker had ignored a chairman in order to grant the request of a freshman, which theoretically was the kind of leadership they sought, but Albert had done so to promote an amendment many Class members found objectionable.

During the floor debate on the rule establishing debate parameters for the bill, Dingell and Staggers joined with Class members to try to block Krueger's amendment. It was a curious irony: reformers who just a year before had argued vehemently against rules that restricted junior members from offering amendments now joined with senior committee leaders to block a fellow Class member from offering an amendment. For his part, Krueger was furious that committee leaders who opposed his amendment were supported on the floor by their staff while he was compelled to communicate through written notes with a staff person in the gallery. On this point as well, the freshmen reformers abandoned their colleague's argument for equity.

After a brutal three-day floor battle, during which Kruger's opponents publicized the role of the energy industry in liquidating his massive campaign debt, the vote ended in a dramatic tie. As the official count remained open, senior legislators buttonholed their colleagues to persuade them to support the committee position. This was the kind of strong-arm tactic that Class reformers had resented the leadership employing but that they embraced now because it served their goals on the natural gas vote. When the gavel finally came down at Albert's direction, signaling the official end of the vote, Krueger had been defeated 201–205, a loss that stunned energy industry leaders. An "ashen-faced Krueger [admitted,] 'I feel whipped'" by the environmentalists.[41] The victorious Eckhardt, meanwhile, was delighted to once again best Krueger, dismissing his freshman colleague from Texas as "not a very good politician."[42] In August, a "terribly disappointed" Ford signed a compromise continuing price controls for at least three additional years, but, later in the summer, the Federal Power Commission used its regulatory power to allow companies to raise gas rates anyway.

The anti–energy company sentiments of many in the Class were better reflected in amendments offered by Chris Dodd to bar major oil companies from joining together to pursue leases on public lands, and by Toby Moffett to increase fines for companies that violated pricing and allocation provisions. Regardless of who won and lost the battles over deregulation and pricing, it was highly significant that freshman members played so important a role on both sides of the debate, a development attributable to their ability, thanks to the reforms they had supported, to secure a large number of seats on the crucial Commerce Committee and the Energy and Power Subcommittee where the legislation was developed.

Freshmen also played a prominent role on a specially created energy panel, the Ad Hoc Select Committee on the Outer Continental Shelf (OCS), cobbled together by the leadership to modernize the outdated 1953 law governing the development of offshore energy reserves on federal lands. Of the 13 Democrats drawn from the three committees with OCS jurisdiction, five were freshmen: Hughes, Dodd, Russo, Zeferetti, and Miller. The latter was appointed after Burton complained about the absence of a California Democrat on the initial list of members, a serious political omission given the lingering anger over the disastrous Santa Barbara platform blowout in 1969.[43] Many of the provisions in the new law that were designed to expand oceanic and coastal protection for fisheries and beaches, as well as those designed to pry higher royalties from oil companies, were designed and promoted by the Class members anxious to side with consumers and environmentalists.

One of the last actions of the Congress before adjourning for the campaign was the successful effort to override Ford's veto of the perennially controversial Labor-Health, Education, and Welfare (Labor-HEW) appropriations bill. This was the second override of an HEW funding bill, which Ford had vetoed because Congress added $4 billion to the $52 billion level he had requested.[44] Even though bill contained the Hyde restrictions on federal funding for abortions, pro-choice liberals voted to override the veto in order to secure the funding. Even the outspoken New Yorker Bella Abzug, who termed the Hyde restriction "unconstitutional, illegal and discriminatory," voted to allow the rider to go into effect, as did 65 Republicans—nearly half of the GOP Conference.[45]

The second session was a continued lesson in the limits imposed by the legislative system and member politics, and it left many in the Class despairing about the capacity of the House to embrace the kinds of progressive policies the freshmen favored. Certainly progress was made in challenging Ford's frequent vetoes, enacting bills like Labor-HEW, child nutrition, a renewed strip mine law, and the creation of the Energy Research and Development Administration to promote electrical technology innovation. Despite the continuing frustrations with the leadership by Class members, the House's override record during the 94th Congress was impressive. Of 39 vetoes that were subject to override votes, Ford was overridden seven times, or 25 percent of the cases, comparable to Nixon and Reagan.[46]

Statistics aside, many Class members remained frustrated that the leadership failed to persuade fellow Democrats to vote to overturn vetoes. Republicans, for their part, were happy to mock the inability of Albert and others to control the Class or successfully challenge the president more forcefully. "The only difference between the Democrats in Congress and a troop of Boy Scouts," chortled the Senate's Republican leader, Hugh Scott of Pennsylvania, "is that Boy Scouts are led by adults."

Part of the overall sense of disappointment was attributable to a feeling that the legislative achievements of the 94th Congress were far less dramatic than the initial organizational reforms. Ford and the bipartisan Conservative Coalition, who remained formidable obstacles to the policy aspirations of the Class, "thwarted [Democrats] time and time again," observers noted, often by challenging legislation not on policy grounds but as deficit-generating initiatives that raised questions of "fiscal responsibility."[47] This tactic—challenging liberal policies on the basis of cost rather than on the substance of the policy, as did past conservatives like Barry Goldwater—would prove to be a highly effective strategy for conservatives in the Reagan era to avoid appearing hostile to popular programs, pointing instead concern for the impact on the deficit, which often won support from budget-conscious Democrats as well. Framing objections in this fashion is one of the reasons that the success rate of the Conservative Coalition improved during the second session from 50 percent in 1975 to 58 percent in 1976, further assisted by conservatives' success in utilizing open rules to force repeated votes on controversial topics like abortion, busing, and defense policy.[48]

For many in the Class who had believed their generation and their election had signified a new age in politics, the qualified results of the 94th were a disappointment both in the institution and in themselves. They found themselves falling prey to the same kinds of pressures common to their senior colleagues as the realities of political life in the House ate away at some of their idealism. "Sooner or later, this place gets the best of you," the normally upbeat Toby Moffett confided. "You get tired. You get cynical. I think even the best of us get worn down, sidetracked, compromised to death." By the late fall of 1976, as they prepared for reelection in 1976, they were not simply reformers, insurgents, and critics. As Norm Mineta acknowledged, "The system swallowed us up." Now, they were politicians.

8 THE REPUBLICAN REFORMERS

I felt myself a moderate but not accepted by either side. I felt like crying out, "I am a congressman."—Rep. Larry Pressler (R-SD)

The party is in miserable shape.—Rep. Ed Forsythe (R-NJ)

This account of the Class of 1974 has focused, to this point, on the role played by Democrats, who constituted the vast majority of the Class. The role of the Republican freshmen has not been overlooked because of their small numbers in the Class but because the reform efforts occurred within the Democratic Caucus, from which all Republicans were excluded. That decision to utilize the Democratic Caucus to effectuate reforms was a practical one: the bipartisan Conservative Coalition retained formidable strength on the House floor and could be counted on to alter or defeat procedural reforms. Within the Democratic Caucus, however, the liberal reformers had gained the upper hand in 1974 and could design the rules largely as they preferred.

Yet the Republicans of the 1970s also included numerous reform proponents, both of liberal and moderate outlooks (mainly from the Northeast and Midwest), who joined likeminded colleagues who still formed a significant component of the Republican Conference.[1] While a number of the reforms implemented by Democrats affected only members of their own caucus, others had significant impacts on Republicans as well including expanded office budgets, staffing levels, and procedural rights. Democrats granted the minority such concessions without any thought that they might eventually contribute to Republican efforts to topple the Democratic majority, which they considered fanciful despite the analyses of Republican strategists.

Living in a Political Netherworld

Republicans reformers—especially those of the 1974 Class—often described themselves as wedged uncomfortably in a political netherworld: unappreciated and unneeded by the Democratic Caucus, where Republicans were unrepresented, while frequently estranged from an increasingly aggressive conservative faction within their own party that viewed them with suspicion and distrust. Little wonder that by the end of the decade, the ranks of Republican reformers had been winnowed significantly.

One point in any discussion of Republican support for reform bears noting. While sharing the majority's *goal* of democratizing House procedures, the minority's *objectives* often were quite different. Democratic reformers targeted their own party hierarchy and the traditional rules that permitted the caucus's dwindling conservative faction to maintain disproportionate power and influence, denying broader participatory rights to newer and more liberal members. The objective of the caucus reforms was not simply to dislodge conservatives—indeed, many remained in powerful positions including chairmanships for years after 1974—but to replace restrictive procedures that neutralized the power of the growing liberal majority in committees and on the floor.

Republican reformers included liberal and moderate members of the GOP Conference as well as conservatives who understood the strategic advantages of loosening the rules. Less restrictive rules governing the offering of amendments,[2] expanded staffing for committee minorities, greater press coverage of committee and floor operations, greater ease in calling for recorded votes, more independent and policy-specific subcommittees—all these reforms provided minority Republicans with expanded tactical opportunities to raise dissenting viewpoints and to expose the voting records of marginal Democrats. Republicans, particularly the more combative faction that emerged in the late 1970s, believed such changes would prove invaluable in restoring the drive for a majority that had been disrupted by Watergate and the elections of the mid-1970s, which had left them with the lowest percentage of House votes since 1936.

Like Democrats, Republican newcomers had organized during the post–World War II era to promote their interests within their conference.[3] "All of us were young," recalled founding member Richard Nixon, who had won a California seat in 1946. "All of us were new members of Congress. All of us were veterans of World War II." These newly arrived Republicans created the Chowder and Marching Club in 1949 to successfully defeat a veterans' pension and continued the organization to educate freshmen who were "unfamiliar with committee operations," recalled Bob Michel of Illinois.

Bipartisanship of the kind marking passage of the Legislative Reorganization Act of 1946 was a well-established fact in the House of the late 1950s and early 1960s. The Congress of that period was described by one member as "a club [with a] feeling of camaraderie [that] transcended party lines."[4] Moderates and progressives within both parties bristled at the leaders and the bipartisan Conservative Coalition that obstructed numerous legislative initiatives from civil rights to federal support for education. This bipartisanship was evident in the 217–212 vote in 1961 to expand the Rules Committee to check the power of Chairman Howard Smith. The rule change passed the full House only because Speaker Rayburn was able to secure the votes of 22 moderate Republicans who defied their leaders and offset the opposition of conservative Democrats. Similarly, liberal Republicans were vital to the success of the 1964 discharge petition that forced the stalled Civil Rights Act out of Smith's committee and onto the House floor.[5]

Republican Reform Initiatives

Republicans launched a concerted reform initiative in July 1968 after the same House Rules Committee unanimously killed the reform recommendations of the Madden-Monroney Committee, which included provisions such as allowing for minority committee staff. Independent staff was crucial: without it, the minority party was compelled to rely on the majority's staff, which put Republicans at a serious disadvantage. The bill, which had passed the Senate after six weeks of debate, also called for more open hearings and lobbying restrictions, as well as changes in the jurisdiction of House and Senate committees. Ultimately, the Republican Task Force on Congressional Reform opposed the diluted House version of the measure, which one member declared lacked enough reform "to put in your eye."[6]

Republicans wanted to end closed-door meetings, a "particularly obnoxious" practice that, they asserted, allowed chairmen to cut private deals.[7] Opening hearings to the press and public, many argued, would enable Republicans to expose committee negligence, helping to make the case that a change in party control was required. "Legislative hearings should be open so people can see just how badly some of these programs have been mismanaged," declared Tom Curtis of Missouri. They also promoted more open rules governing floor debate to allow for more amendments, a position from which the majority Democrats had long recoiled, fearing the adoption of amendments that would alter carefully negotiated legislative packages and jeopardize passage.

The failure of the Madden-Monroney bill outraged Republican reform advocates like Donald Rumsfeld. Like McCarthy's Marauders, the "Rumsfeld's Raiders" he organized challenged not only the majority's rules but also his own party's intractable leadership.[8] The Illinois reformer had helped depose House GOP leader Charles Hallack of Indiana after the disastrous 1964 election losses, replacing him with Gerald Ford of Michigan. After the failure of the 1968 reform, Rumsfeld tried to delay the adjournment of the 90th Congress to draw attention to the aborted reform effort.[9] Rumsfeld also led an unsuccessful challenge to replace Whip Leslie Arends with the more moderate Peter Frelinghuysen of New Jersey. After his requests for better committee assignments were routinely denied, the disheartened Rumsfeld declared, "Congressional reform is an issue without a constituency" and departed to "see if I can get a job with the [incoming Nixon] administration."[10]

Two years later, the bipartisan Legislative Reorganization Act of 1970 promised greater transparency by giving subcommittees the autonomy and minority staffing that Republicans had unsuccessfully sought in the Madden-Monroney proposal. Four years later, some Republicans endorsed the Bolling Committee's reform proposals. After unhappy Democrats aborted that effort, the frustrated Republican leader John Rhodes despaired, "Democrats will never agree to the kinds of reform that are needed" because doing so would dismantle the "self-interest factor that . . . has served them well. Genuine congressional reform," he argued, "will not take place until the American people place control of Congress in the hands of another political party." Anticipating arguments that would be articulated a decade later by a new generation of Republican activists, Rhodes argued that only the "switching of party control" could produce a House that "keeps itself institutionally fit."[11]

Shortly after the beginning of the doomed, second Nixon administration in 1973, young conservatives including Phil Crane of Illinois, Barry Goldwater Jr. of California, and Jack Kemp of New York organized the Republican Study Group, whose members would send occasional notes of defiance to the established leadership, much like their DSG counterparts. The RSG's director, Edwin Feulner, later president of the Heritage Foundation, a conservative think tank in Washington, drew a sharp distinction between these younger activists and senior House Republicans.

"The new conservatives tend to be harder," he wrote. "They know they are coming in as a minority. They have a sense of mission in the House," which was to confront Democrats and strategize a GOP majority.[12]

Party moderates viewed the conservative faction as a throwback to the disastrous Goldwater debacle of 1964 from which most Republicans were anxious to escape association. New Yorker Barber Conable described the RSG as "the most negative group" of Republicans in Congress and strongly disapproved of their focus on divisive social policies instead of the fiscal discipline that was "the heart of conservatism." Others ridiculed the strategy of demanding votes on controversial topics to differentiate conservatives from liberals. "They're tilting at windmills," observed Al Quie of Minnesota.

The loss of 49 Republican seats in 1974 produced a sharp setback to Nixon's "southern strategy" for resuscitating the party. Although Republicans had held just 15 percent of southern House seats in 1964, the regional percentage had risen steadily through the next four election cycles to nearly one-third. With the victory of many Class Democrats in 1974, however, the GOP's share of southern seats slumped back to just 25 percent. Deputy party chairman Richard Obenshain termed the losses "no obstacle to long-range party-building in the South," although he admitted they could delay "some of the party realignment" and discourage party switching by Democrats.[13] In fact, it would take more than a decade for Republicans to regain the number of seats they had held in the House before the 1974 electoral tsunami.

Conservatives Go on the Offense

Shortly after the 1974 election that brought the Class to Washington, the hard-liners made a play for a leadership slot. John Rousselot, a Californian known for his membership in the extreme John Birch Society, ran for chairmanship of the House Republican Campaign Committee. In his early days in the House, Rousselot had been considered so extreme that he had been blackballed from the Chowder and Marching Club, an embarrassing rebuke he never forgot. Observers warned that selecting a hard-liner might send a message that the Republicans could be viewed as "less tolerant of divergent views than the Democratic party," a perception that moderate Republicans feared would consign the party to another period of dwindling membership. "The outcome will say a lot . . . about what the party's national profile will be in the wake of the 1974 election," one writer noted.[14] The warnings were heard, and the position went instead to the more centrist Guy Vander Jagt of Michigan.

The lone reformer in the 94th Congress's GOP leadership was the new conference chairman, John Anderson of Illinois. Anderson began his career in 1960 as a traditional conservative, introducing a constitutional amendment in every Congress to "recognize the law and authority of Jesus Christ" over the United States. But the tumult of the 1960s had an enormous impact on Anderson. "We were undergoing social upheaval," Anderson said, "and the change began to register itself on my conscience . . . to convince me that times had changed, and that some of us—grudgingly—were going to have to change." While remaining an unwavering fiscal conservative, Anderson embraced civil rights legislation. His support for Harlem's controversial Adam Clayton Powell, who had been expelled from the House for misconduct, led Rep. John Conyers, a liberal African American, to observe, "John Anderson has shown more awareness of the existence of black people in America than any other Republican in the House . . . He is one guy who will listen."[15]

The arc of Anderson's ideological views offered a contrast to the shifting stance of the increasingly conservative House Republicans. By 1971, his moderation on social issues like civil rights, consumer protection, open housing, and foreign aid left him "unpopular with the Neanderthals of his own party."[16] At the beginning of the 93rd Congress in 1973, the conservative Sam Devine of Ohio fell just five votes short of ousting Anderson from his conference chair.[17] Later, he barely survived the challenge from Rousselot, who denounced Anderson as "not one of us." By the late 1970s, the Republican Study Group issued a report declaring that Anderson's votes as a member of the Rules Committee "rub Republican regulars the wrong way."

The GOP Reformers

Republican reformers continued to stress the need for more open House operations and an expanded role for the minority. Some of their supposed reforms were thinly disguised efforts to pare back programs they lacked the votes to eliminate, such as an automatic "sunset" terminating all federal programs every four years, necessitating a renewed effort to reauthorize them. Republicans ended the exclusive reliance on seniority for awarding the top minority committee position—known as "ranking member"—several years before Democrats. In addition, Republicans continued to press for greater transparency in committee operations and the inclusion of minority witnesses in hearings.

In particular, Republicans favored rules changes to facilitate their ability to offer floor amendments and demand recorded votes that would place marginal Democrats in uncomfortable situations. "When you are a beleaguered minority," one key Republican floor aide noted, "the recorded vote helps put things on the record." Former Republican rules staffer Don Wolfensberger noted that the goal of the GOP reform task forces that created these legislative initiatives was also to keep "Republicans together railing against Democrats."[18] Asked whether this strategy of offering controversial amendments highlighted Democratic vulnerabilities had changed the tone of the House by more clearly separating the parties into distinct camps, Florida's Lou Frey acknowledged, "I think that's right."[19]

The loss of nearly 50 Republican seats in 1974 had little impact on the moderate Republicans, such as those in the "Wednesday Group." Those who had been critical of Nixon, Watergate, and Vietnam escaped virtually unscathed, while droves of Nixon defenders and other conservatives— especially those on the Judiciary Committee—were defeated. Nearly half the members of the Republican Study Group's Steering Committee lost their seats. "The contrast of the comfortable reelection of moderates should have an impact on the deeply conservative nature of House Republicans," Democratic analysts optimistically concluded.[20] The Republican Party chairman in Mississippi, Clarke Reed, was downhearted after the election, observing, "Conservatives are down, defeated." Many in the GOP grew more concerned early in the 94th with the ouster of Democratic chairmen with whom they had often been able to fashion legislation.

The Class of 1974 bolstered the ranks of Republican reformers, several of whom had defeated more conservative challengers in primaries.[21] They expected to enlist in bipartisan efforts to liberalize the House but, more often than not, found themselves relegated to observer status by Democrats who did not need the support of Republican moderates. As a result, incoming Republican reformers often felt unappreciated by Democrats and untrusted by their more conservative conference colleagues. "I felt like a man without a country," bemoaned one of the reformist Class Republicans.[22] As much as they challenged the Democratic majority, noted one report shortly after the 1974 election, the Republican Class members also created "factional friction" within the Republican Party and with their own leadership.[23]

Willis "Bill" Gradison of the 1st District of Ohio was such a Republican, a low-key former mayor of Cincinnati, educated at Yale and Harvard. Like Norm Mineta, he became familiar with his party's leadership as mayor and had testified before House committees on behalf of the mayors' association earlier in the decade. He first ran for the House in March 1974, in a special election to fill the seat of a Republican who had resigned midterm. The House had just voted to authorize impeachment hearings against Nixon, and the political atmosphere was poisonous for anyone with "Republican" associated with his name. "I felt," Gradison recalled, "like a cork bobbing on the waves," incapable of influencing the direction of the race, which he narrowly lost. Shortly after the defeat, Republican House members invited him to brief them on the public mood all House members would be facing in November. "What's it like out there?" Bill Frenzel of Minnesota queried. Gradison heard a distinct lack of empathy for Nixon among House Republicans, who felt their own careers were suffering as a result of the scandals. Yet, despite the antagonistic mood and the Ford pardon, which dogged Gradison throughout the fall rematch, he was one of the few Republicans to defeat a sitting Democrat in November 1974.

Unlike Gradison, Gary Myers was a novice whose political experience had been limited to "knocking on doors and handing out literature" in local campaigns. In 1972, Myers was a 34-year-old shift foreman at the Armco steel plant near Pittsburgh. Annoyed that Frank Clark faced little opposition for the House seat he had securely held since 1954, Myers tried and failed to convince his brother, a Republican committeeman, to challenge Clark. One evening, Myers returned home from the night shift and announced to his startled wife, "I think I'll run for Congress this year." Echoing Mrs. Zeferetti's incredulity and indifference, Mrs. Myers told her husband, "Well, if you're going to do that, you're going to do it on your own," although she soon became his main strategist.[24]

Others shared her skepticism. Requesting filing forms at the registrar of voters office, he was asked if he was picking up Rep. Clark's petitions. "I was just a foreman at the mill," he recalled. "I really hadn't done anything like this before, but from the first door I knocked on, I got nothing but encouragement." However, the local GOP organization provided little support since its leaders had agreed not to oppose Clark in return for his supporting a Republican state senator. Remarkably Myers spent only $1,900 to win the primary, demonstrating the low threshold to entry that still marked congressional politics in the early 1970s.

Casting himself as "just an ordinary citizen," Myers criticized Clark for using official funds to promote his record in office. Outspent more than seven to one, Myers ran a surprisingly competitive though unsuccessful race, his numbers likely buoyed by ambitious Democrats who wanted to dispense with Clark so they could challenge Myers as a weak incumbent in 1974. Returning to the steel mill, Myers remained engaged in local Republican politics, and, early in 1974, he decided to challenge Clark again. Still radiating relative youth and optimism, Myers enunciated a humble message that sounded like the script of a Jimmy Stewart film. "If you are not comfortable with me, don't vote for me," he told voters. "I'd rather lose than be deceptive." After winning his improbable victory, Myers took a leave from the steel plant, packed his possessions and his family into an "awful lime green Ford Maverick," and set off for Washington, rolling into their new home in McLean, Virginia, "like the Beverly Hillbillies."[25]

Millicent Fenwick of New Jersey was no hillbilly. At 64, Fenwick was the oldest member of the Class on either side of the aisle, and she arrived with a lifetime of unique experiences. Rail thin, impeccably dressed in expensive tweeds, and often puffing on a pipe, Fenwick had once been a model for *Harper's Bazaar* and spoke with the faux-British accent of the affluent, mid-Jersey horse set. With her high cheekbones and aristocratic air, she was dubbed the "Katharine Hepburn of politics," exhibiting the casual elegance of the affluent by driving a dilapidated Chevrolet with a foxhound hood ornament.[26]

Despite her upper-class affect and her fluency in Italian, French, and Spanish, Fenwick never actually graduated from high school, let alone college. Born into wealth, the daughter of Calvin Coolidge's ambassador to Spain and a mother who perished on the *Lusitania*, Fenwick grew up in a 50-room mansion and inherited $5 million. Hitler's rise in Germany during the mid-1930s "horrified" her, but Fenwick's career path veered toward the elite, not the electorate.[27] She became an editor, eventually producing *Vogue's Book of Etiquette* (which included her invaluable advice that " 'tomato' is better pronounced 'to-mah'-to' ").

Fenwick, who married young, once, briefly and scandalously (her husband had left his wife for Fenwick), enjoyed her status as a woman in politics. She held minor appointive positions in New Jersey for years before Gov. Robert Meyner (whose wife would join Fenwick as a 1974 freshman) appointed her to the New Jersey Committee of the US Commission on Civil Rights in 1958. Eleven years later, she won a seat in the state assembly, where she once castigated a male colleague who objected to an amendment she offered. "I've always thought of women as kissable and cuddly and smelling good," he responded. Her voice dripping with disdain, Fenwick archly replied, "That's the way I've always felt about men. I only hope *you* haven't been disappointed as often as *I* have." She later served as the state's director of consumer affairs.

When a Republican-leaning House seat opened up in 1974, assembly GOP leader, Tom Kean, nearly half her age and the scion of a New Jersey political dynasty, presumed he would be the nominee. But Fenwick bristled at the expectation she would yield to a man, "as I've done so often before," and she defeated Kean—a future governor—by just 86 votes out of 25,000. In the general election, she maintained her iconoclastic style by denouncing Nixon, opposing Ford's pardon, and refusing special interest contributions while supporting civil rights, consumer rights, public housing, and campaign finance reform. Her opponent highlighted her advanced age by displaying photographs that emphasized her many wrinkles, but to little effect. Although New Jersey's Republicans lost four of the seven House seats they held, Fenwick won with 55 percent of the vote. It was, one observer noted, a "geriatric triumph" and by far her closest House election.

Hailed as "a new star," Fenwick, like some of her new Democratic colleagues, would display behavior that irritated senior members unused to freshman outspokenness.[28] She stunned senior Republicans by brazenly insisting (unsuccessfully) that she be given Frelinghuysen's prized seat on the Foreign Affairs Committee. Early in her term, she challenged Wayne Hays's plan to increase members' official expense accounts, leading the irascible chairman to threaten to withhold her staff's paychecks "if that woman doesn't sit down and keep quiet."[29] When Hays was forced by scandal to resign his chairmanship and his House seat, Fenwick delivered an unsympathetic floor speech that was so vituperative that it was expunged from the *Congressional Record*.

In Vermont, another scion of a distinguished family also displayed his independent Republican spirit. The son of a state supreme court justice and a product of Yale and Harvard law school, Jim Jeffords had already served in the Navy and the state senate by the late 1960s. As Vermont's attorney general, he had led a successful fight against highway billboards and sued the International Paper Company for polluting Lake Champlain, offending the local business community and dooming his 1972 race for governor.

Jeffords lacked a comfortable fit with Vermont Republicans; he declared Nixon "a national disgrace and a liability to the party" at the same time the state's Republican leadership heaped praise on the embattled president's "matchless record of accomplishment." A dismayed Jeffords declared that resolution an example of the "Vermont Republican pattern of head in the sand."[30] When California governor Ronald Reagan proclaimed at a state party dinner, "My loyalty to Richard Nixon is 100 percent," Jeffords left the dinner shaking his head.

In 1974, the state's five-term Republican senator, 83-year-old George Aiken, decided to retire, and Vermont's lone congressman, a Republican, opted to run for the Senate. Jeffords decided to run for the vacant House seat. "I didn't defend the Republicans," he recalled, but neither did "[I] take it upon myself to castigate the party." Sensitive to the charge he was too liberal for the state's GOP voters, Jeffords endorsed some core conservative positions, including a balanced budget constitutional amendment, opposition to gun control, and a national health plan that resembled what would become known as Obamacare four decades later.

After winning a primary against two opponents who divided the conservative vote, Jeffords faced the Democratic mayor of Burlington and a third-party anti-war activist. As with Fenwick and Myers, the party leadership offered him little support. "I was definitely the epitome of the post-Watergate Republican Party," he recalled, "limping along and barely making it financially," living out of a trailer. Nevertheless, on Election Day, he emerged one of the rare Republicans to win an open seat and "was about as happy at that moment as I have ever been."

His joy did not last long. Wearing a neck brace from a car accident, he and another freshman, Charles Grassley on crutches from an injury, called themselves the "walking wounded" both metaphorically and perhaps in actuality. His lifestyle in Washington was Spartan, compared to that of Fenwick, who rented rooms she called a "shack" in the upscale townhouse of Rep. Pierre S. DuPont of Delaware. Every morning, she told Jeffords, she would "throw open the drapes of my apartment and see the Capitol and I say, 'How lucky I am.'" Jeffords dourly described waking up in a Holiday

Inn, miles from the Capitol, looking out on an alley filled with garbage cans.

Jeffords shared the bipartisan conviction of junior members that the seniority system "stacked the odds against someone new like me," and he quickly felt isolated in the conservative atmosphere of the Republican Conference. In 1975, Congress was not yet a "sharp-edged partisan body," he noted. "That would come later." Representing a heavily agricultural state, he found himself in agreement with outraged Democrats when Ford vetoed farm bills that included higher milk support payments he had authored.

Although neither wealthy nor from a respected political bloodline, Larry Pressler shared an interest in bipartisan reform. Raised in a lower-middle-class family, he had won a Rhodes Scholarship to study in England, based largely, he believed, on his discussion of livestock crossbreeding with bemused interviewers who "had never met anyone who raised pigs." After earning a law degree from Harvard, he served two tours of duty in Vietnam, which would earn him the distinction of being one of the first Vietnam veterans to serve in the Congress. Like Harkin, his experiences in Southeast Asia altered his views on America's involvement in the war, leading him to favor withdrawal of US forces. His other progressive credentials included having marched with Martin Luther King in support of civil and voter rights, and he became a vigorous supporter of Common Cause.

Pressler joined the State Department, with hopes of becoming an ambassador, but the war and Watergate left him "upset with the direction the country was going." In April 1974, he resigned and headed home to South Dakota, planning to challenge incumbent Frank Denholm, a Democrat who had held the House seat since 1971. Like several future colleagues, Pressler felt compelled to run despite a lack of confidence about his prospects. "I don't have any organization, I don't have any plan, I don't have any money," he explained. "I gave myself only a small chance of winning either the primary or the general election." But he vowed to be "a different kind of congressman," limiting his service to eight years, and rebating 10 percent of his congressional salary. "I was prepared to run a campaign on those ideas," Pressler declared, "and let the chips fall where they may."[31]

Criticized for his long absence from the state, his recent registration as a Republican (he acknowledged that might have registered once as a Democrat), and his lack of membership in the South Dakota bar, he faced questions common to unknown candidates, especially whether he would continue to listen to unfamiliar constituents after the election. The Republican organization offered little support, dubious of a young outsider who called for Nixon's impeachment and endorsed the moderate Nelson Rockefeller for vice president. He also allied himself with controversial local issues, raising environmental objections to the Oahe water development project even though it would benefit South Dakota farmers.

"There just isn't that rapport between myself and the traditional party types," he acknowledged. But, like many of his future colleagues, Pressler proved adept at using the emerging technologically of the modern campaign. While Denholm depended on the traditional bumper stickers and billboards, Pressler invested early in television advertising, attacking the incumbent as slow to address the expanding scandals in Washington despite claiming to be "one of the foremost reformers in Congress." In an era of increased transparency, Pressler accused Denholm of being the only member of the state's three-person delegation to refuse to disclose his finances. Those attacks attracted many reform-minded Democrats, whose votes enabled him to defeat Denholm handily despite a Democratic wave election elsewhere in the nation.

Once in Washington, Pressler, like other Republican moderates, grew frustrated with their exclusion from the reform efforts developed by the Democratic Caucus. His credentials were confirmed by press observers, who noted, "Pressler's frankness stands out bluntly," but to no avail.[32] "Democrats didn't even acknowledge that we existed," Pressler bitterly noted. "I felt like an abandoned orphan or stepchild." With few exceptions, "it never dawned on [Democrats] that I was more for reform than many of them." Surrounded by talk of reform, the South Dakotan remembers thinking, "How about *me*? *I* ran on a reform ticket. But no one seemed to recognize that. No one paid much attention to me."

While many of the Democrats' innovations won praise from GOP reformers, that was not true of the decision to grant the majority two-thirds of the seats on key committees irrespective of the future ratios of the parties in the House. The fixed ratios reflected the majority's expectations that Democrats would always be in the majority, although not with the overwhelming advantage enjoyed in the 93rd Congress, and were "indicative of precisely the type of partisanship . . . the country cannot afford," charged Republican leader John Rhodes. The conference chair, John Anderson, often the target of conservative disdain, denounced the change as a "naked grab for power [that is] blatantly unconstitutional."[33]

But Republicans did not simply respond to Democratic rule reforms. At the beginning of the 94th Congress, Anderson proposed television coverage of the floor, open hearings, a ban on the proxy (absentee) voting in committees that enhanced the power of the chairmen, and a requirement that committee records be open for public inspection.[34] His proposal to allocate equal membership to both parties on the Intelligence Committee, in the interest of a bipartisan foreign policy, was rejected by a party-line vote of 265–141, and even Class reformers dismissed the notion of equity. "If the people wanted the responsibilities to be divided 50–50 between the two parties," Bill Brodhead declared, "they would have voted that way."

Republicans were especially supportive of loosening restrictions on the ability to offer floor amendments, a change that would provide them numerous opportunities to tinker with legislation shaped by committees on which they had been outvoted. Open floor rules also enabled Republicans to offer amendments that appealed to conservative Democrats and that forced marginal Democrats either to vote against their own chairs and caucus or to support the party position and risk constituent censure. The new rules resulted in a sharp increase in the number of recorded votes, a 141 percent rise between the 92nd and the first session of the 94th Congress. Additional votes were also facilitated once electronic voting replaced the teller vote process. Throughout the remainder of the decade, the number of recorded votes grew exponentially. From just 177 recorded votes in 1969, four years before the introduction of electronic voting, the number of recorded votes had risen by 1973 to 541. In the two sessions of the 94th Congress, the number rose to more than 600, and by 1978 the number exceeded 830.

Offering controversial amendments was just one of the tactics used by the outnumbered Republicans to force concessions from Democratic leaders. Others included making multiple quorum calls and other procedural votes to slow down the legislative day and objecting to unanimous consent requests to pressure the majority to offer them concessions. A pioneer in such mischief was Iowa's crusty H. R. Gross, who was pleased to be known as a "useful pest" for his floor antics.[35] Originally elected in 1948 by ousting a fellow Republican, Gross delighted in confusing the Democrats' schedules through his mastery of the intricate rules of the House. He would park himself on the floor, meticulously reviewing legislation, raising innumerable procedural questions, shouting out points of order, and raising parliamentary inquiries, all designed to throw the carefully scripted procedure off track. "Read 'em all," he counseled young floor aides on bills and amendments. "Look for what's not in them. I look them up, and then I nail them."[36] One of Gross's young acolytes, Bill Pitts, even earned praise from Democratic rules mavens like Richard Bolling and Bernie Sisk when he discovered opportunities in the rules to trip up chairmen.

The greatest power exercised by the Republican minority was its ability, together with conservative Democrats, to sustain most of Ford's numerous vetoes. In these efforts, as with Democrats, tensions arose when some of the newly elected moderates would balk at demands for party unity. Although Pressler supported Ford "as much as I could," he recalled that the Republican leadership was "pretty tough" in those cases when he voted against the party's position. Assistant Whip Charles Thone would disapprovingly inquire whether Pressler was "abandoning us again," and conservative political groups in South Dakota would send out critical mailings.

The Republican reformers' anguish as a marginalized minority was a long-standing theme. Early in the century, Republicans had sat helplessly as the Democrats' "King Caucus" rammed through Woodrow Wilson's New Freedom legislation enlarging the regulatory role of the federal government. Six decades later, GOP Conference chair John Anderson lamented his party's continued marginalization as the increasingly assertive Democratic Caucus rode "roughshod over outgunned House Republicans." Anderson warned that "Democrats were . . . restor[ing] the iron grip of King Caucus over the legislative process." When the Democratic Caucus passed its resolution against additional funding for Vietnam early in 1975, he predicted, "King Caucus is making a comeback in all the worst senses of that term," asserting that the minority needed better protection in the legislative process.[37]

Democrats acknowledged they ignored potential allies among the Republican Class members because their small numbers were irrelevant to effectuating the reforms. Even decades later, when Chuck Grassley of

Iowa was mentioned as one of the few remaining Class members still in Congress, Berkley Bedell demurred. "Chuck really wasn't one of our class," Bedell protested. "He was a Republican." Henry Waxman agreed, recalling, "If we have a United Democratic position, Republicans are irrelevant."[38] Even a moderate Class member like Matt McHugh affirmed Pressler's sense of insignificance. "Republicans were not the problem," he recalled. "They weren't even relevant. They were not a threat to take the majority [so] we didn't need to feel threatened by them if we didn't do the right thing."[39]

But Pressler was puzzled by the dismissiveness of reform Democrats whom he thought "should have been delighted to have someone on the Republican side saying the same things." Instead, he noted, the younger Democrats generally "seemed annoyed or irritated, not willing to share the spotlight." It was easier, he found, to work with more senior members of the majority like Education and Labor Committee Chairman Carl Perkins, "an old country boy who liked to talk about hogs." But his cordial feelings did not extend to the Democratic leadership, whom he dismissed as "hard-nosed partisans" who "would have nothing to do with [Republican] moderates."

There was a strategic rationale for Democrats not collaborating with moderate Republicans who occupied the House seats that Democratic strategists believed represented the strongest opportunities for successful challenges. As a result, Democrats had little motivation for collaboration that would demonstrate the Republicans' ability to work constructively with the majority, blunting a central argument in favor of replacing them with Democrats.[40] As competition for seats and for majority control grew in the ensuing years, this unwillingness to vouch for the reasonableness of members of the opposite party would prove a key element in the rise of partisan division in the House.

The progressivity of these reform-oriented Republicans on policy matters should not be exaggerated. As noted, far less moderate Republicans also enthusiastically supported some of the reforms, because they enhanced the minority's opportunities for obstructing, dividing, or embarrassing the Democratic majority. Democrats were quick to note that most of the Republican Class members, despite describing themselves as "moderates," retained strong conservative credentials on key legislation. While Fenwick, Jeffords, Pressler, and Myers were more centrist than many veteran Republicans, they still earned strong ratings from conservative-leaning organizations like the Chamber of Commerce and the American Conservative Union.[41]

Resigned to Minority Status

If Democrats did not worry about the prospect of losing control in the mid-1970s, few Republicans anticipated their party might secure the majority anytime soon, a fatalism that prompted many to cooperate with those who controlled the gavel. "The mindset was we would always be in the minority," Gradison acknowledged. A plausible path from the party's diluted state to electing a Republican Speaker "never crossed my mind," the Ohio freshman acknowledged. That fact did not make it any easier for Gradison to accept being kept in the dark about legislation. But, given the seeming unlikelihood of the power arrangement shifting, Gradison was fatalistic. "We understood the distribution of power and the roles we played," he acknowledged. "We had our roles and we played them out."[42] Fenwick, familiar with minority status in the New Jersey Assembly, shared a similar fatalism. "We are very few," she said of her fellow GOP reformers. "We don't struggle for committee chairmanship. We never get knocked out, because we are not in."[43] A key Republican floor aide, Bill Pitts, echoed the same frustration. "We were a minority of 144," said Pitts, an anti-war college activist who followed his father into important House Republican staff positions. "We had no power to stop anything."[44]

But Republican reformers were also dismayed by the scorn they encountered within their own conference. There was "no percentage in being moderate," Pressler wistfully concluded. "Moderates were disliked" in the party and "southern Republicans didn't even regard me as a Republican." Just as conservatives doubted Anderson was truly "one of us," they speculated that the South Dakotan Pressler might be a "McGovern plant" inside the conference. He often was refused permission to speak by Republican floor managers, who suggested he request time on the floor from Democrats, since he often supported the majority's legislation. Republican leader Bob Michel once objected to a routine unanimous consent request from Pressler to insert material critical of the Ford White House in the *Congressional Record*, a rare breach of House comity. Fellow South Dakotan Vern Loen, a member of the White House's congressional relations team, became so incensed at Pressler's repeated votes for Democratic motions and overrides that, ignoring Ford's admonition, he told the *Sioux Falls Argus-Leader* that Pressler was "not a good congressman."[45]

The Emerging Conservative Activists

One reason for the feelings of estrangement by these moderate reformers from their own party was their frequent differences of opinion with the emerging conservative activists. Although the 1980 election, in which Ronald Reagan won the White House and Republicans gained control of the Senate for the first time since 1955, is often cited as the key moment in the ascendency of the Republican faction in the Congress, the origins of this modern conservative House majority really lie in the issues, activists, and organizations that arose in the 1970s. By mid-decade, most of the energy—intellectual, political, and financial—behind the drive for a Republican majority was centralized in the reviving conservative wing of the party, which viewed collaborators—whether freshmen or within the leadership—with disdain. The Jeffordses, Fenwicks, Andersons, and Presslers had long had a significant home within the GOP, but their influence was waning as the party revived in the suburbs and the South, luring conservative Democrats through appeals to patriotism, law and order, and race. Religious conservatives who emphasized divisive cultural issues were rapidly displacing the old-school patrician Republicans who were reliable supporters of civil rights, the environment, education, and other bipartisan legislation. Moreover, if a conservative majority could be fashioned from establishment economic conservatives and emerging religious and cultural conservatives, the GOP felt no need to moderate its positions to retain these outliers: the road to money, message, and the majority veered to the right, and the levers provided by congressional reform provided valuable mechanisms for achieving their objectives.[46]

Sharpened partisan language targeting Democratic policies and leaders increasingly marked the congressional debates of the mid-1970s. Accusatory language even appeared in typically collaborative committees like Ways and Means. In July 1975, Bill Ketchum of California castigated the energy policies of the committee's majority as "the height of absurdity . . . a new plateau of folly" and an act of "perverse determination of the majority to exacerbate our energy shortage." Bill Frenzel decried the Democrats' absence of effective leadership, asserting the majority members "made fools of themselves" by offering an energy plan that he called "a joke."[47] Within a couple of years, the level of partisan rhetoric would escalate beyond anything employed previously.

Republicans were particularly angered by the Democrats' persistent battles with President Ford. Barber Conable, normally a moderate pragmatist, castigated Democrats for refusing to work cooperatively with Ford, which he termed "a partisan waste." Bob Michel, the Republican whip, warned in mid-1975 that Congress "cannot afford a permanent stalemate" with the White House. Without better cooperation, he cautioned, "we [could] slide into a real deadlock, where neither side will permit the other to dominate and where government approaches paralysis."[48] In particular, Republican critics singled out the Democratic Class members as "wild, uninhibited, and . . . feeling their oats." Some of the newcomers, they charged, were "downright rude, intemperate, and immature."[49] By the fall of 1975, Republicans were accusing marginal Democratic freshmen of being "worse than Bella Abzug," the abrasive New York liberal.

The Emergence of the Conservative Activists

The financial energy behind the Right's resurgence originated with a 1971 memo prepared for the US Chamber of Commerce by Lewis Powell, a renowned Virginia attorney and future Supreme Court justice. Powell's memo warned of a "frontal assault" on the business community by liberal activists like Ralph Nader, whose condemnation of American business had grown from a stunning exposé of the auto industry into a far broader indictment of corporate practices and political influence. "Business must learn the lesson," Powell had warned, "that political power is necessary" and that "it must be used aggressively and with determination."

Into the Republican vacuum created by the chaos of Watergate stepped a new generation of conservative activists, including Richard Scaife and Joseph Coors, who spent millions of dollars from their considerable fortunes to create conservative think tanks like the Heritage Foundation in 1973; the Business Roundtable; the National Conservative PAC, run by John Dolan and Charles Black; and the Moral Majority, founded by Virginia minister Jerry Falwell in 1977. These research centers generated valuable studies, analyses, and legislative proposals that were eagerly utilized by conservative legislators on the Hill. Some of the New Right groups focused on specific issues, including the Gun Owners of America; the anti-union Employees Rights Committee; and the Committee for

Responsible Youth Politics, created by Richard Viguerie, a pioneer direct mail fundraiser who boasted that he had "raised tens of millions of dollars for the conservative movement."[50] Opposition to the Equal Rights Amendment, which had been rapidly ratified by 22 states by 1972, was led by Phyllis Schlafly, whose vituperative rhetoric and grassroots activism earned her the title of "probably the best political organizer we've seen in American history," according to 1970s historian Rick Perlstein.[51]

Coors, a Colorado beer manufacturer, created the Committee for the Survival of a Free Congress (CSFC) in 1974 under the direction of Paul Weyrich, who had worked for the Senate leader of the New Right, Jesse Helms of North Carolina, as well as James McClure of Idaho and Paul Laxalt of Nevada. CSFC was patterned after the Democrats' successful National Committee for an Effective Congress and had the goal of raising $2 million and building grassroots support to defeat 100 liberal House members. Strategists for President Ford, warily monitoring the challenge by former governor Ronald Reagan, noted the rising financial and political power of the Right that lay outside the traditional Republican establishment. "We are in real danger," a memo informed Ford, "of being outorganized by a small number of highly motivated right-wing nuts."[52]

Alarmed Democrats traced the sudden growth in conservative spending to 1974's campaign reform law, which expanded political action committees (PACs) that were "funnel[ing] individual corporate contributions to pro-business candidates," creating the specter of the "largest campaign fund in the history of the nation."[53] Within two years after the law's enactment, the number of business and professional PACs had grown from 99 to 412, while PACs associated with organized labor had dropped from 225 to 160. Hal Wolfe of NCEC warned the conservative fundraisers were "just beating us to hell."

Conservatives Target GOP Leaders

Just as the formal Republican leadership was worried by the emergence of independent conservative organizations beyond its control, the activists voiced contempt for a party hierarchy they viewed as collaborationist and ineffectual. "The Republican Party is an institutional disaster," declared Dolan of NCPAC, which supported Reagan's primary challenge. "Anybody that marries himself to the Republican Party at this point is crazy." Conservative fundraiser Richard Viguerie, who had honed his skills as an advisor to Alabama governor George Wallace's independent presidential race in 1968 agreed. "I don't think you can come to power in America with the Republican Party," Viguerie concluded.[54]

Instead, the new conservatives sought to build grassroots networks throughout the nation that could grow a new constituency to displace the traditional, ineffective Republican leadership. "Our bag is in organization," declared Paul Weyrich. "We preach and teach nothing but organization. Conservatives are notorious for feeling that if they are right on the issues, they will win elections. This is nonsense."[55]

Like the Class, which targeted the Democratic leadership, the contempt of these conservative activists was focused not simply on the opposing party but on their own leadership, which they accused of acquiescing in remaining a permanent minority party in Congress. Republican leader John Rhodes, they asserted, was too focused on institutional and electoral minutia and was neglecting his broader responsibility to promote conservative policies in the House. They were especially furious that John Anderson still remained a member of the party leadership as chairman of the GOP Conference. Indeed, some conservative activists were even contemptuous of the man many Republicans increasingly viewed as the party's rising star. "Reagan is not a savior," Howard Phillips of the Conservative Caucus group sneered, after the Californian selected moderate Pennsylvania senator Richard Schweicker as his prospective 1976 running mate. "He's a lightweight."[56]

These conservative activists were the first to perceive, in the gloom enveloping House Republicans after Watergate and the 1974 election, a glimmer of hope that the GOP could revive its stalled momentum toward a Republican majority. Their central premise was that cooperation with Democrats was a prescription for continued electoral failure because it meant that Republicans would share responsibility for policies they had little role in shaping; collaboration blurred the difference between the parties and mainly benefited the majority, which received credit for fashioning the coalition and the outcomes. What was needed instead, the hardliners argued, was a *refusal* to cooperate and a determination to exploit every opportunity to challenge and stigmatize Democrats, to raise issues that resonated with conservative voters and drew a clear differentiation between the parties, while taking advantage of the recent finance laws and congressional rules to raise money and exploit the ability to inject divisive issues into the legislative sphere.

The strategy soon appeared to be working. As the second session of the 94th Congress wound down in 1976, second-term representative Bill Armstrong of Colorado declared, "Republican conservatives spend less time complaining." Morale in Congress, he reported, was "surprisingly good, considering that we're outnumbered two to one. We're not hunkering down" in fear of Democrats.[57] No Republican played out that strategy with greater impact than Class member Henry Hyde. Although raised in a Democratic family, Hyde grew increasingly conservative during his college and law school years. By the time of his first race for Congress in 1962, an unsuccessful challenge to Chicago's Roman Pucinski, he was strongly opposed to labor unions and a vigorous anti-communist. Elected to the state legislature in 1966, Hyde rose rapidly, and by 1971 he was the majority leader. When nine-term House incumbent Harold Collier retired in 1974, Hyde won the Republican seat.

A large, hulking figure with a shock of white hair reminiscent of Tip O'Neill, Hyde's personable nature and political acumen were quickly recognized by his party colleagues, who elected him president of the freshmen Republicans. But, as an experienced legislator used to serving in the majority, Hyde quickly became frustrated that "Republicans were relegated to holding spears" in the House. Yet, by the end of his first term, Hyde's name had become synonymous with his amendment to the Labor-HEW appropriations bill preventing the use of federal funding to pay for abortion procedures, which had been ruled constitutionally protected by the Supreme Court's *Roe v. Wade* decision in 1973. By 1975, NCPAC was referring to Democrats opposing the Hyde amendment as "baby killers," an epithet first used by Sen. Robert Dole in his 1974 race against Rep. Bill Roy, a physician who defended the court's decision. The following year, in response to growing conservative opposition to *Roe*, Republicans dropped support for abortion rights from their national platform.[58]

Conservatives determined that using every opportunity to raise such differentiating issues would play a central role in peeling conservative Democrats away from their traditional Democratic loyalties. Despite the steps taken by the Class and others in 1974 and 1975, Minority Leader Rhodes declared, only the "periodic switching of party control . . . will result in a Congress which keeps itself institutionally fit."[59] The effectiveness of the strategy appeared to be confirmed in a special House election in April 1976, when hard-liner Ron Paul, an antiabortion Texas conservative, captured a longtime Democratic seat. A few weeks later, Reagan crushed Ford in the Texas primary by a two to one margin, sending "a message to conservative Republicans in other states," noted *Congressional Quarterly*, that the Right was clearly ascending.[60] "I want a massive assault on Congress in 1978," Richard Viguerie declared at the end of 1976, "in a way that's never been conceived of."

A Disappointing Election

Republicans began the final race to the November elections with enduring divisions from the bitter convention battle in which Ford eked out a last-minute victory over Reagan. Worried that Ford's "coattails will be so short as to be non-existent," leaving House candidates to fend for themselves, Rhodes declared that House Republicans "must be doing something wrong" and should "set their own sails," outlining legislative objectives a GOP House majority would pursue.[61] Eighteen years before Newt Gingrich's "Contract with America," Rhodes embarked on a virtually unheard-of effort to nationalize the congressional contest, a difficult objective in any year but especially so in the midst of a competitive presidential campaign that was certain to overshadow House races. His "Program for Progress" embraced a litany of mainstream conservative goals including tax incentives for private energy producers, a relaxation of government regulations, a purging of ineligible welfare recipients, tax simplification, and mandatory prison sentencing.[62]

Rhodes and other senior Republicans were quick to assure party leaders that their new agenda was "a blueprint to be shown to voters to tell them what the GOP can do if it gets back into power" in the Congress, not "a slap in the face for Ford," although he did advise House members they could not depend on "presidential shirttails." Not surprisingly, White House chief of staff, the former Republican House reform advocate Donald Rumsfeld, and other administration officials viewed the "Program for Progress" as a perfidious "stab in the back" intended to distance House Republicans from Ford's presidential campaign.[63] The lone moderate in the House GOP leadership, John Anderson, downplayed the seriousness of the agenda—and dismissed the likelihood Republicans might implement it—by characterizing his colleagues' work as "an intellectual exercise, and nothing more."[64]

The weak performance of House Republicans in the 1976 election did little to improve mainstream Republican spirits. "The party is in miserable shape," Rep. Ed Forsythe of New Jersey bemoaned. Some questioned the wisdom of turning toward the right or the effectiveness of basing party hopes on a Republican resurgence in the South. "The fabled southern strategy this year doesn't make any sense" in light of former Georgia governor Jimmy Carter's unique appeal in the region, said moderate Washington State governor Dan Evans. In Minnesota, the party actually changed its name to Republican-Independent to try to heighten its appeal.[65] Indeed, shortly after the election, one highly regarded publication speculated that the entire GOP House Conference might collapse into "a conservative rump group likely to have meager legislative impact."[66] Congressional scholar Norman Ornstein concurred with the pessimistic assessment, asserting that Republicans were "at the point where they have to be concerned about their long-term viability in the House." Further losses, he warned, might "exacerbate the deep ideological differences" that could change the nature of the Republican Party and cleave significant partisan difference between the parties.[67] By the end of the 94th Congress, that chasm was a growing trend within the Republican Party. Moderates increasingly became the targets of party activists who scorned the bipartisan collaboration that Class members like Gradison, Pressler, and Fenwick reflexively embraced.

"The atmosphere in and around Congress today is far more acrid than at any time during my career," complained Rhodes, but who bore the responsibility for the growing partisanship was a matter of opinion. Rhodes ascribed the diminished "feeling of camaraderie [that once] transcended party lines" on Democrats, who had developed reforms unilaterally within their own caucus rather than on a bipartisan basis, as with the Legislative Reform Act of 1970. He pointed accusingly at the Class members as "louder, more uptight, hostile and devious" than those with whom he had long served. As liberals in the Democratic Caucus checked the influence of the conservatives, with whom Rhodes and others had long cooperated, Republicans were being unfairly "cut out of the action." Citing as an example the Democrats' decision to establish a permanent 2:1 party ratio rule that gave them "absolute control," Rhodes observed, "It has never [been] so partisan as it is today."[68]

Republicans Adopt a Harder Edge

Republicans who had long prided themselves on their pragmatism now chastised colleagues who were too "fat, dumb and happy" to fight for majority status."[69] Bill Steiger, just 38 but already a 10-year House veteran, worried that the prolonged minority status had "debilitate[d]" many party members. "You end up developing a mind set of the minority," he observed. "You become so accustomed to that condition that you tend to be more cautious in what you do . . . You are not willing to strike out to find a new position." Some even doubted whether the current cohort of Republicans could function as a majority. "We'd have a difficult time," Conable admitted, "if we . . . would have to adopt a positive program [because] so many of our members are used to blocking." Al Quie, a longtime, deal-cutting member of the Education and Labor Committee, agreed that Republicans had "become too cautious," and Ed Derwinski of Illinois predicted that without a "Democratic president who stubs his toe," Republicans could not win control of the House. Freshman Republican Bill Gradison shared the sense of futility. "We know when the trains are leaving," he noted, "but the engineer doesn't care whether we're on board or not. It leaves when he's ready." Even John Anderson admitted to mounting frustration with the Democratic majority. "It becomes very inhibiting and discouraging," he noted, "when you find yourself blocked in exercising a positive legislative role."[70]

Frustrated with their seemingly permanent status in the minority and irritated by the suspicion radiating from their own conservative colleagues, many Republican Class members looked for career paths outside the House. Not even through his first term, Pressler determined to seek an open Senate seat in 1978. Indeed, within their first few terms, other Republicans from the Class including Fenwick, Grassley, Bob Kasten, and David Emery launched Senate campaigns hoping to find a more welcome environment and enjoy more impact.[71] Gary Myers, frustrated and feeling unappreciated, simply quit after his second term, returning to his job at the steel plant. The moderates' leader, John Anderson, continued to face conservative challenges to his leadership position and even to his House seat. Challenged in the next Republican primary by a fundamentalist television minister who won support from conservatives, Anderson ironically survived only because of crossover support from Democrats. Shortly after the new Congress took office, John Birch Society member John Rousselot nearly defeated him for conference chairman. Anderson resigned as chairman in 1979 and undertook an independent race for president in 1980 against the champion of the rising conservative movement, Ronald Reagan.

The incoming Republican activists of 1978 were energized by conservative activism, and their charges against party leaders paralleled those leveled against Speaker Albert by the Democratic Class of 1974. The attacks inspired the same response as in 1975, with one critic castigating the incoming Republicans as "kind of a Red Guard of the right," a virtual echo of Mary Russell's 1975 description of Democrats as the "Red Guard of the Revolution."[72] These activist Republicans proved particularly adept at using the freedom of the floor afforded by Democrats' reforms—open rules, transparency, and nonlegislative floor speeches—in a fashion that "eroded [Democratic] party loyalty and aided the growth of the Republican Party" in districts where "folks back home . . . can now watch House debate on cable television."[73]

"We want to be activists," declared Jim Courter, who defeated 1974 Class member Helen Meyner. "None of us believes in Sam Rayburn's dictum that to get along, you have to go along." By late 1979, the parallels between the Democrats of 1974 and the rising conservative Republicans of 1978 were evident. "The current class of Republican newcomers to the House of Representatives is making a lot of noise and attracting a lot of attention," the *New York Times* observed. Just as the Class of 1974 had been labeled the Watergate Babies, this new crop of Republicans might be known as "Proposition 13 babies [who] rode into office on the same antigovernment, pro-austerity sentiment that fueled that [1974] revolt."[74]

The Republican reformers of 1978 shared none of the desire for collaboration with Democrats that characterized many in the Class Republicans of 1974. Of the 25 new GOP freshmen in 1978, only one—Charles Dougherty of Pennsylvania—regularly voted with the Democratic majority, and his career lasted only four years before he was ousted by a Democrat. More common were the sympathies of Tom Tauke, who defeated Class member Mike Blouin with a very 1974-like promise of "shaking things up."

"Many of these newcomers are convinced," reported the *New York Times*, "that they can convert such sentiment into a Republican majority in the House," an implausible prediction just four years earlier. The Republicans of 1978, not unlike Democrats four years earlier, believed the obstacles to achieving their goals lay within their own party, not simply with the opposition, and they castigated GOP leaders as fatalistic about remaining a permanent minority, which rendered them willing to compromise with Democrats to secure their limited share of largesse, instead of girding for battle. "I guess that's inevitable when you've been in the minority for years and years," Courter said unsympathetically.

Little noticed in the postmortem of the 1976 election was the outcome in one of the evolving southern districts, Georgia's 6th, where veteran Democrat John J. Flynt, who had rarely faced any challenge, had eked out his second victory—by just 2,000 votes—against a little-known college professor. Republicans had added thousands of conservative suburbanites, many of them recent arrivals from northern cities, to the district, lifting hopes of beating Flynt, and were determined to try again. In 1978, Flynt decided not to tempt fate and retired. The two-time Republican challenger, a onetime moderate who had moved steadily to the right, assimilating the conservatives' prescription for confronting Democrats, and determined to challenge not only Democrats but his own party's somnambulant leadership as well, won his seat in Congress. His name was Newt Gingrich.

9 REVOLUTION OR SKIRMISH?

This was a real reform Congress.—Rep. Abner Mikva (D-IL)

The grandiose plans never got anywhere.—Rep. Jerry Ambro (D-NY)

Bullshit . . . They were very important changes—decentralizing power in the House, democratizing the House.—Rep. Tim Wirth (D-CO)

early a half century after the election of the Class of 1974, the breadth, success, and implications of its impact on the 94th Congress and American politics remain uncertain and confused. Most frequently, historians have highlighted the removal of the three chairmen—Edward Hébert, Bob Poage, and Wright Patman—as the signature moment of the 94th Congress while exaggerating the Class's overall assault on the seniority system.[1] The actual record of the 94th Congress, and the Class, was more complex.

There was no shortage of contemporary criticism of the new House or its recent arrivals. President Ford, in constant battle with the young reformers over Vietnam, deficits, vetoes, and more, called the 94th "the most unproductive Congress" he had ever seen, and an aide, Jerry Jones, decried it as "an unproductive, lurching mechanism."[2] But such hyperbolic interpretations have misconstrued the record of the Class and the 94th Congress, embellishing a stereotype of its members and distorting their actions while minimizing achievements that had far-reaching implications for the Congress and American politics. As this account has already chronicled, Class members were less the inciters than the co-implementers of changes developed and promoted for years before the election of 1974. "It was a media myth that we fomented the sudden change in procedures," Phil Sharp acknowledged. "We provided the votes in the final step. [Others] plowed the land, and we helped harvest the crop."[3]

Certainly, the House was "in the midst of a historic transition between old and new ways of legislating" that were "virtually unrecognizable" compared to those of the House of the 1950s or 1960s. The internal reforms had shaken up but not completely dislodged the existing power centers and given vast new autonomy to the caucus, junior members, subcommittees, and others who had been previously excluded from much of the decision making, including the minority. Certainly the election of a number of less politically experienced, idealistic, combative members in the Class demanded that attention be paid to a "new breed of Members" who were less willing to tolerate the conservative domination and sluggish nature of the legislative process.[4]

Given the size and diversity of the Class—which itself should caution against stereotyping—it is not surprising that even its own members voiced conflicting opinions about the record of the 94th Congress. Abner Mikva, a veteran of earlier Congresses where the reform initiatives had been stymied, had no qualms about characterizing the work of the 94th. "This was a real reform Congress," Mikva declared. Most Class members shared the unbridled assessment of Tim Wirth, who dismissed criticism of the Class as having minimal impact. "Bullshit," he declared. "They were very important changes—decentralizing power in the House, democratizing the House."

The harsh evaluations of the 94th Congress were attributable, at least in part, to the unrealistically high expectations created by the wave election that had sent dozens of new faces to Washington. With Democrats enjoying seemingly veto-proof majorities in both the House and Senate, it was broadly—but naïvely—anticipated that the 94th Congress would have the muscle to assert legislative equity with a severely weakened presidency. But such an expectation overlooked harsh realities and real challenges that constrained the reformers. As Fred Wertheimer of Common Cause once declared, "There never was a veto-proof Congress. Just Congress with majority of 'national Democrats.' "[5]

Despite the infusion of 76 freshmen Democrats and the removal of three senior chairs, substantial power remained with the bipartisan Conservative Coalition. This mix of Republicans and largely southern Democrats retained substantial power on the House floor, especially in sustaining Ford's vetoes, which required the low barrier of only one-third of those voting. Moreover, both the Class and the House faced the considerable challenges of crafting legislative solutions to extraordinarily complex issues—the energy crisis, the debt, tax reform—in a volatile political atmosphere in which an unelected president faced a serious challenge within his own party and many Class members themselves faced aggressive electoral challenges from Republicans seeking to recapture dozens of seats unexpectedly lost in 1974.

Legislative Record of the 94th Congress

The legislative achievements of the 94th Congress have been inaccurately minimized by the contemporary press and by historians. While falling far short of being "an overall policy on energy," the 1975 energy law elevated the issue of conservation, rather than simply expanded production, as a key component of a national energy policy, including mandates for improved appliance efficiency and the imposition of fleet mileage standards. Considering the political turmoil in the nation resulting from the abruptness with which the energy crisis had hit the world, the complexity of energy policies, and the many crosscurrents that ran through the House involving regional, economic, regulatory and political sensitivities, it was impressive that the Congress was able to fashion the legislation it did. It was unrealistic to expect that Congress could achieve greater consensus on such an intricate policy in the midst of a weak economy and broad political uncertainty. Indeed, the enormity of the challenge faced by the 94th is reflected in the fact that numerous issues from 1975, like tougher mileage standards and increased gas taxes, remained highly controversial into the twenty-first century.

Criticism of the 94th also overlooked the ability of the expanded Democratic Caucus to break long-standing legislative logjams on legislation that did not attract a veto. Congress passed the first major revision to the copyright law in 67 years, rewrote trade laws for the first time in 40 years, and pared back the oil depletion allowance that had resisted reform for decades. Congress also enacted innovative environmental and consumer protection laws addressing the regulation of solid chemical waste and price fixing on consumer products, as well as a mandate that states provide all children an appropriate public education regardless of their disabilities. The "trial run" of the new Budget Act proceeded "with a degree of efficiency remarkable for a body which has so many new members," despite opposition from Conservative Coalition members who recoiled at the $74.1 billion deficit and liberals who favored more countercyclical spending to ameliorate the recession.[6] Perhaps most satisfying for members of the Class, Congress used its power of the purse to force an end to the wars in Southeast Asia, concluding nearly a decade of bitter domestic division and costly combat.

As the 1976 election neared, Congress worked at a "frantic pace" to complete its legislative business. Despite obstinate opposition initially from Ford, Congress provided vital assistance to New York City during its financial crisis. The Government in the Sunshine Act, an early "transparency" law that built on the earlier reforms that opened committee deliberations to public scrutiny, also became law. So, too, did changes to tax laws that included an early version of the Earned Income Tax Credit to boost the income of low-wage workers.

Unquestionably, the legislative record was uneven, and many of the highest legislative priorities of Class members—clean air improvement, health care, and a toughening of the campaign finance law—remained unaddressed as the session wound down. Reformers both inside and outside the House, including Common Cause, which had heavily promoted the Class, blamed both parties for blocking action on these policy initiatives. The press joined in as well, subjecting the 94th Congress and the Class to withering criticism that has long colored the historical portrayal of its actual record.

Critics Voice Disappointment in Reformers

In particular, critics focused on the inability of Congress to design a comprehensive national energy policy. More than two years had elapsed since the Arab embargo and the sharp spike in oil prices, the *New York Times* disapprovingly observed, but "the country still has no overall policy on energy or even a general philosophy of how the difficulties should be remedied."[7] The *Washington Post*'s David Broder targeted the freshmen, who were "insecure about their political futures" and lacked the courage to join Ford in telling their constituents that oil prices would have to rise through decontrol and higher taxes at the pump.[8] "The big on paper Democratic majority disappears when an issue, such as energy, pits one region against another, divides producer and consumer states, and splinters further among oil, gas, coal, hydroelectric and nuclear power advocates," Broder observed.[9] Even Class member Les AuCoin dismissed the new Energy Conservation and Development Act as an "empty bag."

But the critiques went deeper than energy and began less than six months after the new House had taken office. Broder, an influential columnist, in particular had quickly soured on the Class. "No one can lead men and women who refuse to be led," he wrote, targeting for criticism the freshmen who "have been unwilling to follow the example of senior and more politically secure members." He castigated the Class as "so insecure about their political futures that they cannot see beyond any issue in terms that reach beyond the next election." Likely in response to their opposition to raising taxes to discourage energy consumption, he criticized them for hesitating to cast controversial votes that "more politically secure members" were prepared take.[10] The two to one Democratic House often appeared "to be losing at every turn to President Ford or, even worse, . . . to itself," another commentator noted.[11] "Rarely has a party in Congress promised so much and accomplished so little," the *New York Times'* Tom Wicker scolded, noting the more senior Democrats and their leaders were "bewildered by the freshmen, [found] them politically naive and accuse[d] them of seeking instant solutions to complex problems."[12] After a promising start, the *Post* noted, "Nine months later, it has all turned to ashes. Democratic programs have gone down to cinders under successful presidential vetoes."[13]

Class members who had been heralded as future leaders, like Tim Wirth, were castigated for suggesting reforms like a per diem payment of $100 for members (a common practice in state legislatures, where salaries were considerably lower than in Congress) or a "scheme" to make every fourth week a "recess" to permit members to return to their districts.[14] "Republicans, Democratic centrists and traditionalists of all stripes," as well as commentators and cartoonists, lambasted the seemingly hapless Democrats "clumsy oaf[s] who had the foolish presumptuousness to think that [they] could govern."[15] Congress, one observer wrote, had "lapsed into its traditional pattern of spasmodic productivity, rampant inefficiency, [and] Hydra-headed parochialism."[16] The freshmen bore special responsibility for having failed "to make this 94th Congress something different from its predecessors and more worthy of public esteem," wrote Broder. The record of the new Congress, he concluded, was "a cop out" and a "long way from the brave rhetoric of last winter" about "greedy oil companies" and promises of rollbacks in oil costs.

But others painted a more sympathetic portrait of a Congress that clearly was in transition. *Congressional Quarterly* concluded that, on balance, the record of the 94th Congress was "respectable," although it bore "only slight resemblance to its Democratic leaders' ambitious legislative blueprint."[17] In many cases, the critiques were based on comparisons to the wildly inflated expectations raised by the analysts themselves, not promises made by the Class members or by leaders who had far a more realistic perspective on what might be achieved. House Majority Whip John McFall, far from a leading reformer, rejected the dire analysis. "The record clearly shows," he declared, "that this has been an effective, responsible, 'do-much' Congress."[18] Nor did numerous freshmen, including Tim Wirth, apologize for their positions against removing price controls on energy, a step that could cost recession-ravaged consumers more than $12 billion over the following year.[19]

Dick Conlon, who as staff director of the Democratic Study Group was one of the chief architects of the reforms, agreed the Class's first Congress was largely a success. Despite the "press reports of ineptitude and internal dissention, Presidential charges of do-nothingism, and polls showing public dissatisfaction at an all-time high," Conlon argued that the record was impressive on many fronts. And while the Conservative Coalition still frustrated the ability of the majority to overcome Ford vetoes, the override battles had "reawakened [Congress] to a new appreciation of its Constitutional powers and role."[20]

Vetoes Limited Achievements of the 94th

Indeed, a major factor that prevented the 94th from achieving greater success was the heavy use of the veto by President Ford, a new executive positioning himself for a 1976 campaign and anxious to confront a heavily Democratic Congress. Although many observers anticipated that the large Democratic majorities would allow the Democratic Congress to enact virtually any legislation it favored, such predictions were fanciful at best. Indeed, most bills passed with less than veto-proof margins because of conservative Democratic opposition, and the bipartisan Conservative Coalition remained so entrenched on the floor that, in many cases, it was futile to even bring a vetoed bill up for an override vote.

As a result, legislation governing strip mine regulation and allowing freer construction site picketing failed when conservatives in both parties united to sustain Ford vetoes. Even so, as the second session wore on, the success rate at overturning Ford's many vetoes improved markedly, often due to the overwhelming unity of the Class, which banded together to oppose Ford's efforts to slash its favored domestic programs.[21]

While many in the White House expressed surprise at Ford's effectiveness given his weak claim to the presidency and the huge Democratic congressional majorities, in fact, Ford prevailed on only 61 percent of the votes on which he had taken a position in 1975, the second-weakest record for a president in his second year since the early 1950s.[22] The House's record of challenging vetoes improved in the second session, and overall, despite the anger at so many vetoes being upheld, the 94th Congress had a strong record on the proportion of vetoes overturned. This improved success cheered Democrats. When, in August 1976, only seven Democrats (all senior conservatives) voted to sustain Ford's veto of a health services bill that included popular family planning programs, Pennsylvania Democrat William Moorhead exulted, "Well, *now* we have a veto-proof Congress!"[23]

Class members were clearly pleased at their role in passing legislation and the procedural changes that enabled them to play a significant role in the debate. "The legacy of the 94th [class] is that the system can be changed," observed Bill Hughes. "The process can be made to work for the people who sent [us] to Washington. [We] sought election to Congress to legislate—to make a difference in the lives of people—to make our country stronger."[24] "We [freshmen] produced the majorities," Andy Maguire noted. "It was an amazing accomplishment."[25] There was, South Carolina freshman Ken Holland said, a "conscious rejection of [the] 'get along go along'" philosophy that had marginalized earlier groups of freshmen.[26] A review of the role of freshmen in key floor activity during the 94th Congress confirmed a marked increased over freshmen in earlier Congresses in such areas as floor managing a bill, offering floor amendments, offering and winning amendments in subcommittee and full committee, and service on conference committees.[27] Bob Krueger, despite his losses in the deregulation battles, nevertheless marveled that, because of the rules changes, "it's been easier to take an active role here as a freshman congressman than it was the young professor in academic life."[28] In their first term, more than a third of the Class members managed a major bill or amendment on the floor, a dramatic change from a decade earlier. Virtually all Class members offered floor amendments (compared to just 12 percent of those entering in 1965), and they were victorious two-thirds of the time. In addition, 70 percent of Class members served on House-Senate conference committees where the respective chamber's bills were reconciled into a single, identical package.[29]

Accomplishments aside, many Class members remained frustrated that the House moved too slowly and remained in the grip of special interests and parochialism. Class members blamed Speaker Carl Albert for failing to convince wayward Democrats to embrace priority issues like national health insurance, strip mining reform, and the Humphrey-Hawkins jobs creation bill. Albert "did not even try to avail himself of his new powers," one account noted, because he remained largely deferential to the chairs and was unwilling to compel his members to cast risky votes on legislation that faced an unlikely path to enactment. "Any bill the Senate is not going to pass," the Speaker declared, "I don't want to see brought up here, no matter how strongly I am for it."[30] The leadership "had broken faith" with the Class of 1974, charged Phil Sharp, annoyed that Albert and others seemed incapable of enforcing the discipline "that any corporation or any well-run University or any well-run executive agency would."[31] Far from unfairly chastising the leaders with their demands for tighter scheduling and greater party discipline, Norm Mineta explained, the freshmen were trying "to make the leadership more assertive."

Others advised that not all Class members shared the liberals' irritation with the leadership. "The ones who are happy the way things are, are not aggressive in saying so," John Jenrette explained. The South Carolina freshman sympathized with the need of conservatives, even chairmen, to reflect district opinions that conflicted with the liberal caucus majority, and noted that his own duties as the only freshman in the whip organization were "causing problems in his conservative district." Similarly, Glenn English pushed back against criticism of the leaders, expressing confidence they were doing "as fine as job as you could."[32]

In fact, however, the freshmen were being inconsistent. Class members insisted on using the caucus to impose party positions on unwilling caucus members and expected the leaders to enforce the will of the majority. At the same time, the Class members chafed when leadership pushed them to accept strategic decisions needed to manage the House. The conflict between looser rules that enabled broader participation and the need for a strong leadership to effectuate policy and timing decisions illustrated the conundrum facing the leaders. After watching one "chaotic and confused debate," AuCoin confessed to a senior member that he was losing his confidence in his "great notions of congressional government" and was even becoming sympathetic to "a strong Presidency." Lud Ashley, a 20-year veteran, exploded in laughter, telling the freshman he was "learning quickly" that Congress was never designed to be "efficient."[33]

Class Votes Demonstrate Cohesion

Contrary to the argument that Class members were difficult to discipline and unrealistic purists on matter of legislation, the freshmen demonstrated cohesiveness in their support for party positions. At the outset, Dick Conlon argued, the Class performed as a "cohesive bloc," with nearly unanimous support for the reforms that emboldened the caucus and elevated the liberal Phil Burton to chair it. Despite regional, ideological, and stylistic differences, members of the Class continued to display a "remarkably consistent [and] unusual cohesiveness" throughout much of their first term.[34] Overall, Class members voted more reliably in support of Democratic positions—72 percent—than did more senior party members (64 percent). Outside the South, the Democratic freshmen scored high levels of party unity, not only those representing safe districts like Jim Oberstar (94 percent loyalty), Mineta (93 percent), and Stephen Solarz (92 percent), but also many from marginal districts like Paul Tsongas (90 percent), Helen Meyner (89 percent), Herb Harris (89 percent), and John Krebs (82 percent).

Class members with the most conservative voting records including Jack Hightower (87 percent), Larry McDonald (86 percent), Marilyn Lloyd (84 percent), and the former class president, Carroll Hubbard (83 percent), as well as Oklahoman Glenn English (88 percent), all represented southern districts with strong conservative (if not yet Republican) bases. Only one western Democrat, Jim Santini of Nevada, who later in his career would become a Republican, voted with the Conservative Coalition more than half the time.[35] Yet virtually all of these southern members supported the internal House reform, even though the changes blunted their own region's influence by curtailing the power of senior chairs.

Indeed, a 1976 report stated that the southern Democratic Class members were more likely than their non-freshmen regional colleagues to support party positions (63 percent versus 53 percent) and more likely to oppose Conservative Coalition positions (37 percent versus 25 percent), although, as the 1976 election drew nearer, Class support for coalition positions increased.[36] Not only did urban southerners like Harold Ford, Herb Harris, and Joe Fisher cast more progressive votes than their rural southern colleagues did, but so did Jenrette and Holland of South Carolina, who were cited as "among the most liberal Democrats in the Class."[37] "I felt no great problem in voting more conservatively on labor issues and military spending," recalled Jenrette, "and with the progressives on social and economic issues" like the Equal Rights Amendment.[38] To help offset their liberal votes, the moderate southerners catered assiduously to district interests like the textile industry, the military, and tobacco growers. The marked progressiveness of many of these southern freshmen led at least one analyst to speculate that "the sectional division between northerners and southerners within the Democratic party may be reduced in the years ahead, assuming a significant number of the freshmen are re-elected in 1976 and thereafter."[39]

The unity of the Class members and rise in the number of liberal members led to a slight reduction in support for White House positions from the prior two-year period, from 41 percent to 36 percent, while opposition to administration positions rose from 45 percent to 57 percent. Several southern Class members who represented urban districts—Herb Harris, Joe Fisher, and Harold Ford—were among the most frequent Ford opponents, at levels comparable to northern Democrats and more than double the average of all southern Democrats. Democrats from swing districts, including Norm D'Amours, Bill Hughes, and Meyner were also among those most frequently opposing Ford—more than 76 percent of the time.[40] Many of these Democrats from traditional Republican districts were also among the strongest opponents of the Conservative Coalition and seemed unconcerned about the political ramifications of breaking decisively with their predecessors' records. Maguire, who represented a district that had previously elected Republicans for more than a half century, asserted, "The political attitudes of my district changed over the years, and I think I reflect them now." Gladys Spellman of Maryland, and Fisher and Harris of Virginia, also consistently ranked as among the members of the House with the most liberal votes, although they had replaced conservative Republicans.

While the Conservative Coalition was far from defeated in the 94th Congress, the loss of reliable southern votes reduced its successes in the 94th Congress, helping to create an impression that a conservative resurgence was merely wishful thinking by Republican strategists. In 1975, the coalition was successful on just 52 percent of the key votes, 15 percentage points below its 1974 success rate and its lowest level since 1966, and that rate rose only slightly to 58 percent in 1976.[41] Because of the nature of some of those votes, particularly around cultural and religious issues like abortion, the coalition was able to win support from some usually reliable liberal and moderate Class members like Oberstar, Sharp, and Berkley Bedell as well as southerners like Krueger, Elliott Levitas, Butler Derrick, and Holland.[42]

However divided the Class members were on policy questions, they demonstrated discipline in addressing the need for reform. Republican or Democratic, freshmen had little invested in a system that squelched the views of all but the senior-most majority members. Regardless of ideology, Class members agreed with the reform objectives that enabled them to participate in committee and floor activities. "The changes are really revolutionary," concluded Mo Udall of Arizona. "This House bears little resemblance in its basic power structure to what it was 10 years ago."[43] The *Washington Post* acknowledged, "A revolution has occurred," largely because "the seniority system as the rigid, inviolable operating framework of the House has been destroyed."[44]

Of course, the seniority system was not "destroyed," and a "revolution" had not occurred, but very significant changes had taken place because reformers checked the autocratic power of the chairmen and also served notice the Congress would not remain the "sapless branch" described by Sen. Joseph Clark. "There's an insistence that we're a co-equal branch, and we want to be consulted," said Udall, even with a new, incoming Democratic president. The sentiment was not so much anti-White House, he cautioned, as "pro-legislative power and pro–checks and balances."

As important as the deposing of the three chairmen was, there were far more extensive changes in the leadership of committees during the 94th Congress. Wilbur Mills had fallen even before the replacement of the other three southerners, producing a new Ways and Means chairman from Oregon. Then, midway through 1976, the irascible Wayne Hays became embroiled in a tawdry scandal involving a mistress on his official payroll that forced him to vacate his powerful House Administration position and soon to resign from Congress. In addition, five additional chairmen chose to retire at the end of the 94th Congress, perhaps fearful of the next round of elections or resentful of their seeming loss in status. As a result, by January 1977, fully half of the House's standing committees had installed new chairmen during the preceding two years, an unprecedented infusion of new leadership.[45]

Class Members Consider Their Legacy

Class members held mixed opinions about the significance of the Class itself. Tim Wirth spoke for many when he contradicted Broder's charge that the freshmen had "settled comfortably into the grooves of the old politics." Refuting allegations that "the so-called revolt had been a failure," Wirth declared his colleagues had helped achieve "one of those watershed moment of history, . . . a moment of ideological realignment." Wirth believed that the new transparency rules, which he termed "the politics of sunshine," would spell the end of "the days of the lavish reception and the campaign contribution" and the dawning of a less partisan political environment. Speaking like the technocrat he would become, Wirth envisioned a new information age that would replace ideology with pragmatic problem solving, ending the "triangular relationship [that] some might call a *ménage a trois* among the interest groups and the Executive and Legislative branches of government . . . [that] has thrived on privacy and secrecy."[46] Wirth was not alone in his expectation that the reforms would produce a more open and less polarized congressional environment. Bob Krueger, the Texas English professor, asserted, "People are too complex and multidimensional to be put along a liberal conservative continuum."[47] But the predictions of a post-ideological, technocratic, pragmatic politics proved fanciful. Not far under the surface, the prospects for reduced partisanship were rapidly diminishing rather than improving.

One facet of the 94th Congress that did not diminish was the sense of being a member of the Class, which profoundly affected virtually all its members, creating a personal connection that endured over time. "It was a great class," Steve Neal remembered. "Really good guys. Honest. Not beholden to special interests, [trying to] do what is good for whole country. That's what motivated nearly the whole class." The intense personal relationships, Matt McHugh agreed, persisted despite disagreements on policy matters. In addition to their "common agenda at the outset," he noted, we "developed personal relationships that carried on . . . that lasted longer than most. Developing those human relations was important in making Congress work." Four decades later, Bill Hughes agreed, "We wanted to make a difference in our districts and for our country. While we did not always agree on every issue, there was a clear understanding that the willingness to listen and respect other points of view was important to success; that compromise was essential. Our respectful interaction as a group that wanted to make a difference . . . led to the bonding and sense of identity that is with us to this day."[48]

What did inevitably dissipate was the notion of being a distinct subgroup within the House. Maguire dismissed "the childish, rah-rah, nostalgia, fantasizing notions" that had been created about the Class but sentimentally recalled, "Without question, we . . . shared an identity and we knew it." The freshmen believed it was advantageous to sustain the sense of being a Class as they adapted to their new environment. They felt the need to "work harder to maintain their identity because of the institutional pressure of the House," Ken Holland of South Carolina said. "We felt the system was operating to fragment and diffuse the new members group. We had to put on a little more effort into staying together."[49] Paul Tsongas agreed it was necessary to "resist integration into the House for the time being . . . You have to countervail pressures to become part of the system. There's a danger that we'll forget why we were elected."[50]

Those with longer experience in legislative settings seemed less interested in maintaining a separate Class identity, likely because they recognized the need for building collaboration among a broader membership than one based on common electoral experience. Paul Simon, an experienced politician with an eye to higher office, applauded the New Members Caucus for helping helped freshmen acclimate to Capitol Hill but declared that he did not "want to be identified as a freshman; I want to be identified with one issue or another."[51] Les AuCoin, a former leader in the Oregon legislature, similarly emphasized that "integration into the House" was his top priority, rather than maintaining an exclusive freshman organization or even using the caucus to enforce party positions. "It's more important for freshmen to learn as much through their committees and rise through the ranks," he advised, rather than devise unofficial mechanisms like freshman task forces.

Tensions within the Class

Early in the Congress, senior Republican Barber Conable of New York had expressed skepticism that the Class's "reformist sentiment will hold Democrats together once they start dealing with economic complexities," and few Class members were surprised when the early cohesion on reform dissipated.[52] "I always thought we would be split up when we got into our committees and begin working on separate areas of legislation," Maguire acknowledged. "We were never a monolith. [We reflected] different geographical areas and a wide spectrum of ideology."[53] Dave Evans agreed. "Anybody who thought the freshmen would be doing anything together beyond the first 6 months was mistaken," he said, and Dick Ottinger, a Class president, agreed the idea of a distinct "class was a short term state of mind."

Tensions arose within the Class over concerns that some were focused excessively on self-promotion and by perceptions that liberals were insufficiently sympathetic to the political constraints of their colleagues in marginal seats. "There were so many hot dogs in that class," Tom Harkin laughingly recalled. A few of the Class "wanted to elevate their importance, [to] stand out," said Elliott Levitas, which affected others who "resented a few trying to speak for the whole class." As a result, he noted, a "backlash set in against the more militant leaders" who acted as though they had been designated as spokespeople for all Class members.[54] Bill Hughes spoke for a number of freshmen in disapproving of such self-promotion, which implied that all Class members shared a point of view on policy matters, while Hughes considered himself "more moderate in my views on many issues than many in the class."

Decades later, after his voting record and personal relationships had solidified his ties to the liberal faction in the caucus, Marty Russo still seethed over his ill treatment by some progressives who questioned his votes on issues like hospital cost containment and regulation of funeral homes. A junior member of Judiciary, Russo was skeptical in February 1976 when fellow subcommittee members insisted he support an investigation to assess whether President Ford had lied to Congress about having made a deal to grant Nixon a pardon in return for resigning the presidency. "All hell is breaking loose down here," a staff person excitedly told Russo, summoning him to the subcommittee. "Oh shit," Russo thought, realizing he would not be called unless he represented the tie-breaking vote. "Here I am a freshman and I have to decide whether to impeach the President? My heart was thumping!" Arriving at the meeting, a senior member excitedly whispered, "This is how we can take down Jerry Ford and win presidency in '76!" As Democrats swarmed over the freshman, Henry Hyde facetiously urged them to "leave my dear friend from Illinois alone." Russo, a former prosecutor, had carefully reviewed the transcript of Ford's testimony and voted no.[55] Russo recalled, "My liberal buddies wanted to kill me." One senior Democrat seethed, "We ought to kick you out of the caucus!"[56]

But Russo recalled he had never promised to be a partisan warrior or even a reformer. "I didn't go to Congress with the intention of bumping off some chairmen," Russo explained. He was surprised to find himself enmeshed in changing rules and disciplining chairman he had never met at the direction of senior members he neither knew nor trusted. "These guys had this all arranged!" he recalled thinking as he listened to one of the liberals spin out a strategy for the Class. When Wirth announced he was leaving one freshman meeting to "go out there [and] talk to the press," Russo rebuked the charismatic Coloradan. "Who the hell do you think *you* are?" he queried Wirth. "Who told you to be *my* spokesman? When you go out there and say 'the Class,' then I get a call from the press in my district saying, 'Do I agree?' So when you go out there, you say what you want to say, but say it's on behalf of Tim Wirth."

Sharp also worried that several of the liberals were "pushing the envelope" in trying to set the Class's agenda on policy questions where differences of opinion existed. Anxious to demonstrate that he was not part of the liberal cabal growing in the caucus, Krueger inaccurately assured his constituents that despite what they heard from the so-called leaders, "most of the new members come from basically conservative districts, like ours, and I doubt those members campaigned in favored of big new spending programs. Further I doubt that they will vote for such programs."[57] He was wrong on both counts.

Occasionally, their colleagues' aggressive behavior shocked some in the Class. Mike Blouin recalled a White House breakfast he attended along with several Class colleagues who lacked his experience in a small state legislature, where diplomacy and conciliation were prized. After Class colleagues launched a sharp attack on President Ford during a meeting in the White House, Blouin expressed astonishment at his colleagues' confrontational style. "My God," he recollected thinking, "*that's* not the way you play this thing . . . in his own home. Try to work together."[58]

Such divisions on policy and personal style did not, however, dissuade most Class members from supporting each other when possible. Carroll Hubbard, despite being more conservative than many Class colleagues, recalled voting for an amendment on the floor if he discovered that a Class member was the author, even if he wasn't completely sympathetic to the proposal. Harkin agreed, noting, "Unless there was a real problem in the district, we tended to be supportive of each other's amendments." Of course, Class collegiality did not always determine how they voted when their constituencies were impacted. A proposal by Joe Fisher to raise the gasoline tax to encourage energy conservation was vigorously opposed by northeasterners including Maguire, Toby Moffett, and Jerry Ambro, who feared the impact on consumers in their energy-consumptive districts. And some Class members' proposals drew opposition on philosophical grounds, as when Maguire and Bill Brodhead, on the grounds of separation of powers, strongly opposed Levitas's signature initiative to check the powers of bureaucrats who had "evolved into a fourth, non-constitutional branch of government."[59] Class members would also rely on the expertise of fellow Class members more than advice from other members regardless of the colleague's ideology. On military issues, for example, the liberal Jerry Patterson would solicit the advice of his conservative colleague Jim Lloyd, a retired military pilot whom Patterson regarded as "a solid guy."[60]

Freshmen Legislative Achievements

By the end of their first term, given their expanded opportunities on subcommittees to focus on specific issues, many Class members had already demonstrated significant legislative achievements, winning recognition from senior members and from advocacy groups. In addition to the formal committee structures, they gained expertise with the formation of informal caucuses and study groups, pooling staff resources, inviting outside policy experts to meet with them, and developing initiatives that frequently exasperated the formal committee leaders. "We thought we could master everything," recalled Tom Downey, who organized a group on military policy that continued to meet years after he departed the Armed Services Committee. Miller collaborated with the venerable Sen. Hubert Humphrey to expand the Supplemental Nutrition Program for Women, Infants, and Children's (WIC). Other freshmen legislative initiatives included restrictions on military aid to Indonesia (Bob Carr), allowing Congress to bar military aid to Chile (Harkin), ending US aid to Angolans battling Soviet influences (Don Bonker), imposing tighter restrictions on toxic waste (Jim Florio), tightening clean air standards (Henry Waxman), restricting federal funding for abortions (Henry Hyde), promoting consumer affairs (Moffett), South Africa and military reform (Downey), famine relief (McHugh and Floyd Fithian), Vietnam humanitarian aid (Harkin and Bob Edgar), small farmers (Rick Nolan and Oberstar), and deregulating oil and gas prices (Krueger).[61] Steve Neal won support for an amendment requiring that federal agencies prepare cost and benefit statements on proposed regulations. Hughes won approval of a hugely popular ban on the dumping of New York's sewage sludge into waters impacting his New Jersey shore district.

Class members were also appointed to special panels to bolster their standing at home and to take advantage of their expertise. When a task force was created to investigate problems in the US auto industry, Jim Blanchard chaired hearings, winning local publicity and building institutional credibility that proved valuable when a bankrupt Chrysler sought federal aid in the late 1970s. And when the Ad Hoc Select Committee on the Outer Continental Shelf was cobbled together to modernize the laws on offshore oil and gas leasing, 5 of its 13 Democratic members were freshmen.[62] Class members authored all of the environmental restrictions contained in the final OCS law, as well as those designed to pry higher royalties from distrusted oil companies that enjoyed royalty rates far lower than those permitted by other countries. The heightened profile provided by these appointments resulted in district and national recognition for Class members before they were even reelected once.

Senior Members Express Irritation

Not surprisingly, the self-assured legislating and skilled self-promotion of the Class, sometimes outside formal channels, rankled powerful senior members who dismissed the newcomers as "rambunctious radicals . . . hasty reformers, big spenders."[63] Too many of the freshmen, one senior northeasterner complained, violated the sacred Rayburn rule, choosing to "sound off on all issues without proper in-depth study." The freshmen were "in a hurry to make a record," agreed a veteran Republican from the Midwest, and they sometimes inadvertently trod on powerful feet.[64] Approached by the Foreign Affairs Officers Association to offer an amendment that would assure that more ambassadorships went to professional, career diplomats instead of to campaign contributors, Don Bonker readily agreed, believing "it seemed like the right thing to do." But Bonker's amendment drew a harsh rebuke on the floor from Wayne Hays, who chaired the Subcommittee on State Department Operations. Bonker's heart sank as Hays explained that "I fully expect some day to be named Ambassador to France, and I will be damned if this amendment will get in my way!" Bonker was stunned. "It was a rude awakening!" he later recalled, admitting he had been "naïve" to offer the amendment.

Senior members were especially perturbed that the Class's obsession with the Vietnam nightmare had left them instinctive "opponents of a strong defense establishment" at a time when heavy military spending was still required.[65] Norm Mineta acknowledged that a clear polarization existed between freshman and older members who regarded the Class as "opponents of a strong defense establishment," a conflict illustrated in the consideration of a floor amendment by Berkley Bedell. Theatrically displaying a pair of pliers he had purchased at a local hardware store for $3.95, the Iowa freshman denounced the Pentagon for spending $4,200 for what appeared to be a similar tool. Both the Ford administration and the Armed Services Committee's bipartisan leadership criticized Bedell's amendment to tighten purchasing criteria and reduce sole bid contracts as a way of controlling excess costs, but the dramatization was effective and his amendment passed.

Although Tip O'Neill complained that the 1974 New Members Caucus survived for five years, in fact, the weakening of the formal organization was evident by the end of the 94th Congress. The exhausting demands of members' schedules—the frequent meetings of committees and subcommittees, delegation breakfasts and lunches, constituent demands, fundraising and district travel—cut deeply into the time most had to devote to an ad hoc institution like the NMC. "The institution began to eat us up," one recalled. By the middle of 1976, the New Members' Caucus was meeting infrequently, and its plans for freshman whip systems and task forces had been largely forgotten.

Rather than looking only to fellow freshmen—what one senior staffer called an "incestuousness" that would enhance isolation and ineffectiveness—Class members focused on building tight relationships with more senior members and committee allies. "We can't bring change all by ourselves," Mineta argued. "We have to reach out to our natural allies," particularly the other reformers in the Democratic Caucus. Recognizing that many senior members suspected many of the self-assured freshmen would prove to be one-term wonders—a flash in the pan tossed out by voters in 1976—Mineta advised, "If we come back in large numbers, then we will be taken seriously."[66]

Assessing the 94th

On balance, then, it seems unwarranted to rate the 94th Congress as "notably unproductive" for having passed "no monumental laws," as did the

New York Times upon its recessing for the 1976 election. Congress and Ford "slugged it out like two heavyweights," the *Times* concluded, before ending in "stalemate."[67] While it is true that several complex issues were not resolved and others remained unaddressed, the lack of progress properly belongs to a multiplicity of factors including the complexity of the issues, the continuing power of the Conservative Coalition, the aggressive use of the veto, and the natural political divisions that existed in a group of more than 70 members of Congress.

Nor is it accurate to assert that the Class members' self-righteousness prevented them from acting as loyal party members. In fact, Class members were "more liberal and more loyal to their party" than were other House Democrats, voting with their majority and against the majority of Republicans 72 percent of the time compared to 64 percent for non-freshmen.[68] Southern Class members were more loyal to the party position (51 percent) than their non-freshman southern colleagues (44 percent), although they did oppose the party significantly more frequently than did their non-southern Class members. Class members tracked their non-freshmen regional colleagues almost exactly in their support for the Conservative Coalition on floor votes, demonstrating recognition by Class members of what was needed to survive politically on votes scored by conservative organizations.

Any accurate evaluation of the Class and the 94th Congress must look beyond the number of bills passed or defeated, or vetoes sustained or overridden, or other formal measures of legislative productivity. Special attention must be given to the extensive reforms effectuated by the Democratic Caucus in late 1974 and early 1975 that altered the structure and operations of the House. Far beyond the well-known removal of three aged and autocratic chairmen, the revisions in subcommittee selection and chairmanships, the expanded participatory rights of less senior members, the autonomy that allowed issues long submerged by chairmen and special interests to percolate into the formal legislative process, the reassertion of congressional authority through aggressive oversight and veto overrides—all these mark the 94th as the culmination of a decade of effort by reformist forces to democratize and energize the House. Long-standing goals of the growing liberal faction—revision of the oil depletion allowance, the abolition of the hated Internal Security (formerly Un-American Activities) Committee, and, particularly, the end to US involvement in the Vietnam War—marked a historic shifting of power within the majority caucus that would have significant implications in policy and party realignment in the decades ahead.

Still, the inescapability of compromise and the frustrations at not achieving more sweeping policy goals took a toll, leading some to question whether the dramatic shift in American politics described by Wirth and others had really occurred at all. Shortly after the July 1975 retreat at Airlie House, several freshmen asked Rick Nolan why he had neglected to attend. "The Class has been retreating ever since we walked in the door," replied Nolan, who, disenchanted, would voluntarily retire from the House after three terms (although he returned 32 years later in 2012, after the longest sabbatical in congressional history). "The freshman have felt more frustration than fulfillment," declared *Washington Post* writer Mary Russell. Many attributed the sense of disappointment to the "overblown expectations of the press, the public, and Members themselves, [including] especially many of the freshmen," as Dick Conlon of DSG observed.

A greater sense of achievement by the Class and Democrats in general, many concluded, would have to await the election of a Democratic president in 1976 who would not employ the veto to obstruct legislation that a Democratic Congress had approved. But, first, members would have to be reelected, something they had carefully prepared for by "vot[ing] their districts on certain issues rather than personal inclinations or party."[69] But whether members of the Class could replicate their unlikely victories of 1974 and return as more seasoned legislators remained a very uncertain prospect as they headed home for the 1976 election.

10 BEFORE YOU CAN SAVE THE WORLD, SAVE YOUR SEAT

Right now they are operating on the principle of "We've got to protect our asses."—Daniel Rapoport, *Washington Post*

My ass was on the line in the district.—Rep. Phil Sharp (D-IN)

I don't even try to defend Congress anymore. I just try to defend my *own* votes.—Unnamed freshman

I got [constituent] calls about clogged toilets, refrigerators on the street, gravel in alleys, alley repairs; it was hot and heavy.—Rep. Marty Russo (D-IL)

Two crucial questions loomed as the nation braced for the election of 1976: First, how many of the House seats won in 1974 could Democrats hope to retain, particularly the marginal southern and suburban seats they had wrenched from Republicans in the aftermath of Watergate? And, second, could the largely unknown Democratic nominee, Jimmy Carter, a former one-term governor of Georgia, defeat the accidental incumbent, Jerry Ford, an essential step in eliminating the veto threat that had prevented enactment of so many Democratic priorities throughout the 94th Congress?

Class president Jerry Ambro of New York remained confident his classmates would defy the predictions of the first-term curse. "The freshmen have been running scared," he noted. "They literally are crawling all over their districts . . . accessible and available." Dismissing projections of major setbacks, he declared, "If we lose 15, that's a lot."[1]

The early signs of constituents' mood were, once again, not encouraging for Republicans. As in early 1974, special elections suggested Republican optimism about resuming their march to the House majority might be unwarranted. In late January, James Hastings, an upstate four-term Republican indicted on corruption charges, resigned from a seat that had not been occupied by a Democrat in more than a century. The surprise victory of the Democrat, Stan Lundine, heightened Republican uncertainty about the election in the nation's bicentennial year.

Almost from the time they arrived on Capitol Hill, Class members recalled the special efforts that had gotten them elected two years earlier and planned for their first reelection effort.

- Through much of 1974, Max Baucus had trudged, with icicles hanging from his nose, across 630 miles of the state of Montana to introduce himself to voters. "I wore out as much shoe leather as I knew how," Baucus recalled upon ending his trek in the Dirty Shame Saloon in Yaak. The stunt, borrowed from "Walkin' Lawton" Chiles's 1970 Senate campaign in Florida, taught him that "listening to Western Montanans is the best way to understand and to know the district I intend to represent."[2]

- In Ohio, the crew-cut veteran state legislator Ron Mottl had won just 35 percent of the general election vote against a Republican and four independents. Mottl spent his first term in the House focused on local issues including veterans' needs, opposing school busing, and fighting Republican efforts to weaken clean air laws.

- In Washington State, Don Bonker "did not have a prayer of winning" a House seat in 1974.[3] His improvised answer to a reporter's question opposing exporting raw logs, a subject he knew nothing about, persuaded a local plywood manufacturer to promote Bonker's long-shot candidacy. "My campaign slogan was: 'I pledge to stop exporting logs and jobs,'" Bonker recalled. "It's what got me elected."

- Bow-tie- and suspender-wearing Butler Derrick paid close attention to the unraveling South Carolina textile industry. As a freshman, Derrick fought for brown lung disability benefits for textile workers, opposed a national nuclear waste dump in South Carolina, and solicited the growing black electorate. "I believe you're elected for two reasons," said Derrick, "to represent the people who elect you and [to] use your best judgment to do your best on their behalf."[4]

Baucus, Bonker, and Derrick personified the axiom subscribed to by all Class members: a close connection to their constituencies was crucial to winning and retaining a seat in the House. As they geared up to defend the seats many had improbably won, they embraced Tip O'Neill's admonition that "all politics is local." For the many marginal members whose 1974 victories were widely regarded as reversible flukes, special attention was needed in the face of the resurgent Republicanism, especially in the

South and traditionally GOP suburban districts. Members in those districts were not anxious to advertise their progressive voting records and asked the liberal Americans for Democratic Action to defer their long-standing ratings for the campaign season.[5]

Learning the Lesson of 1966

Both the freshmen and senior party leaders were well aware how, following the Democratic landslide of 1964, just 38 out of 71 freshmen members were reelected in 1966. In Republican districts, like many of those won by Class members a decade later, only 23 of 47 had survived their first reelection campaign. That purge effectively ended the Great Society legislative juggernaut and raised Republican hopes of a resurgent drive to a House majority. An additional 1976 worry for freshmen was a primary challenge from a veteran Democrat they had defeated or from a predecessor who had unsuccessfully sought another office, like Jerome Waldie, who was reportedly eyeing his former California seat now held by George Miller.

At an early caucus briefing in 1975, they were warned, like so many college freshmen, that many of them probably would not return. "Based on statistics and voting patterns," one report concluded that nearly half of the 1974 freshman class faced "a real risk of defeat." Less bleak projections estimated losses in the 15- to 30-seat range, a setback that would revitalize the Conservative Coalition and significantly weaken the liberals' hold on the caucus. One certain outcome, a Democratic source acknowledged, was that "nobody seriously thinks we will go up from 290 this time no matter what happens."

Despite their focus on reforming House operations and on sweeping policy aspirations, Class members understood the formula for their political survival. "Before you can save the world," Phil Burton cautioned them, "you have to save your seat!" Freshmen like South Carolina's Derrick took the advice to heart. "You were supposed to do bold things," his aide Marcia Hale recalled, "but you couldn't do that if you couldn't get yourself reelected."[6]

Many of those in marginal districts often expressed a Stoic view of their futures, declaring an unwillingness to squander what might prove to be a brief time in Washington. Toby Moffett even dismissed the wisdom of staying in Congress very long. "If I'm there over 10 years," he asked a high school friend, "call and remind me" why he ran.[7]

From the outset, Class members regularly spoke with each other about strengthening connections in their districts. The "Santini Series," a group of 8 to 10 marginal Democrats organized by the Nevada freshman, held discussions in the Capitol every three weeks to share reelection strategies, meetings that were "instrumental in assisting . . . most all in the group."[8] At the July 1975 Airlie House conference, Floyd Fithian recalled, Class members held "a group help-and-think-session" to discuss constituent communications, effective messaging, and "how we might help each other combat the rising tide of criticism of Congress [that] affects our re-election prospects."[9]

Only one member of the Class voluntarily chose not to seek reelection in 1976, and he had grander plans. Philip Hayes was persuaded by Indiana colleagues to launch a primary challenge against the state's four-term senator, fellow Democrat Vance Hartke, whose presence on the ticket many feared would jeopardize other Indiana Democrats, especially the other four House freshmen. Although Hayes narrowly lost the Senate primary, the concern about Hartke's dampening impact proved unfounded. While Indianapolis mayor Richard Lugar defeated Hartke in November, all five of the Indiana House seats remained in Democratic hands.

Given the large number of Class members seeking reelection, as well as the financial demands on the party from several dozen nonincumbents seeking to replace retiring members or Republicans, House freshmen understood that they would bear primary responsibility for their own reelection. "The Class of '74 freshmen were operating on the principle of, 'We've got to protect our asses,'" the *Post* reported.[10] Marty Russo recalled that he spent much of time his first term "just trying to figure out how to be a congressman [and] get reelected." One widespread technique was to continue to run as outsiders, distinguishing themselves from the institution they came to reform by emphasizing their individual service and accomplishments. "I don't even try to defend Congress anymore," one Class member noted. "I just try to defend my own votes."[11]

A mid-1975 *New York Times* analysis suggested they had reason for concern, reporting they were vulnerable to Ford's charge of being uncooperative. Only 17 of the 76 freshmen Democrats were truly safe, the report estimated.[12] It was "their recognition of this [fact that] keeps the freshman together," the analysis concluded, "even though they may differ on specific issues."[13] Republicans "could well recapture many of the House seats they had lost in the Watergate disaster of 1974," the *Washington Post* warned in mid-1975, while predicting that President Ford had "a good chance of reelection."[14] A year later, analysts predicted "modest" success for House Republicans, who seemed likely to pick up 20 to 25 of the 49 seats they had lost in 1974.[15]

Republican strategists had considerably bigger aspirations, targeting 109 Democratic incumbents. Nearly half had won with less than 55 percent of the vote, the standard definition of a vulnerable seat. Democrats agreed that of the 50 most vulnerable, 45 were first-termers, including high-profile freshmen like Andy Maguire, Tim Wirth, Tom Downey, Ab Mikva, and Bob Carr. Even before they had been sworn in, these members had been identified as "Democrats who sailed in on the Watergate tide [who] are . . . more liberal than the people who elected them."[16]

Republicans were especially confident they could defeat southerners whose votes had been more liberal than their districts appeared: Herb Harris and Joe Fisher in Virginia, Elliott Levitas in Georgia, Harold Ford in Tennessee, and Steve Neal in North Carolina.[17] Republicans noted how these freshmen often emphasized deficits and spending controls in their statements to send a conservative message to their districts. "We are beginning to see Liberal Democrats talk about fiscal responsibility and too much government in Washington," noted Steve Stockmeyer, the executive director of the National Republican Congressional Committee.[18] Indeed, rival Democratic presidential contenders Jimmy Carter and California governor Jerry Brown both advocated a reduced federal role and stricter attention to federal spending, helping to validate the conservative message.

Large Number of Retirements

Although every freshman except Hayes fought to remain in Congress, the largest number of incumbents since 1940 decided to retire or seek another office. Their departures may have resulted from a variety of causes included the growing workload and the punishing demands to stay in touch with constituents, as well as enhanced pension benefits that encouraged departures. Some complained of the "more partisan session[s] in recent years," and many may have disliked the new rules that diminished the prestige and power they had long enjoyed; some may well have resented having to endure the demands, questions, and challenges of junior colleagues who were less deferential to senior members than they had been in the past.[19] John Burton speculated that the new rules restricting the ability of those veteran members to occupy multiple subcommittee seats and chairmanships might have encouraged some retirements.

All of the Democratic retirees had begun their service prior to 1968, and five had first been elected in the 1940s. While a sizable number of seats, however, the departures did not provide many clear opportunities for Republicans, since virtually all were considered secure for Democrats. By contrast, a number of the open GOP seats were considered potential pickups for Democrats.

Of particular importance was the departure of five additional chairmen who retired and another who was defeated in a primary, providing new leadership in several additional committees.

- Thomas "Doc" Morgan of Pennsylvania, who had seen his authority as chairman of the International Relations Committee undercut by caucus resolutions on Vietnam, bowed out after 18 years as chairman and more than 30 in the House.
- James Haley, chairman of the Interior and Insular Affairs Committee, announced his retirement on June 1. The Floridian, whose frail condition had led Burton to help him evade an interview by the incoming freshmen in January 1975, was barely functioning as chairman. Most of his power already had been relegated to the subcommittees in a deal between Burton and Republican Sam Steiger in 1971.[20]
- Robert Jones of Alabama, chairman of the Public Works and Transportation Committee, retired, seemingly clearing the way for Jim Wright to assume the chairmanship.
- Joe L. Evins, chairman of the Small Business Committee, had first been elected to the House in 1946. His seat would be filled by the son of Tennessee's former Democratic senator, Al Gore Jr.
- Leonor Sullivan of Missouri, whose career in the House had begun as an assistant to her husband during his service in the House, retired as chairwoman of the Merchant Marine and Fisheries Committee after complaining of the intensified workload. Her seat was won by future Democratic leader Dick Gephardt.
- In addition, Ray Madden, the 84-year-old chairman of the Rules Committee, was easily defeated in the Democratic primary by Adam Benjamin Jr. Madden had told his Indiana colleague Dave Evans that his primary campaign would consist of "a few ads in the paper."[21] His defeat illustrated how a new generation of politicians could outmaneuver the entrenched incumbents wedded to antiquated campaign techniques.

Further departures from the Old Guard included Wilbur Mills, who, disgraced, dethroned, and possibly even detoxed, declared on March 5, "I am tired," and announced he would retire at the end of the 94th Congress. Two days later, House Dean Wright Patman died at Bethesda Naval Hospital only three days after marking his 47th year in the chamber, the fourth longest in history to that point.[22] Later in the month, the ousted Armed Services Chairman F. Edward Hébert announced his retirement. In June, the chairman of the House Administration Committee who had escaped removal by the caucus, Wayne Hays, stepped down after the disclosure that he had a girlfriend on his payroll who confessed, "I can't type, I can't file, I can't even answer the phone." Hays would only deny that Elizabeth Ray's salary was awarded "solely for sexual services." Three months later, his reputation in shambles, Hays quit the House altogether.

The exodus of such a sizable group of senior members cost the House substantial institutional memory but did not jeopardize Democratic strength. Indeed, each of these senior retirees was succeeded by a Democratic freshman in 1976. But the mass turnover produced vacancies that rippled through all House committees, allowing Class members to capture prized committee and subcommittee seats, gain seniority and even chairmanships, which enabled them to accrue institutional influence and seniority within an unusually short time.

One departure in particular had deep significance for the House and the Class. In June, 68-year-old Speaker Carl Albert, beleaguered for much of the 94th Congress, announced he would retire.[23] Albert had earlier pledged to leave before reaching his 70th birthday, but the persistent disapproval of his management style had "made life miserable" for him, one observer wrote.[24] "He'd been through a lot, and he just wore out," agreed fellow Oklahoman, Glenn English. Many Class members shared Jerry Patterson's lament that Albert was "the nicest man [but] not a strong Speaker."[25]

The freshmen had proven to be a persistent frustration for the Speaker. Initially insisting he had no intentions of retiring, he lashed back at Class critics whom he accused of having "an inferiority complex and are afraid they won't be elected again. Just take me on [and] I'll teach you how little impact you have in the House," he pledged. "And what's more, I'll teach your district how little impact you have in the House."[26] "I tried to be the leader of this group that refused to be led," Albert reflected in his autobiography, resenting the lack of credit given him for the reforms that had occurred.[27] "None of this [reform] stuff could have happened had he been an active opponent," former aide Joel Jankowsky insisted, an observation seconded by House Parliamentarian Charles Johnson, who agreed that Albert had been "smart enough to allow [reform] to occur."[28] As much as the Oklahoman wanted to appease the reformers, his responsibility to appease moderates, whose presence and votes he needed to pass legislation and preserve the Democratic majority, left him without strong sympathy among many in the Class.

Class members seemed to live by a double standard when it came to Albert, harshly critical when the Speaker could not convince conservative members to go along with the caucus majority but insisting on the right to oppose leadership requests themselves when expedient. "People . . . want leadership for the other guys," one staff person recalled, "the guys who don't agree with them. They want the leadership to get those who defect from the positions they desire, but they don't want to be told what to do."[29] Class member Don Bonker empathized with Albert's conundrum, recalling, "Only fourteen out of seventy-five freshmen backed the leadership . . . [on] the crucial 'bullet-biting' tax provisions" in the bill. In a letter to Albert, Bonker had criticized his "freshmen colleagues [who] were so adamant about party discipline and critical of those who deserted the 'party vote,'" a decision he termed "probably the greatest setback this Congress will experience. Where were the freshmen when the leadership desperately needed them on this important issue?" An appreciative Albert had instructed his staff to tell Bonker "how grateful I am for his confidence."[30]

From their earliest days in Washington, Class members had been counseled to build tight connections to their districts, utilize the benefits of incumbency, and raise money to ward off challengers. North Carolina's Charlie Rose, a Burton acolyte, counseled they would make mistakes, "but if you don't make too many of them, you will be back in 1976." "I needed to get across the point I was looking out for the people back home on bread and butter issues," said English. "That was my reality if I was going to stay in Congress very long." Phil Sharp was in fully agreement. "My ass was on the line in the district," he recalled.

Not even a month after their election, Class members received a Democratic Study Group briefing on how to exploit their incumbency: issue publicity statements (advice: keep them brief); exploit the free franking privilege to mail letters, referring to the printed facsimile of the member's signature that substituted for normal postage, including newsletters, town hall announcements, even baby care books and calendars emblazoned with their names; spend the expanded travel allowances to go home frequently; utilize emerging technologies like the new "fax" machines that transmitted documents over telephone lines, producing wet, foul-smelling copies that had to be hung in the hallways to dry; and take advantage of the reduced-price WATS long-distance telephone lines. "You are all joining a new club now," DSG chairman Tom Foley advised. "It's called the 'incumbency club.'" They exploited their subcommittee assignments to conduct oversight investigations, publicized their committee and floor activities, and demonstrated a high degree of sophistication in dealing with the press. Although freshman Les AuCoin was disappointed by the "emphasis on congressional self-interest," others were enthusiastic about exploiting the benefits of incumbency.[31] "We used the frank to a fare-thee-well," Downey recalled. "I wanted to communicate better with my constituents to win the election."[32]

Institutionalization of Oversight

The freshmen proved eager to participate in the oversight hearings that allowed them to promote themselves as relentless critics of government waste and corporate misconduct. Decades had passed since complex programs like Social Security had been thoroughly reviewed; agencies like the CIA and FBI were rarely scrutinized. Vietnam and Watergate effectively ended such passivity, and members eagerly tore into administration and private sector witnesses. More than simply creating controversy, however, these investigations provided legislators with "a golden opportunity to bring public attention to an issue which instantly made it a higher priority for Congress" such as domestic surveillance by the Central Intelligence Agency, rail safety, the oil industry's profits, the dangers of the nuclear industry, the weak economy, wasteful Pentagon spending, and abandoned toxic waste sites. The new transparency rules allowed gavel-to-gavel coverage, which elevated the profile of the Class as well as the Congress as a whole.[33]

Aggressive oversight meant Congress was "fulfilling its obligation under the Constitution to hold the president responsible," noted Henry Waxman, who would become an expert practitioner of the art.[34] Mineta endorsed the practice as well, recalling the years of his childhood in a

Japanese American relocation camp because no one in Congress had raised questions about the fairness of the internment policy. Elliott Levitas viewed oversight as "one of the most important tools Congress has. Clearly one of the messages of our class," said Levitas, was to "hold people accountable for what they did." Russo saw the hearings as letting "fresh air into our government and cut[ting] down on 'smoke-filled room' judgments."[35] Miller, who became a skilled inquisitor of Western irrigators and the nuclear power industry, noted that oversight allowed Congress "to examine existing programs of the federal government, rather than simply to extend them or create new ones."[36] Indeed, oversight allowed legislators to gain high visibility without the risks associated with casting votes on legislation. Hearings provided a veto-free way "of challenging the Imperial Presidency," in Levitas's words and, occasionally, even "ruffling establishment feathers within the Congress itself. I was a marginal member," noted Levitas, "yet I perfected a major tool of the Class: oversight."[37]

A rules change at the beginning of the 94th Congress required most committees to devote one subcommittee specifically to conduct oversight of all of the programs under its jurisdiction, and by March 1975, twice the number of committees had created oversight panels as had existed in the prior Congress. A few cautionary voices were raised about focusing so much attention on investigation as opposed to legislation. Republicans in particular were concerned the Ford administration was being eviscerated by congressional inquisitors and proposed creating task forces to "goad the Democrats" and expose Democratic malfeasance. John Anderson worried about the tendency to focus on "scandals, corruption à la Watergate, or Executive Branch hanky-panky . . . to bring headlines and turn on the TV klieg lights." Even some Democrats, like Richard Bolling, worried that a post-Watergate obsession with oversight could diminish legislating (although his reform plan from the prior year had mandated that every committee have an oversight subcommittee). Looking back, even Norm Mineta's chief of staff, Les Francis, later mused, "We created a monster in a sense."

No directive to the Class was more important than the need to cultivate close relationships with constituents, and the members proved creative and inexhaustible in doing so. Phil Burton repeated the same message he had given Dave Obey after his special election in 1969: "Go home, go home, go home."[38] English, whose Oklahoma district included 23 counties, had successfully attacked his predecessor for failing to stay in touch with voters. English scheduled frequent public meetings throughout the district, all announced in massive mailings proclaiming his presence. Veterans cautioned Class members to avoid falling prey to the charge that they had "gone Washington. Personal relationships with constituents," they were advised, "were far more important" in winning loyalty than explaining their votes.[39]

Delivering for Constituents

Class members did use the legislative process effectively to secure victories for constituents. Tip O'Neill often counseled, "All politics is local," and for all their success of ending the war in Vietnam or reforming the seniority system, members needed to demonstrate effectiveness in addressing problems unique to their own districts. Sometimes that meant behaving parochially. When a senior member told Glenn English a controversial vote was something he "need[ed] to do for the country," English brushed aside the request. "Not everybody sees it that way," he responded. "What does it mean to us and our districts?"

During the 1974 campaign, incumbent Republican Charles Sandman had claimed credit for keeping the National Aviation Facilities Experimental Center (NAFEC) in his New Jersey district. "You elect that young squirt to Congress," Sandman warned, referring to his opponent, Bill Hughes, "and you can kiss NAFEC goodbye." Once in office, Hughes forced a reversal of the decision to relocate the facility, earning valuable local support. Hughes also used his position on the Merchant Marine Committee to stop New York City from dumping sludge in waterways adjacent to the district. Nearby, New York's Jerry Ambro also fought for more stringent rules on dumping of toxic waste in Long Island Sound. Water quality was an issue as well for George Miller, who launched highly publicized investigations into federal irrigation practices that degraded his constituents' water supplies. Herb Harris promoted creation of the new Washington metro subway system that benefitted his northern Virginia constituents, and Les AuCoin authored legislation to expand federal mortgage assistance for home construction, which helped his timber-dependent Oregon district, where unemployment remained at 20 percent.[40]

Such local successes insulated Class members from allegations they were more concerned about activities in Washington than about the voters back home. When Steve Neal's opponent declared the congressman's vote for foreign aid proved that he "didn't care about people in North Carolina, and was always up in Washington," Neal countered by championing locally important issues like textiles, tobacco, and furniture. This ability to deflect criticism was what Jim Florio called "building the constituency while developing the policy."

In May, Hays's committee authorized a "constituent communication allowance" to cover the cost of two newsletters a year, each one filled with stories and photos highlighting the incumbent's achievements and "anything else 'eligible to be mailed under the frank,'" a loosely applied restriction.[41] Members sent newsletters and "polls" to gather information from constituents about their major areas of interest so that subject-specific mailings could be mailed on a regular (and publicly funded) basis. Members also sent hundreds of thousands of notices of town hall meetings that prominently displayed their photographs and names. Like other Class members, Neal sent out tens of thousands of invitations declaring he was "interested in your opinion," knowing that the mailing served mainly as an advertisement since "only one percent would show up."

Town hall meetings, at which the congressman would report on recent developments and respond to questions from constituents, were a popular way to introduce oneself to voters. In Iowa, Berkley Bedell would ask attendees to suggest topics and recommend how he should vote. Afterward, his staff would tabulate the results and send a letter to those who had been at the meeting. Like many other freshmen, Bedell also created district advisory committees of local small business leaders, veterans, farmers, teachers, and others with whom he would regularly consult. Bedell credited those relationships with insulating him from criticism when he cast unpopular votes, as when he opposed an extension of the ratification period for the Equal Rights Amendment (because he considered it unfair to alter the rules). "All hell broke loose among my Democratic friends in the district," Bedell recalled, but, thanks to the close relationships he had built, he won his next election by his typical margin.

Class members also kept in close touch with voters by opening a number of district offices where constituents could meet with staff or the representative during recesses. Dave Evans opened four offices in his Indiana district, and Martha Keys operated several in Kansas to service her 15-county district, where only one sparsely staffed outpost had previously sufficed. Another innovation was the use of "mobile offices"—

leased vans emblazoned with the officeholder's name and image—that drove through their districts, setting up shop in mall parking lots and on street corners to hear constituent complaints and to offer aid. The idea was not only used in large suburban districts, like those of Sharp and Downey, but in far-flung Western districts where it was impractical to have numerous offices. All these additional offices were made possible by increased resources provided to members' official accounts by Hays and the House Administration Committee, which also expanded each member's staff limit from 16 to 18, increased the permissible number of free trips home, and allowed members to withdraw travel expense money in cash. The windfall from Hays's benefaction relieved many of the younger cash-strapped members from having to supplement their strained office needs out of their own pockets. "In 1976, I actually discussed leaving Congress," one class member admitted, because of the financial pressures compounded by limitations on earning outside income.

The concentrated outreach effort contrasted with the behavior of their predecessors, many of whom had grown lackadaisical about responding to constituents. Russo was invited to an event by a local Republican official who complained his predecessor was "an SOB who doesn't come to a single thing I invite him to." He eyed Russo and asked, "Are you comin' or not?" When he appeared at the 2,000-person dinner, Russo was rewarded with an introduction as "someone who will stay in touch with us." Tim Lee Hall of Illinois attended a steady round of parades, fairs, town halls, and other public events declaring, "I'll talk with anyone no matter how long it takes." Ambro admitted he was amazed by the reports of rural voters who would flock to meet House members. "In New York," he said, "you could put 20 congressmen on a street corner and you couldn't draw flies!"

These close personal associations superseded policy positions in determining whether to support Class members, many reported. "People don't care that much about issues," Bedell noted. "If you can get to know them and they like you, that's more important than how you vote. The question is, 'Does he really represent us. Do we like him, can we trust him?'" Matt McHugh similarly felt that the time spent "develop[ing] my personal relationships" encouraged constituents to overlook particular votes with which they disagreed. "They would say, 'I don't agree with you, but I know you work hard,'" he noted. "In most cases, they will not throw you out because of this or that vote. By and large, people would give me the benefit of the doubt, and that was my protection."[42] In Texas, Bob Krueger worked his district from 4 a.m. until 10 p.m., telling constituents, "I can't promise you'll like all my votes, I will look at each issue, and you judge me." He found that "if you were straightforward" with voters, "you were OK. People trusted me because they knew me personally."[43] As a result of the personal contact, noted Les AuCoin, the first Democrat to represent his district in a century, although "Congress is held in low esteem, like a used car salesman, people have a high respect for their individual congressman. I didn't fully appreciate that until I got here. My constituents distinguish between me and the Congress."[44]

Using the Perks of Incumbency

When personal visits proved impossible, the enlarged office accounts paid for new technology that mass-produced personalized form letters that were often signed with autopens that replicated the member's signature. Virtually everything mailed from congressional offices used a frank in place of postage. The printing of materials took place in the subsidized Democratic and Republican print shops located deep in the bowels of the Rayburn House Office Building. The costs of producing and mailing these materials, laden with photos and honorific stories about the incumbent, were minimal and entirely covered by public funds.

Offices were authorized to purchase mailing lists from private vendors to better target mailings to the predilections of the individual constituent. Government-printed booklets entitled "How Our Laws Are Made," "Our Flag," and "Your Baby at One" were mailed to thousands of constituents in every district. Surveying the innovative campaign techniques he and other freshmen employed, even Moffett—considered a "media star" in the Class—had to wonder whether the expansive attention to constituents "is really more service, or is it show business?" The Class appreciated both realms: "I don't think another class had understood the techniques of communication as well as this one," Ned Pattison observed.[45]

All these early technological advances allowed legislators to put their names and ideas before voters many months before the commencement of the official campaign season, and at no expense to their campaigns. As a result, by early 1976, some of the early trepidations about the vulnerability of Class members were dissipating. The *Washington Post*'s chief Hill correspondent confirmed that the Class members "have minded the store in their districts very well."[46] A discouraged Republican who would lose to a supposedly vulnerable freshman forlornly noted, "I was campaigning as a nonentity in a district where the guy had been around for two years . . . He [had] absolutely deluged the district with mail."[47]

Close contact with constituents was not without its drawbacks. One downside of such availability was an increased expectation that members of the House could solve problems that lay outside the realm of federal officeholders to remedy. Sharp found it "painful" when people showed up to request aid with nonfederal problems he couldn't solve, including a constituent who had fallen into a water tank.[48] Russo remembered responding to complaints about clogged toilets, refrigerators on the street, and alley repairs, which he referred to local officials.[49] Since anyone could show up at the numerous town halls scheduled by Class members, confrontations with angry constituents would occasionally erupt. Helen Meyner of New Jersey was "shocked" at the expectations of voters. "People came in and said the most God-awful things about Congress," Sharp remembered, including racial epithets. "There was no diminishment of low-ball intellectual capacity at town halls. It was a style of theater." Still, his willingness to take the public abuse itself won points with some constituents. Town halls were "a chance to show my seriousness," Sharp recalled, "to say, 'I work hard, I take you seriously, and I take the job seriously.' "[50]

The constant demands took a huge personal toll on the young members and their families. Frequent travel home was a regular feature of freshman life, even to the West Coast, and many would fly home on Thursday or Friday evenings to conduct two or three days of town halls, site visits, and constituent meetings before boarding a red-eye flight back to begin the workweek in Washington. Butler Derrick, knowing he was "way too liberal for his district," as his top aide admitted, threw himself into every Christmas parade, Rotary club luncheon, and town hall meeting; his large district staff was required to respond immediately to constituent requests, and those who fell short were fired. He "won because he just went home," an aide said, on 45 weekends in 1975, creating "an impression he was a hard-working fella."[51] Dave Evans, whose election had been called 1974's biggest upset by the *Almanac of American Politics*, visited his district 50 of the 52 weeks of his first year in office to ensure his "reelection in 1976 isn't perceived as a fluke" like his first victory; the two weekends he missed were due to his appendectomy.[52] His Indiana colleague, Floyd

Fithian, regularly visited towns whose residents had never seen a live congressman, drawing 800 people to breakfast meetings. Ned Pattison spent 42 weekends in his district in 1975, and Republican freshman Dave Emery was in his Maine district for 152 days that year. Mike Blouin remembered spending 25 to 30 weekends a year, and every recess, traveling throughout his Iowa district. Russo was advised by his Republican colleague Ed Derwinski to "go to everything the first two years, even if only 2 or 5 people show up. After two years, they'll think you were everywhere." Russo followed the advice but "had no life for two years," attending multiple events every Saturday and Sunday.

Some Class members developed innovative events to publicize their dedication to constituents and the district. John Jenrette, whose constituents "criticized me for non-availability" (as well as for divorcing his wife) compensated by creating a Congressional Tourism Caucus to promote South Carolina travel and by innovatively hiring a number of African American women to work in his local office.[53] One Jenrette plan took a tragic turn when a fly-in of Minnesota sunflower farmers intended to encourage tobacco growers to diversify their crop ended in a disastrous plane crash.

Tom Harkin returned to his 1974 gambit of working at everyday jobs in the district to demonstrate that becoming a member of Congress had not inflated his ego. The press delightedly covered his days working in a grain elevator, on a railroad, or as a nurse's aide. Jim Lloyd spent day in a wheelchair to highlight the challenges faced by people living with disabilities. In Connecticut, Toby Moffett advertised a "Citizen Congress Day" and "Talk with Toby . . . from Washington" free call-ins, which his staff followed up with notes back to the callers.[54] Tom Downey took advantage of his seat on Armed Services to make an unannounced visit to West Point to investigate a cheating scandal involving a constituent. "Go tell the superintendent I am here," he directed a startled official who doubted the boyish 25-year-old was really a congressman.[55]

Republicans complained about the skillful use of the perks by Class members, although their members were equally entitled to use them, and did. Future House member and vice president Dick Cheney, who was serving as White House chief of staff in 1976, grumbled that the Class had "expanded the hell out of the powers of incumbency," allowing them to retain districts that Republicans believed should they should have regained.[56] Other Republicans, however, gave the Class "immense credit" for being "very canny [at] keeping the home fires burning" by using the tools of the trade for their electoral advantage. "It pissed off Republicans," GOP staffer Donald Wolfensberger admitted. "They got credit for constituent services, and were not held accountable for liberal votes."[57]

The press marveled at the ability of the freshmen to play the dual roles of legislator and candidate. "They have been remarkably effective in their districts," the *National Journal* reported, "able to . . . play an unusually substantive legislative role and serve their districts." Early in 1976, the *New York Times* abandoned earlier predictions of large-scale losses, observing that while many Class members represented what "would appear to be hostile Republican districts," thanks to their "aggressive activity back home . . . the careful wooing of constituent views, the scrupulous replies to mail and the accessibility of the representatives," many believe "a number of the freshman Democrats have a good chance at this stage to win re-election." *Congressional Quarterly* reviewed the 1976 summer schedules of the freshmen and noted, "Virtually all have placed special emphasis on constituent services, and have committed large amounts of resources to the maintenance of active district offices and staffs." The *Washington Post* noted the irony that "the freshman Democrats who swept into the House two years ago with lofty promises for change are running for re-election on the most homely virtue: their constituent casework."[58]

Not all reviews were so admiring, however. The Class's methodical attention to the 1976 campaign struck some senior Democrats as an example of the freshmen's narcissism. Groused Neal Smith of Iowa, "They decided the most important thing in the world was to get re-elected." Critics decried the use of millions of dollars in public funds spent to bolster the freshmen's name and image, expressing disappointment that Class members were just as willing to engage in self-promotion as any other politician. Quoting one Class member who had asserted the freshmen had been "elected because we ran against Congress," the *Baltimore Sun* also reproved the freshmen for emphasizing constituent services and communications, charging, "The instinct for survival is strong even in idealists."[59] The ever-critical David Broder, who frequently criticized the freshmen for failing to achieve a standard he had set for them, echoed the complaint. "The freshmen, one by one, are peeling off from formation and beginning to concentrate on tactics that give them, individually, the best chance to survive," Broder asserted. "That is the old game of politics, the game that members of Congress have been playing for years. And it raises disturbing questions about what has gone wrong with the promising 94th."[60] Broder also chastised the freshmen for catering to their districts at the expense of good public policy. "Conscientious members know they have to lead their districts, even if it entails a degree of political risk," he admonished. But "there is little sign that the juniors in Congress recognize" that obligation.[61]

These accusations were unfair and inaccurate. Class members ran in support of progressive policies and even, as we have seen, in some cases to reform the institution, but they were far from "idealists" who disavowed the instinctual political urge to retain their jobs. The freshmen had never suggested they would not aggressively seek the reelection that was obligatory to achieve their legislative objectives. Rebuking them for utilizing the perquisites of incumbency to promote their achievements holds them to a standard that they never set for themselves. Nor is there any evidence that they ignored serious legislating or abandoned party positions to concentrate on the electoral aspects of their jobs. "Everybody was interested in being reelected," Tom Downey admitted. "But we were more interested in educating ourselves and doing a better job."[62] Maguire agreed, dismissing the criticism as "a cheap and wrongheaded story line." Indeed, Maguire and others representing traditionally Republican districts often professed they would not hesitate to jeopardize their careers by remaining silent on issues of concern. "We told each other," said Maguire, " 'We're not in Congress to perpetuate ourselves. We're there because things need to be done. We are here to make a difference, to be the best public servant, however long it lasts.' "[63]

Such fatalistic attitudes may also help explain the disinterest of some in building the collegial relationships on which long congressional careers are based. "We weren't worried about offending people," agreed McHugh, who represented a district with a five to three Republican registration. "We had no stake in the status quo." Iowa's Mike Blouin offered a similar analysis: "Some people didn't care" about offending others, he recalled. "They weren't there to make friends."[64]

In their campaigns, Republicans often tried to characterize the Class as "big spending radicals," but many Democrats countered with the examples of wasteful spending they had uncovered, often in agencies Republicans had protected. Sharp could have passed for a conservative Republican when he condemned the federal government as "a vast, shapeless creature, with duplicative programs, some of which bear no resemblance to what was originally intended." Unusual for a Democrat, he even targeted unemployment insurance as "a year-round welfare program." Others like Downey and Bedell became knowledgeable critics of spending by the Pentagon. Miller emerged as a critic of the low royalties paid by oil companies on oil and gas produced from public lands, and Derrick opposed local water projects. As a result, the Republican attempt to label the freshmen as big spenders mostly "flopped."[65]

The theme of fiscal responsibility was echoed by presidential nominee Jimmy Carter, whom many in the Class had met in 1974 when he traveled the country in support of House candidates on behalf of the Democratic National Committee. "We can have an American government that's turned away from scandal and corruption and official cynicism," he had told the Democratic convention in words that echoed the views of many in the Class. His focus on the environment, energy, and consumer protection also echoed objectives of many Class members, who optimistically believed his election would allow the Congress to enact Democratic priorities with simple majorities instead of having to marshal two-thirds margins to overturn vetoes.

Surviving the Election

The outcome of the presidential election was anything but overwhelming. Carter defeated Ford by less than 2 million votes, winning fewer electoral votes (297) than any victorious candidate since Woodrow Wilson 60 years earlier. In the House, however, the election's outcome was not ambiguous, with Democrats actually gaining one seat in the House. Carter's strength in the South—he was the first Democrat to sweep the region since the pre–civil rights victory of Franklin Roosevelt in 1944—helped many Class members retain marginal seats crucial to sustaining the House supermajority. Elsewhere, the story was just as decisive. "There's an enthusiasm, even a euphoria, in some quarters," one Democrat exclaimed.[66]

The victory was not altogether unexpected. From more ambiguous prospects early in the year, by September polls were indicating preference for Democrats in House races of 57 percent to 34 percent, a lead projecting a substantial victory. While early estimates had anticipated a loss of 20 seats or more to Republicans, only two Class members were defeated: Tim Lee Hall of Illinois, who was attacked as a big spender, and Allan Howe, who had been arrested for soliciting a prostitute, an offense that did not play well in conservative Utah.

Democratic losses befell mainly legislators who had served six to eight terms although several recent arrivals—including Ed Mezvinsky in Iowa and Richard Vander Veen, who had replaced Ford in 1974—were defeated. Most surprising was the ease with which most of the freshmen won their campaigns. There were a few nail-biters—Mikva won by 201 votes, Wirth, Meyner, Robert Cornell, Keys, Blouin, and Mark Hannaford barely exceeded 50 percent—but the freshmen's assiduous cultivation of the electorate paid electoral dividends. Downey won with 57 percent, Russo 59 percent, Bedell 67 percent, and Rick Nolan 60 percent. Indiana freshmen Fithian, Sharp, and Evans all received more than 55 percent. Many more in districts with long records of Republican representation swept to easy victories. Southerners like Levitas, Neal, Jenrette, and Harold Ford benefitted from Democrat Carter's regional strength; Ken Holland defeated legendary New York Yankee shortstop Bobby Richardson, and other conservatives like Carroll Hubbard, Ted Risenhoover, Mottl, and English all romped to easy victories. In many cases, Class members easily outdistanced the presidential ticket's performance in their districts; in his Texas constituency, Krueger ran 20 points ahead of Carter. Without question, Democrats, an observer noted, "taught the Republicans a lesson in the power of incumbency."[67] The size of the victory, *Congressional Quarterly* reported, "stunned [Republican] party strategists who had expected a substantial GOP comeback."

Peering out from the electoral rubble, Republican House strategists were shocked by the breadth of the defeat. Only a year earlier, the press had been reporting that many of the Class of 1974 would not survive; on election eve, Republicans anticipated winning 15 new seats in the South, but they actually lost 2. "We underestimated the value of incumbency," admitted a glum Steve Stockmeyer, executive director of the Republican Congressional Committee. Indeed, one analyst concluded that "a large percentage of the first-term Democrats . . . appear to be within striking distance of locking up their districts" and, with them, any hope for a Republican House majority in the near future.[68]

The Class of 1974 quickly met with the incoming 1976 class of nearly 50 Democratic winners to share the lessons learned, but the newly elected members faced a very different landscape from that of two years earlier. No longer was there a need to confront the seniority system that protected aged, autocratic chairmen. Indeed, with the removals, resignations, defeats, and retirements, well over half the chairmen for the 95th Congress would have less than four years with the gavel, and all the chairmen understood the need to pay attention to the will the caucus. None of the prospective chairmen for the 95th would face a challenge to their right as the senior member to chair their committee.

A more collaborative White House and new leadership also greeted the incoming class, with a notably more charismatic and liberal Speaker Tip O'Neill waiting to take up the gavel. But O'Neill was clear that Congress would not abandon its determination to assert its coequal role in governing simply because a Democratic president had been elected. In his early discussions with Carter's team, he insisted on proper deference to the House and its leaders. "You're in the big leagues," he advised the head of Carter's congressional team when he heard that Frank Moore was planning a White House meeting for newly elected Democrats. "Don't meet with freshmen. The *Speaker* meets with freshmen. He tells *you* what went on."[69]

There were other early points of potential tension with the new Democratic president that had been overlooked during the campaign. While sympathetic to the reformers' views on deficit control, reform, energy, and the environment, Carter held strong views on the need to keep the legislative branch in check based on his experiences as governor. He had criticized Ford for "not leading Congress," which he believed was too complex and disorganized to direct policy. "That has got to come from the White House," Carter said, "and in the absence of that [leadership], the country drifts."[70] Even some in the Class who had recently advocated an enhanced role for Congress sympathized with Carter's outlook. The institution he had sought to reform as "an enthusiastic knight" in 1974, Wirth concluded, had become "stymied by relentless and pointless maneuvering for short-term political advantage" and the relentless search for campaign funds.[71] He had become "frustrated with the posturing and paralysis of Congress."[72]

Many Class members would quickly lock horns with Carter over his insistence on spending constraints that precluded action on long-frustrated policy initiatives. Years after leaving the White House, Carter encountered Harkin and Wirth, who reintroduced themselves as Class members. "We were in the class of 1974, two years before you got there," Harkin reminded the former president. "I remember you guys," Carter responded. "You were kind of a pain in the rear." "Yeah," Wirth fired back, "we thought the same of you!"[73] Still, an analysis prepared for Carter by the White House congressional relations staff midway through the Carter presidency revealed the members of the Class of 1974 as Carter's most supportive group, voting to back Carter 78 percent of the time. By comparison, the class of 1976 that arrived with Carter supported him in 71 percent of votes. Indeed, nearly half of the 32 House members supporting Carter more than 95 percent of the time were from the 1974 Class.[74]

That analysis illustrated significant differences between the Class and the group that was elected in 1976. Like their 1974 colleagues, many of the incoming members were supportive of reform, but their version ran more to the broad governmental reorganization enunciated by Carter than to internal House democratization. Adam Benjamin, who had defeated the 84-year-old chairman of the Rules Committee in his Indiana primary, contrasted his class as having run "more against bureaucracy and the tentacles of the federal government" than had the 1974 Class, which "probably ran against Congress more than anything except Watergate."[75]

Nor did the class of 1976 seek to organize itself as distinctly as did the Class of 1974. "I see no necessity to 'one up' the class of 1974," said freshman Norm Dicks of Washington State, a longtime Appropriations staff person. One of the new class's leaders, former Arkansas attorney general Jim Guy Tucker, seemed to reject the very concept of a "class" that the '74 contingent had embraced. "I don't think we want to institutionalize being newcomers," Tucker said. In California, former Republican and Nixon administration official Leon Panetta, who had ousted a six-term veteran Republican, declared, "We're a more practical group. We came up through the process."[76] Indeed, 46 percent of the new class had served in prior elective office, compared to 37 percent of the class of 1974.[77] A staff member agreed the new class was "less rah-rah, less starry-eyed, less naive" than that of 1974.[78]

Veterans of the Class of 1974 drew a similar distinction from their new colleagues. The newcomers, Toby Moffett sniffed, were "totally different" from members of his own class, terming them "young fogies, the children of political organizations and hand-picked."[79] The *Washington Post*'s Capitol Hill specialist agreed, describing the 1976 cohort as "more restrained, more politically experienced, more accustomed to working

within the system than their 1974 counterparts [and] had no apparent desire to make a similar impact." Mineta observed that, unlike many in the
1974 Class who had beaten Republicans, most of the 1976 group had replaced retiring Democrats and therefore had trod a very different path to
their seats in the House Chamber. The circumstances of 1974 had given a
sense of urgency to those members, a belief that "they arrived feeling
they would have to make an impact if they were going to keep these
formerly Republican seats," whereas the 1976 class felt less pressure.[80]

Despite the differences, the advice the Class of '74 shared with the newcomers was the lessons drilled into them two years earlier. "Communicate," advised Jenrette, who had been reelected despite his well-publicized
divorce. "Remember, it's the folks back home who vote." McHugh promoted the frequent town halls that he believed were responsible for his
victory. Other veterans shared their strategies: hire competent staff, return to the district weekly, do not miss floor votes, send out frequent self-
promotional mailings, and fly flags above the Capitol for constituents.[81]
"I hired a staff geared to providing great constituent service," Jenrette recalled. "I return to the district probably 75 percent of weekends, and spent
lots of time there during the recesses. We did town halls, newsletters,
and even were among the first to generate computer letters addressing a
wide range of substantive issues. I was very active in speaking engagements
throughout the district." As a result, he later thought, "it never crossed
my mind I wouldn't be reelected."[82]

While not demanding further changes to the rules, the newly elected
members wanted to be sure they benefitted from the recent reforms. "We
want to make sure the leadership continues [the] practice" of assigning
freshmen to major committees, Tucker noted, pointing to the large size
of the 1976 class. There wasn't much chance the leadership would ignore
the newcomers. Combined with the remaining members of the Class of
1974, as well as the pre-1974 liberals, the reformers now held more than
half the seats in the caucus. Any effort to pare back reforms or limit the
role of newer members would surely be repulsed.

The Class had protected its members and the hard-won reforms of the
94th Congress. Significantly, its skillful use of the powers of incumbency
had allowed Democrats to solidify their grip on the House majority, which
only a few years earlier had been on the trajectory to far narrower margins, if not a genuine contest for control. Evolving events within the conservative movement, including the rise of evangelicals, the emergence of

hard-edged fundraising and grassroots organizations, and the growing appeal of Ronald Reagan, seemed to present little threat as Democrats consolidated unified control of government. And yet that control was far more tenuous than it appeared, and, in only a few weeks, the spirit of reform that had dominated the caucus over the preceding four years would come to an abrupt end.

11 CODA FOR REFORM

The House won't stand for anyone who's going around whacking asses.
—Lionel Van Deerlin (D-CA)

[Wright was] an unctuous Evangelical with a pocket full of chits from the Chicago and New York guys. None of us took him seriously.
—Rep. Abner Mikva (D-IL)

Bolling was a God to a lot of people.—Rep. Tim Wirth (D-CO)

s in 1974, the 1976 House Democratic Caucus confronted major decisions even before its new members were sworn into office. Unlike two years earlier, however, there was less need for sweeping changes in the rules to make the House a more transparent, accountable, and participatory institution. But the Class of 1974, and the rest of the caucus, did have one momentous decision to make—the election of a new majority leader—and the unpredictable results of that contest would shape the future of reforms and the arc of partisanship in the House in ways both unintended and unforeseen.

The battle had been years in the making, a much-anticipated clash between two brilliant but headstrong personalities who had planned, plotted, and shaped the recent democratization of the House: Phillip Burton and Dick Bolling. While they shared a commitment to House reform, they diverged sharply on its ultimate design. Neither could abide the thought of the other playing a significant role in leading the Democrats, and years of relationship building, personal coddling, strange alliances, and unspoken vendettas would play out in the caucus's secret voting.

The Democratic Caucus that convened in early December 1976 received three sets of reform recommendations: one from Democratic Study Group, another from the Committee on Administrative Review chaired by Dave Obey, and the third, a product of the Committee on Organization, Study, and Review chaired by Neal Smith. The proposals were the outgrowth of nearly four dozen propositions presented to members, including the still-unresolved reorganization of "inappropriate and fragmented committee jurisdictions."[1]

It quickly became apparent that reform fatigue was setting in. "Reform is pretty well complete," Mo Udall declared, suggesting a need only to "fine tune a little more."[2] And, indeed, compared to the sweeping modifications approved two years earlier, the only changes adopted in late 1976 were minor, including a requirement that conference committee meetings be open to the public. Additional proposals to limit the concentration of power—imposing a term limit on leadership positions and committee chairmanships—were rejected by a more than two to one margin. Similarly, a proposal to require election of Ways and Means subcommittee chairs failed by a 22–98 vote despite support from Bolling and Burton, who declared that "no single reform [was] any more important."

One structural change was reflected in the determination of incoming Speaker Tip O'Neill to include more minorities and women on the Steering Committee. The traditional means of promoting candidates for priority committees—votes within the various regions—had failed to reflect the diversity of the caucus membership. "The House is not the most efficient system, but it is the freest," he noted. Although the "autocratic methods" used by the prior Speaker may have been efficient, the House would benefit from greater diversity on the crucial Steering panel.

Abuses of Liberalization

Wariness about additional rules modifications was prompted in part by growing irritation that Republicans had taken advantage of looser rules governing floor procedures to disrupt proceedings and force embarrassing votes. The frustration with these maneuvers had flared earlier in the year, prompting a proposal to raise the number of members required to secure a recorded vote on the floor from 20 to 33.[3] Even a committed DSG reformer like Dave Obey had become exasperated by Republican maneuvering and obstructionism. "I have been wrong, based on what has happened [during the] last session," Obey asserted, noting the nearly 1,300 roll call votes—a vast increase—in the prior four years. "I don't think it makes much sense to allow our rules on roll calls in effect to be used as a filibuster," Obey argued. "That is getting a little silly. How many nights have we been here . . . for three or four or five hours, having amendment after amendment that didn't mean a damn . . . and we wind up not being able to get sufficient time spent discussing major amendments?" he asked his caucus colleagues. If proponents could not round up 33 members to demand a vote, Obey asserted, "it probably isn't that important."[4] Other veteran legislators chimed in to support Obey. The minority had a natural tendency, added Leo Ryan of California, "to stall, to delay, to cut back, to make . . . things not happen." Neal Smith agreed that the minority was abusing its privileges. "[You] can't have strong leadership when 21 people can [undermine] the will of the leadership," he argued, rendering the majority and the leadership "almost powerless." Otis Pike of New York agreed the House was "spending too much time doing nothing . . . [taking] vote after vote on junk, which is unnecessary and trivial and non-controversial."[5]

But the Class of '74 members, who recalled how tight restrictions had constrained liberals from securing recorded votes on issues like Vietnam, remained wedded to the reforms. "There are often amendments of significant policy consequence for which only relatively few are willing to put the House on record," argued Class member Steve Solarz. "If this proposal was adopted, it is going to make it more difficult to get roll calls[, which] will make it more difficult for the House to work its will."[6] George Miller heatedly rejected Obey's amendment as undermining democracy in the House. "Each of us represent[s] a half million people and maybe those half million want Congress' feet put to the fire," even if they were conservatives trying to embarrass Democratic members, Miller argued. "If John Ashbrook and John Rousselot [two hard-line conservatives, from Ohio and California, respectively] and others want a recorded vote they are entitled to it." Looking into a future few thought likely, he argued, "Someday it will be a [Democratic] Minority that wants a recorded vote . . . That, my friends, is democracy, and that is what has to be preserved here. We cannot risk being efficient and do away with a democracy. We need to preserve the free speech and the exchange of ideas in this House."

Miller also noted that it was difficult to find just twenty members willing to demand a recorded vote on controversial issues like nuclear power. "The special interests are lobbying to keep people off the floor day and night" to prevent recorded votes they might lose. Voters, he declared, had a right to know "where their representatives stand on these issues."[7] Other Class members including Bob Carr, Phil Sharp, and Tom Downey rose to agree with Solarz and Miller, as did several senior liberals, and the proposal to raise the votes required was defeated.

This often-overlooked confrontation in January 1976 provides new insights into the principled motivations of the Class, and perhaps their naïveté as well. At this early stage in their careers, their self-perception as outsiders remained greater, in some respects, than their role as majority policymakers. They were moved by their own early experiences to defend transparency and accountability, even if doing so benefited Republicans.

By the end of 1976, however, another session of GOP tactical maneuvering had persuaded most Democrats to reconsider their earlier decision. DSG had polled its members, and 40 percent favored raising the threshold for a recorded vote to 33. While hailing the earlier reform as "one of the major changes that we made in the last 4 or 5 years [that] brought democracy to the House," Udall acknowledged it was being abused by "small groups [that] should not be permitted to take up the time of the House to vote on any particular thing they happen to think is important to them."[8] Jack Murtha, a conservative Pennsylvania Democrat elected in early 1974, agreed that the "minority uses this tactic so many times to stall the procedures of the House." Some Class members like Andy Maguire remained unconvinced, while longtime reformers like Carr endorsed raising the threshold, which the caucus voted to do, infuriating Republicans.

Bolling versus Burton

The main question before the caucus, the race for majority leader, presented a rare opportunity for the members to "vent their frustrations on the party leadership."[9] The election forced many of the Class to confront their seeming contradiction: a desire for someone strong enough to discipline the caucus while not interfering with member autonomy; a leader who would "mobilize support for legislation without appearing tyrannical" while also being "committed to the major institutional and procedural changes we want to see in the House." Above all, they wanted a leader who would be sympathetic to their own personal and political needs without demanding absolute obeisance. The next leader, one member added, must be "approachable [and] concerned with my problems. That's as important as where a guy stands on policy and reform questions."[10]

The race included not only Burton and Bolling, but also Majority Whip John McFall, a courtly Californian appointed in 1973 by Carl Albert after Burton's failed effort to be elected whip. McFall's claim rested largely on his brief occupation of the low rung on the "leadership ladder" that typically propelled lower-level leadership into the higher ranks. But caucus sentiment was unsympathetic to such automatic promotion. Brock Adams of Washington State, the first Budget chairman, and Jim Wright, the likely incoming chairman of the Public Works and Transportation Committee from Texas, were also mentioned as "dark horses."[11] Tom Foley, the DSG chairman and the one member Burton feared could defeat him, opted to run for caucus chair.[12]

The stakes of a Burton-Bolling confrontation had grown as they promoted alternative versions of a reformed House. Bolling's special committee had produced the complex set of rules changes in 1974 only to have Burton successfully sabotage his years of intellectual effort over disagreements about modifications to committee jurisdiction. Burton dismissed Bolling as a "white collar liberal" intellectual who promoted reform for reform's sake, without having any distinct legislative objectives behind his plan. For his part, Bolling viewed Burton as "a threat to the system" who was "trying to move ahead too quickly."[13]

Bolling favored greater centralization of power in the speakership (a role he intended to occupy) as a necessity for efficient House operations. His "sole reform," one reviewer wrote, was to allocate power away from the chairmen, with the Speaker serving as "the organizing instrument."[14] Burton viewed reforms as a means to an end, the end being a progressive policy agenda with him directing the caucus and likely the House as Speaker. For a decade, these two had warily circled each other, offered dueling proposals and fighting proxy wars. "They understood each other," recalled David Cohen of Common Cause, "and they hated each other."[15]

There were policy disagreements between the two as well. Bolling was a supporter of activist government whose liberalism was tempered, as was frequently the case with postwar progressives, by Cold Warrior tendencies on foreign policy. Unapologetically ambitious, he had challenged Carl Albert for majority leader in 1962 but suffered a humiliating defeat. He had proven his willingness to defy caucus instructions when he killed a resolution to end funding for Vietnam, a decision that alienated many Class members.

A Phi Beta Kappa graduate of the University of the South, Bolling's writings had earned him a reputation as the intellectual father of reform, but he was widely regarded as a "lone wolf."[16] One review of his *House Out of Order* described him as "an unemployed errand-boy, a no-work specialist, a playboy, and an ineffective operator with only one foot in the Democratic Study Group."[17] Such a dismissive review must have wounded a temperamental ego such as Bolling's. Others, however, held him in high regard, including members of the Class. "Bolling was a God to a lot of people," Tim Wirth declared, and Elliott Levitas called him "a giant." John LaFalce admitted that Bolling "made me feel good," while Bob Krueger agreed Bolling was "respected as . . . a reformer . . . intelligent, [with] integrity."[18]

But Bolling's icy personality was a liability in a profession where cordiality and joviality were valuable traits. The Missourian liked to dismiss colleagues by asserting, "I wouldn't give that prick the time of day if I had the only watch in town." Such haughtiness led O'Neill to observe, "Dick treaded on a lot of toes he could have avoided if he wanted to." He did not hesitate to excoriate individual members or even the caucus, and he once dismissed the entire Congress as "a lobby for arrogant brokers of special privilege." "Bolling knew what an elitist he was," David Cohen recalled. "He didn't suffer fools, people who [he thought] were lesser than he," and, as one journalist noted, he "let it be known he considered many colleagues fools." Bolling charged the dysfunctionality of the House was "entirely the responsibility of House Democrats," and especially liberals whom he denounced as "totalitarian in temperament and occasionally seized with fits of voodooism." Those who refused to regard "the liberal program as a holy tablet," he warned, were "read out of the liberal ranks." He was not above making personal attacks, as when he asserted that the attention span of Harlem's Adam Clayton Powell, the chairman of the Education and Labor Committee, lasted "between forty seconds to two minutes." He also denounced the conservative William Colmer, chairman of the Rules Committee on which he served, as "inhabiting a political position perhaps slightly to the left of Ivan the Terrible."

Such comments illustrate why members of all opinions shared one impression of Bolling: he was gratuitously arrogant, especially in displaying his superior knowledge of House history and procedure. "He was a stuffed shirt," Tom Harkin declared, intent on "sending a message, 'I'm smarter than you are.'" While he was "good and honest," Ab Mikva agreed, he also possessed a "very big ego [and had an] overly high opinion of himself." At hearings of the Rules Committee, Bolling would dismiss chairmen who could not explain their bills to his satisfaction, admonishing them to return after they had studied their own legislation more thoroughly. Even his admirers acknowledged the shortcomings of his personality. When he asked Obey, who described himself as "a disciple of Bolling," to recommend a first step in preparing his campaign for majority leader, Obey unhesitatingly said, "Stop being such a prick!" Bolling promptly agreed, "I think you are absolutely right." He later confided to Udall, "I think I'm too arrogant to win."[19] Nevertheless, he declared, "I am not going to change my personality, god-damn it."[20]

Phil Burton possessed his own odd mixture of personality quirks. As chairman, he had transformed DSG "from a tea-and-talk party into a muscular anti-establishment invasion force," one observer described. Unlike the intellectual Bolling, he fancied himself "a Maoist, a revolutionary, a street fighter," who contrasted his own bellicose, in-your-face style with the more cerebral and effete manner of his opponents.[21] While Bolling and Wright handed out their books about Congress to promote themselves, Burton preferred to talk with colleagues, often displaying a voluminous knowledge of sports statistics. "He does not need to be loved," wrote the *Nation*'s Mary Ellen Leary. "He has no interests, no hobbies, no tastes outside politics." Amazingly, he succeeded in the political realm despite this "abrasive manner" because of "his perfectly apparent ambition."[22] Josiah Beeman, a longtime staffer, noted that Burton was "a hard man to work for," possessing "a very bad temper" that could be directed toward members and his own staff. Lobbyists would wait for hours for a meeting before Burton would "bring them in for a minute, abuse them mercilessly and throw them out. He had no use for them."[23]

Colleagues often encountered the caucus chairman's wrath. Burton was a big man, and "when he came over and took your coat by the collar and pulled you towards him and told you what he was going to do to you if you didn't support his bill," Beeman recalled, "it was pretty intimidating." Obey recalled Burton's willingness to "run over" members with whom he disagreed, and Marty Russo witnessed the caucus chair "screaming obscenities" at John Krebs on the floor, demanding the freshman "get over here" and change his vote. Such outbursts raised doubts about Burton's suitability as a party spokesman. "The House won't stand for anyone who's going around whacking asses," predicted veteran California Democrat Lionel Van Deerlin, recalling Burton's threat against Al Ullman when the new chairman opposed placing freshmen on the tax subcommittee.[24]

Even officials in his San Francisco district often had strained relations with the hard-driving Burton. When queried about his relationship with

Democratic mayor Joseph Alito, Burton assured a reporter, "There hasn't been a bad word between us in two years." Dubious, the reporter asked how long it had been since San Francisco's congressman and mayor had spoken. Burton drolly replied, "Two years."[25] House colleagues could suffer more than a bruised ego if they offended Burton. "More guys lost their seats in California in reapportionment due to crossing Phil than you can imagine," recalled Beeman.

Burton may well have been "the most unpleasant man in American government," the *Los Angeles Times* observed, as well as "the most competent congressman in the country."[26] Largely bereft of the interpersonal skills and bonhomie common to those seeking leadership positions, Burton was consumed with "the mastery of the political game, at which he is phenomenally adept," the *Nation* described. "He has no time for such niceties as cultivating the media, placating rivals, or being diplomatic with allies."[27]

The descriptions of his methodical, profane, indefatigable pragmatism elicited colorful observations from friend and foe alike, and there were many of both. Carr recalled how Burton served the freshmen as a "mentor, a tutor" during their initial campaigns, and Norman Mineta credited him with "pushing for change." Carr admitted, "We were only too happy to follow him as our Pied Piper." Moderates from the Class of '74—from Leo Zeferetti, who never met Burton before winning his primary, to John Krebs, who had known him for many years as in the reformist California Democratic Council—all recalled how Burton had reached out to help them, and they loyally lined up behind him. Bill Brodhead remembered being surprised at how many southern conservatives counted Burton as a close friend, but Burton knew the caucus needed them. "Get to know southerners and conservatives," Burton would presciently advise liberals. "Be nice to those guys, listen to them. Without them, there is no Democratic majority."[28]

But others were leery of Burton; some liberals distrusted his willingness to cut deals with conservatives on textile imports and tobacco subsidies in return for their support for expanded food stamps. Even so, Burton "scared some of our guys" from the South, John Jenrette admitted. Krueger from Texas viewed Burton, whom he barely knew, as "a narrow-minded, doctrinaire liberal, arrogant, self-centered, not particularly smart or open-minded. He was a corrupt politician," he charged, without any evidence, "and I had no reason to support Burton; I didn't like him."

His rude and confrontational behavior was legendary, and he could be as arrogant as Bolling. Burton was "one of the weirdest people I have ever met," one member said. As his close ally and lieutenant, Ab Mikva, understatedly admitted, "He could be quite abrupt with people." Many people could recall Burton's explosive and personal attacks, often on people whom he considered friends and colleagues. He "didn't see many as his equal," one former staff person noted. He firmly believed that the "end justified the means," and if that meant cutting deals with tobacco defenders to win a key labor or welfare vote, Burton never gave the deal a second thought. He was contemptuous of "boy scouts" who were too uncompromising in their standards to play the political game successfully, like Udall, who "thought everything was legitimate" in the Congress.[29]

"He had a very strong sense of right and wrong," recalled a staffer, who remembered how Burton would instruct his staff to withhold information so that other committee members would have no choice but to rely on him to cut the best possible deal. Burton considered himself a "master of the politics, not of the substance. The less people know what is in the bill, the better," the staff remembers him advising. "He kept people in the dark except when it served his interests." He wanted to avoid having to answer "what about this and that," questions that parsed individual sections but missed the comprehensive nature of the package. To persistent skeptics who questioned whether they would be compromised by voting for a fabrication of Burton's, he would authoritatively declare, "You're in your mother's arms; trust me." "Not since Lyndon Johnson was in Congress," an observer wrote, "had there been so many lapels pulled, arms twisted, ears whispered in, and deals made—or so much personal power amassed—by one man with a genius for legislative strategy."[30] He was purely operational, said one member, comparing him to the emotionless genius of Sherlock Holmes.

Despite his temper, crudity, and lack of manners, Burton impressed friends and foes alike as a man of his word, not a minor attribute in House politics. Jack Tomlinson, a California political leader, said that Burton's ability to work with conservatives was premised on the fact that "they know his words can be relied on." He would collaborate with Republicans, like his San Francisco colleague William Maillard, on policy issues when necessary. He would not let lobbyists buy him a meal, Beeman recalled, and he often picked up the entire check himself. Burton also enjoyed support from many of the younger southern or conservative Democrats like Glenn English and Charlie Rose, whom he had supported in their campaigns, in seeking committee assignments, and in promoting issues important to their region. He even received support from the hard-line Democratic conservative Larry McDonald, who acknowledged to Burton that he "always [had] been fair" despite their ideological disagreements. After McDonald walked away, Burton told his aide, Ben Palumbo, "If you ever say a word about this, I will kill you."

Heavy use of alcohol undoubtedly fueled much of Burton's bellicose behavior, damaging feelings not easily repaired. A good friend remembered spending many hours drinking with Burton, whose prodigious consumption of whiskey and vodka often raised the "possibility of disaster." Even this loyal lieutenant admitted Burton's drinking "would have disqualified him [from my vote for leadership], except he was my friend." Others could not excuse the behavior. "Phil just drank too damn much," Obey recalled. After having "really abuse[d]" a House colleague, a contrite Burton "couldn't understand the next day when he sobered up why this guy was not a great friend anymore," Beeman noted.

One particular evening of excessive drinking years earlier may have doomed Burton's aspirations for a leadership position. At a Beverly Hilton party in Los Angeles attended by major Democratic contributors, Burton unleashed a string of obscenities, causing Tip O'Neill to remark that his wife would have washed out the mouth of a child uttering such vulgarities. Burton "went berserk," O'Neill recalled, challenging the future Speaker to a fistfight. "I ought to run against you, I'll run against you for Speaker," he shrieked, red-faced, calling O'Neill "a dog" and lunging across the table. Only the intervention of his wife (and successor in office), Sala, calmed the irate congressman, but he never apologized. From that day forward, O'Neill firmly opposed Burton's rising in the leadership.[31] Some in the Class agreed that Burton must not gain a foothold on the leadership ladder. "I thought Burton was crazy," one recalled, "and simply did not want to give him an avenue to the Speakership."[32]

The remaining candidates were given little chance of success. As chairman of the Transportation Subcommittee on Appropriations, John McFall was in an ideal position to deliver earmarked funding for local projects, but many of the 123 Democrats who had entered the House since 1970 had not yet profited yet from his largesse. Ominously for McFall's candidacy, their votes were likely to determine the outcome of the race.

McFall's prospects were further undermined when he, along with several other members, were implicated in a bribery scandal involving Korean businessman Tongsun Park, the "Onassis of the Orient." "Koreagate," as the scandal became known, "blew his chances," in the opinion of Bernie Sisk, a supporter.[33]

Wright: The Sleeper Candidate

The fourth candidate was Jim Wright, whose profile seemed the antithesis of everything that had recently been written or said about the changing nature of the Democratic Caucus. A senior member of the Public Works and Transportation Committee, a devoted practitioner of congressional pork, his reddish hair parted in the middle, his voice oozing flowery rhetoric, Wright seemed a relic of an earlier era, what columnists Roland Evans and Robert Novak called a "pompous prototype of Hollywood-style congressman."[34] Others were less generous. Mark Gersh, a top strategist, dismissed Wright as a skilled orator but a "hack." But Wright was also a genial institutionalist, one well-placed staffer recalled, and the "guys who mattered knew that Tip was for Wright," as illustrated by the fact his chief of staff, Leo Diehl, made calls on Wright's behalf.[35]

Worried about Burton's strength, O'Neill instructed Dan Rostenkowski, the Illinois member of the whip organization, to find a credible alternative, and "Rosty" determined to support Wright. Chicago mayor Richard Daley saw the possibility for a win regardless of the outcome: if Wright won, he would owe the Illinois delegation, and if he lost, he would likely be chairman of the Public Works Committee and could still provide earmarked assistance to Daley's favorite projects. Burton understood the need for Illinois Class members to follow Daley's directive. "I won't be mad at Illinois," Burton said in forgiving Russo. "I know you have to do what the Mayor wants."

Like Class members Downey, English, and Jim Blanchard, Wright had aspired to public office since childhood. "From my junior year in high school, my conscious and undeviating goal had been to serve in Congress," he wrote late in life, what he termed "the noblest calling of all."[36] He had recently returned from 31 combat missions in the South Pacific during World War II when he won his first race to the Texas Legislature in 1946. Just 23, Wright was "full of zeal and hankering hungrily to go on and start building that 'brave new world'!" As a freshman, he recalled feeling the same kind of "disappointed zealotry of the newly elected member and his/her desire to participate in making policy changes" as Class members 28 years later.

As a freshman in Austin, he actively promoted a litany of progressive issues. He advocated ending the discriminatory poll tax, supported allowing women to serve on juries, and favored integration of the University of Texas law school. He led more than 100 other young members of the legislature in sponsoring a bill to raise severance taxes on oil, gas, and sulfur production to finance public schools, raise teacher salaries, and improve rural roads. Based on his service in the military, he endorsed giving the vote to 18-year-olds. "To lots of Americans, each of these was a 'radical' idea," he declared, "so some of them figured I was a 'dangerous radical'!" His personal experience helped him appreciate "that it's perfectly natural for newcomers to American politics to want to make big changes."

"If there was a mistake I didn't make," he later recalled, "it was because I didn't think of it!" As the Texas political climate soured in 1948, Wright reverted to a more traditional southern stance in a futile attempt to save his seat. "I believe in the Southern tradition of segregation," Wright declared, "and have strongly resisted any and all efforts to destroy it." His loss that year, some recalled, led him to an instinctive hesitation about getting too far in front of any movement.[37]

Like some of the southern freshmen of 1974, Wright had won his House seat in 1954 by defeating an incumbent Democrat who enjoyed the support of the political establishment. He quickly fell under the influence of Speaker Sam Rayburn, who became his "most appreciated source of good advice and inspiration." Two years later, Wright refused to sign the "Southern Manifesto," a declaration by 101 southern congressmen and senators denouncing federal efforts to force desegregation of public facilities, and the following year Rayburn advised that he vote for the controversial civil rights law. "The old gentlemen said—'Jim, I think you *want* to vote for this bill. I *know* you're getting a deluge of angry mail, threatening you with retribution if you do. But I think you are a *big enough man* to overcome that. And I know you'll be proud in future years that you did.' "[38]

Seven years later, however, after losing a race to fill the unexpired Senate term of the new vice president, Lyndon B. Johnson, Wright voted against LBJ's landmark civil rights law. Citing his experiences living in Weatherford, Texas, he believed he "should respect and defend the rights of all those small individual operators to make whatever rule he or she might wish in his or her private property." It was, he admitted late in life, the vote he most regretted, although he remained convinced that "my general record of supporting racial equality and equal individual rights will stand the test."

Wright's personal style could not have been more different from Bolling's or Burton's. Disagreements were met not with bellicose outbursts or haughty condescension but with solicitous, even unctuous, friendliness. His style was born of advice from his father after losing his 1948 reelection bid. The voters who opposed him "are not evil men," his father had told him. If voters disapproved of him, it was not because "they don't like you, it's because they don't know you. That's a correctible mistake." The approach to winning over adversaries by befriending them, Wright found, "is almost magic."[39]

The genial style worked to Wright's benefit. "You didn't need to get beat up" speaking to him, an aide recalled, a marked contrast to Burton's excoriating a colleague or Bolling's aloof dismissals. "He really would listen to you. He might say 'no,' but with a gentlemanly personality." As a southerner and moderate, Wright sympathized with members who felt bullied by the caucus's aggressive efforts to compel votes on controversial topics. "We recognize that members in close districts must have a certain latitude of independence in order to represent their districts—and stay in Congress," Wright advised. "We tend to back off some of those fellows."[40]

On many of the key policy questions important to the Class, Wright was regularly aligned with the non-reform side. A steady supporter of the war in Vietnam, Wright had been largely aloof from the reform movement, although he had briefly chaired a panel that made suggestions for improving House operations. During the chairmen purges in 1975, Wright spoke up in defense of Texas colleague Wright Patman. During the key energy debates of the 94th Congress, he was a supporter of Texas's oil and gas industry. Nor was Wright a thoughtful analyst of Congress. In contrast to Bolling's heavily reviewed tomes, Wright's book, *You and Your Congressman*, was dismissively described by a *New York Times* reviewer as "well-intentioned." A photo of him with the disgraced President Nixon still hung on his office wall in late 1976. He was so seemingly unsuited to the caucus climate that some speculated Wright was merely a plant by Burton designed to draw votes away from Bolling and McFall to facilitate his own election. Mikva labeled Wright "an unctuous Evangelical with a pocket full of chits from the Chicago and New York guys. None of us took him seriously."[41]

Wright argued that moderates and southerners, who had been represented in the leadership by Albert, Hale Boggs, and McFall in recent years, needed continued representation in what might otherwise be a team that tilted unfairly toward the growing liberal bias of the caucus. Southerners feared Burton might "ride roughshod" over opponents, and even some liberals shared Wright's argument that the "leadership team ought to be balanced . . . [able to] communicate with the moderate members . . . [and] communicate across party lines." Fred Richmond, a liberal who was very close to many Burton supporters, nevertheless declared he would support Wright because he thought an O'Neill-Burton leadership team would prove "disastrous." As a result of such statements, Wright believed he would win 75 percent of McFall's votes and half of Bolling's should he make it to the runoff.[42]

Wright openly courted the 1976 freshmen, sponsoring a luncheon for the new members at which some in the Class reportedly warned the new freshmen not to "be taken in by Burton's solicitude, as we were."[43] Burton made a rare error when he urged those attending the lunch to heed the advice of Carroll Hubbard, whom he had helped win election as first president of the Class of 1974, although he was later shocked when Hubbard endorsed Wright. Wright made a point of continuing to hold such lunches and dinners for the entire time he served in the leadership, to get to know new members and "[size] up the individual talent in the room."[44]

Inside the Caucus Vote

Although in November *Congressional Quarterly* considered the majority leader race a "wide open contest," Burton entered it the "front runner," confident of the loyalty of "issue-oriented" Class of 1974.[45] He had already won important races for DSG chair and caucus chair, and he was convinced his assistance to the newer members during their campaigns and acclimation to the House, combined with his own strategic acumen, would overwhelm his three competitors. Asked about his plans should he lose, Burton was dismissive. "The thought hasn't crossed my mind for even a fraction of a second," he declared. He was so certain of victory that he repeatedly refused entreaties from senior aides to create a whip organization to assess his support.

Up to half of his own California delegation was likely to defect, led by his old caucus adversary, Bernie Sisk, whom Burton had defeated for caucus chair. "I respect his political knowledge," Sisk said, but "I and many other Democrats felt his attainment of a position of leadership could be disastrous." Class member Mark Hannaford was also put off by Burton's demeanor, which was "a lot more dominant than is my style."[46] California veterans, including Leo Ryan and James Corman, also opposed Burton. Outside California, a Class member from the Northeast who had supported him for caucus chair pulled back from support for the leader slot, explaining, "Phil's problem is that he's overly ambitious, not a pleasant guy and has a bad temper."[47] Russo agreed, conceding that Burton had looked out for the 1974 class but was "so belligerent, it is hard to like him." But Burton knew how to work the members. "That's fine," he confidently told Downey, when the New Yorker informed him he would not support him on the first ballot. "You'll be for me on second ballot."

McFall dropped out after placing fourth in the opening tally, but an ominous sign for Burton was that his own total fell six votes below his projection. The frenetic maneuvering on the second ballot became the subject of decades of intense speculation. Many believe that Burton, presuming Wright would be easier to defeat in the third ballot runoff, encouraged a few supporters to back the Texan, hoping to push Bolling to third place and elimination. But, according to his aide, Ben Palumbo, Burton issued no such directive, always believing he would face Wright in the final balloting. "His answer was, an emphatic 'no, never, I play straight football,'" Palumbo declared. "He flatly told these guys, 'It could get around the chamber and I'd be flat on my ass.' His orders were absolutely firm: 'Vote for me.'"[48]

The speculation that Burton was throwing votes to Wright was fueled by his gaining only one additional vote in the second round, in which Bolling was ousted by just 2 votes, 95–93. Confident of his broad support throughout the caucus, Burton ignored staff recommendations to take a pause in the balloting to form a whip system to check on his pledges. But Burton was wary of any break in the balloting, long nursing a suspicion that his agreement to such an intermission in the balloting for an elective whip in 1973 had allowed opponents to rally votes against his position.

As the members prepared to vote, the last-minute maneuvering began in earnest. "I was leaning towards Phil simply because he was a passionate reformer and was very helpful to our Class," Bill Hughes recalled. But

Wright had New Jersey colleagues on the Public Works Committee, including Jim Howard and Bob Roe, urge a vote for Wright, whose departure from the committee would elevate their own seniority. "They convinced me that he would be a much more balanced [leader]," Hughes recalled, "one who could work with all segments of the Democratic Party . . . and get things done." He also acknowledged Wright and the Public Works Committee could help him retain a crucial Federal Aviation Administration facility in his district.[49]

Bill Cable, who worked for Frank Thompson (also from New Jersey), assumed his boss would support fellow reformer and Education and Labor colleague Burton. "Hell no, fuck Burton!" responded Thompson, who resented Burton's support for Hays during Thompson's chairmanship challenge in 1975. Thompson, who believed Burton had forced him out of DSG leadership, told his staffer, "I already made my deal. We're going to show him what it means to fight us! Jim Howard promised me Jim Wright will deliver [projects for New Jersey]." He had already secured older members of the delegation including Dominick Daniels, Joseph Minish, and Edward Patten and was confident of his ability to "round up all the New Jersey liberals" except for Class member Andy Maguire. "He's the only guy I've got to sit on," Thompson declared. "I don't trust that son of a bitch as far as I could throw him."[50]

Many carefully kept their yellow ballots close to their chests to prevent others from seeing their choice. Wright, unlike Burton, had an active whip operation that was buttonholing members on the floor. One Wright whip, Carroll Hubbard, noticed that his friend Dave Evans of Indiana had marked his ballot for Burton. "Your district wouldn't want a majority leader as liberal as Burton!" warned Hubbard, who had once driven more than 300 miles in a snowstorm to attend an Evans fundraiser in Indianapolis when airports had been shut down. Evans admitted he was chafed that Burton had never reached out to solicit his vote and changed his vote to Wright. Meanwhile, Toby Moffett pleaded with his reluctant Class colleagues including Wirth, Max Baucus, and Chris Dodd. "Don't lose perspective," he implored, "don't vote for Wright."

California colleague and former Class president Norm Mineta had signed a letter supporting Burton but was viewed suspiciously by Burton loyalists who feared that Mineta, like other Public Works members, stood to benefit from Wright's departure from the committee by moving up in seniority and by having a sympathetic ear in the leadership. Others suspected that Mineta harbored his own leadership aspirations and wanted to prevent the elevation of a California competitor that could short-circuit his own ambitions. Burton dispatched his lieutenant, Mikva, to monitor Mineta's voting. Showing Mikva his ballot with "Burton" clearly marked, he implored, "Tell Uncle Phil I voted for him!"

Mikva reported back, but Burton remained dubious. Two years earlier, he had cautioned Brodhead, "Be sure you know X voted for Y. Demand to see the ballot before it is dropped in the box." Brodhead was surprised. "Is it common to show whom you voted for?" he inquired. "No, it's a question of trust," Burton replied, explaining that some members would have two ballots, one to demonstrate fealty and another that was actually cast when no one was looking. Fifteen years later, in a 1991 letter to the *Washington Post*, Mineta remained adamant that he did not support Wright on the third ballot, denouncing suggestions he did so to be named a deputy whip or to gain seniority on Public Works as a "cheap piece of gossip." Yet one account reported that Wright's whipping sheet showed Mineta as a Wright vote on the third ballot.[51]

The multi-decade obsession with Mineta's vote has obscured the fact that many other freshmen, like Baucus, Hughes, and Wirth, *did* vote for Wright. Numerous members of Burton's own California delegation joined Sisk in voting for Wright for a variety of reasons, including Glenn Anderson, who had never forgiven Burton's opposition to his appointment to Ways and Means. Later, when Burton explained that he had supported his appointment, Anderson sighed, "If I had known that, I would have voted for you!"[52]

Many colleagues recalled Burton's warnings to be certain that you got the answer you *wanted*, not the one you wanted to hear. "You're going to win" or "You're going to be a great Leader" was not the same, he reminded people, as "You have my vote." One chronicler reported "many double crosses" against Burton, including Education and Labor colleague Joe Gaydos. Rostenkowski reportedly strong-armed Lud Ashley to change his vote from Burton to Wright. Columnists Evans and Novak claimed that many of the former state and local lawmakers in the 1976 class voted for Wright. Barbara Mikulski, an incoming Maryland member, voted for Wright to minimize Democratic infighting between President Carter and the congressional leadership that she believed more likely with a Burton victory.[53] Mikva was convinced that Paul Simon and even the very liberal Sid Yates of the Illinois delegation voted against Burton because of his drinking. Indeed, numerous members were quoted as explaining that Burton seemed "too driven too ambitious, too manipulative, too contentious," and that, after the tumult of the last two years, "we're tired of confrontation."[54]

Others saw the election as an opportunity to right old wrongs, including senior members who struck back at the person they saw as largely responsible for enhancing the role of the caucus at their expense. Glenn English believed Texans, and southerners in general, blamed Burton personally for the humiliating caucus defeats of Chairmen Patman, Hébert, and Poage in early 1975, the Mills resignation, the grudging retirement of other southern and conservative chairs, and the region's diminished influence. Joe Waggoner and "Tiger" Teague vented their anger at Burton for refusing to recognize them during caucus debates, and Jim O'Hara and Neal Smith resented Burton's role in weakening the Hansen-Bolling reform package. Some chairs resented Burton's use of the caucus to declare party positions on issues within their jurisdiction, including the oil depletion allowance, the Vietnam funding termination, and the killing of the antibusing amendment.

The Dramatic Outcome

There was a "tense and dramatic" atmosphere in the House Chamber during the final balloting as the ballots were collected in three boxes, taken into the cloakroom, and dumped onto the three tables.[55] One by one, the tellers appointed by the candidates turned over the ballots. The middle box, containing the most ballots, took longest to complete. Charlie Wilson of Texas, a Wright teller, turned over the final ballot. It read, "Wright." One Burton observer was so stunned, he claimed, "I nearly stained my drawers!" Krueger left the cloakroom and signaled Wright on the floor, holding up one finger. By a vote of 148–147, Wright was elected.

It fell to Ben Palumbo, his lone aide on the floor, to inform Burton, who was standing in the tiny vestibule connecting the back of the House Chamber to the lobby. Burton's head was cocked to one side, his hands jammed deep in his pockets. "Sorry, Phil," Palumbo consoled, "you lost." Burton took the news bitterly, blaming "deviousness" by many members who had lied to him, but he refused an offer by the caucus chairman Tom Foley to conduct a recount. "Don't feel sorry for me," he told Palumbo. "Now, we have to protect the guys who were for me."

"Wright proved to me he could count a lot better than I do," he joked afterward, but the mood at the DSG's offices was glum. One member hurled a glass at a wall in frustration, startling attendees with its tremendous shattering. Bolling took a more philosophical view. "The day I lost to Burton, I went home and had two drinks," he recalled, "first to commiserate with myself for losing, and second, to toast to myself for winning" by blocking Burton.

Wright, in victory, was gracious. He embraced the vanquished Burton and Bolling, declaring, "We Texans are not new to landslides," a reference to Lyndon Johnson's controversial 87-vote victory in his 1948 Senate race. Wright declared that the victory was "not a mandate" for him personally and, employing the rhetorical flourishes for which he was renowned, asserted that his goal was "to lift Congress to the pinnacle of respect [it] deserved in the world."[56] While promising to pass progressive legislation, Wright portrayed himself as "bridge between liberals and conservatives."[57]

Sala Burton traced the loss back to that drunken confrontation with O'Neill years before, which had convinced the future Speaker that Burton was ill suited to the leadership. That account, which was disseminated widely, created a sense there was a "big potential for disaster if a guy like that is Majority Leader."[58] The DSG's executive director, Dick Conlon, long a Burton ally, was brutally frank in analysis. "What the hell did you expect?" he asked Burton. "You drink too much, your clothes are rumpled, you're overweight." He may have been a political savant, Palumbo agreed, but Phil Burton "couldn't deal with his own shortcomings." Sisk concurred, not surprisingly: "I think there was a strong feeling by a substantial bloc of Democrats that Burton shouldn't win the leadership fight."

Certainly there were additional explanations; many saw the vote as retribution for Burton's many slights over the years. Tim Wirth stated that several Class members who "had all been staunch Bolling supporters" were surprised that Burton, who "fancied himself as the master vote counter [had] never asked [us to support him]. He had assumed our votes."[59] Some recalled Burton's defense of the subsequently disgraced Wayne Hays as illustrative of his willingness to cut unsavory, self-serving deals. One report suggested that half the California delegation "had scores to settle with him" and might have voted for Wright. However, Burton was not the only one with delegation problems. Within the Texas delegation, Bob Eckhardt had been a close ally of Burton on issues ranging from

Vietnam to energy and House reform, and he and Jack Brooks signed a letter of support for Burton.[60]

Unquestionably, too, the freshmen of 1976 did not share the strong loyalty to Burton felt by many in the Class of '74. And with an incoming Democratic administration, following eight years of tumult under Republican presidents, the large Democratic majority simply may not have seen the value of electing as leader a man whose bombastic style, however effective, promised years of tension within the caucus, both as majority leader and perhaps Speaker, whenever O'Neill's reign ended.

While it will never be known how specific votes were cast, interviews with many who participated in the election were persuasive on several key points. First, concerns about Burton's temperament were highly salient in influencing votes. However impressive his legislative legerdemain, his style of denigrating and castigating colleagues left many wary of placing him in such a commanding and visible position. Second, ideology mattered less in determining votes than did personal relationships. Liberals opposed Burton and conservatives supported him based on how much he had done, or might do, on their behalf. And, lastly, the Class voted very much like others in the caucus. Many supported Burton in recognition of his key role in reform and in placing them on committees, but, for others, local concerns or delegation politics drove the decision. In the end, the majority leader race, like most leadership races, was largely determined by what a candidate could do for a caucus member, not simply by ideological compatibility or a shared commitment to reform. The caucus, by the narrowest of margins, was not comfortable giving Burton the power and profile that went with being majority leader and potentially Speaker.

The indefatigable Burton refused to abandon his hopes of entering the leadership. The day after his defeat, he floated the possibility of running for whip if that position were made elective, and the *Washington Post* speculated, "O'Neill may not be able to prevent an election this time." But the caucus wanted to allow the new Speaker to select his team, and the proposal to elect the whip failed dramatically, 39–98, with O'Neill leading the opposition.[61] O'Neill and Burton were "on different planets," one observer noted, and the Speaker believed "he would never have had a peaceful day with Burton part of the leadership inner circle."[62] The new Speaker instead elevated Chief Deputy Whip John Brademas, a respected Indiana liberal with a 94 percent Democratic loyalty voting record and a reputation as "Mr. Education."[63]

The chastising loss did little to dampen Burton's explosive behavior. Tim Wirth remembered that in apparent retribution for his vote for Wright, Burton "tried to retaliate against me by . . . objecting to a suspension vote on my . . . first real bill in Congress." Fortunately for Wirth, fellow Interior Committee member Teno Roncalio of Wyoming, who had attended high school with Wirth's mother, "charged onto the floor and really went after Burton[, whom] he could not stand. They had a major set-to, and Burton stormed off the floor and the bill passed."[64] A few years later, flying with Vice President Walter Mondale aboard *Air Force Two*, Burton consumed multiple vodkas before launching into a vituperative tirade against "fucking Carter" and "fucking Mineta" that left the vice president and his staff stunned. Yet Burton harnessed his prodigious energies in the improbable role of chairman of the Subcommittee on National Parks and Territories, transforming the panel into a dynamo of legislation, creating numerous parks and wilderness areas across the nation. A new term for doing favors for members—"park-barreling"—was coined to describe his technique of delivering public land designations to members. Because of his extensive promotion of America's Pacific insular territories (for which he won nonvoting delegates to the House), it was said the sun never set on Phil Burton's empire.

For the next two years, angered by the leadership's "lack of production" on situs picketing and other labor legislation, Burton nursed the idea of challenging Wright. "I am certainly headed in that direction," he told union leaders. "I certainly don't expect to wait until the next century."[65] Alternatively, he contemplated waiting until O'Neill completed his term as Speaker and then challenging Wright for the top position.

But Burton had risen as high as he ever would, and, it may be argued, so had the period of intense reform in the House. By late 1978, Wright was firmly established as the majority leader, facing no opposition to his re-election, which was significantly seconded by Norm Mineta. "No member of this caucus, regardless of what region, of what seniority, or of what ideological bent will ever lack for a sympathetic ear, a supportive friend and a ready hand of assistance with Jim Wright as Majority Leader," Mineta told the incoming 96th Congress.[66] In 1979, Bolling ascended to the chairmanship of the Rules Committee, the position he coveted almost as fervently as the speakership, and in which he began to tighten down the open rules that had granted Republicans the flexibility to force controversial votes and delays on the floor.[67] In 1983, having risen no higher than the chairmanship of his Interior subcommittee, Burton died suddenly from a massive heart attack. Half of the dozens of members flying to his memorial service in San Francisco were said to have attended just to be certain he was truly dead.

For many of the younger members, the election was a dramatic, almost inexplicable, setback. "The advent of a Jim Wright era in Congress gives heartburn to younger Democrats, who fear for their party's future and their own," observed the liberal *New Republic*. Wright seemed too much "the stereotypical genial, backslapping legislator with more than a hint of the snake-oil salesman about him."[68] Seasoned political observers speculated that Wright's election illustrated "some mellowing by House Democrats" that would result in a less assertive House of Representatives during the Carter administration and perhaps well beyond it." Columnists Evans and Novak credited Wright's election to the desire of Democrats to "consolidate . . . after several years of turnover and turmoil in their ranks." Some predictions about Wright's impact were proven wildly inaccurate. An insider wrongly predicted that Wright would be a "very quiescent Majority Leader" who might never rise to the speakership.[69] The defeat of Burton, it was argued, constituted a "moderate counter-revolutionary re-action following turbulent radical reform" that would move "the House power equation rightward."[70]

The Waning of Reform

But there was no conservatization of the House Democrats under Wright. With the exception of raising the number of votes needed to secure a recorded vote, the reforms effectuated in the 94th Congress were not weakened. True, the pace of change slowed but mainly because so many major innovations had been implemented in the period 1973–1976 and because so many of the old guard had retired by 1977. With a Democrat in the White House and the threats of vetoes seemingly lifted, however, many considered it time to focus more on legislative production and less on internal changes.

Additional efforts to identify areas for reform included a special panel chaired by Dave Obey in 1977. Obey's recommendations were managerial in nature—creation of an administrator to handle the management of the House, appointment of a comptroller to manage the financial system, and a proposal to "bring a greater degree of candor to House travel procedures."[71] Little in the package sought to alter the power relationships in the House like those during the zenith of reform in 1973–1975.

Two years later, the Select Committee on Reform undertook a renewed effort to revise jurisdictional realignment under the chairmanship of Jerry Patterson. O'Neill also charged Patterson with addressing the proliferation of subcommittees, which had grown in number to more than 140 by 1979, which "fragment[ed] the legislative process and spread members too thin," the *Post* charged.[72] As a result, for example, 84 committees and subcommittees shared jurisdiction over some aspect of energy policy. After months of work, the effort encountered the same massive institutional resistance that had stymied the Madden-Monroney Committee in 1968 and the Bolling Committee initiative of 1974. Member self-interest, including among Class members who had begun to accrue seniority and chairmanships, outweighed appeals for efficiency. The "biggest thing we were trying to do, we didn't get done," Patterson wistfully acknowledged. "I was very naïve, very idealistic." Even a recommendation to limit each committee, except Appropriations, to 6 subcommittees and a 3-year phaseout of 26 subcommittees met with vigorous opposition because it meant fewer members would get to chair panels.[73]

With liberals now dominant in the caucus, a more progressive Speaker in O'Neill, and a Democratic president, there seemed less urgency for the kinds of reform that had targeted a more conservative and unresponsive leadership. In one important regard, however, the spirit of revitalization so inflamed by the Class continued apace: efforts to reassert the Congress's coequal status with the presidency, regardless of who occupied the White House. Although it had been predicted in 1976 that he had "no interest in continuing hell-bent democratization of the House or constant congressional assault on presidential prerogatives," by the time of his accession to the speakership in 1986, there was no stronger exponent of congressional equity with the executive branch. Wright promoted an "unprecedentedly proactive agenda" as Speaker, and, despite the expectation that he was, among Burton, Bolling, and himself, the one with "the soft touch," Wright challenged both the Reagan White House and a resurgent Republican Conference in the House aggressively.[74] Even a hard-line Burton disciple like George Miller would laud Wright's "risk taking[, which] has given the House back some of its pride."

The dissipation of the reform agitation was illustrated by steadily decreasing attendance at caucus meetings in the 95th Congress. Resentment continued to grow over the perceived abuse of the open amendment process and the frequent quorum calls and recorded votes (which doubled in 1978) to delay floor action. But there remained little interest in caucus dictates to the leadership regarding the management of the House. At the organizing meetings after the 1978 election, the caucus rejected a proposal by freshman Ted Weiss of New York to prohibit voting on the floor between 2 a.m. and 8 a.m. Longtime reformer Mo Udall disparaged the proposal, noting that Republicans would simply drag their feet until 2 a.m., forcing an adjournment that would necessitate another legislative day to be consumed. "What it says," explained Udall, "is we don't trust our own leadership."[75]

Committees also began to push back against dictates by the caucus. In the 1978 organizing caucus, after Democrats had suffered a 15-seat loss, Class member Christopher Dodd asked for the caucus to direct Ways and Means to take action on Social Security tax rates, a motion seconded by the progressive John Seiberling of Ohio, who noted the committee had ignored an earlier caucus directive. Subcommittee chairman Jake Pickle of Texas acknowledged the caucus's impatience but asked for and received additional time to consider the proposal. Another Dodd proposal to bar chairmen from also chairing a subcommittee on their own panel drew strong opposition despite a qualification that grandfathered all current chairs. Speaking in opposition were longtime reformers Obey, Seiberling, and Maryland's Parren Mitchell, as well as Phil Burton, who confessed he once has been "a zealot" in support of such a restriction.[76] The more conservative Bob Duncan, who had raised warnings in 1975 that the aggressiveness of the liberal caucus faction could jeopardize the seats of members in marginal districts and endanger the future of the majority, noted that past reforms had so "diffused power throughout this body as to almost divest our leadership of the tools" needed to run the House. While not endorsing a rollback to pre-1974 rules, Duncan suggested it was "time to put on the brakes and avoid any further diffusion of power and responsibility."[77] Dodd sensed the "slaughter afoot," and the proposal was defeated.

A proposal by Bob Carr directing the Speaker to include as a conferee any member whose amendment had been adopted by the House was ridiculed as naïve. Carr's proposal "ignored the realities of the way we legislate around here," insisted Interior Chairman Udall, a startling observation coming from one who just a few years earlier had been at the forefront of advocating changes in House procedure.[78] Another plan, by freshman Al Gore of Tennessee, to require advanced notice of conference meetings, infuriated Sam Stratton, who skewered the freshman by noting that "a lot of these things sound great to people who have never had to deal with the situation . . . It doesn't work that way."[79]

Reform proposals from 1974 Class members were also rejected, including an initiative to allow one-third of the caucus to consider an issue rather than a majority. Moffett and other Class veterans argued that although reforms allowed just 50 members to call a caucus, actual participation had dropped so significantly in the past Congress that caucus meetings frequently were incapable of promoting issues. A smaller quorum, as he proposed, would prompt attendance and "make the caucus a vibrant thing again." Maguire echoed that sentiment, asserting that the "Democratic caucus has not functioned in even a minimal way." Downey agreed, denying the goal was to create "a tool for just a small group of people who want to cause mischief" but rather "to revitalize the Caucus as a policymaking body," rather than "what the Caucus has turned into."

But that was precisely the concern of many caucus members who, like John Anderson in 1975 has speculated that "King Caucus would become supreme," driven by "a very small percentage of people." The caucus "should not be a substitute for the committee," explained Class member Paul Simon. Policy decisions ought not be made "by whim rather than on the basis of substantial study." Small groups should not be "trying to speak for the party," in the words of Jack Murtha, elected early in 1974, as was Bob Traxler, who explained that he sometimes avoided caucus meetings specifically to *ensure* the absence of a quorum that might take votes on issues he would rather avoid.

The defeat of the Moffett proposal by a 33–74 vote illustrated the transformation of the Class and the weakening of the argument that the caucus needed to force recalcitrant committees to address priority issues. As if to make the point about the diminished caucus, only 38 percent of the members even attended this meeting. The Class, and power, had moved from the caucus back to the committees and the leadership, although both were now more responsive to the members than they were before the reforms were enacted. Committees were no longer the bastions of senior conservative despots; the activists and dissidents of 1974 were now, just four years later, subcommittee chairs and senior members driving the agenda. The reforms, and the reformers, had been institutionalized.

12 REFORM AND THE RISE OF POLARIZATION

Politics got ugly.—Rep. Mike Blouin (D-IA)

Campaigns became more vicious . . . go for the jugular. And the kind of people coming into the House was changing, too, as was the language they were willing to use to get and stay there.—Rep. Dave Obey (D-WI)

Michel would never challenge O'Neill about corruption in the Democratic Caucus. [He] liked to have cocktails and smoke cigars, but wouldn't challenge O'Neill on their legislation or organize to beat their members until Newt came along. —Rep. Larry Pressler (R-SD)

y the late 1970s, the contour, style, and operation of a new kind of congressional politics were underway. Battles were taking place within each party for dominance; money and independent organizations were promoting issues and financing campaigns in an unprecedented fashion; and with the question of House control increasingly a focus, particularly after the 1980 election of Ronald Reagan and a Republican Senate, there was a persistent emphasis on exploiting issues that served to emphasize the differentiation between the parties.

Many have argued this shift—the emergence of a distinctly partisan and confrontational style—occurred at later points in our political history: the election of Ronald Reagan, the Republican capture of the Senate in 1980, the bitter 1984 House battle over the 8th District of Indiana, the challenge to, and downfall of, Speaker Jim Wright at the hands of the Republican activists led by Newt Gingrich. As this account has already shown, the transition to a more polarized and competitive atmosphere was underway in the late 1970s, bolstered by changing forces both within and outside the Congress.

Although the significant reforms to House rules were largely complete by 1978, intended and unintentional impacts emerged over the subsequent decade and a half of Democratic majorities. While often achieving the reformers' goals of democratization and transparency, many of the reforms designed to check the accumulated power of conservative *Democrats* inadvertently facilitated the rise of a new generation of conservative *Republicans* who, like the Class of 1974, challenged not only the opposing party but their own ossified leadership. A Republican in the class of 1978 reflected that "senior Republicans on a committee have sold out to the Democratic leadership on the committee," citing the decision of the ranking member, Frank Horton of New York, who "was leading the charge" to support the Democrats' initiative to create a federal Department of Education. Another of the junior, more confrontational Republicans, leveled a similar charge at the Republican leader, Bob Michel of Illinois, who supported Democratic bills moving through the Appropriations Committee on which he served. While Michel may have secured funds for his own priorities in the legislation, this critic noted, "the rest of us don't feel under any constraints at all—at least I don't—and . . . the junior members, don't, partly, I suppose, because we are not consulted when it comes time to construct major deals."[1]

Late in 1975, Colorado freshman Tim Wirth declared that arrival of the Class had signaled an "ideological realignment" in American politics, a "new [politics] that emphasizes openness and the non-systematic use of power [to achieve] not only material but moral aspirations as well."[2] While politics was indeed changing, Wirth and many others misread the emerging fault lines; the new political topography would result not in his postpartisan ideal but rather the most partisan and polarized era in modern American politics.

Ironically, Wirth's career itself was marked by a souring of his faith in Congress as an institution of political change. Throughout the 1980s, as the levels of partisanship in the House markedly rose, Wirth became increasingly "frustrated with the posturing and paralysis of Congress" and dismayed by the failure of the Class's well-intentioned efforts to make politics more open and collaborative.[3] "There was bad leadership in House," he asserted, but he also blamed himself (and perhaps by extension, the Class more broadly) for being "excessively self-important." Whatever the explanation, he concluded, "The energy was gone in the mid-'80s. We went flaccid." Elected to the Senate in 1986, his discouragement grew with the rising partisan confrontations. "People run for the right intentions," he said after announcing his retirement in 1992, "but politics takes over." Congress was overwhelmed by a "sclerotic" lack of intellectual fervor. "Fresh voices must speak out for institutional change," he declared.[4]

Fresh voices were indeed "speaking out," and they were increasingly combative, more partisan, and more engaged in what political scientist Frances Lee has termed "the perpetual campaign" for control of Congress.[5] By the late 1980s, Republicans were successfully challenging incumbents in districts they believed had been inappropriately electing Democrats since the Class's victories of 1974. Under their relentless assault, Democratic House seats shrunk from the "veto-proof" halcyon level of 292 in 1975 back to the pre-Watergate surge in the mid-250s a decade later.

The pace of reform slowed in part both because the members elected after 1974 did not share the Class's enthusiasm and because the success of the modernization efforts diminished the need for additional change. Moreover, many of the more aggressive freshmen had departed the House by the mid-1980s either in defeat or by seeking another office, and those who remained were taking full advantage of their swiftly accumulating seniority to join the ranks of chairmen.

But there was also a rising disquiet, a sense that perhaps the reforms had gone too far, had damaged the capacity of the institution to function effectively, jeopardizing the ability to achieve political goals. "We had no idea how good we had it," Wirth said later, reflecting on his early years in the House.[6] As early as mid-1975, some feared that disseminating power was complicating, not facilitating, the legislative process. Even some of the reformers accepted the unintentional consequences of some of their decisions. "You make the rules more democratic," one senior staff observer noted, "and things are bound to look messier."[7] One of the prime ways things became "messier" was the rapid increase in the ability to raise and force recorded votes on highly volatile political and cultural issues. The "ideological realignment" Wirth had confidently predicted was underway, but it was far from post-partisan. Indeed, a new era of unabated political warfare was suffusing Congress. Dave Obey, whose own efforts at reform were largely ignored, declared that the House "stopped being fun in 1978."[8]

Unintended Consequences of Reform

This unease did not translate into recommendations that Congress return to the hierarchical system.[9] "No one is pleading for a counter-reformation or a return to a pre-Watergate political standards," assured Duke University political scientist James David Barber although he worried the swift reforms might have confused voters into believing Congress's many problems could be solved with a "traumatic quick fix."[10] "If you're asking would I like to see us go back to where we were," wrote James Sundquist of the Brookings Institution, "I'd have to say no."

Others were more circumspect. Scholars who had bemoaned the lethargy of the Congress in the 1960s now questioned whether reformism might produce, in the words of Henry Graff of Columbia University, "a generation of political cowards . . . either virgins or eunuchs fearful of making consequential decisions" because of expanded public scrutiny and competitiveness. George Reedy of Marquette, a former press secretary to Lyndon Johnson, predicted, "We are going to regret a number of these reforms," and Herbert Alexander, the longtime director of the Campaign Finance Institute, worried that new rules could complicate the management of Congress, "where party discipline is already minimal."

An especially sharp critique came from conservative intellectual Irving Kristol, who likened Congress's periodic reform efforts to "spasmodic self-abuse." Far from resolving the problems of the Congress, Kristol warned, the "reforms aiming to solve today's problems are likely to constitute the problems of tomorrow," promoting partisan division by demanding an unattainable "insistence on a degree of political purity." Sunshine laws, Kristol argued, penalized candor and rewarded "grandstanding" by self-promoting legislators skilled at taking advantage of their newfound access to round-the-clock coverage by the media. The transparency rules, he predicted, would do little but "provide opportunities for mischievous intervention by various publicity-hunting busybodies" while complicating the search for compromise and forcing deliberations even further behind closed doors.[11]

Within the Congress, no less a reform advocate than Richard Bolling cautioned about "the demagoguery" of some of the changes approved by the House. In the Senate, where fewer changes had been effectuated, Alan Cranston of California concluded, "in some reforms, we overreacted, as if we have to prove our morality and ethics." Sen. Bill Brock, a Tennessee Republican defeated in his 1976 reelection campaign, warned, "The reforms may have contributed to increased alienation of citizens from the political process." Most of the House reformers disputed such instant revisionism, arguing divisive and demoralizing experiences like the Vietnam War, Watergate, and the Nixon impeachment had fueled what Mo

Udall termed "a healthy skepticism about government," not their reform initiatives.[12]

Yet some of the reforms did have serious operational consequences. The adoption of the O'Neill-Gupser Amendment in 1970 made it easier to call recorded votes in place of the traditional secret teller counts, and subsequent reforms similarly forced previously private actions and statements into full public view. Although members obviously still could conduct private conversations, the horse-trading aspect of retail legislating was diminished; the opportunity for amendments that might have improved legislation and facilitated bipartisan floor approval was impaired when nearly every motion was subject to a vote.

As early as 1976, Wayne Hays argued that the presence of the press and public had generated "more partisanship and more hardenings [of positions]."[13] The votes on procedural rules were transformed from inconsequential procedural decisions into votes on which members were held as accountable as on the substance of a bill itself. These rules battles became far more frequent (twice as frequent in 1983–1984 as in the prior three Congresses) and partisan, leading to a "striking increase in partisanship" and a "prickly relationship" between the two parties.[14] Opening conference committees chilled the atmosphere in the meeting room, asserted Sam Stratton of New York, compelling members to stake out contrary positions that complicated reaching agreement. "We will not get any compromise," asserted the conservative Stratton, unless members "go into the corner drugstore or the [Rayburn Building's] Gold Room to conduct your conferences." Veteran John Dent of Pennsylvania speculated that "if you would have had an open conference, there would never have been an Election Reform Bill [or] a Minimum Wage Bill. I beg of you young people," he implored the freshmen, "wait for a few months of experience."[15] A Judiciary Committee staffer agreed: "Behind closed doors, some southern Democrats could cut deals they wouldn't have been able to do in public." "You can't get things done if everybody knows what's going on," another senior staff person advised. Within a year of the decision to open conferences, it was acknowledged that whenever conferees "encountered fundamental disagreements," they simply recessed to finalize negotiations. "The accommodations," it was noted, "have been made, as usual, in quiet."[16]

The historic decision to allow live television coverage of the floor and virtually all committee hearings had profound, if not unexpected, consequences. Although there had been occasional television coverage of major hearings like the Army-McCarthy inquiry or the Watergate inquiries, coverage of floor debates had long been resisted on a bipartisan basis. Republican David Dennis had warned that live floor coverage would encourage "prima donnas . . . who will be spending more time making hay on the TV camera than in doing the business that we are sent there to transact."[17] Tip O'Neill was even more blunt. "Some of us aren't very smart and we won't look so good," he predicted. "If you think the public's rating of Congress is low now, just wait till we get television! If a guy was picking his nose or scratching his ass, that's what you'd see."[18]

Increasingly, presidential use of television left many in Congress feeling at a decided disadvantage, and a 1974 joint Senate-House report endorsed the need to counter the "growing imbalance between executive and legislative power."[19] The enormous popularity of the Watergate and impeachment hearings—which gave tens of millions of Americans their first live look at extended congressional hearings—increased the pressure. By October 1975, a joint committee recommended that both the House and Senate allow TV coverage of committees as well as the floor.[20] When the House turned on the floodlights and cameras on March 19, 1979, the first speaker on the airwaves was the technology-savvy sophomore from Tennessee, Al Gore, who optimistically predicted, "The solution for lack of confidence in government is more open government at all levels. Television will change this institution just as it has changed the executive branch . . . but the good will far outweigh the bad."

Yet the decision to televise proceedings contributed to the rise of heightened partisanship in the House by encouraging "grandstanding[,] and that has led to more focus on contentious issues," Class member Bill Hughes observed. With the ability to watch floor proceedings (and even some committee hearings) in their offices, many members opted against spending time on the floor where valuable collegiality had long developed. "You didn't see people on the floor, talking to each other," complained Class member Leo Zeferetti, who wistfully recalled the days when Tip O'Neill might wander over, drape a burly arm over his shoulder, and propose they "get Shirley [Chisholm] to go along" on a key vote.

The lure of the camera proved powerful. As Dennis and others had warned, members delivered speeches and offered motions that had less to do with legislating than with appealing to partisans, funders, and the press not only during formal House business but also during the legislatively irrelevant "one minute speeches" and "special orders" at the beginning and end of the day (and sometimes well into the night). Where such speeches previously had typically been honorific—congratulating the local sports team or a spelling bee winner—in the televised era, they became vehicles for inflammatory criticisms of the other party that required no countervailing response from those under attack. Precluded from bringing legislation to the floor, minority Republicans employed these informal procedures to present alternative policy goals to national audiences, knowing that most observers were unable to distinguish genuine legislative debate from the rhetorical spectacle. As partisan lines hardened in the early 1980s, the tone of these ancillary floor remarks grew increasingly accusatorial.[21] Newt Gingrich, first elected in 1978 and among the most aggressive in the practice of inflammatory floor debate, credited TV coverage with having "provided a group of media-savvy House conservatives with a method of . . . winning a prime-time audience."[22]

In the first year of the reforms, 93 percent of congressional hearings and markups were open to the press and the public, as were the majority of conference meetings, a reform that had met with sweeping bipartisan support.[23] The goal, said freshman Bill Brodhead, was to "put everybody on record, no hiding from press or constituents."[24] Wariness about being subjected to nationally televised challenges discouraged some members from speaking. "No one trusts anyone," declared Zeferetti.[25] The number of recorded votes, which had risen from 177 in 1969 to 537 at the time of the 1974 election, grew to 661 during the Class's first session, and in 1976 to more than 800 recorded votes, often on controversial issues like abortion, school busing, and flag burning.[26] By the late 1970s, Republican strategists were skillfully forcing Democrats to choose between their constituents and the party leaders on sensitive votes.[27] It was this rapid expansion in votes, with the related delays in the legislative calendar and promotion of controversial topics, that convinced even members of the Class in December 1978 to "do away with all other dilatory tactics," in the words of Majority Leader Jim Wright.[28]

Republicans responded harshly, characterizing the reversal as an effort by a partisan majority to stifle their voices. Pleas for "a little more fairness, a little more openness, a little more balance," John Anderson complained, "always seem to fall on deaf ears on the other side of the aisle. We are stuck with the futility and frustration of being in the minority."[29] The restrictions energized conservatives to find ways around the new limitations, led by hard-liners like John Ashbrook, Bob Bauman, and John Rousselot, who proved adept at honing germane amendments that skewed marginal Democrats. Bauman bragged about his efforts to impose abortion restrictions to "create political difficulties for the Democratic incumbents," and it worked.[30] Steve Neal, the moderate North Carolina member of the Class, credited Bauman and other conservative activists with setting effective political traps. "It was a huge nuisance," Neal admitted.

Frustrated Reformers React

By August 1979, Class member John LaFalce had had enough. LaFalce was no partisan warrior; he had served as a minority member in the Republican-dominated New York legislature, represented a Republican district, and had even rationalized Ford's pardon of President Nixon as "an act of mercy, not an act of justice." But now he believed that Republican exploitation of the open rules had "strangled democracy," empowering a "mobocracy" intent on promoting an atmosphere of "anything goes."[31] He was heartened that 42 colleagues, including many reformers like Bolling, supported his proposal to limit each side to six floor amendments on any bill instead of the hundreds that often were filed. "No one in their right mind thought amendments could be unlimited," he asserted. "You can't run a representative democracy that way. You need fair rules [to produce an] efficient, egalitarian form of government. You need to run the railroad on time."[32] His New York neighbor, Matt McHugh, agreed. "With more democratization, [there is] more leeway for amendments, more openness, an increased prospect for more amendments that can be controversial and polarizing," he noted. "And that did happen over time. In a participatory system, you need members who are non-polarizing."[33]

After the caucus raised the number of members needed to demand a recorded vote, the number of bills considered under permissive rules shrank from 86 percent in the reform-driven 94th Congress to 66 percent four years later, to barely half by the early 1980s. On the more significant or controversial legislation, 64 percent were considered under open rules during the 94th Congress, but that number had shrunk to just 13 percent a decade later.[34] Similarly, the percentage considered under closed rules that permitted only leadership-approved amendments quadrupled over the same period. Both of these changes, which reimposed efficiency lost through earlier reforms, met with the vigorous protests of Republicans, who accused Democrats of arrogant and partisan mismanagement of the House.

Another strategy for protecting bills from punishing amendments was the use of the "suspension of the rules" procedure, which required a two-thirds vote to pass a bill, barred amendments, and tightly limited debate time. Because the minority could generally produce the one-third needed to block such a bill, the process was typically employed only for noncontroversial measures like commemorative resolutions and the naming of post offices. But with Democrats enjoying a two-thirds majority in the mid-1970s, the leadership resorted to expanded use of the suspension process to curtail Republican interference. The maneuver encountered opposition from Class members still committed to open floor participation. Christopher Dodd complained that utilizing the non-amendment strategy meant "we are not following the guidelines" intended to allow open floor debate.[35] Republicans responded by more regularly opposing suspension bills on partisan grounds, defeating 25 in the 94th Congress as compared to just 1 before the Class's election. In the next Congress, 31 suspension bills failed, often winning votes from some frustrated Democrats who opposed the bill's substance or objected to being precluded from offering their own amendments.

The reformers' decision to expand the number of subcommittees spread power to members who otherwise might have waited years to gain seniority. Limitations that restricted the service of senior members on multiple subcommittees further allowed newer members to have an unusually substantive impact on key policy areas and even to chair significant subcommittees early in their congressional service. The greater independence accorded the panels allowed junior members to raise issues long suppressed in full committees. But the proliferation of specialized subcommittees also fueled what some viewed as a "Balkanization of the caucus," where small groups fashioned complex legislation and most members remained unaware of subjects until they appeared on the House floor.

An additional complication was that the range of viewpoints on subcommittees, where membership was determined by self-selection, often was far narrower than on full committees, to which members were appointed by the Steering Committee to ensure a wide perspective of opinion. The domination of the subcommittees by like-minded Democrats often minimized the need to incorporate Republican ideas into a bill, feeding the minority's sense of exclusion from the legislative process. With the new campaign finance rules allowed by the 1974 reforms, lobbyists also found it easier to target these highly specialized subcommittees to ensure legislative outcomes favorable to their interests.

For the leadership, the proliferation of panels and the active legislative activity they produced served to complicate the management of the House. "New members once were seen and not heard," Tip O'Neill nostalgically recalled, "but now it seemed that even the lowliest freshman could be a power in the House." Although O'Neill had sanctioned the creation of additional subcommittees, select committees, and task forces to give younger members greater exposure, he came to believe power, or at least profile, had been too widely disseminated. "Almost before we knew it," he later wrote, "there were 154 committees and subcommittees, each with its own chairman."[36]

Even many reformers agreed the expansion of subcommittee autonomy complicated management of an already unruly House. Richard Bolling, who had long warned about excessive dissemination of power, charged that some of the reforms "have had a much deeper impact and have transformed the character and operations of the House, [making] the legislative process much more untidy, freewheeling and unpredictable." Don Fraser, a former DSG chair and longtime reform advocate, worried about the impact of the proliferation of subcommittees. "Now everybody has a subcommittee and everybody wants to do their thing," he asserted in 1976. "[Members] are in subcommittee hearings and committee hearings[,] and that is why they are not on the floor." Walter Kravitz, a former Budget Committee staff director, warned that the new rules could grant too much power to the subcommittees, risking a return to the disorganization that existed in the era before the 1946 legislative reforms were implemented.[37]

Inevitably, it fell to the leadership to sort out the profusion of legislation that poured from the subcommittees, not all of which could find its way to the floor. *Congressional Quarterly* in 1978 noted that the legislative process had slowed because "more members demanded consideration of more bills and amendments."[38] "The responsibility for saving subcommittee government from itself . . . falls largely to the party and party leadership," Lawrence Dodd and Bruce Oppenheimer concluded in 1981.[39] Subcommittees reported legislative proposals on an array of issues including consumer protections, energy, education, environment, children, and many other policies that strong chairmen might have restricted or staggered in earlier times. "You need to deal with and negotiate with a lot [of] congressmen," Bob Giaimo of Connecticut acknowledged, and many of the new players were less deferential, less patient, and less seasoned.[40] Often, when their bills reached the floor, the subcommittee chairs rather than the full committee leaders managed the legislation. Whereas, a decade earlier, subcommittee chairs had been allowed to manage their own bills only 42 percent of the time, during the 94th Congress, that percentage rose to 66 percent.

Even Class members acknowledged that service on a large number of subcommittees, together with other official and political duties, stretched the freshmen thin. "There was a sense of loss of control and information, an ability to control your own time," Carr reflected. The increased specialization of the panels meant "more legislation was coming to the floor that we knew less about. The committees and subcommittees were the knowledgeable people, and in effect, the floor became an appellate body to little legislatures," battling out issues that previously had been resolved in committees and were then ratified by the overall House. The profusion of subcommittees also contributed to greater infighting, as multiple panels claimed jurisdiction over portions of complex legislation, slowing down the pace of decision making.[41] Years later, after he had become the chairman of the Public Works Subcommittee on Surface Transportation in 1992, Norm Mineta agreed that "dispersion of power and increased jurisdictions" of the subcommittees had "probably contributed to the [floor] logjam."[42]

Yet some Class reformers, while acknowledging the heavy workload and dispersal of responsibilities that came with the expansion of subcommittees, challenged the notion that the reforms had altered the fundamental power structure of the House. Although the younger members might show "a kind of lack of deference to some degree in some situations," as Andy Maguire phrased it, the leaders and chairmen remained in command. "You still knew who was in charge," George Miller said, pointing to the strong chairmen like John Dingell, Dan Rostenkowski, Bill Natcher, and Jack Brooks who remained in power for many years after the reforms were implemented. Disagreements with more senior members did not prevent the creation of "coalitions with senior like-minded members [and] with leadership," and, rather than standing apart from the leaders, Maguire asserted, "we integrated ourselves into the ongoing work of Congress and the Democratic party and the goals of leadership."[43] Waxman rejected the labeling of Class members as disturbers, calling them instead "talented people [who] wanted to be active in issues." The critics, he believed, were "creating conspiracies where none exist[ed]."[44] And while Majority Whip John Brademas argued that many of the reforms had "increased the obstacles to passage of all bills," fellow Indianan Floyd Fithian reminded his colleagues that "an open and more free, more democratic system is not efficient. Democracies are not efficient; they never were intended to be."[45] Still, reformers believed the changes were worth the frustrations, and Tom Foley, the Agriculture chairman, acknowledged the while the hierarchical old system had provided "efficiencies, they were not efficiencies I would like to go back to."[46]

Class members rejected accusations they bore particular responsibility for problems associated with the reforms since virtually all the rules changes had been designed prior to their election. "[We] may have exacerbated the impact of reform," Toby Moffett agreed, "but we certainly didn't give rise to it."[47] Other reformers placed the blame with the leadership for failing to impose greater discipline. Ab Mikva faulted O'Neill for refusing to twist arms when members opposed a position endorsed by the caucus. "He never would call you in and say, 'do the right thing or you will lose your seat,'" Mikva noted.

The institutionalization of oversight activities, while granting Class members greater visibility and elevating Congress's role in scrutinizing the executive branch, also contributed to a rise in partisan tensions. Members quickly learned that a hearing on a controversial topic, with a reluctant witness and a shrewd line of questioning, could turn an obscure freshman into a national media figure in short order, and many became skilled performers. As the number of investigations doubled beginning with the Class's 94th House, the nature of oversight increasingly reflected the "new polarized, winner-take-all Congresses featuring sharp partisanship and polarization in the new technology age."[48] Fueled by the Watergate inquiry and the new generation of investigative, exposé-oriented journalists it spawned, oversight became "weaponized," in the words of political scientists David Parker and Matthew Dull, serving as a crucial tool for attacking the opposing party, especially during periods of divided government when the rate of investigations, often "framed by alleged negligence, abuse of power, violation of law, and ethical misconduct," increased substantially.[49]

Even the budget process produced unintended consequences that fueled partisan rancor. Support for a strengthened congressional hand in writing the budget blueprint was initially bipartisan because of broad anger at President Nixon's impoundment of congressionally approved spending. "The culture then was that the president has too much power," recalled Republican representative Bill Archer of Texas.[50] The law, one analyst has written, "threw out the old president-led and appropriator-controlled system, replacing it with a less hierarchical, more inclusive process," but one that "invited more conflict among legislators, and created more access points for proliferating interest groups."[51]

The budget process also constrained and delayed the work of the Appropriations Committee, long among the most collegial of congressional activities since both majority and minority ensured funding for their own priorities. By contrast, the budget process, which allocated no actual dollars, quickly devolved in a distinctly partisan exercise in which conflicting party priorities were reflected in competing blueprints at the outset of each session. As a result, one top Republican staff aide agreed, the budget procedure immediately divides the House sharply into "our budget versus theirs."[52] Appropriator Dave Obey argued that budget reforms made the annual decision-making about spending "far more political and far more partisan."[53]

Yet another area of reform that veered far from its anticipated objective was the complex issue of campaign finance. Although the law was enacted in 1974, prior to the arrival of the Class, it had dramatic impacts on Class members like Dave Evans and Bob Edgar who spent only a few thousand dollars to win their seats with little organizational support or dependence on special interest contributors. With the proliferation of political action committees, which reformers had hoped would make campaigns more transparent and accountable, such low-budget, outsider campaigns became virtually impossible. PACs quickly arrayed themselves along partisan lines, and candidates were forced to appeal to one side or another. Within a year, 137 business PACs had been created, and another 244 had been set up by labor organizations. Even more problematically, during the 94th Congress the Supreme Court declared the law's spending limits unconstitutional, leaving in place the special interest fundraising machinery but imposing few constraints on the level of expenditures. The goals of the law were further weakened when, in March 1976, the court ruled that individuals could spend unlimited personal funds on their campaigns while weakening the ability of the regulating body, the Federal Elections Commission, to function.[54] Combined with the emergence of divisive issues and the proliferation of special interest organizations, the loosening of campaign financing laws helped to fuel the emerging field of negative attack ads and further increased candidate dependence on well-endowed partisan sources.

Personal Relations Deteriorate

The partisan atmosphere contributed to a deterioration in the personal relationships that had customarily softened the damage from legislative combat. Into the late 1970s, liberals like Ab Mikva recalled having cordial relations with Illinois conservatives like Republican leader Bob Michel and antiabortion activist Henry Hyde, both of whom supported his nomination for a federal judgeship in 1979. Bipartisanship was also evident when it came to taking ethics actions against miscreant members. In April 1976, Bolling led dozens of colleagues from both parties in filing a complaint against senior Democrat Robert Sikes, chairman of the Military Construction Subcommittee on Appropriations, for his failure to disclose income from the defense industry. Opposition to Sikes, who blamed his troubles on "flaming liberals" as well as Republicans, led the House to reprimand him 381–3.[55] Such bipartisan agreement on an ethics issue would become a rarity in the years ahead, as investigations took on a partisan cast beginning in the late 1980s.

Members had long enjoyed bipartisan friendships during pickup basketball and handball games in the House gym. Bill Gradison recalled how the "young guys with a lot of testosterone" would spend hours together burning off excess energy, free from the need for public posturing and even discussing the current issues before the House. But the increasingly partisan atmosphere and the superheated, accusatorial rhetoric of debates made it "harder to come there and . . . to be buddy buddy with 'the gentleman from Kentucky,'" Ab Mikva recalled. More frequent commuting back to districts, necessitated by growing competition for marginal seats, meant less free time in Washington for the traditional fraternizing that had facilitated cross-aisle friendships. Since the additional office account funds provided in 1975 meant that members had the financial capability (not to mention the political necessity) to return to their districts almost weekly, many families chose to remain in their home districts, further fraying the apolitical social network that had bridged official party differences. By the early 1980s, one member of the 1978 class noted, "The collegial system is disintegrating. We are seeing it begin to disintegrate."[56]

Many in the Class recognized and were troubled by the growing bitterness in the House. Matt McHugh had been attracted to political service by the "bipartisan sense among people that government was not working well" in the wake of Watergate, the Nixon resignation, and Vietnam. The reforms of the mid-1970s, he asserted, were a "bipartisan effort to make the system work, [become] more powerful," and did not reflect "a partisan agenda. We didn't see ourselves as partisans." And, indeed, although some reforms—like the creation of permanent committee ratios that benefitted the majority—had unmistakable partisan ramifications, many others, including the allocation of staff and the liberalized rules for offering amendments, benefitted both parties. Sympathy for bipartisanship was echoed by Berkley Bedell, himself a former Republican. "If ever anyone in Congress was nonpartisan, I'm it," he declared. "I'd cut [red] tape to help a Republican, and Republicans would cut tape to help me." He fondly recalled how his unsuccessful opponents often called to congratulate him on his reelection victories.

Like Bedell, Tom Harkin would sponsor bipartisan social events, and Dick Ottinger recalled regularly having drinks with fellow New Yorker Hamilton Fish and collaborating legislatively with Sen. Lowell Weicker of Connecticut. A willingness to look past party was crucial, Henry Waxman explained, because "patience, a knack for finding allies (especially unlikely ones), and the ability to persevere for very long stretches are the qualities that ultimately distinguish the best legislators."[57] Even as liberal a legislator as Waxman recalled proudly his collaboration with conservatives like Hyde and Orin Hatch, just as George Miller teamed up with John Birch Society member John Rousselot on children's issues, and with the unlikely duo of Sen. Bob Dole of Kansas and liberal George McGovern on child nutrition. Class Republican Bill Gradison recalled his close working relationship with Ways and Means Democrats during the 94th Congress, even sharing a "cockroach infested room" at a bipartisan retreat where legislators could "let your hair down," an atmosphere more conducive to compromise than the "big conference room in [the Ways and Means hearing room in] Longworth with the lights shining in your eyes, and cameras."[58] Vermont Republican freshman Jim Jeffords worked closely with subcommittee chairman John Brademas on the landmark legislation mandating education for individuals with disabilities. When a witness from the Ford administration upbraided them for the $20 billion cost of compliance, Jeffords fired back, "That's *your* problem!"

"I was interested in good policy, and I didn't care if came from the Democratic Party or the Republican," deregulation proponent Bob Krueger said. "I didn't think it was treason to work with Republicans. Rayburn and LBJ did it, and government worked a hell of a lot more effectively when they did."[59] Jim Florio collaborated with conservative Republicans like Norm Lent of New York and Ed Madigan of Illinois, and Jim Blanchard recalled similar efforts on the Banking Committee. "Involve everybody," he remembered Mo Udall advising. "You argue with some Republican one day, but you might need him the next." Ultimately, Blanchard made his mark in the House on aiding the failing auto companies in Michigan, and he counted as crucial allies Republicans Stewart McKinney of Connecticut and Tom Evans of Delaware. Based on his experience working in state government in Lansing, Michigan's Bob Carr worked closely with moderate Republicans, and one staff person recalled that liberal Dave Obey was "asshole buddies since college" with conservative fellow Wisconsinite Bill Steiger, a strict conservative.

Regional interests often brought members of disparate ideologies together through groups like the Northeast-Mid-West Coalition that worked across party lines on economic, trade, and environmental legislation affecting their states. GOP leader Bob Michel and Dan Rostenkowski, who became Ways and Means chairman in 1981, would often collaborate on behalf of Illinois. As late as the mid-1980s, one member recalled Speaker Tip O'Neill wandering into the office of Gene Snyder of Kentucky to play cards, have a few drinks, and do a little horse trading. On one visit, knowing Snyder was seeking an earmark for an important local project, O'Neill put his feet up on Snyder's desk and said, "Gene, you've got your bridge." Such genial feelings existed even among the leaders who constantly maneuvered against each other. Michel was renowned for traveling with O'Neill on foreign trips, or congressional delegations, often teaming up to sing songs around a piano.[60]

Few Democrats appreciated that the reforms might unintentionally help to undermine these bipartisan traditions or provide Republicans with enhanced means for planning an assault on the House majority. Democrats remained in control of the House as they had since 1933 with only four years of interruption, fueling a mind-set among many that a

Democratic majority was "an entitlement" unthreatened by biennial elections or the granting of minor concessions to the Republicans.[61] On reflection, Mike Blouin agreed, the Class's actions unintentionally "fueled the fires. Had we known," he said, "we could have done something." But until the later 1980s, threat of losing control was too far-fetched for many senior House members to contemplate seriously. In the aftermath of the Reagan landslide in 1981, in which Democrats lost 33 House seats and the Senate shifted to Republican control for the first time since 1954, a group of Class members including Toby Moffett, Tom Downey, and George Miller had visited with Speaker O'Neill to raise concerns that, unless the trend were arrested, the House might soon have a Republican majority. The Speaker dismissed them as alarmists.[62]

Jim Free, a savvy Tennessean serving as a White House congressional liaison for President Carter, agreed, "The party missed the changes in American politics. The marginal guys in the South were voting pretty much on line with other members of the Class—Levitas, Holland, Jenrette, and Derrick. They were voting just like those guys in Boston, in a way that put them at risk."[63] The replacement of older conservatives by more progressive Class members moved southern Democrats' party loyalty closer to the average than in recent memory, and yet most of the Class's southern members won reelection so often that they were confident of the loyalty of constituents even as the region grew demonstrably more conservative. When a liberal organization enthusiastically rated Butler Derrick's voting record as liberal as that of Bella Abzug, the irrepressible New Yorker, his district director "pointed out to him that Bella Abzug represented the Upper West Side of Manhattan," not rural South Carolina. But Derrick voiced little concern, asserting he was "proud of the fact that he was a progressive southern Democrat representing a conservative district."[64]

"I thought we would be in the majority continually," Class member Don Bonker admitted, a common belief. "I signed up with an understanding the Democrats would always be in power," Waxman recalled decades later. Affording Republicans the tools that allowed them to expose marginal Class members in areas like the South and suburban districts did not appear, for most, to convey much of a risk. Even a numbers-driven analyst like Mark Gersh of the National Committee for an Effective Congress dismissed the biennial fluctuations of House Democrats as insignificant given the party's continuing dominance. Between 1978 and

1982, despite the election of Ronald Reagan and the capture of the Senate by Republicans in 1980, Gersh noted, Democrats still held 272 seats to 163 for Republicans, nearly 64 percent of the members. "There was natural loss," Gersh acknowledged, "some seats eventually going the other way."[65] But important signs of change were being missed; with the retirement of many of incumbents from the Class and subsequent elections, reapportionments that reduced the Democratic electorate in many cases, or simply the Republican Party gaining greater traction and recruiting stronger candidates, these seats were at increased risk and, with them, the Democrats' "entitled" grip on the gavel.

Certainly, the newer generation of Republican House members rejected any notion of being doomed to minority status. They were painfully aware that, since 1955, no Republican had ever served in a Republican-led House, had ever presided over the House of Representatives, or had ever chaired a hearing. Little wonder that many GOP leaders and members had grown resigned to their inferior status.[66] But with the advent of the reforms, by 1976, observers noted a sharp rise in partisan voting in the House fueled by the promotion of sharply divisive cultural, religious, patriotic, and economic issues. Race, in particular, was believed by many southern Democrats to be the favored issue for driving whites out of the Democratic coalition.[67] On many of these issues, Democrats became more unified during the 1970s, with party unity rising from 33 percent in 1972 to 48 percent by 1975, a change viewed as "significant" by *Congressional Quarterly*.[68] By contrast, bipartisan voting was recorded at its lowest in a decade, with Democrats slightly more likely to cast bipartisan votes than Republicans, reflecting the large number of moderate Democrats who needed to cast votes to appease their constituents in Republican-leaning districts.

Defining and Divisive Votes

The ability to force votes on highly divisive political and cultural issues, and the infusion of members who were happy to do so, drew deep cleavages between the parties. On the Democratic side, those issues involved reduction in military spending, environmentalism, and expanded rights for minorities and women. For Republicans, "cutting-edge" issues like school busing, reducing welfare, crime, and curbing the growing "permissive and irreligious" lifestyle served as valuable differentiating organizational and tactical devices.[69] The sheer number of floor votes on these controversial topics—the number of amendments allowed in the House more than quadrupled between the 1950s and 1980s—"contributed to the sense of uncertainty and instability that was pervasive" in the House.[70]

By the end of the 94th Congress, Republican strategists—many from outside the Congress itself—had "brilliantly figured out the evangelicals, the single issue voters" on abortion, the Panama Canal, busing, and more issues, Pat Schroeder recalled, "and started harvesting them in the South" and elsewhere, including her Colorado district. "A lot of Democrats were asleep and didn't understand what they were doing."[71] The approach was developed by Republican strategists like South Carolina activist Lee Atwater, a "really important . . . genius," in the words of Derrick aide Marcia Hale. A 1981 Atwater memo on conservative messaging techniques described how the harsh racist terminology of the 1950s had been replaced in the late 1970s with terms like "forced busing, states' rights, and all that stuff," Atwater noted. "Now, you're talking about cutting taxes, and all these things you're talking about are totally economic . . . 'We want to cut this,' is much more abstract than even the busing thing."[72]

"We saw the southern conservatism emerging," recalled top Republican House strategist Bill Pitts, "and [we] took advantage of it" to target vulnerable Democratic seats. One of the Republican activists later recalled it was "our job to so structure the confrontations that swing Democrats and marginal Democrats will have no choice." By using floor procedures to fashion amendments on divisive issues that put Democrats in conflict with their constituencies or their party, these strategists found a political game plan that reforms had inadvertently facilitated. "They've either got to leave their leadership or get defeated at the polls," the Republican declared. "That's how we're trying to design every confrontation."[73] While it took two decades for House Republicans to exceed the number of seats lost in 1974, most Republicans who entered the House after 1976 were allied with the more conservative wing of their party.[74] Ultimately, changing demographics and reapportioned district lines, as well as the defeat and retirement of southern Democrats who had utilized their incumbency to retain marginal seats, left Democrats incapable of withstanding the growing Republican strength in southern districts.

The southern members of the Class understood they were in the crosshairs of the growing conservative juggernaut in the South. "Whew!" Derrick would tell his staff. "We're in trouble!"[75] The savvy Derrick, who survived assaults until retiring in 1994, constantly could feel the "tug and pull on him, where he was and where the district was and where it was going." Southern Democrats in the Class believed they survived as long as they did after the rise of the conservative cultural activism purely because of the millions of new black voters who gave them overwhelming support. "I received a lot of help from national civil rights leaders," John Jenrette recalled, calculating that he needed solid support from black voters, who constituted up to 40 percent of the primary voters, and one-third of whites to win reelection.

By the late 1970s, the ideological sorting already had left the minority faction of each—the conservative Democrats and the liberal Republicans— sharing a sense they were ill treated by their party's majority. Mineta noted the rise in "polarization between freshman and some older members of Congress, who regard them as hasty reformers, big spenders and opponents of a strong defense establishment."[76] Republicans took note of the diminishing number of conservative Democrats who could be counted upon as natural allies. Republican John Ashbrook, an Ohio conservative who had challenged Richard Nixon's renomination in 1972 over the president's alleged domestic policy liberalism, recalled there had been "a few southern conservative Democrats" with whom he could ally himself. "But now," he hyperbolically asserted in 1976, "you don't have anything but liberals" who were unchecked by the remaining moderates in the party.[77]

Dave Obey, a liberal, sympathized with the plight of the moderates, criticizing both "right-wing interest groups" who were making politics "simultaneously meaner and more trivial" as well as "knee-jerk liberals" who emphasized what he termed "fringe issues."[78] Class member Marty Russo felt unfairly stigmatized as an industry apologist for his votes against hospital cost containment, regulating the funeral industry, and abortion. "I wasn't set in my views as a liberal or a conservative," he recalled. The liberals "thought they had these overwhelming numbers and could shove things down [the moderates'] throat." He would tell his liberal friends, "You guys have a great idea, but you can't pass crap" without moderate Republicans because of the defection of southern conservatives. "You have the easiest jobs," he told his fellow Illinois representatives, liberal Ab Mika and conservative Phil Crane, one of the rising conservative activists. "You can always be liberal or conservative. I am a moderate. I have to choose on every issue."

Republican moderates similarly resented the rising influence of the hard Right in the 1976 and 1978 campaigns. "Moderates were not liked in the [GOP] conference," Larry Pressler said, acknowledging they were viewed as "softy, squishy [and] not interested in being harshly partisan. Being independent was a problem in getting things done." Caught between those in his party who accused him of being a "McGovern plant" and Democrats who generally behaved "as if I wasn't there and didn't even acknowledge we [moderates] existed," Pressler admitted he felt "like a ship in the night, sailing along [while] no one noticed or cared." As early as 1976, a quarter of the membership of the moderate GOP Wednesday Group voluntarily retired from the House. The later departures of moderate Class Republicans like Pressler, Dave Emery, Millicent Fenwick, and Jim Jeffords not only further diminished the ideological diversity of their conference but also allowed more recently elected conservatives to move up into more senior and influential positions on committees to confront the majority.

The conservative activists in the Republican Study Group, which had 75 members in the 94th Congress, did not regret the departure of their "moderate and liberal brethren [whom they viewed] with deep suspicion." The RSG had issued reports like *The Case Against the Reckless Congress*, a hard-edged attack against the Class and the 94th Congress, and regularly attacked fellow Republicans it viewed as insufficiently confrontational.[79] The "mission" of the "harder" Republicans entering the House, RSG director Ed Feulner said, was to draw clearer distinctions between the GOP and Democrats by promoting culturally divisive issues that might enable them to win the House majority denied them by the Class surge of the mid-1970s.

Pennsylvania's Bob Walker, elected in 1976, epitomized the keen edge of the younger Republican activists who, like many in the Class of 1974, viewed his own party leaders with almost as much disdain as anyone in the other party did. "Many of our more senior members didn't see any way out of minority status," he recalled. "They found it easier to cooperate with Democrats to get a percentage of the action," which blunted the GOP's ability to distinguish itself and left the party with "no real case to take to the country."[80] These new conservatives, *Congressional Quarterly* noted, were "scornful of the Republican Party" and its congressional leadership, and were dedicated to "carefully raising money and building the organization . . . to move Congress sharply to the right over the next several elections." Achieving that goal required promoting issues that defined conservatism distinctly, pressing contentious votes, raising money, and identifying prospective candidates for office. During the

94th Congress, conservative groups utilized the 1974 campaign reform law to increase their House fundraising from just $250,000 for the 1974 election by more than ten times, to $3.5 million for the 1976 House cycle with little notice.

By 1978, the new conservatives had the capacity to target some of the Class members they viewed as occupying seats that rightly belonged to Republicans. It was the year "when conservatism started to raise its head," recalled Class member Mike Blouin, who lost his Iowa seat that November. Another Class victim was Martha Keys, battered by criticism for her votes on issues meant to sound improvident, like a National Science Foundation study of why gorillas grind their teeth. One of the conservative groups sent a New Yorker to Keys's district to facetiously thank her for providing taxpayer funds to rehabilitate Yankee Stadium. Such tactics appalled less confrontational Republicans, but the conservatives had a symbolic issue and, as Keys recalled, "loads of money to market it."[81]

Democratic special interest groups used many of the same tactics to target Republicans. "Single issue [groups], with deep pockets, took control of the process," recalled Blouin. "It was scary." In April 1976, the League of Conservation Voters issued its "Dirty Dozen" members targeted for defeat, including several insufficiently pro-environmental Democrats in conservative-leaning districts. Gary Myers, the moderate Pennsylvania Republican, found himself pilloried by both sides in the abortion debate and by women's groups because he opposed extending time for states to ratify the Equal Rights Amendment, which he supported.

One junior Democrat who fancied himself a moderate remembered being shocked by the emerging partisanship in the very early 1980s. "I remember . . . a Republican said that if there were an incumbent Democratic member even if he were a friend—he would still go out and support the Republican opponent because the important thing was to elect a Republican Congress," the Democrat recalled, "and I remember disagreeing very strongly." But soon, he admitted, he embraced the same combativeness. "You want to know something?" he asked. "I have become the most partisan person going, and I have been actively campaigning against Republicans for incumbent Democrats, and I will continue to do so. So I have changed."[82]

Few partisan actions by Democrats did more to confirm the analysis of the conservatives than the 1985 decision to seat Frank McCloskey after a disputed election in Indiana's 8th District. The decision to recognize

McCloskey as the winner, despite a state official's ruling in favor of the Republican candidate, led junior Republican Newt Gingrich to charge, "A seat in the U.S. House of Representatives is being stolen, not by a rump group, but by members of the Democratic Party."[83] Republicans walked out of the House Chamber on May 1, 1985, in protest, but in an action that tainted his reputation further with his increasingly militant conference, Minority Leader Bob Michel returned soon afterward to shake the hand of his newly ensconced colleague. Gingrich and others would long cite Michel's chivalrous act as evidence of his accommodationist instincts.

Partisanship Consumes the House

Increasingly, even moderate Democrats became frustrated with the skill of Republicans in devising symbolic and exploitable votes, leading to still further rollbacks in the open amendment procedures initiated in the mid-1970s. Jim Wright, who became Speaker in 1987 expressing a hope of restoring the "collegial, bipartisan" atmosphere of an earlier era, determined to challenge not only what he viewed as Republican mischief-makers in the House but President Reagan's unilateralism in foreign affairs as well. Wright clashed bitterly with Reagan over the president's intervention in Central America and the perceived lack of progress on arms control with the Soviets. "I trust [Soviet leader] Mikhail Gorbachev more than I trust Ronald Reagan," Wright once told a stunned group of House members. "[Reagan is] an SOB who doesn't want to end the damn arms race. *Gorbachev* cares more about peace than Reagan does!" Noting the members' astonishment, Wright told the group, "I'd prefer you not repeat what I said a while ago."[84]

Republicans chaffed bitterly under Wright's action "tightening the screws" to restrict Republican strategic opportunities within the House.[85] Although just 15 percent of bills were debated under "restricted rules" that limited amendments in the 95th Congress (1977–1978), a decade later under Wright, that percentage had more than doubled, and then doubled again through 1992 under his successor, Tom Foley. By the time of the Republican takeover of the House in 1994, more than three-quarters of all bills were debated under a rule sharply limiting amendment opportunities.

Wright also invented maneuvers to spare marginal Democrats from casting difficult votes, including the novel "deeming" process by which a bill could pass without the House actually casting a vote. In another 1987 maneuver, Wright circumvented rules preventing a second vote on a bill in one legislative day and then ignored the official time limit on voting to secure its passage. These muscular tactics infuriated Republicans, who argued that the misuse of power by Democrats could only be remedied through election of a Republican majority.

The growing partisan fervor was evident in the evolving views of Republican Dick Cheney, Ford's former chief of staff who won Wyoming's seat in 1978. As late as 1984, Cheney had asserted the GOP "still [has] a place for the moderates, liberals and progressives [because] we can't become the majority party by trying to read people out."[86] By the end of the 1980s, Cheney had become a no-holds-barred antagonist. "What choice does a self-respecting Republican have except confrontation?" he asked. "If you play by the rules, the Democrats change the rules so they can win. There's absolutely nothing to be gained by cooperating with the Democrats at this point." Even the moderate New Yorker Barber Conable agreed. While Republicans used to get their share of amendments, he asserted, now "all you get . . . are fang marks."[87] Left with bills that were "take it or leave it," moderates voted no, and legislation lost the bipartisan imprint.[88] "Wright ran the House with an iron fist," recalled Michel's chief of staff at the time, Ray LaHood. "He really poisoned the well" by jamming legislation through in a manner that infuriated the minority. "That really ticked people off. Even [Republican Leader] Bob Michel felt that way."[89]

Even so, the young conservatives remained skeptical of Michel's willingness to engage in the "frontal assault" they believed was needed to oust Democrats from the majority. Hard-liners including Gingrich, Bauman, Walker, and Vin Weber of Minnesota decried Michel's "country club manager" leadership style as "too fat, dumb, and happy" to win the majority.[90] Michel "liked to have cocktails and smoke cigars" with his long-time friend, Tip O'Neill, recalled Pressler, "but he wouldn't challenge O'Neill on their legislation."[91] Although a frustrated Michel chastised the hard-liners for their "refusal to negotiate or compromise," even moderate Republicans became increasingly frustrated as Democrats rescinded the reforms that had been utilized to launch attacks on liberals.[92] The patrician Hamilton Fish of New York came to agree that "those of us who were not inclined to confrontation have now discovered that pressure, and tough pressure, is the way to get results."[93] The Democratic message to moderate Republicans, Fish recalled, was "stay in line or get nothing." The Democrats were "not willing to share spotlight," becoming "harshly partisan" during the late 1970s, "push[ing] away" moderates, Pressler believes. Although he had been the target of hostile conservative attacks during his 1978 Senate race for his moderation, Pressler speculated that, had he remained in the House, he would likely have supported Gingrich's confrontational tactics. The temperate approach, he admitted, was "too squishy."

Looking back at their experiences and actions in the House, Class members disclaimed any idea that the reforms they promoted were intended to promote partisanship; indeed, as they noted, their criticisms often were aimed at their own leadership, including chairmen who were unresponsive to the broader caucus. Nevertheless, they acknowledged that the open floor procedures, expanded transparency, and dissemination of power they supported helped provide the mechanisms by which a skilled generation of Republicans could launch an unforeseen battle for control of the House. "Liberals were thinking we were winning," recalled Scott Lilly, a senior DSG and committee staffer. "But we were about to get shit kicked out of us."

Class Democrats tied the decline in collegiality and collaboration to the new generation of Republicans who arrived in 1978 and the early years of the Reagan administration, those who successfully exploited the reforms of the mid-1970s to push conservative priorities. In particular, they pointed to Newt Gingrich as the most tactical and methodical of Republican strategists, who emphasized the need for message discipline over legislative mastery and who employed viscerally partisan rhetoric atypical of either party. "Newt was a game changer," Don Bonker said, employing a mixed metaphor. "He came in throwing grenades, with a machete." "Newt wouldn't say 'bad,'" Florio recalled, "he said 'pathetic,' which drove polarization." Harkin highlighted Gingrich's pedagogical writings that taught Republican candidates to "speak like Newt," employing harsh epithets aimed at "personally destroying your opponent," including terms like "sick," "pathetic," and "traitors" to impugn Democrats who "cheat" and "lie."[94]

"Campaigns became more vicious" by 1979, Dave Obey noted, as a new generation of Republicans launched a "campaign of personal destruction . . . the 'go for the jugular' approach. The kind of people coming into the House was changing, too, as was the language they were willing to use to get and stay there." As a result, the traditional comity and collaboration seemed to be dissipating rapidly, with the House increasing "resembl[ing] a poisonous snake pit."[95] "Politics got ugly," remembered Iowa's Class member Mike Blouin, who lost his seat in the

Republican resurgence of 1978. "The brickbats came out, and campaigns got mean." The new Republicans arrived in Washington "filled with bitter partisanship," Elliott Levitas recalled. As a result, under Gingrich's growing influence, George Miller noted, interparty collaboration was viewed as "trading with the enemy," and those who engaged in bipartisan efforts risked being labeled "not loyal to the ideology."[96]

Despite the rise in partisan feuding—culminating in Gingrich's stunning purge of Speaker Wright in 1989—few anticipated that the Democratic majority itself might be endangered. Even with the elections of Ronald Reagan and George H. W. Bush, the six-year Republican majority in the Senate, and the erosion of House seats during the 1980s, the permanency of the Democratic control seemed beyond question. In 1988, Professor Burdett Loomis noted that Congress had become far less collegial but concluded the escalating "partisanship clearly disadvantages minority Republicans." Loomis concluded Democrats not only had "determined the nature of the House since 1955 [but] will continue to do so for the foreseeable future."[97] Three years later, journalist Alan Ehrenhalt could not "find any consistent pattern of Republican progress" and described Democrats as "the natural majority."[98] Indeed, only one month before the wave election of 1994 that gave Republicans their first House majority in four decades, political scientists William F. Connelly Jr. and John J. Pitney Jr. reported "many House Republicans had succumbed" to the inevitability of serving in a "permanent minority." The publishers added the question mark to the title of Connelly and Pitney's book, *Congress' Permanent Minority? Republicans in the U.S. House*, as the last-minute election wave suddenly rose.

Class member Les AuCoin, who had lost a close race to incumbent Sen. Bob Packwood in 1992, had sensed "a deeper, undetectable shift in the tectonic plates," a swing away from the confidence in government activism the Class had brought to Washington. More than the careers of most in the Class was at an end; it was a new era with a new set of empowered conservative activists practicing a combative form of politics in pursuit of very different objectives for the House and for the country. "The Great Society was over," AuCoin noted, as was the Class's reform era, "but no one knew it."[99]

CONCLUSION
A HINGE POINT IN HISTORY

It was a glory time.—Rep. Tim Wirth (D-CO)

It was a hinge point in history but we didn't know it.—Rep. Les AuCoin (D-OR)

I believe we . . . shook things up a little.—Rep. Berkley Bedell (D-IA)

We gave politics a better name, which this country sorely needs.
—Rep. Mike Blouin (D-IA)

The White House was abuzz on March 23, 2010, as President Barack Obama and congressional Democrats gathered for the signing of the national health care law. The event had special significance for members of the Class for whom expanding health insurance to all Americans had been a career-long objective. George Miller, now nearly 65 years old and white haired and mustached, had been a 29-year-old House hopeful when Sen. Ted Kennedy flew into his California district 36 years earlier to promise voters that Miller's election would speed enactment of health reform.

The young president circulated among House and Senate leaders in the mansion's elegant Blue Room, thanking them for guiding his signature priority to passage. Included in the reception were the chairmen whose committees wrote the law, including Henry Waxman (House Commerce), Max Baucus (Senate Finance), Tom Harkin (Senate Health, Education, Labor, and Pensions), who had replaced Kennedy upon his death the previous August, Chris Dodd (Senate Banking), and Miller (House Education and Labor).[1] All five had begun their congressional service as members of the Class on the same cold day in January 1975, part of "a new generation of Democrats, many of whom wanted to change their own party and reform the Congress as much as they wanted to punish the party of Nixon."[2] All had won election to the House in their late twenties or early thirties; all now were well into their sixties. Beckoning the youthful president to join them for a historic photograph, the chairmen informed Obama that they had entered the House together in 1975 promising to enact national health insurance. The president laughed, "Oh, I was just 13!"

Their presence in the Blue Room as chief architects of the landmark bill of their long and productive careers was itself a testament to their durability in office and, ironically, to the very seniority system they had challenged in their earliest weeks as congressmen. The long-standing relationships and trust they had developed over decades of service played a crucial role in facilitating the passage of this complex law, helping them avoid the convoluted jurisdictional tangles that had proven so difficult to unravel. "[We] all arrived here the same day 35 years ago," Dodd noted. "We all know each other very well."[3] The White House bill signing illustrated the extreme end of what scholars have called "the 'long tail' of decisions that voters made [in] 1974," decisions that endured for decades.[4] Five years after the signing ceremony, the era had formally ended: all had left the Congress.[5]

The health care negotiators were not the only Class members to serve long tenures or rise to high ranks in official Washington. Thanks to the rapid turnover of seats in the 1970s, their elevation to power was swift despite the endurance of the seniority system. Within just eight years of their first election, virtually all of the 39 remaining members of the Class either served as a subcommittee chair or on one of the powerful exclusive committees. Norman Mineta, John LaFalce, and Jim Oberstar would also wield gavels as chairmen of House committees, and Mineta would serve as a two-time cabinet member under Presidents Bill Clinton and George W. Bush. Nine moved to the Senate, four of whom—Dodd, Paul Simon, Harkin, and Larry Pressler—would run unsuccessfully for their party's presidential nomination.[6] Less successfully, several—John Jenrette, Fred Richmond, Carroll Hubbard, and Richard Kelly of Florida—went to prison. None rose high within the elected leadership of the House, choosing policy-driven legislative careers instead while benefitting from the seniority system they had once challenged.

Neither the veteran Bill Barrett nor freshman Class member Tom Downey, at the time of their awkward introduction on the House floor in January 1975, could have foreseen the sweeping institutional and political changes that would result from the historic election of 1974. There had been reform and reformers before the arrival of the Class in January 1975, but, with its election, the rules of the House, of committee and floor activity, and campaign strategy changed dramatically. Like much of the congressional tradition the Class helped to upend, Barrett did not survive the 94th Congress; he died in office in April 1976.

"A Different Kind of Congress"

The Class brought more than support for reform to archaic House procedures: it brought generational change, a merging of the external activism of the streets—the campus, civil rights, and anti-war movements, the battles for women's rights and consumer protection, the drive for energy innovation and transparent government. "They arrived feeling they would have to make an impact if they were going to keep these formerly Republican seats," the *Washington Post* declared in 1976.[7] Joe Crapa, who came to know the Class as staff to the New Members Caucus, viewed them as a unique collection of members. "They had a sense that the people had selected a different kind of Congress," he recalled, and they set about to prove it. Their politics had not emerged from smoke-filled rooms or the ward heeler's organization for the most part. "They were children of the '60s, activists who came up in politics by working outside the system," Crapa said. "For the most part, they were not party people, but outsiders, ministers or PhD's and even one house painter. They were fairly sophisticated about using television. They were not out of the old labor background. They were suburban, well-educated in good schools . . . clannish and self supportive and not dependent on anyone."[8]

Many of them brought personal experiences that would fuel their passion for the issues they pursued; many even relished confronting powerful forces within their own constituencies. Liberals southerners like Elliott Levitas and Jenrette promoted civil and voting rights, Miller fought local asbestos and oil companies that compromised his constituents' health, Waxman battled the air pollution that clogged Los Angeles, where he grew up. They "revel in taking on formidable opponents," one account noted, "often in the name of protecting both country and consumer," even if in doing so they came across to critics as "brash, abrasive and arrogant[, utilizing] tactics [that] cause resentment."[9] "We were the first class that was like that," declared Phil Sharp, "and now the whole place is."

They may have been "the most rebellious freshmen class in memory," criticized by veteran members as "hot shots . . . who feel they've got the world by the tail . . . quite arrogant with their colleagues," but their intelligence and commitment won them "grudging respect from House colleagues." In short order, by House standards, they were recognized as leaders by the press and citizen groups, and they wielded genuine power in their committees. By 1984, even the crusty Richard Bolling admitted many in the Class "have become effective legislators."

Although they are remembered for having thrown out three aged committee chairmen, most came to Washington to work on policy issues, not to reform the institution of the House itself. The Class brought a "sense of mission[, a] mandate . . . to have an impact on the legislative process," as James Sundquist of Brookings concluded.[10] While most credit the Class with the reforms that challenged the autocratic management of the Congress, most of its members were unaware of the struggles to pry open the closed committee system, empower subcommittees and more junior members, and energize the Caucus until they arrived, although they quickly became enthusiastic participants. "We didn't create the agenda," Dick Ottinger acknowledged, "but we were excited about making change."

Their 49 additional votes did make the difference in the implementation of reforms that had been successfully resisted for more than a decade during which the bipartisan Conservative Coalition, with the support of the committee chairmen, dominated the House. After years of liberal ennui, the Class's arrival produced an activist majority faction in the caucus "that suddenly had the votes to do what it wanted to do."[11] "It was a hinge point in history," recalled Les AuCoin, "but we didn't know it." Tim Wirth called it "a glory time," filled with "a tremendous sense of mutual mission. You really had a sense of why you were there and what you were doing." They not only displaced chairmen but, in doing so, sent a powerful reminder to other senior leaders that the caucus majority was not to be ignored. By the end of their first Congress, not only had three chairmen been displaced, but also another half dozen, doubtless annoyed by their diminished hegemony, decided to depart the House, as did the oft-criticized Speaker, Carl Albert. As a result, well over half of the chairmen for the 95th Congress were in their first or second terms, and there was a new leadership team including Speaker Tip O'Neill and Majority Leader Jim Wright.

The members and the achievements of the Class are often characterized as a one-dimensional "noisy, faction-ridden collection of individuals," as illustrated by the frequent widespread use of the moniker "Watergate Babies."[12] But their rambunctiousness was exaggerated.

Even their most celebrated action—the removal of the three chairmen—was not a blind rebellion against all conservative or aging chairs but a surgical assault. "Our targets were the old bulls in the Democratic Caucus who were not open or accountable," Matt McHugh recalled, the "old line Democrats who were secretive, who hoarded power, and didn't want to share participation in the process."[13] The reformers did not, as some concluded, destroy the seniority system or significantly undermine the authority of the party's leadership. "Anybody that thinks the seniority system is dead is wrong," Ned Pattison had noted. "But you don't make yourself slaves to it."[14] They did not weaken the power of responsible chairmen or disable the House from functioning. Overall, the centers of power survived, although they were compelled to acknowledge the views and welcome the participation of a wider range of the caucus membership. As William Greider and Barry Sussman summarized early in the 94th Congress, it was important to distinguish between the Class members' unconventionalities and the substance of their ideas and legislative skill. The freshmen "might stand apart because of their style, but not their ideas," they wrote. "They are not as original as they seemed." Another writer in 1975 observed, "If you get beyond style and rhetoric, beyond the hurry-up activism, the freshmen are remarkably orthodox [and] do not stand out from their elders on most crucial issues."[15]

The reforms the Class helped implement, together with the forceful personalities who took advantage of the reforms, dramatically enhanced the ability of junior members to play constructive and even leadership roles in the promotion of policy matters and to empower them to raise significant and controversial issues that the old-line leadership had resisted. As this account makes clear, the targets of the reformers were not all of the conservative or southern members of the caucus but those who used the seniority system to run the House like a personal fiefdom, as well as those leaders who did not have the fortitude or determination to challenge the old order that had rendered the Congress little more than "the sapless branch" of the federal government. The objective was not simply to shift power from the conservatives to the liberals as much as to *disseminate* power more broadly to younger members who had waited for years to participate fully, to chair subcommittees, and to impact the legislative agenda of the House.

Intraparty Tension

Not surprisingly, the style, impatience, and impertinence of some members of the Class—their irreverence and occasional unwillingness to bow to tradition—irritated those who clung to the traditional House organization. "Young members got to participate earlier and have power," Glenn English said, and the expanded democracy of the House understandably annoyed those "old bulls" who had long enjoyed unchallenged access to the levers of power. Tip O'Neill spoke for many, including some reformers, when he worried that some changes had led "many Members to question the conventional ways of doing business in the House," undermining the functionality of the institution.[16] "Congress became more difficult to control than ever before," O'Neill wrote. "Party discipline went out the window."[17] From his side of the Capitol, 1974 freshman senator Gary Hart of Colorado speculated that reform had replaced parliamentary order with "a controlled madhouse."[18] "They were mostly radical reformers," recalled House officer Donnald Anderson, who "treated our Democratic leadership shabbily and disloyally."[19] That critique was shared by President Ford, a longtime Republican House leader who found he could no longer cut deals with a small number of bipartisan friends. "All they did was screw it up," said Ford, referring to the Class and other reformers. "They took away the benefits of seniority, which [had] created stability. They undercut the capability of the leadership, both Democrat and Republican . . . to effectively handle the problems that are on its doorstep." Even longtime reformer Mo Udall considered whether the reform impulse had gone too far. "We tend to overkill when we get involved in some of these reform things in the House," Udall remarked.

But, of course, Ford and many others who complained about the impatience of the Class portrayed the pre-reform House in an idealistic and distorted light. The House of the 1950s and 1960s was *not* effectively addressing the "problems that [were] on its doorstep." The conservatives who occupied a disproportionate share of the chairmanships were not creating "stability" but obstructing legislation favored by the majority of the caucus while voting against their own party's priorities. Issues that had strong support within the majority and the country as a whole, including energy, the environment, consumer protection, health care, Pentagon reform, and, especially, ending the war in Vietnam, were routinely ignored by this supposedly stable and effective leadership. With the election of 1974, the balance changed. Joining with the existing reformist wing of the party, the Class provided the crucial component needed to overwhelm the conservative faction's intransigence and finally effectuate a modernization of the House.

The reforms that opened the Caucus and the House to greater scrutiny, transparency, and accountability also left members more vulnerable to criticism from their local or national party constituencies.[20] The reforms allowed more junior members unprecedented opportunities to serve on key committees and subcommittees, to raise issues and shape legislation, and to steer the attention of the caucus toward long-suppressed concerns. They checked the power of the old guard to establish agendas for committees and the floor by empowering the caucus and the subcommittees to investigate and legislate in areas ignored by the full committees, often responding to the growth in advocacy organizations that had been routinely ignored by the leadership of the committees and the House.

Although united on the need for internal House reforms, members of the Class held a range of ideological, regional, and district views on policy questions. Critics were scathing in their disappointment at the legislative achievements of the 94th class, particularly the freshmen, and especially the failure to override Ford vetoes. But the idea that Class members would be unified on major policy matters was an invention of the critics, not a characteristic ever professed by the Class itself. Indeed, Class members expressed the likelihood they would not agree once the decision making moved from reform to policy questions. Given the wide variety of districts they represented, it would have been miraculous if they had voted with the unanimity critics expected of them.

Still, Class members voted with greater consistency for positions supported by a majority of House Democrats than non-freshmen party or regional colleagues. Most of those who represented traditionally Republican seats voted with their more secure colleagues, defying critics who accused them of caring more for their seats than for their principles. To compensate for voting records that sometimes strayed from their constituents' outlook, the Class developed innovative mechanisms for heightening their profile and gaining recognition, including a skillful use of emerging technology, pioneering constituent outreach, and sophisticated press relations. Older members marveled at their success in retaining seats that few had anticipated Democrats would hold. The day after the publication of the gushing profile "The Startling New Man from

Texas" highlighting Bob Krueger's role in the oil deregulation fight, a flabbergasted veteran sat down next to the former professor. "Krueger, I can't get over you! First year in the House!" Sonny Montgomery of Mississippi marveled, recalling that Kruger's longtime predecessor, O. C. Fisher, "got a lot of pussy, but he never got in the *New York Times!*"

The Republican Revival

Democrats were not alone in feeling the influence of growing grassroots movements. By the end of the 1970s, Republicans reflected the growing demands of conservative activists for a litany of initiatives including restrictions on abortion, law and order, gun rights, neighborhood preservation, and traditional Christian values, in addition to more the traditional hostility to taxes, government spending, and the expanded role of the federal government. As with the 1974 Class, these conservative activists viewed their own leadership as insufficiently aggressive and resolved to promote a more confrontational and strategic challenge to the bipartisan presumption of a permanent Democratic majority.

Many Republicans had long supported the kinds of reforms promoted by DSG and various committees in hopes of expanding their ability to have an impact in committee and on the floor. Like the Class's southern Democrats, many of the freshmen Republicans were members of a moderate House faction that embraced issues like women's rights and the environment and even abortion rights. But the Republican class also included members like Henry Hyde, precursors to the harder-edged conservatism that would be supplemented by the incoming GOP classes of 1976 and 1978, a faction that joined with other conservatives to promote the partisan agenda of the rising New Right and the evangelical movement that provided much of its base support. Indeed, several of the Republicans elected in 1974 chafed at the growing conservatism within their own party as well as their exclusion by Democrats from efforts to democratize the House.

Many of the reforms implemented by the liberal reformers to expand their own participation unintentionally strengthened the conservatives. The novel opportunities for procedural motions and amendments enabled GOP strategists to target Democrats in marginal seats that conservatives believed never should have been lost. Assuming that Republicans could not make up for their enormous numerical disadvantage created by the massive victory in 1974, Democrats provided the minority with independent staff, hearing witnesses, and other resources that expanded the Republicans' ability to launch effective attacks in committee and on the floor. As Democrats responded by rescinding reforms and shrinking the legislative opportunities, Republicans cited the crackdown as evidence of partisan mismanagement and evidence of the need to replace the House majority.

Unlike much of the supposed Washington cognoscenti, these conservative activists rejected a central premise of mid-twentieth-century House politics: that Democrats would retain majority control of the House indefinitely. Just four years after the Class's landslide victory and reshaping of the House, it was clear that a new generation of Republicans was entering the House prepared to challenge the bipartisan presumption of Democratic control, and that calculation profoundly changed the nature of congressional politics. This new generation of Republican—including Newt Gingrich, Vin Weber, and Tom DeLay, together with earlier activists like Bob Bauman and Henry Hyde—proved inventive in devising opportunities for prosecuting their case against Democrats and against their own Republican leaders, who remained seemingly reconciled to minority status. This faction was confident that a more aggressive strategy could shake loose the seats that had slid into Democratic control and that the "emerging Republican majority" envisioned by Kevin Phillips in 1969 might soon be in reach. The huge majorities created by the 1974 election did not last long. By 1980, one-third of the 76 Class Democrats was gone as a result of defeat or retirement; others left to seek another office. A decade after their election, after setbacks in the 1980 and 1984 Reagan landslides, half of the Class was no longer in the House. When the Republicans finally won control in 1994, just 8 of the original 76 remained.

Ultimately, the arc of the Class's reform movement from liberalization of House rules to the tightening of participatory procedures even before the end of the 94th Congress raises a profound and very contemporary question about the nature of managing large legislative bodies that inherently contain formal parties inevitably riven by factions. While the calcified system that confronted the Class upon its arrival in 1974 governed unresponsively and unfairly, those who raised warnings about the impact of reform proved prescient, even if they were mainly motivated by their own political self-interest. The conservative New York Democrat Sam Stratton prophetically warned that reforms "instituted with great fanfare, in the desire to spread the action around and to put the old fogies in their place" might "hamper their activities," and often not in ways anticipated by the promoters of looser rules.[21] Even Class member Paul Simon, who would move to the Senate in 1990, observed, "We have ended up a weaker legislative body." By the end of the decade, many Democrats recognized the freer rules and constraints on chairs were jeopardizing legislative outcomes and empowering conservative rivals, and they turned to their leaders to exercise greater control over the legislative process.[22]

The promotion of issues by the majority liberals in the caucus, including Class members, did create obstacles for southerners trying to survive in marginal districts where Republicanism was resurgent, and the loss of those seats during the 1980s cut deeply into the margins that assured a Democratic majority. When, in the mid-1970s, Georgia senator Richard Russell inveighed that "the southerners' time has passed," he was only partially correct: the southern *Democrats'* time of controlling the House was waning, but the rising power of Republican southerners, who would dominate the party in the early 2000s, was just dawning.

Did Reform Hurt the House?

The tendency to misrepresent the impact of the reforms of the 1970s continues into contemporary political studies. The post-Watergate 94th Congress foreshadowed the emergence of "the new polarized, winner-take-all Congresses featuring sharp partisanship and polarization in the new technology age," wrote David C. W. Parker and Matthew Dull, replacing the more "bipartisan, accommodating, and 'compromise' Congress" of an earlier era.[23] A recent analysis entitled "How American Politics Went Insane" concludes that the origins of the current gridlock can be traced to the reformers of the 1970s, when "seniority and committee systems came under attack and withered." The failure, Jonathan Turley argued, lay with reformers like the Class of 1974, who bear responsibility for "favoring amateurs and outsiders over professionals and insiders; by privileging populism and self-expression over mediation and mutual restraint; by stripping middlemen of tools they need to organize the political system. All of the reforms promote an individualistic, atomized model of politics."[24] Similarly, Republican political aide and Gerald Ford biographer James Cannon asserted, "The election of 1974 swept aside the House and Senate traditions that respected experience and ensured accountability." In its wake, Cannon argued, "Congress became a loose congregation of independent operators serving parochial interests, local constituencies, and the highest goal—the next election."[25] "Now, every-body's a baron," Norm Ornstein wrote, and President Ford remarked that Congress had devolved into "435 prima donnas . . . who have no allegiance to their party or their leaders." Even the respected political scientist Barbara Sinclair described the post-reform House as "anarchies where members participated on their own terms and without restraint."[26]

While it is unquestionably true the post-1974 House was less easily controlled by a small coterie of aging leaders who routinely defied the caucus majority, any notion that the "Peoples' House" had descended into anomic dysfunction or that substantial bipartisan collaboration ceased to occur distorts the subsequent history. In the post-reform era, there was no shortage of disciplined and forceful leaders including Speakers Tip O'Neill and Jim Wright and chairmen like John Dingell, Dan Rosten-kowski, Jack Brooks, and Jaime Whitten. True, the House was more difficult to manipulate and a greater challenge to manage, but it was hardly a disorganized or chaotic body. Partisanship was certainly on the rise, but most major legislation continued to enjoy a significant measure of bipartisan support for decades. "The secret to crafting legislation," wrote Class member Henry Waxman, a liberal, in summarizing his years of legislative achievement, "is not ramming through a partisan bill, but rather designing one that is acceptable to all parties."[27] Bill Hughes, a moderate, concurred with Waxman's observation. "The bottom line is that the system works well when you listen to other points of view and reach across the aisle to accommodate and compromise," he noted. "That is our legacy."[28]

While many Class members acknowledge that they (like many others) missed or misread underlying changes that were working their way through American society, they nevertheless retained a confidence that the significant role they played in the transformation of Congress was decidedly for the better. "We gave politics a better name," recalled Mike Blouin, "which this country sorely needs." Berkley Bedell agreed: "I believe we . . . shook things up a little." But they also shared the disappointment that more was not achieved in the 94th Congress and in the years immediately following it, and that they were incapable of sustaining the optimistic fervor they brought to Washington.

By 1980, the national optimism that had marked the arrival of the Class had soured, and the reaction to cultural and political turmoil of the previous decade and a half had helped persuade nearly 40 percent of voters that "moral threats cut right through the social fabric." Rather than the confident issues of equality, peace, and transparency that had fueled the early careers of the Class, voters highlighted ominous factors that represented a "serious threat to the American way of life" including the inefficient federal bureaucracy, high and unfair taxes, the demands of minorities and women for greater equity, and a "lack of unity and patriotism."[29] Intractable problems and crises fed the doubts about the capability of government to solve problems: the enduring energy crisis, the inability to free American hostages held in Iran, the persistence of corruption and scandals among politicians. A succession of crippling developments, both foreign and domestic, further sapped faith in government: renewed war in the Middle East, the Three Mile Island nuclear plant meltdown, and the catastrophic failure of the Teton Dam.

If Democrats and analysts missed the changing currents of American politics, so, too, did Republican moderates who winced at the rising contentiousness within their own party. Bill Gradison, a Republican Class member, termed Newt Gingrich's use of bombast to challenge Democratic domination to be "mission impossible" and predicted the Georgian was "wasting his energy [because] nothing is going to come of this."[30] While the movement of moderate Republican reformers like Millicent Fenwick or Dave Emery to the Senate failed to materialize, a growing number of hard-liners—labeled "the battered children from the House" by Republican senator Alan Simpson—did achieve that transition, helping to significantly elevate the partisanship level in the upper chamber as well.[31] One of them, Trent Lott of Mississippi, recalled seething under the "bullyboy tactics [which House Democrats had used] to enforce their power" and described his former conservative House colleagues who had moved across the Capitol to the Senate in words that could easily apply to the Democratic Class in 1974 or the GOP activists who followed them soon afterwards. "We were hungry," Lott said. "We intended to make a difference and eventually capture the leadership."[32]

Lessons from the Class of '74

Four contemporary lessons can be drawn from the experience of the Class in the 94th Congress. First, despite the continuing cooperation between Democrats and Republicans on legislative objectives following the election of 1974, the recognition that ideological realignment would put control of the House in play meant that sentiment for bipartisan collaboration diminished. Both parties asserted the other was abusing the rules and procedures of the House for partisan gain. Both parties believed that control by the other would present a political and legislative danger, and, as a result, the trend increasingly became one of conflict rather than of bipartisan collaboration. The reforms implemented in the 1970s presented valuable opportunities for differentiating political and cultural issues to be promoted than would have been possible in a more rigorously controlled House, and the decision to roll back some of the reforms accentuated the rising division between the parties.

Second, the experience of the Class, as with contemporary Republicans in the age of the Tea Party and Freedom Caucus, affirms the need for leadership-imposed discipline in a large and diverse legislative body like the House of Representatives. Reform was essential in the 1970s because those in control were abusing their power, refusing to allow junior members to fully participate, squelching the views of the majority of the caucus, and repressing discussion of issues important to these members and the electorate. During the 94th Congress, the Class sent confusing signals: frustration that the leadership did not crack down on senior members who defied the will of the caucus but hostility to efforts by the leadership to influence and pressure junior members. But, within two years, most of the reformers recognized the need to reimpose some restrictions so that the House might function more effectively.

Third, the experience of the Class, as well as that of subsequent reformers, casts doubt about the ability of the Congress to truly achieve the co-equal status with the modern presidency that waves of reformers have sought. Certainly, their activism as aggressive proponents of procedural reforms, their enthusiastic embrace of aggressive oversight, and their eagerness to challenge the White House presumption of superior authority helped to recast Congress as a proactive force in the political life of the nation. By its size, design, and complex operational rules, Congress is inevitably a far slower, more collaborative, and more bureaucratic institution than the executive. As Thomas Cronin has noted, there are "dangers in expecting efficiency from a Congress that is never going to be fast on its 1,070 feet." In extraordinary periods of large majorities or during national crises, Congress can play a commanding role in shaping public policy, even when the presidency is controlled by the opposing party, as during the Class's freshman years of 1975–1976 or the last two years of George W. Bush's presidency. And, certainly, presidents have learned they cannot bully their legislative programs through an unwilling or divided Congress. But, generally, the inevitable negotiation and compromise, as well as the procedural rights of the minority, preclude Congress from the type of bold initiative the presidency commands, just as the multiple individuals who claim to "speak" for Congress inevitably produce a more diffused and discordant message than the singular declaration of the president.

Lastly, the experience of the Class and the era in congressional politics it so influenced illustrate the deep roots of the current polarized and highly partisan state of American politics. One needs to go back much further than the emergence of Newt Gingrich in the early 1990s (to which Democrats invariably point) or the efforts by Jim Wright to constrain the rights of the confrontational New Right in the late 1980s (which Republicans highlight) to appreciate the antecedents of today's deep divisions and gridlock. The origins arguably date to the mid-1970s examined in this book, when the momentum of a radically changing political atmosphere fueled by the emergence of a host of socially and culturally divisive issues remained largely concealed by the "abnormal Democratic resurgence" that followed the tumult of Watergate and Vietnam with the election of the Class.[33] Wright's tightening of rules to disadvantage the minority exacerbated the isolation that prompted complaints from Republicans in the mid-1970s, leaving them, in the words of Nelson Polsby, "no place to go but into the camp of the Republican militants." Unlike O'Neill, charged Gingrich acolyte Vin Weber of Minnesota, Wright managed the House in a manner that Republicans found "fundamentally unfair" because he appeared to lack "respect for the institution . . . [D]eep down he is a mean-spirited person, ruthless in the truest sense of the word."[34]

A 10-year retrospective recalled "the Fabled Class of 1974" as "bold newcomers, young, brash, independent and reform-minded [who] shunned tradition and wanted to do things their way. They were the most rambunctious freshmen Democrats the House had seen in years . . . born out of the national discontent."[35] They brought a fearless willingness to challenge the activities of other institutions, especially in the military and corporate world, which substituted for the deference earlier generations of legislators had provided. Unquestionably, the *Baltimore Sun* noted in mid-1975, "the voters wanted something different."[36]

Yet, even as the national mood changed, the confidence of some Class members was cooled by the incessant demands of campaigning and fundraising, the inevitability of compromise, the slow pace of change, and the rising levels of partisan conflict. The optimistic Tim Wirth, who had envisioned a new era of nonpartisanship, became dismayed by "an overwhelmingly polarizing force" driving the parties apart, inflating the importance of special interest organizations and the campaign money they commanded, and wasting valuable legislative time on policy chimera like the funding of controversial photographic exhibits and bans on flag burning—issues designed to embarrass the opposition rather than formulate serious public policy. In 1992, after 18 years in Congress (the last 6 in the Senate), Wirth decided to "leave the field to younger, more enthusiastic knights, as I was 18 years ago." Gary Myers, the Pennsylvania Republican steelworker, became "fed up with constituent demands" and "useless" social engagements, and quit after just two terms. "Congress is a long way from making any real changes in the way it runs," he concluded in 1978. "I'm glad I'm going home."[37] Fourteen years later, Matt McHugh joined more than 50 colleagues in retiring just before the Republican takeover, many after having been ensnared in a controversy involving the House bank. "There is now too great a gulf between my hopeful belief in what our institutions can be and the public perceptions of them," he remarked.[38] Bob Carr, who had enjoyed notoriety in 1975 for calling on Speaker Albert to resign, came to recognize it was an act of "sheer, naïve stupidity" akin to "putting a gun in my mouth. It took years for people to look at me rationally." A decade later, a sobered Carr—who had lost his seat in 1980 and regained it two years later—admitted, "I pick and choose my battles more carefully. You cannot go through life being an angry young man."[39]

Others, while recognizing the limits of reform, took comfort in the incremental changes they had achieved, much like those who gathered to sign a historic, if imperfect, health care law in 2010. "There are plenty of things to discourage you . . . pettiness, expediency, selfishness, crassness, opportunism, cruelty, demagoguery and assorted other evils . . . slowness in which change occurs," Les AuCoin wrote in his diary as a freshman. "And yet, you can also see numerous examples of quiet courage, flashes of individual inspiration and moments of genuine greatness each day."[40]

"Maybe we were a little oversold from the beginning," mused Mark Hannaford of California.[41] John LaFalce agreed. "We're fantasizing when we give greater grandeur to our class" he asserted. But whether they served briefly or enjoyed long careers, whether their service in Congress was marked by ousting chairmen or by becoming chairmen themselves, virtually all Class members retained a special affection for those with whom they began their journey in the House. A decade into his House service, the southern moderate Butler Derrick declared that when he needed support, "I go to my buddies in the Class of '74."[42] There was a sense of unity, Elliott Levitas recalled, and, even decades later, many continued to "share a sense of bond between us . . . more than nostalgia."

Others concluded that, despite their special bond, "it was the freshmen who changed most, from practicing idealists to idealist pragmatists."[43] "You've got to be able to operate in this institution," Moffett noted in his second term. "You can't stand to one side and just shout." As part of the process, he noted, "even the best of us get worn down, sidetracked, compromised to death."[44]

Ultimately, the Class should not be judged on the criteria typically used to define its historical role—the removal of three chairmen and the changing of House rules—but rather by its longer-term impact on the institution. Many of the members, I discovered in conducting interviews for this book, minimized their personal impact on the House and on American politics, having served only a few terms and then having moved on, at a relatively young age, to another phase of their lives. But as the scene at the White House in March 2010 reflects, the footprint of the Class extended far beyond rules changes and heated rhetoric. From this Class emerged many of the talented legislators of the last quarter of the twentieth century, not only those few who rose to chair committees, but those who shaped key legislation on welfare, international relations, transportation, health, defense, banking and finance, environmentalism, energy, and civil rights during years of service. If, in their exuberance and impatience, they were impertinent or confrontational, then such behavior was far more short lived than the decades of sclerotic, autocratic conservatism their actions had challenged. Tom Foley helped write the pre-1974 reforms, then rose to a committee chairmanship because of the Class's challenge to the crusty chairs in 1975, and ultimately became the embodiment of the leadership as whip, majority leader, and Speaker himself. It was the Class of '74, Foley noted, these "new kind of reformers [who] tried and succeeded in changing this place and making it more responsive and more interesting."[45]

EPILOGUE

Whatever became of . . . the Class of 1974?

California

Mark Hannaford served two terms before being defeated in 1978. He served as an assistant secretary of commerce in the Carter administration and made several unsuccessful attempts to return to the House. He died in 1985.

John Krebs was defeated in 1978 by Republican Charles Pashayan. His greatest achievement was preventing the commercial development of Mineral King Valley, which was named for him in 2009. He died in 2014.

Jim Lloyd won three terms in the House in a Republican-leaning district before being ousted in the Reagan landslide of 1980. An Air Force veteran, he later went to work for an aerospace company. He died in 2012.

George Miller, at 29 the second-youngest member of the Class, enjoyed the lengthiest House career (along with Henry Waxman) among the Democrats, retiring in 2014 after serving as chairman or ranking members of three committees (Committee on Natural Resources, Committee on Education and Labor, Select Committee on Children, Youth, and Families) for three decades. He was a prodigious legislator in areas including child and family policy, water reform, labor safety, education, and health care.

Norman Mineta rose to become chairman of the Transportation and Infrastructure Committee before retiring in the middle of his 10th term to go to work for a major defense contractor. He returned to government as secretary of commerce at the very end of the administration of Bill Clinton and then served as secretary of transportation during the administration of George W. Bush.

Jerry Patterson survived the first Regan landslide of 1980 but was defeated in 1984. He resumed his law practice and was active in local education activities, serving on the board of several community colleges in Orange County.

Henry Waxman served in the House for 40 years, chaired multiple committees (Committee on Oversight and Government Reform and the Committee on Energy and Commerce), and authored many of the most significant laws enacted during his tenure including clean air and water, health care, and tobacco safety.

Colorado

Tim Wirth served for six terms in the House before successfully running for the Senate in 1986. On the Commerce Committee, Wirth rose to chair the Telecommunications Subcommittee. He retired from the Senate voicing discouragement with politics in 1992 but then became an assistant secretary of state and worked closely with Vice President Al Gore on environmental issues. He later served as chairman of the United Nations Foundation.

Connecticut

Christopher Dodd served in the House for three terms before winning election to the Senate in 1980, serving for 30 years (the longest tenure in the state's history). He gained fame in his later years in the Senate for authoring major Wall Street reform legislation (with Rep. Barney Frank of Massachusetts) following the 2008 financial market collapse, and he also played a key role on health care following the 2010 death of Sen. Edward M. Kennedy. After retirement, he headed the Motion Picture Association in Washington. Dodd also served as chairman of the Democratic National Committee in the 1990s and unsuccessfully ran for the presidential nomination in 2008.

Toby Moffett served four terms in the House, where he chaired the Subcommittee on Energy, Environment, and Natural Resources. He unsuccessfully ran for the Senate in 1982 and subsequently lost races for governor and the House. He later became a lobbyist in Washington.

Florida

Richard Kelly, a former judge, served for three terms in the House before becoming involved in the Abscam scandal. He lost his primary in 1980 and, despite his claims he was running his own undercover investigation into the bribery scandal, was convicted and spent 13 months in prison. He died in 2005.

Georgia

Elliott Levitas served in the House for a decade before losing in the Reagan landslide of 1984. He later returned to the practice of law.

Larry McDonald, true to his John Birch Society background, compiled a staunchly conservative record during his five terms in the House. He opposed legislation protecting gays and lesbians, fought gun control, and was a virulent opponent of the Soviet Union and the United Nations. His death aboard a commercial airliner shot down by Soviet jets in 1983 prompted unproven allegations of a conspiracy.

Idaho

George Hansen unsuccessfully ran for the Senate three times before defeating a Republican incumbent in the 1974 House primary. A strong conservative, he was reprimanded by the House in 1984 for failing to make disclosure on required forms and subsequently narrowly lost his reelection bid. He was convicted and imprisoned for 25 months, but the conviction was later overturned. He died in 2014.

Illinois

Tim Lee Hall won a surprise victory in 1974, replacing the retiring Republican whip, Leslie Arends, but his service was short lived. In 1976, he was one of just two members of the Class to be defeated. He lost a comeback attempt in 1978. He later served in an appointed state government job and died in 2008.

Henry Hyde was majority leader in the Illinois House before winning his seat in 1974. He quickly became a national figure when his amendment barring the use of federal funds for abortions became law in 1976. Hyde later chaired the International Relations Committee and the Judiciary Committee, in which role he managed the 1998 impeachment of President Bill Clinton in the House. He served for 30 years and died in 2007.

Abner Mikva, who returned to the House in a new seat in 1974, retired in 1979 when he was appointed to the US Court of Appeals in Washington by President Jimmy Carter, and he was later appointed chief judge by President Bill Clinton. Mikva became one of the rare Americans to serve in all three branches of government when he left the judiciary in 1995 to become White House counsel to Clinton. He later became a

law professor and received the Presidential Medal of Freedom, the
nation's highest civilian honor. He died in 2016.

Marty Russo served on the Commerce Committee and the Ways and
Means Committee, becoming a trusted lieutenant of the latter's
chairman, Dan Rostenkowski. Despite his initial moderation, he
became a close ally of several liberal leaders including George Miller,
Nancy Pelosi, and Charles Schumer. He was defeated in the 1992
Democratic primary after reapportionment placed him in the same
district as Rep. William Lipinski and later became a prominent
Washington lobbyist.

Paul Simon served for 10 years in the House and in 1984 won a surprise
victory in a Senate race against incumbent Charles Percy, where he
served until retiring in 1996. One of the older members of the Class,
he was distinguished by a formality, his moderation (he was a strong
supporter of a balanced budget amendment to the Constitution and
opponent of the rising use of obscenity in entertainment), and the
bow tie he always wore. He made an abortive race for the 1988
presidential nomination and died in 1993.

Indiana

Dave Evans, like Fithian, lost much of his base in the Indiana
reapportionment in 1982 and was forced into a primary contest with
fellow Class member Andy Jacobs, who won the race. Evans became
a political consultant in Washington.

Floyd Fithian saw his district carved up and become more conservative
in the 1982 reapportionment, leading him to run for the Senate. He
won the Democratic nomination but was defeated by incumbent
senator Richard Lugar. In an unusual career twist, Fithian returned
to Capitol Hill as a staff person, serving as chief of staff for his Class
colleague, Sen. Paul Simon. He died in 1993.

Philip Hayes remained in the House only one term, choosing to
challenge incumbent senator Vance Hartke in the 1976 Democratic
primary. His seat was won by a Democrat, who held it for only a
single term. In 1982, it was won by Democrat Frank McCloskey whose
disputed reelection two years later helped inflame Republican
charges of corruption against the Democratic majority.

Andy Jacobs, who was one of three Class members to have previously
served in the House, remained in Congress until retiring in 1996,

becoming a respected expert on Social Security (and chairing the Ways and Means subcommittee on that subject). In 1975, he and fellow Class member Martha Keys made history when they became the first members of Congress to marry each other while in office. He died in 2013.

Phil Sharp remained in Congress for two decades before retiring in 1994. He remained an influential member of the Commerce Committee on both energy and clean air issues, and chaired the Energy Subcommittee, which had been source of bitter battles over deregulation in the 94th Congress. After retirement, he served as director of the Kennedy School at Harvard and then as president of Resources for the Future, a Washington think tank.

Iowa

Berkley Bedell served in the House until his retirement in 1986 as a result of health problems. Well into his 90s, he remains active in both Iowa and national politics, and has authored several books promoting economic and political reform.

Michael Blouin served only two terms in the House before being defeated in 1978. Blouin lost support among Republicans, who shifted to a more antiabortion position, and his pro-choice views also cost him support among Catholic Democrats. He attempted a comeback in 2006 but lost the gubernatorial primary to Chet Culver, the son of the Democrat he had replaced in the House in 1974 following the elder Culver's election to the Senate.

Charles Grassley served in the House for three terms before being elected to the Senate in 1980. A strong conservative, he has chaired both the Judiciary Committee and the Finance Committee. He is the last remaining member of the Class of 1974 who has served continuously since 1975.

Tom Harkin served in the House until his election to the Senate in 1984, where he served five terms. He was a vigorous proponent of education, people with disabilities, and health care, and served as chairman of the Committee on Health, Education, Labor, and Pensions following the death of Sen. Edward Kennedy. Harkin unsuccessfully sought the Democratic presidential nomination in 1992.

Kansas

Martha Keys served two terms in the House before being defeated in
1978. One of the few women in the Class, her career was
distinguished by her appointment as a freshman to the Ways and
Means Committee. Keys was a major supporter of legislation to
expand women's opportunities in college sports and to revise Social
Security law to benefit women. She later worked in several positions
in the Carter administration. During her brief service in the House,
she married fellow Class member Andy Jacobs.

Kentucky

Carroll Hubbard remained in Congress for 18 years, while also seeking
the Democratic gubernatorial nomination in Kentucky in 1979.
Hubbard became embroiled in the controversy involving checking
overdrafts at the House bank in the early 1990s, which contributed to
his defeat in the 1992 primary. After being convicted of misusing
campaign funds, he spent two years in federal prison. He was
unsuccessful in seeking a seat in the Kentucky Senate in 2006 and
2008.

Louisiana

Henson Moore was the last member of the Class elected, on January 5,
1975, in a special revote ordered because of voting irregularities. He
was the unsuccessful Republican nominee for the Senate in 1986,
after which he became deputy energy secretary. Toward the end of
the George H. W. Bush administration, he briefly served as deputy
White House chief of staff.

Maine

David Emery was just 26 when he was one of the few Republicans
to defeat an incumbent Democrat in 1974. He rose to become chief
deputy Republican whip before running an unsuccessful race for the
Senate in 1982. In 2005, he unsuccessfully ran for governor of Maine.
In 2016, he was defeated in a race for the state Senate.

Maryland

Gladys Noon Spellman was a vigorous advocate for federal employees
and retirees in her suburban Washington district. One of her

proudest (and most popular) achievements was the repaving of the notoriously bumpy Baltimore-Washington Parkway. Her career was cut short by illness, which left her permanently incapacitated, and the House declared her seat vacant in 1981. Spelman remained in a coma until passing away in 1988.

Massachusetts

Joseph Early was a district-focused member, serving on the Appropriations Committee. He was known as someone who could "deliver the dough," steering federal funds to his Massachusetts district, as his 2012 obituary noted.

Paul Tsongas served two terms in the House, championing the designation of Lowell, Massachusetts, as a unit of the National Park Service, which helped revitalize a key city in his constituency. In 1978, he was elected to the Senate, defeating the Senate's only black member, Edward Brooke, and served until 1984. The prior year, he had been diagnosed with cancer, which led to his decision not to seek reelection. Declared clear of cancer, he reemerged in 1992 as a candidate for the Democratic presidential nomination, adopting a strong anti-deficit message. Tsongas died in 1997, and his widow, Nikki, was elected in 2012 to serve in the seat he had occupied in the House.

Michigan

Jim Blanchard served four terms in the House and played a major role in securing financial support for the ailing Chrysler Corporation. His leadership in rescuing the state's leading industry helped propel Blanchard to the governorship in 1983, where he served two terms before being defeated in a bid for a third term. He was credited by *Newsweek* magazine with leading "one of the most dramatic economic turnabouts in the recent history of state government." He was later named ambassador to Canada by President Bill Clinton.

William Brodhead served for four terms before surprisingly retiring in 1982 to practice law. In 1994, he was defeated in the Democratic Senate primary by fellow Class member Bob Carr.

Bob Carr won reelection three times before losing his seat in the 1980 Reagan landslide. However, two years later, he regained his seat and held it for a dozen years, serving on the Appropriations Committee, before retiring to unsuccessfully run for the US Senate in 1994. He subsequently became a Washington-based consultant and faculty member at George Washington University's Graduate School of Political Management.

Minnesota

Thomas Hagedorn served four terms in Congress before losing his primary in 1982.

Richard Nolan won three terms in the House before retiring in 1980 and returning to Minnesota to work in international trade. In 2012, he won election to the House again, after the longest absence in congressional history.

Jim Oberstar enjoyed a long tenure in the House before losing in a surprise upset in 2010 during the Tea Party upsurge. Like his former employer, Rep. John Blatnik, whom he replaced, Oberstar rose to become chairman of the Transportation and Infrastructure Committee, with a special focus on aviation policy. Oberstar remained a reliable liberal except on abortion issues. He was also a vigorous proponent of bicycling and had taken a long ride the weekend before his sudden death in 2014.

Montana

Max Baucus won reelection to the House from his Montana district and then successfully ran for the Senate in 1978, the first of six victories. Baucus eventually became chairman of the Senate Finance Committee, in which position he was a major figure in crafting the Affordable Care Act in 2010 along with Class colleagues Chris Dodd and Tom Harkin in the Senate, and George Miller and Henry Waxman in the House. In 2014, Baucus resigned from the Senate to become ambassador to China.

New Hampshire

Norm D'Amours served five terms in the House before departing in 1984 to unsuccessfully challenge Republican senator Gordon Humphrey. An expert on banking issues, he served for seven years as the chairman the National Credit Union Association in the 1990s following appointment by President Bill Clinton.

Nebraska

Virginia Smith was active on farm and rural issues and Republican politics for more than two decades before seeking a seat in Congress in 1974. A member of the Appropriations Committee, she provided crucial support for the Reagan administration but opposed his policy of supporting the Nicaraguan Contras fighting the government. She retired in 1990 and died in 2006.

New Jersey

Millicent Fenwick was the oldest and arguably the most charismatic freshman in 1974. She compiled a moderate to liberal voting record during four terms in the House and was called "the conscience of Congress" by CBS news anchor Walter Cronkite, although she also sought to protect asbestos manufacturer Johns-Manville, a constituent, from legal prosecution. She was defeated in her race for the Senate in 1982 and later served as ambassador to the Food and Agriculture Organization of the United Nations from 1983 to 1987. She died in 1992.

James Florio served in the House until 1989 and was best known as the principal author of the Superfund law. He was elected governor of New Jersey in 1989 on his third attempt and was defeated after a single term. He unsuccessfully sought the Democratic senate nomination in 2000. He has continued to practice law in New Jersey.

William Hughes served in the House for 20 years before retiring in 1994, playing a major role in a large number of laws involving drug trafficking, terrorism, and chemical safety. The following year, he was confirmed as the US ambassador to Panama and served during the turbulent period leading up to the transfer of the Panama Canal and the Canal Zone to Panama, an issue that had been stirring controversy since his initial term in the House.

Andrew Maguire played a key role in legislation promoted by members of the Class including energy, health, and clean air. He was defeated after serving three terms in 1980. Two years later, he lost a primary for the Democratic Senate nomination. He subsequently worked on environmental policy, international farm development, and childhood immunization efforts.

Helen Meyner served two terms in the House before being defeated in 1978. After leaving the House, she served on several corporate boards. She died in 1997.

Nevada

Jim Santini served four terms in the House, leaving in 1982 to challenge incumbent senator Howard Cannon in the Democratic primary. One of the more conservative Democratic members of the Class, Santini became a Republican in 1986 and won that party's nomination for the US Senate. He was defeated in the general election by Rep. Harry Reid, who had succeeded him in the House. He later worked as a lobbyist for the tourism industry. He died in 2015.

New York

Jerome Ambro, one of the Class's presidents, focused primarily on local environmental and jobs issues during his three terms in the House He was defeated for reelection in 1980 and died in 1993.

Thomas Downey served in the House until his defeat in 1992. A member of the Armed Services and Ways and Means Committees, Downey was prominent on legislative issues in both areas, particular welfare reform and childcare, and also played a major role in effort to reform Pentagon spending. He became a prominent Washington lobbyist following his defeat.

John LaFalce spent his entire 28 years in the House working on financial services, banking, and housing issues, rising to become one of the Class members to chair a full House committee, the Small Business panel. He also was the ranking Democrat on the Financial Services Committee. He retired in 2002.

Matt McHugh served for nine terms before retiring in 1992. After leaving Congress, he served as vice president of Cornell University and worked at the World Bank.

Henry Nowak served nine terms in Congress, all of them as a member of the Public Works and Transportation and Committee. He was forced to shift to a new district following the 1980 census, and following the 1990 census his second district also was eliminated. He retired in 1992.

Richard Ottinger had previously served in the House (1965–1971) before an unsuccessful Senate race in 1970, which he lost to Conservative Party nominee James Buckley. His return to the House lasted until 1984, when he retired. He continued his work on environment and energy issues and became a law professor in New York.

Ned Pattison, one of the surprise winners in the Class, served for two terms. Narrowly winning a second term with only 47 percent of the vote, Pattison was an obvious target in 1978. The district's Conservative Party united with the Republicans to return the seat to Republican control. He returned to the practice of law and died in 1990.

Frederick Richmond left a legacy of promoting of urban gardens, supporting food stamps, and challenging agribusiness, a product of his unusual (for a Brooklyn congressman) appointment to the Agriculture Committee. His career ended in scandal, however, when he was indicted for possession of marijuana and for paying a bribe, and he was forced to resign from office.

James Scheuer was one of four Class members who had previously served in the House (1965–1972), losing his seat in 1972 in a Democratic primary where, because of reapportionment, he was forced to run against Rep. Jonathan Bingham. He returned to the House in 1974 representing another district. He was forced into another district following the 1980 reapportionment but was able to win and remained in the House until retiring in 1993. After leaving the second time, he briefly served as president of the European Bank for Reconstruction and Development. He died in 2005.

Stephen Solarz in the House for 18 years, focusing primarily on foreign policy issues. Having won his House seat by defeating an incumbent Democrat, he himself was ousted in the 1992 primary following reapportionment that fragmented his district. He later served as chairman of the Central Asian-American Enterprise Fund. He had aspired to be named ambassador to India, but the nomination encountered severe political opposition. He remained active on international policy issues until his death in 2010.

Leo Zeferetti, a former police union official, served four terms in the House before the 1982 reapportionment radically altered his district. He was thrown into the same district as Republican incumbent Guy Molanari of Staten Island, who won the 1982 election.

North Carolina

Bill Hefner, a gospel singer when he was elected in 1974, served in the House until 1998, when he chose to retire. He served briefly as a local official in Alabama and died in 2009.

Stephen Neal served for 20 years in the House before retiring on the eve of the Republican victory in 1994.

Ohio

Bill Gradison was an influential member of the Ways and Means Committee, playing a key role in tax and Social Security reform legislation in the 1980s. He resigned in 1993 to become president of the Health Insurance Association and later worked with the law and lobby firm of Patton Boggs in Washington.

Ron Mottl was one of the most vulnerable of the Class of 1974, winning election in a six-way race (including four independents) with just 35 percent of the vote. He developed a moderate to conservative voting record during his four terms in the House, supporting much of President Reagan's legislative agenda. He was defeated in the 1982 primary and later served on a local school board and in the Ohio assembly.

Oklahoma

Glenn English served for nearly 20 years as one of the most conservative Class members, before resigning in January 1994 to become the head of the National Rural Electric Cooperative Association.

Ted Risenhoover, an Air Force veteran, was among the more conservative members of the Class. His defeat in the 1978 primary was largely attributed to exposés about his personal lifestyle. He later worked for the House doorkeeper and at the Pentagon before resuming a career in publishing. He died in 2006.

Oregon

Les AuCoin was active on environmental, abortion rights, and foreign policy issues during his 18 years in the House. He retired in 1992 to challenge Republican senator Bob Packwood, narrowly winning the primary and then narrowly losing to Packwood. Following the election, it was disclosed that the *Washington Post* had delayed printing information about numerous women alleging abusive behavior by Packwood, who resigned the seat in 1994. He later became a professor at Southern Oregon University.

Bob Duncan had served as Speaker of the Oregon House of Representatives and as a member of the US House (1963–1967) prior to being reelected to a new district in 1974. He ran unsuccessfully for the Senate three times, including as a pro–Vietnam War Democrat, losing to the anti-war Republican Mark Hatfield, who was endorsed by the state's Democratic senator Wayne Morse. Duncan returned the favor by running against Morse in the 1968 primary but was defeated. He died in 2011.

James Weaver served until 1986, when he unsuccessfully ran for the Senate. In 1980, Weaver conducted an official filibuster against a controversial public power bill by filing 113 amendments to delay action on the measure, which prompted the House to modify its rules to restrict such practices. During his Senate race, Weaver came under criticism from the House Ethics Committee and was forced to withdraw from the race.

Pennsylvania

Bob Edgar, who had to look up the address of the Democratic Party in 1974 to know where to announce his candidacy, served in the House until 1986, when he ran unsuccessfully for the Senate against incumbent Republican senator Arlen Specter. He later served as the president of the Claremont School of Theology, the chief executive officer of the National Council of the Churches of Christ, and president of Common Cause before passing away in 2013.

Bill Goodling served in the House until 2001, rising to become chairman of the Education and Workforce (formerly Labor) Committee. He focused on education policy and, after his retirement, worked on his family's foundation on adult literacy. He died in 2017.

Gary Myers was a mechanical engineer prior to his election to the House, where he served on the Public Works and the Science and Technology Committees. He retired after two terms and returned to work at a steel plant in his district.

Rhode Island

Edward Beard served three terms in the House, always carried a small paintbrush in his pocket as a reminder of his former profession as a

housepainter. In 1980, he was defeated by moderate Republican
Claudine Schneider. He later operated a bar and hosted a talk radio
show.

South Carolina

Butler Derrick served in the House for 20 years before retiring in 1994.
He became a senior member of the Rules Committee and was a
vigorous defender of his state's textile industry, chairing the
Congressional Textile Caucus and opposing trade laws he argued
would hurt local industry. He embraced unconventional positions
for a South Carolina Democrat including abortion rights,
environmental issues, and tough restrictions on guns. He died in
2014.

Kenneth Holland served four terms, narrowly winning a second term
against New York Yankee shortstop Bobby Richardson. He retired in
1982 to resume his legal career.

John Jenrette served three terms in the House, creating the Tourism
Caucus as one of his major achievements. Jenrette's career was
marred by personal controversies including a divorce and highly
publicized remarriage, and ultimately by his involvement in the
Abscam bribery scandal, which landed him in prison.

South Dakota

Larry Pressler served three terms in the House before his election to
the Senate in 1978, where also served three terms before being
defeated in 1996. He has been involved in higher education and law
since leaving the Senate and ran unsuccessfully as an Independent
for the Senate in 2014. He endorsed Barack Obama for president in
2008 and 2012 and Hillary Clinton in 2016.

Tennessee

Harold Ford Sr., the lone African American freshman in 1974, served on
the Ways and Means Committee and was an expert on welfare policy,
chairing the subcommittee on Public Assistance. His career was
tarnished by indictment on bank fraud charges in 1987, which cost
him his chairmanship, but he remained in the House and was
acquitted in 1993. He retired in 1996 and his son, Harold Jr.,
succeeded him.

Marilyn Lloyd served for 20 years after replacing her husband, the 1974 nominee who was killed in a plane crash en route to his victory party. Lloyd served on the Science and Technology Committee throughout her career in the House, as well as on Public Works and Armed Services. She was also a strong advocate for breast cancer treatment and famously reversed her long opposition to abortion.

Texas

Jack Hightower, a moderate member of the Class, served for five terms before losing his seat in the 1984 Reagan landslide. He later served as first assistant attorney general of Texas and was elected to the Texas Supreme Court in 1988. He died in 2013.

Robert Krueger was a dean at Duke University before returning to Texas to win a House seat in 1974. He narrowly lost a 1978 Senate race to incumbent Republican John Tower and lost a primary for the open seat six years later. He served as an ambassador-at-large for Mexican affairs from 1979 to 1981, and as ambassador to Burundi (1996–2000), about which he wrote a book. In 1990, he won a seat on the powerful Texas Railroad Commission, and, when Sen. Lloyd Bentsen resigned in 1993 to become treasury secretary under President Bill Clinton, he was appointed to the seat by Gov. Ann Richards. He lost a race for the seat six months later, running what the *Houston Chronicle* called "the single worst [race] in Texas' modern political history."

Utah

Allan Howe was one of just two Class members to be defeated after serving a single term. His career was cut short after he was arrested for soliciting a prostitute. He died in 2000.

Vermont

Jim Jeffords was noted as a moderate to liberal Republican, known for being the only House Republican to vote against President Reagan's 1981 tax cut. He gained a reputation on issues involving education and disability rights. He was elected to the Senate in 1988. In May 2001, angered by President George W. Bush's tax cuts and by the refusal of the Senate to fund disability laws, he announced, "Increasingly, I find myself in disagreement with my party" and became an Independent, choosing to caucus with the Democrats, which had the effect of switching control of the Senate to the Democrats. After a special election 18 months later, however, Republicans regained the majority. He retired in 2006 and died in 2014.

Virginia

Joseph Fisher, an economist with a strong interested in the environment, served for three terms before being defeated. He founded the think tank Resources for the Future, which was later chaired by classmate Phil Sharp. He later worked for the Wilderness Society and was an economics professor. He died in 1992.

Herb Harris served for three terms before losing in 1980 to the same person he had originally defeated in 1974. He resumed his legal career and died in 2014.

Washington State

Don Bonker served in the House until 1988, when he unsuccessfully sought the Democratic nomination for the Senate. He chaired the Subcommittee on Trade on the Foreign Relations Committee and was active in trade legislation. He has worked in the private sector since leaving the House. In 1988 and 1992, he unsuccessfully sought the Democratic US Senate nomination. He continues to work in Washington, DC, on international affairs.

Wisconsin

Alvin Baldus served three terms in the House, losing in the 1980 general election. He died in 2017.

Robert Cornell, one of two Roman Catholic priests in the 94th Congress, served two terms in the House. He planned to run again in 1980, but declined to do so when Pope John Paul II ordered priests not to serve in public office. He died in 2009.

NOTES

INTRODUCTION

1. Interview with Thomas J. Downey. Coincidentally, Speaker Carl Albert—a diminutive man when he arrived as a freshman in 1947—had a similar experience with a veteran member and did deliver the papers as requested.

2. Five of the incoming Democrats—Richard Ottinger (NY), James Scheuer (NY), Abner Mikva (IL), Bob Duncan (OR), and Andy Jacobs (IN)—had previously served in the House.

3. Loomis, *New American Politician*, 4.

4. "Freshmen Have Never Been Treated So Well," *Washington Post*, January 15, 1975.

5. Richard Arenberg, "Fond Farewell to the 'Babies' of Watergate," *Conversation*, January 7, 2015 (online column); Ronald D. Elving, "Rebels of '94 and 'Watergate Babies' Similar in Class Size, Sense of Zeal," *CNN All Politics*, January 24, 1998.

6. John Jacobs, *Rage for Justice*, 248.

7. Granat, "Class of 1974."

8. Ibid.

9. Letter from James C. Wright to John Lawrence, September 24, 2014, John A. Lawrence Papers, Library of Congress, Manuscript Division.

10. James Sundquist, "The Decline and Resurgence of Congress" (Brookings, 1981), referenced in Smith, *Call to Order*, 371.

11. David Broder, "The Fading Promise of the 94th," *Washington Post*, August 10, 1975.

CHAPTER 1. TOOTHLESS, SAPLESS, AND SECRETIVE

1. Shapiro, *Last Great Senate*, prologue.

2. Richard Fenno, "Interview with Rep. Charles S. Joelson," Center for Legislative Archives (April 1964), Special Collections, Oral Histories and Interviews, National Archives, Washington, DC, https://www.archives.gov/legislative /research/special-collections/oral-history/fenno/joelson.html.

3. Clarke, *Ask Not*.

4. Julian Zelizer, quoted in Tanenhaus, "The Power of Congress," 70.

5. Ibid.

6. Interview with David Cohen. Bingham remained a member for nearly 20 years. His father, Hiram, an explorer who discovered the Machu Picchu ruins, is thought by some to have served as the model for the Indiana Jones film adventurer. The elder Bingham served as a Republican US senator and governor of Connecticut in the 1920s and 1930s.

7. Nathanson, "Caucus vs. the Barons."

8. President Harry S. Truman coined the epithet to describe the Republican-controlled Congress elected in 1946.

9. Interview with Jim Oberstar.

10. Zelizer, *On Capitol Hill*, 49; Loomis and Barnett, "Thinking about My Generation." In the Senate as well, the elections of 1956 and 1962, in particular, led to an infusion of younger, progressive Democrats with strong liberal credentials, including Joseph Clark of Pennsylvania and William Proxmire of Wisconsin in 1956, and Abraham Ribicoff of Connecticut, Gaylord Nelson of Wisconsin, George McGovern of South Dakota, Birch Bayh of Indiana, Daniel Inouye of Hawaii, and Edward M. Kennedy of Massachusetts two years later. See Shapiro, *Last Great Senate*, 11–13.

11. Richard Reeves, "How Kennedy Won the House and Lost the South," *New York Times*, March 9, 2009.

12. Interview with David Cohen.

13. Shannon, "Revolt in Washington," 662.

14. Zelizer, *On Capitol Hill*, 54.

15. Ibid., 662ff.

16. See Black and Black, *Rise of Southern Republicans*.

17. Bolling, "What the New Congress Needs Most," 79–81.

18. Walter J. Oleszek, "The Evolving Congress: Overview and Analysis of the Modern Era," in Congressional Research Service, *Evolving Congress*, 23.

19. Zelizer, *Fierce Urgency of Now*, 170.

20. Hathorn, "Changing Politics of Race," 228.

21. Powell lost his chairmanship of the Education and Labor Committee, and was expelled by the House in 1967 for ethics-related reasons. He promptly ran for, and was reelected, to the seat from which he had just been removed, serving until his defeat in the 1970 Democratic primary.

22. Albert, *Little Giant*, 316, 138.

23. Stevens, Miller, and Mann, "Mobilization of Liberal Strength in the House," 667–681.

24. Norman Ornstein, "Causes and Consequences of Congressional Change," 4; "The Democratic Study Group: A Winner on House Reforms," *Congressional Quarterly* 31, no. 22 (June 2, 1973); Interview with Abner Mikva.

25. Interview with Jim Oberstar, who had served as Blatnik's administrative assistant prior to his own election to the House in 1974.

26. See Democratic Study Group (DSG) Records, Library of Congress, Manuscript Division. DSG also developed a campaign fund to assist progressive candidates in their campaigns.

27. Interview with Abner Mikva; also see Mikva Oral History, Historical Society of the District of Columbia Circuit (1996). Mikva was the kind of reformer unwelcome to the Chicago Democratic organization. "Who sent you?" one of the ward heelers asked when Mikva appeared to volunteer for the 1956 campaign. "Nobody sent me," Mikva replied. "Well, we don't want nobody that nobody sent," the functionary told him.

28. Interview with William Cable.

29. Bolling, *House Out of Order*, 244.

30. Ibid., 52–53. Bolling was not alone in his frustration with liberals. Freshman David Obey, a former whip in the Wisconsin legislature who won a special election in 1969 for the longtime Republican seat vacated by Melvin Laird, Nixon's new defense secretary, declared that "one of the most frustrating characteristics of so many liberals or progressives in Congress throughout the years was that they were simply not operational. While they could give eloquent speeches that would stir souls, many could not strategize their way through a phone book." Obey preferred to "work things out." He viewed DSG chairman Jim O'Hara as an exception. Obey, *Raising Hell for Justice*, 123.

31. Bolling, *House Out of Order*, 235.

32. Rohde, *Parties and Leaders in the Postreform House*, 18–19.

33. Rohde, "Committee Reform in the House of Representatives and the Subcommittee Bill of Rights"; also see Voorhis, *Confessions of a Congressman*, 59, referenced in Congressional Research Service, *Evolving Congress*, 26.

34. Bone, *Party Committees and National Politics*, 168; Bolling, *House Out of Order*, 66; referenced in Congressional Research Service, *Evolving Congress*, 27.

35. Interview with David Obey.

36. David Obey, *Raising Hell for Justice*, 311–312. In his autobiography, Albert asserted that he "persuaded John McCormick to reawaken the Democratic caucus," but he may have been embellishing his role since he, too, later came under caucus criticism for being too cautious. He also asserted that some in the caucus urged him to challenge the aged McCormack for the speakership, and while he was convinced that he could have won, he deferred because he was the elder man's "ally, and supporter and his friend."

37. "Rayburn Is Dead: Served 17 Years as House Speaker," *New York Times*, November 17, 1961.

38. David Obey, *Raising Hell for Justice*, 122.

39. Albert, *Little Giant*, 310.

40. Conlon, "Putting the 94th in Perspective," 29; "DSG: A Winner in House Reforms," *Congressional Quarterly* (June 2, 1973): 1367; Ornstein, "Causes and Consequences of Congressional Change," 4–5.

41. Galloway, *Legislative Process in Congress*, 646.

42. "Congressional Reform Bill Dies in Rules Committee," *Congressional Quarterly Almanac*, 1968, 24th ed. (Washington, DC, 1969), 657–658. The bill also established several new standing committees, required expanded budgetary data and new procedures on appropriations bills, and revised the Regulation of Lobbying Act.

43. "2 Liberals in Congress: One Excited, One Disgusted," *New York Times*, May 31, 1969.

44. An amendment was unsuccessfully offered by Rep. (later Sen.) William Hathaway (D-ME) that would have required that a committee quorum be present to vote to close a meeting. Chairmen objected based on the difficulty of assembling a quorum.

45. A number of additional members would claim credit as well for restricting secretive teller voting, including Carl Albert and Richard Bolling. Interview with Joel Jankowsky. Interview with Charles Johnson.

46. The Senate has never moved to an electronic voting system, retaining the calling of the roll that consumes enormous quantities of time in the upper chamber and helps to facilitate legislative obstruction.

47. Ornstein, "Causes and Consequences of Congressional Change," 9, 13.

48. Interview with Don Bonker; Interview with William Cable.

49. House Republicans had already instituted a conference vote on proposed ranking members of committees in 1970.

50. Ornstein, "Causes and Consequences of Congressional Change," 102–103.

CHAPTER 2. SEEDS OF REBELLION

1. "Congress and Government, 1975 Overview," *Congressional Quarterly Almanac 1975*, 31st ed. (Washington, DC, 1976), 695–698, http://library.cqpress.com /cqalmanac/cqal75-1211994.

2. "The Man from Bugtussle Made National Impact," *Norman (OK) Transcript*, June 1, 2007.

3. Obey, *Raising Hell for Justice*, 135.

4. John Jacobs, *Rage for Justice*, 239.

5. Robinson, *You're in Your Mother's Arms*, 227.

6. Cong. Rec., "The Seniority System in the U.S. House of Representatives" (February 25, 1970), H5169–H5172.

7. Under long-standing rules, the Ways and Means Committee functioned as the Committee on Committees that made committee assignments and recommended chairmen to the full caucus.

8. Riegle, *O Congress*, 268. "Home Rule," Rarick declared, "would invite takeover by Black Muslims."

9. Obey, *Raising Hell for Justice*, 135.

10. Interview with Joel Jankowsky, assistant to Speaker Carl Albert.

11. Obey, *Raising Hell for Justice*, 129.

12. Interview with Tom Harkin.

13. Russell, "Hill Change." Forty-one of the 69 freshmen were Republicans, many replacing incumbents who might well have tired of their perpetual minority status and opted for the pension bonus.

14. For this section in general, quotes are from Democratic Caucus minutes, January 22, 1973, Democratic Caucus Papers, Library of Congress, Manuscript Division.

15. Democratic Caucus notes, January 22, 1973, Democratic Caucus Papers, Library of Congress, Manuscript Division, 34.

16. Remini, *House*, 433.

17. Holifield read the rising levels of reformist displeasure, however, and retired in 1974.

18. The vote on Patman was 155–40 and on Diggs, 154–36.

19. *Congressional Quarterly*, 33, no. 18 (May 1975) 242.

20. Norman Ornstein and David Rohde, "Seniority and Future Power in Congress" (manuscript, 1974), 13. Later included in Ornstein, *Change in Congress*;

Rohde, "Committee Reform in the House of Representatives and the Subcommittee Bill of Rights," 39.

21. See Rohde, "Committee Reform in the House of Representatives and the Subcommittee Bill of Rights"; Ornstein, "Causes and Consequences of Congressional Change"; Stephen S. Smith, *Call to Order.*

22. Ornstein, "Causes and Consequences of Congressional Change." Some dismissed the expansion of subcommittee powers as "a bunch of bullshit," particularly the staff accorded the new chairs. "You walk into these offices and you see people sitting on their asses reading the Washington Post. It hasn't changed things a damn bit." Rohde, "Committee Reform in the House of Representatives and the Subcommittee Bill of Rights," 47.

23. Mierzkowski, *Gerald Ford and the Challenges of the 1970s,* 67.

24. Democratic Caucus minutes, January 22, 1973.

25. Albert, *Little Giant,* 347.

26. Nathanson, "Caucus vs. the Barons"; *Congressional Quarterly* 33, no. 18 (May–June 1975).

27. Interview with David Cohen.

28. Democratic Caucus notes, January 22, 1973.

29. Democratic Caucus minutes, February 1, 1973.

30. Democratic Caucus notes, February 22, 1973.

31. Albert, *Little Giant,* 323.

32. Letter from Jim Wright to John Lawrence, September 24, 2014, John A. Lawrence Papers, Library of Congress, Manuscript Division.

33. Cong. Rec., August 3, 1971, 7690.

34. Albert, *Little Giant,* 317. Rep. Tim Wirth (D-CO) would offer a similar analysis about his own class, the freshmen of 1974. "We were the children of Vietnam, not children of World War II. We were products of television, not of print. We were products of computer politics not courthouse politics."

35. Letter from Jim Wright.

36. Interview with Patricia Schroeder.

37. Obey, *Raising Hell for Justice,* 153.

38. Morton Mintz, "The Speaker: Carl Albert to Retire This Year," *Washington Post,* June 6, 1976.

39. *Congressional Quarterly,* 24, no. 25 (June 12, 1976): 335.

40. Mikva Oral History, Historical Society of the District of Columbia Circuit (1996), http://dcchs.org/OralHistory.asp?OralHistoryID=22. Abzug stories are legendary. She reportedly rebuked House Doorkeeper "Fishbait" Miller in a particularly graphic manner when he admonished her to remove her trademark hat before entering the House Chamber, as required by the rules. Another House official recalled being on the receiving end of Abzug's fury when Foreign Affairs chairman "Doc" Morgan (PA) outmaneuvered her and blocked her from filing a discharge petition.

41. Democratic Caucus minutes, May 9 and 10, 1973.

42. Democratic Caucus minutes, July 19, 1973.

43. "The Democratic Study Group: A Winner on House Reforms," *Congressional Quarterly* 32, no. 22 (June 2, 1973).

44. Democratic Caucus notes, April 4, 1973, 5.

45. James Naughton, "Freshmen House Democrats Fight Nixon on Control," *New York Times*, April 12, 1973.

46. Ibid.

47. Special orders occur at the end of the day's legislative business and need not be related to legislation before the House. Nor is there any requirement to grant time to those disagreeing with the views of speakers, as is the case with normal floor debate.

48. Bill Gunther to Carl Albert, Carl Albert Papers, University of Oklahoma, Box 5 Correspondence (April 16, 1973).

49. Cong. Rec., April 18, 1973. Nixon cited rampant spending and a growing deficit as the basis for impoundment. The deficit, indeed, had mushroomed from a $3.5 billion surplus 1969 to a $23 billion deficit by mid-1972 due to spending on both expanded domestic programs and on the war.

50. Handwritten comment by Albert on the Gunther letter.

51. Naughton, "Freshmen House Democrats Fight Nixon Control."

52. Kevin Kosar, "So . . . This Is Nixon's Fault?," *Politico*, October 24, 2015.

53. Russell, "Hill Change."

54. Democratic Caucus notes, May 2, 1974.

55. US Department of State, "Reporting International Agreements to Congress under Case Act," n.p., n.d., http://www.state.gov/s/l/treaty/caseact/.

56. In a bipartisan assertion of the powers of the legislative branch, 87 Republicans joined with 196 Democrats on the House override, which was opposed by 32 of the conservative Democrats. In the Senate, 25 Republicans joined with 49 Democrats in support of the override, and only 3 Democrats voted no.

57. "The Democratic Study Group," *Congressional Quarterly*; Democratic Caucus notes, May 16, 1973.

58. As Joel Jankowsky, Albert's aide remarked, the decision was to put the foxes in the same house.

59. Albert, *Little Giant*, 245.

60. Interview with Mark Gersh. Albert aide Joel Jankowsky referred to Albert and Bolling as "partners in crime."

61. Bolling, "Congress and Its Committee System," 1–14; E. Scott Adler and John D. Wilkerson, "Intended Consequences: Jurisdictional Reform and Issue Control in the U.S. House of Representatives," http://www.congressionalbills.org/Why%20Reform.pdf.

62. *Congressional Quarterly* 34 (July 19, 1976): 1533.

63. Zelizer, *On Capitol Hill*, 144.

64. House Democratic Caucus notes, May 1–2, 1974.

65. Democratic Caucus minutes, May 1, 1974.

66. Malbin, "Congress Report," 1881–1886; Zelizer, *On Capitol Hill*, 150.

67. The Senate Watergate hearings, chaired by Sen. Ervin, had been televised, as had select earlier events including the infamous Army-McCarthy hearings in 1954.

68. John Jacobs, *Rage for Justice*, 234; Stevens, Miller, and Mann, "Mobilization of Liberal Strength in the House," 667–681.

69. Douglas Dibbert interview. Eventually, 35 would win their elections.

70. Mary Russell, "Hill Change: Slow Motion," *Washington Post*, September 15, 1974.

71. Malbin, "Congress Report," 1886.

72. *Congressional Quarterly* 32, no. 52 (December 24, 1974).

73. *Congressional Quarterly* 33, no. 4 (January 25, 1975): 189.

CHAPTER 3. THE CLASS: DIVERSE AND DETERMINED

1. David Broder, "GOP 'Talent Hunt' Beginning for 1974," *Washington Post*, February 21, 1973.

2. Ibid.

3. Interview with Rep. Lou Frey.

4. DeFrank, "Gerald Ford's Pardon."

5. Interview with Lou Frey.

6. DeFrank, "Gerald Ford's Pardon."

7. Bob Woodward, "Closing the Chapter on Watergate Wasn't Done Lightly," *Washington Post*, December 28, 2006.

8. Reportedly, Ford also authorized spending $110,000 on a vault to house Nixon's papers. Congress soon passed legislation barring the transfer of the documents to Nixon.

9. Granat, "Class of 1974."

10. Sen. Charles Grassley (R-IA) remains the lone member elected to the House in 1974 in continuous service since 1975. He was elected to the Senate in 1981. Rep. Rick Nolan (D-MN), retired after three terms in 1980, and then was reelected in 2012 after a 32-year hiatus, the longest on record. Sen. Pat Leahy (D-VT) has served in the Senate since 1974 but never served in the House.

11. Blatnik, first elected in 1946, reportedly introduced Jacqueline Bouvier to John F. Kennedy.

12. Interview with Jim Oberstar. The bill was passed despite Smith's opposition but was vetoed by President Dwight D. Eisenhower.

13. Interview with Tom Harkin.

14. Tom Harkin, "Vietnam Whitewash: The Congressional Jury That Convicted Itself," *Progressive*, October 1970; *Life*, July 17, 1970.

15. Interview with Tom Harkin.

16. Correspondence from Andrew Maguire, January 13, 2014, John A. Lawrence Papers, Library of Congress, Manuscript Division.

17. Ibid.

18. Richard, "Timothy E. Wirth."

19. Wirth, "Diary of a Dropout."

20. Interview with Pat Schroeder.

21. Interview with Tim Wirth; Communication with Tim Wirth, March 17, 2014.

22. "Freshman Have Never Been Treated So Well," *Washington Post*, January 15, 1975.

23. Ronald D. Elving, "Rebels of '94 and 'Watergate Babies' Similar in Class Size, Sense of Zeal," *CNN All Politics*, January 24, 1998, http://www.cnn.com /ALLPOLITICS/1998/01/26/cq/elving.html.

24. Wirth, "Diary of a Dropout."

25. Harmon ran as both a Democrat and a Republican, 18 times in all, winning only in 1958.

26. Mark Patinkin, "A Visit with Eddie Beard, Former Congressman Battling Parkinson's," *Providence Journal*, April 12, 2015.

27. For years, Russo remained sensitive about being labeled a product of the Daley machine.

28. See Lublin, *Republican South*, 21–25.

29. Interview with John Jenrette.

30. Interview with Elliott Levitas.

31. Ibid.

32. "Rep. Mineta to Quit Congress," *Los Angeles Times*, September 12, 1995.

33. Interview with Les Francis.

34. Schneider, "JFK's Children."

35. Interview with Matt McHugh.

36. Loomis and Barnett, "Thinking about My Generation."

37. Ramey and Haley, *Tackling Giants*, 162.

38. Ibid., 165.

39. "Freshman Have Never Been Treated So Well," *Washington Post*.

40. Interview with Thomas Downey.

41. Alison Mitchell, "For One Lawmaker, Allure of Capital Had Double-Edge," *New York Times*, November 8, 1992.

42. Interview with James Blanchard.

43. Interview with Jerry Patterson.

44. For examples of how the term has entered into the historical vernacular, see Ryan Grim, "Watergate Babies, Now Fully Grown, Dominating Health Care Endgame," *Huffington Post*, March 3, 2010; Zelizer, *On Capitol Hill*, 156ff.; "Watergate Babies Take Power," *Congressional Quarterly*, 53, September 2, 1995; Remini, *House*, 447; Steven V. Roberts, "Life of a 'Watergate Baby,'" *New York Times*, May 13, 1986.

45. Interview with Mike Blouin.

46. Remini, *House*, 447.

47. O'Neill with Novak, *Man of the House*, 284.

48. Chris Matthews quoted in Loomis, *New American Politician*, 4.

49. Rimini, *House*, 446.

50. Richard L. Lyons, "Hill Freshmen Seek Strength," *Washington Post*, July 15, 1975.

CHAPTER 4. THE REINFORCEMENTS

1. *The (MIT) Tech*, 94, no. 7 (March 1, 1974): 4.

2. *Congressional Quarterly* 32 (1974): 3122.

3. "Pre-election Final Report: Possible Landslide," *Congressional Quarterly* 32, no. 44 (November 2, 1974): 3011. Generic leads of half that amount typically spell a catastrophic loss.

4. "Republicans May Lose Long-Held House Seats," *Congressional Quarterly*, 32, no. 43 (October 26, 1974): 1965–1967.

5. Two of the unsuccessful 1974 hopefuls would reemerge as major political forces—and adversaries—two decades later: Bill Clinton in Arkansas and Newt Gingrich in Georgia.

6. Just one member of the moderate "Wednesday Group" was defeated, John Dellenbeck of Oregon.

7. Interview with Douglas Dibbert and NCEC materials in his possession.

8. "Southern Republicans: Little Hope This Year," *Congressional Quarterly* 32, no. 43 (October 26, 1974).

9. "The House: New Faces and New Strains, *Time*, November 18, 1974. "Democrats: Now the Morning After," *Time*, November 18, 1974; *Congressional Quarterly* 32, no. 45 (November 9, 1974): 3060; *Congressional Quarterly* 32, no. 46 (November, 16, 1974): 3122.

10. Phillips, *Post Conservative America*, 59–61.

11. Ibid., 57, 60, 69. Phillips asserted that but for Watergate, Republicans could have gained as many as 4 Senate seats and 30 in the House in 1974.

12. *Time*, November 18, 1974.

13. Edward C. Burks, "Toby Moffett: Washington Outsider Settles In," *New York Times*, February 26, 1978.

14. "House," *Time*.

15. *Congressional Quarterly* 34 (September–October 1976).

16. Frank Starr, "A Fight in the House GOP Caucus?," *Chicago Tribune*, December 9, 1974.

17. Granat, "Class of 1974," 498–505; Interview with Willie Blacklow.

18. House seats, unlike those in the US Senate, can only be won in elections.

19. Interview with Pat Schroeder.

20. Elizabeth Kastor, "A Woman's Place: The 1950s Were Not Easy for Females in Congress," *Washington Post*, November 17, 1996.

21. Schroeder, *24 Years of House Work*.

22. Schapiro, *Millicent Fenwick*, 150.

23. Bradley would be elected to the Senate from New Jersey in 1978 and would serve three terms before retiring.

24. "A Breakthrough in Politics," *Time*, November 18, 1974; Interview with Donnald Anderson.

25. John Branston, "The Count Down," *Memphis Flyer*, October 7–13, 1999.

26. See Lublin, *Paradox of Representation*, 37–38.

27. Other minorities registered modest increases with the election of the Class. The number of Catholics rose from 114 to 124, and the number of Jews from 14 to 23.

28. In addition to Mikva and Ottinger, the returning members included James Scheuer (NY), Bob Duncan (OR), Andy Jacobs (IN), and Republican George Hansen (ID).

29. "Freshman Have Never Been Treated So Well," *Washington Post*, January 15, 1975; Interview with Richard Ottinger.

30. Abner Mikva, Oral History, Historical Society of the District of Columbia Circuit (Washington, 1996), 149. Two years later, he would spend more than $1 million in a reelection campaign.

31. Comments at July 8, 2015, Reunion Dinner, Washington, DC.

32. Loomis, *New American Politician*, 4.

33. Interview with Andrew Maguire.

34. Naughton, "Lost Innocence of Congressman AuCoin."

35. Interview with Jim Blanchard.

36. Interview with John LaFalce.

37. Interview with Berkley Bedell.

38. Interview with Tim Wirth.

39. Paul Richard, "Timothy E. Wirth," *Washington Post*, February 23, 1975; Interview with Jerry Patterson.

40. John Jacobs, *Rage for Justice*, 257.

41. Ibid.

42. Interviews with Thomas Downey and George Miller.

43. *Congressional Quarterly* 33 (August 2, 1975): 1677.

44. John Yang, "In Wake of Watergate, Reformers Charged Hill: But Class of '74 Now Draws Some Fire," *Washington Post*, June 15, 1992.

45. Mineta was ultimately succeeded in 1976 by Jerry Ambro (NY) and returning member Richard Ottinger (NY).

46. Interviews with Berkley Bedell and Les AuCoin.

47. Malbin, "Congress Report," 1881–1886.

48. Obey, *Raising Hell for Justice*, 166.

49. Interview with Douglas Dibbert.

50. James Reston, "The Class of 1974," *New York Times*, December 18, 1974.

51. Interview with Bob Carr.

52. O'Neill with Novak, *Man of the House*, 282–285.

53. Loomis, *New American Politician*, 241; Granat, "Class of 1974."

54. NCEC paper (possession of the author). NCEC's history was skewed; the first Congress did not meet until 1789; 1976 was the bicentennial of the signing of the Declaration of Independence.

55. Stephen Green and Margot Hornblower, "Mills Admits Being Present during Tidal Basin Scuffle," *Washington Post*, October 11, 1974.

56. *Congressional Quarterly*, 32, no. 47 (November 23, 1974): 3151.

57. Julian Zelizer, "Learn from the 'Watergate Babies,'" *CNN Commentary*, February 10, 2014.

58. Malbin, "Congress Report."

CHAPTER 5. THE REVOLUTION

1. "Democrats: Now the Morning After," *Time*, November 11, 1974. Political scientist John Patty has written about how larger majorities often contain more unruly factions than narrow majorities.

2. "The Old Order Changing in 94th Congress," *Morning Record* (Connecticut), February 5, 1975.

3. DSG special report, "94th Congress Reform Proposals" (December 1, 1974), Democratic Study Group (DSG) Records, Library of Congress, Manuscript Division, 93-15.

4. Interview with Tim Wirth.

5. Interview with Marty Russo.

6. James Reston, "The Class of 1974," *New York Times*, December 18, 1974.

7. Interview with Bill Brodhead.

8. The other at-large whips were Cardiss Collins of Illinois and Bella Abzug of New York.

9. An effort in July 1970 to restrict the absolute reliance on seniority was defeated by the caucus. Several members had previously lost seniority for refusing to support Democratic presidential candidates, including John Rarick (LA) in 1969, who endorsed independent George Wallace in 1968; as earlier noted, John Bell Williams (MS) and Albert Watson (SC) lost their seniority for endorsing Barry Goldwater in 1964. Indeed, the only chairman to be stripped of his gavel was a black liberal, Adam Clayton Powell (NY), who was expelled from the House for unethical conduct, although he later reclaimed his seat but not his chairmanship.

10. Interview with Les AuCoin.

11. Waxman, *Waxman Report*, 25.

12. Loomis and Barnett, "Thinking about My Generation."

13. Interview with Tim Wirth.

14. Interview with Steve Neal.

15. Interview with Pat Schroeder.

16. Interview with Mike Blouin.

17. Interview with David Cohen.

18. Loomis, *New American Politician*, 55; Mary Russell, "Common Cause Report Hits Hébert," *Washington Post*, January 14, 1975.

19. *Congressional Quarterly* 33, no. 4 (January 25, 1975): 212.

20. Interview with Pat Schroeder. Hébert wrote an autobiography he immodesty entitled *Last of the Titans*. Speaker Albert signed Schroeder's travel voucher.

21. Interview with James Blanchard.

22. Interview with David Obey.

23. James R. Dickenson, "A Too Formidable Reformer?," *Washington Star-News*, n.d. [1974].

24. Mary Russell, "Freshmen-Led Drama Yet to Be Played Out," *Washington Post*, January 19, 1975.

25. Russell, "Common Cause Report Hits Hébert."

26. Interview with Marty Russo.

27. "House Caucuses: Preparing for the 94th," *Congressional Quarterly* 32, no. 46 (November 16, 1974): 3118.

28. Dickenson, "Too Formidable Reformer?"

29. Correspondence from William Hughes to John Lawrence (July 17, 2015), John A. Lawrence Papers, Library of Congress, Manuscript Division.

30. Interview with Glenn English.

31. John Jacobs, *Rage for Justice*, 259.

32. Sisk, *Congressional Record*, 200.

33. Robinson, *You're in Your Mother's Arms*, 233–234.

34. *Congressional Quarterly* 33 (August 2, 1975): 1676.

35. Roland Evans and Robert Novak, "Power Shift in the House," *Washington Post*, December 7, 1974.

36. Naughton, "Lost Innocence of Congressman AuCoin."

37. Reston, "Class of 1974."

38. Much of the following account is drawn from the minutes of the Democratic Organizing Caucus held on December 3, 1974, in the Manuscript Division of the Library of Congress.

39. Nathanson, "Caucus vs. the Barons."

40. Norman Ornstein and David Rohde, "Seniority and Future Power in Congress," in Ornstein, *Change in Congress*.

41. Both the Hansen and Bolling reform commissions had recommended abolishing HUAC and sending its jurisdiction to Judiciary.

42. Democratic Organizing Caucus notes, January 13, 1975, Library of Congress, Manuscript Division; *Congressional Quarterly*, 33, no. 3 (January 18, 1975).

43. Early Democratic Caucus for the Organization of the 94th Congress (unpublished), December 3, 1974, Democratic Caucus Papers, Library of Congress, Manuscript Division, 128ff.

44. Evans and Novak, "Power Shift in the House."

45. "New Congress Organizes: No Role for Mills," *Congressional Quarterly*, 32, no. 49 (December 1974).

46. Robinson, *You're in Your Mother's Arms*, 237.

47. Charles Rangel became the first black Member of Ways and Means in 1975 and rose to chair the committee in 2007. Annunzio, who had denounced Metcalfe earlier in the Illinois Caucus, also disputed Dellums's case for minority representation.

48. Democratic Caucus notes, December 4, 1974, Democratic Caucus Papers, Library of Congress, Manuscript Division, 160, 165.

49. Democratic Caucus minutes, December 4, 1974, Democratic Caucus Papers, Library of Congress, Manuscript Division.

50. Democratic Caucus minutes, December 4, 1974, 251.

51. Ramey and Haley, *Tackling Giants*, 186.

52. John E. Yang, "In Wake of Watergate, Reformers Charged Hill: But Class of '74 Now Draws Some Fire," *Washington Post*, June 15, 1992.

53. "Congress and Government, 1975 Overview," *Congressional Quarterly Almanac* (1975), 31st ed. (Washington, DC, 1976), 695–698.

54. Mary Russell, "Hill Chairmen Return to Meet with Freshmen," *Washington Post*, January 9, 1975.

55. Russell, "Freshman-Led Drama Yet to Be Played Out."

56. Richard Lyons, "Freshman Assess House Chairman," *Washington Post*, January 14, 1975.

57. Russell, "Hill Chairmen Return to Meet with Freshmen."

58. Ramey and Haley, *Tackling Giants*, 186.

59. Interview with Bill Brodhead.

60. Interview with Berkley Bedell.

61. Ibid.; Schneider, "JFK's Children."

62. Lyons, "Freshmen Assess House Chairman"; Interview with Henry Waxman.

63. Ramey and Haley, *Tackling Giants*, 187.

64. *Lubbock Avalanche-Journal*, February 7, 1975; Interview with Marty Russo.

65. Russell, "Freshmen-Led Drama Yet to Be Played Out"; Russell, "Hill Chairman Return to Meet with Freshman."

66. Interview with Bill Brodhead.

67. Russell, "Freshman Led Drama Yet to Be Played Out."

68. "House Democratic Revolt Claims 3 Chairmen," *Congressional Quarterly*, 33, no. 4 (January 25, 1975): 210.

69. *Lubbock Avalanche-Journal*, February 7, 1975; Russell, "Common Cause Report Hits Hébert."

70. *Congressional Quarterly* 30, no. 7 (February 15, 1975). The quote was by Rep. Bob Bergland (MN) who would become Jimmy Carter's secretary of agriculture in 1977.

71. *Texas Monthly*, May 1976, 123.

72. There was a sizeable contingent of rural freshmen on the Agriculture Committee, assigned to commodity-based subcommittees according to their local constituent needs: Livestock, Dairy, Tobacco. Of the new appointees, only Fred Richmond (NY) represented an urban constituency.

73. Democratic Organizing Caucus minutes, January 22, 1975.

74. *Congressional Quarterly* 30, no. 7 (February 15, 1975): 380.

75. Democratic Organizing Caucus notes, January 22, 1975, 548–553. Ralph Nader, the consumer advocate, weighed in to support Patman because of his lengthy battles against corporate banking interests.

76. For a recent account of the vote against Patman, see Stoller, "How Democrats Killed Their Populist Soul."

77. Clem, *Making of Congressmen*, 206.

78. Interviews with Martha Keys and Steve Neal.

79. *Congressional Quarterly* 33 (January 25, 1975).

80. *Lubbock Avalanche-Journal*, February 7, 1975.

81. Interview with Douglas Dibbert.

82. Russell, "Freshman-Led Drama Yet to Be Played Out."

83. Interview with Elliott Levitas.

84. Sisk, *Congressional Record*, 324.

85. Interview with Jim Oberstar.

86. "Old Order Changing in 94th Congress," *Morning Record*.

87. Flat prints file, Phillip Burton Papers, Bancroft Library, University of California (Berkeley), January 22, 1975.

CHAPTER 6. TIME TO PUT ON THE LONG PANTS

1. *Congressional Quarterly* 33, no. 1 (January 6, 1975).

2. NCEC release following 1974 election, n.d., John A. Lawrence Papers, Library of Congress, Manuscript Division.

3. Ibid.

4. "Congress Opens in 'Spirit of Unity,' " *San Francisco Chronicle*, January 15, 1974.

5. James Reston, "The Class of 1974," *New York Times*, December 18, 1974.

6. Mary Russell, "House Chiefs, Freshmen Split on Issues," *Washington Post*, January 17, 1976.

7. Morton Mintz, "The Speaker: Carl Albert to Retire This Year," *Washington Post*, June 6, 1976.

8. *Congressional Quarterly* 33, no. 1 (January 1975).

9. Interview with Henry Waxman.

10. *Congressional Quarterly* 32, no. 1 (January 1975); Interview with Joel Jankowsky; Interview with Les Francis.

11. Leary, "Phillip Burton of the Caucus."

12. Interview with Martha Keys.

13. Interview with Tim Wirth.

14. Freshmen joining the Livestock and Grains Subcommittee included Jim Weaver (OR), Tom Harkin (IA), Jack Hightower (TX), Berkley Bedell (IA), Glenn English (OK), Floyd Fithian (IN), Rick Nolan (MN), and Norm D'Amours (NH). John Jenrette (SC) was careful to gain a seat on the Tobacco Subcommittee, while Nolan, Alvin Baldus (MN), John Krebs (CA) and Matt McHugh (NY) flocked to the Dairy and Poultry panel. *Congressional Quarterly* 33, no. 7 (February 15, 1975).

15. "City Slicker Congressmen Worry Butz," *Milwaukee Journal*, January 15, 1975; "Butz Worried by New Congress," *Lawrence (Kansas) Journal-World*, January 15, 1975.

16. Interview with Bob Krueger.

17. Only one freshman sympathetic to the oil industry, Bob Krueger of Texas, secured a seat on the subcommittee.

18. Staggers, according to one account, "would never recover from his wounds" and retired from the House in 1980, leaving the full committee chairmanship to Dingell. Ironically, Waxman, who would engage in years of battles with Dingell over energy policy, ousted the Michigan veteran as chairman in 2009. David Rogers, "Henry Waxman Hands Off the Torch," *Politico*, February 10, 2014.

19. Sullivan did retain the chairmanship of the full Merchant Marine Committee based on her seniority.

20. Interview with Matt McHugh.

21. Interview with Steve Neal.

22. "Ford and Democrats Offer Differing Solutions," *Congressional Quarterly* 33, no. 3 (January 18, 1975): 131.

23. Les AuCoin diary, January 15, 1975, quoted in Naughton, "Lost Innocence of Congressman AuCoin."

24. Tabb, "The Real Ford Strategy."

25. *Congressional Quarterly* 33, no. 7 (February 15, 1975).

26. *Congressional Quarterly* 33, no. 10 (March 8, 1975; April 1975).

27. *Congressional Quarterly* 33, no. 11 (March 15, 1975).

28. *Congressional Quarterly* 33, no. 10 (March 8, 1975).

29. Albert, *Little Giant*, 355.

30. Abner Mikva Oral History, Historical Society of the District of Columbia Circuit Appeals Court (1996), 154.

31. *Congressional Quarterly* 33, no. 7 (February 15, 1975).

32. *Congressional Quarterly* 33, no. 9 (March 1, 1975).

33. Interview with Elliott Levitas.

34. *Congressional Quarterly* 33, no. 18 (May 1975).

35. Ibid., 31.

36. John W Finney, "Emergency Funds," *New York Times*, April 24, 1975.

37. John Jacobs, *Rage for Justice*, 276.

38. Ibid., 915, 237.

39. Mieczkowski, *Gerald Ford and the Challenges of the 1970s*, 291.

40. Ibid., 62–63.

41. Vern Loen, Charles Leppert, Doug Bennett, "Memo to Max Friedersdorf: Home District Sentiment," April 7, 1975, Gerald Ford Presidential Archives.

42. *Congressional Quarterly* 33 (April 26, 1975).

43. An even more restrictive 10-day limit by Don Riegle failed 97–311.

44. Mikva Oral History.

45. General Accounting Office, "The Seizure of the Mayaguez—a Case Study of Crisis Management," B-133001 (May 11, 1976), 71; Behuniak, "Seizure and Recovery of the S.S. *Mayaguez*," 61.

46. Richard Lyons, "Democrats Intensify Roles in House," *Washington Post*, November 7, 1974.

47. *Congressional Quarterly* 33 (June 28, 1975).

48. Rapoport, *Inside the House*; John Jacobs, *Rage for Justice*, 274.

49. *Congressional Quarterly* 33 (April 5, 1975).

50. The member, Alan Steelman, did not run for reelection to his House seat in 1976, instead challenging Sen. Lloyd Bentsen unsuccessfully. His seat was won by Democrat Jim Mattox.

51. James Lyons, "Democrats Intensify Roles in House," *Washington Post*, November 7, 1974.

52. *Congressional Quarterly* 33, no. 23 (June 7, 1975).

53. Naughton, "Lost Innocence of Congressman AuCoin."

54. "Democrats Worry about Minority Rule," *Congressional Quarterly* 33 (April 5, 1976): 1333.

55. *Congressional Quarterly* 33, no. 23 (June 7, 1975). The members who switched were Fountain Sikes, Stratton, and White (TX). The override failed 278–143.

56. Ibid.

57. Michel Malbin, "A Learning Experience for Freshmen," *New York Times*, August 24, 1975.

58. Mary Russell, "Freshmen Feel Frustration," *Washington Post*, October 27, 1975.

59. "Democrats Worry about Minority Rule," *Congressional Quarterly*, 1334.

60. *Congressional Quarterly* 33, no. 23 (June 7, 1975).

61. Helstoski had nominated Michigan's John Conyers Jr. for Speaker, with seconds from Parren Mitchell and Ron Dellums, but Albert won the caucus vote handily, 202–25.

62. Transcript of 1972 caucus meeting, located in Democratic Caucus minutes, Democratic Caucus Papers, Library of Congress, Manuscript Division.

63. Mary Russell, "The 'Most Frustrating' Year for Albert," *Washington Post*, October 26, 1975.

64. *Congressional Quarterly* 33, no. 38 (September 18, 1975).

65. Ibid., 1333; Malbin, "Learning Experience for Freshmen."

66. Daniel Rapoport, "The House Is Troubled," *Washington Post*, June 22, 1975.

67. "Albert Faces Ouster Drive by Frosh Dems," *Pittsburgh Post-Gazette*, June 16, 1975.

68. Letter from Don Bonker to Carl Albert, Carl Albert Papers, University of Oklahoma, Box 4 (June 16, 1975).

69. Rapoport, "House Is Troubled."

70. "Albert May Face a Revolt in the House," *New York Times*, June 14, 1975.

71. *Congressional Quarterly* 33, no. 18 (May–June 1975).

72. Naughton, "Lost Innocence of Congressman AuCoin."

73. Floyd Fithian to Carl Albert and Thomas O'Neill, Carl Albert Papers, University of Oklahoma, Box 5 Correspondence (June 13, 1975).

74. Ron Mottl to Carl Albert, Carl Albert Papers, University of Oklahoma, Box 7 Correspondence (June 13, 1975).

75. Don Bonker to Carl Albert, Carl Albert Papers, University of Oklahoma, Box 4 Correspondence (June 16, 1975); Richard Lyons, "Hill Freshmen Eye Override Strategy," *Washington Post*, June 18, 1975.

76. Freshman participants included Toby Moffett, Bob Carr, Paul Tsongas, Gladys Spellman, and Herb Harris.

77. "Albert Faces Ouster Drive by Frosh Dems," *Pittsburgh Post-Gazette*.

78. Nearly a decade later, after he had lost his House seat in 1980 and regained it two years later, Carr attributed his attack on Albert to his being "an angry young man" and promised to "pick my battles more carefully." Interview with Bob Carr; Mieczkowski, *Gerald Ford and the Challenges of the 1970s*, 68.

79. *Congressional Quarterly* 33 (September 18, 1975).

80. Interview with James Blanchard.

81. Richard Lyons, *Washington Post*, July 15, 1975.

82. Ibid.

83. Neither the hearings nor the freshman whip system ever occurred.

84. *Lexington Dispatch*, August 2, 1975.

85. Pay in 1969 was set at $42,500, or $270,697 in 2015 dollars. At no time since has congressional pay in real dollars ever been higher than this level.

86. *Congressional Quarterly* 33 (August 9, 1975): 1803.

87. Interview with Don Bonker.

88. No votes included Wirth, Carr, and Downey, Simon, Blouin, Bedell, Tsongas, Hubbard, and Ambro. Bonker voted yes.

89. Freshmen, including Democrats Carr, Harken, Miller, and Sharp, and Republicans, including Grassley and Hyde, returned their pay raise to the Treasury, while others including D'Amours, Dodd, Fenwick, Keys, Maguire, and Nowak donated theirs to charities. Battles over the pay raise continued for another 15 years before adoption of the Twenty-Seventh Amendment, which barred Congress from raising its salary prior to an intervening election, an amendment that had been stalled since the 1790s.

90. *Congressional Quarterly* 34, no. 36 (September 4, 1976); Interview with John Gregory.

91. An excellent in-depth account of the energy politics of the era can be found in Meg Jacobs, *Panic at the Pump.*

92. *Congressional Quarterly* 32, no. 46 (December 7, 1974).

93. *Congressional Quarterly* 33, no. 3 (January 18, 1975).

94. *Beaver County (PA) Times*, June 5, 1975.

95. *Congressional Quarterly* 33 (May 1975).

96. "Congress at Mid-year: Most Issues Unresolved," *Congressional Quarterly* 33, no. 27 (1975); *Congressional Quarterly* 33, no. 3 (January 19, 1975): 159. Only Republican Sen. Jacob Javits of New York dissented from the argument against raising energy taxes. Less than a year earlier, the Joint Economic Committee had drawn the opposite conclusion, describing a new 30-cent per gallon tax an "effective way" to cut oil imports.

97. Among House Democrats in general, support for creation of an energy corporation was just 46 percent. Only 14 percent favored taking over utilities, and 13 percent seizing oil companies.

98. William Greider and Barry Sussman, "Public Mood: The House Today, Badly Tattered," *Washington Post*, June 29, 1975.

99. Lyons, "Hill Freshman Eye Override Strategy."

100. Don Bonker to Carl Albert, Carl Albert Papers, University of Oklahoma, Box 4 Correspondence (June 16, 1975).

101. *Congressional Quarterly* 34, no. 2 (January 10, 1976).

102. A 1969 reform reduced the allowance from 27.5 percent to 22 percent.

103. The conservatives included Waggoner, Landrum, Omar Burleson (TX), Jones, Jake Pickle, and the former chairman, Mills.

104. *Congressional Quarterly* 33, no. 9 (March 1, 1975): 419.

105. *Congressional Quarterly* 34 (January 17, 1976): 100.

106. John Jacobs, *Rage for Justice*, 273. Not surprisingly, Sen. Russell Long of Louisiana, chairman of the tax-writing Finance Committee and a reliable supporter of his home state energy industry, removed the House provision from the Senate tax bill.

107. Interview with Bob Krueger.

108. Krueger would run for the seat and lose in 1978.

109. David Rosenbaum, "Startling New Man from Texas," *New York Times*, May 2, 1976.

110. Keith, *Eckhardt*, 274.

111. E-mail from Andrew Maguire, January 15, 2014, John A. Lawrence Papers, Library of Congress, Manuscript Division.

112. *Congressional Quarterly* 33, no. 34 (August 23, 1975).

113. *New York Daily News*, October 30, 1975, 1; Sam Roberts, "Infamous 'Drop Dead' Was Never Said by Ford," *New York Times*, December 28, 2008.

114. 175 Democrats and 38 Republicans voted for the bill. Two New York liberals, Elizabeth Holtzman and Bella Abzug, opposed the bill because it was too restrictive. Holtzman called it an "illusory remedy" after her amendment requiring federal loan guarantees failed on a 101-9 vote in the House. The Treasury ultimately earned $40 million in interest on the bailout.

115. *Beaver County Times*, June 5, 1975.

116. E-mail from Les AuCoin, March 11, 2014.

117. "Democrats in Disarray," *New York Times*, June 15, 1975, E-17.

118. Mieczkowski, *Gerald Ford and the Challenges of the 1970s*, 64.

119. *New York Times*, June 15, 1975.

120. Malbin, "Learning Experience for Freshmen."

121. Interview with Rick Nolan.

122. "Freshmen in the House: A Sobering Six Months," *Congressional Quarterly* 33, no. 31 (August 2, 1975): 1674.

123. *Congressional Quarterly* 33, no. 36 (September 6, 1975).

124. "Congress Report: A Year Older and Wiser, Freshmen Reassess Their Role," *National Journal* 8, no. 7 (February 14, 1976).

125. Margins of 404-7 in the House and 87-7 in the Senate for the conference report doubtless persuaded Ford a veto was futile. Virtually all the House freshmen supported the bill.

126. Timothy E. Wirth, "Working for a Responsive and Accountable Congress," *Boulder Daily Camera*, March 14, 1975.

CHAPTER 7. THERMIDOR

1. Tim Wirth, "The First 10 Weeks in Congress," *Colorado Daily*, April 9, 1975.

2. Mary Russell, "House Chiefs, Freshmen Split on Issues," *Washington Post*, January 17, 1976; David S. Broder, "Why Congress Is Floundering," *Washington Post*, August 13, 1975.

3. *Wall Street Journal*, December 26, 1975.

4. Foley, the new Agriculture chairman and former DSG chairman, won the support of the freshmen.

5. For a thorough discussion of the challenges in adjusting committee jurisdiction, see Adler, *Why Congressional Reforms Fail*.

6. "Congress Report: A Year Older and Wiser, Freshmen Reassess Their Role," *National Journal* 8, no. 7 (February 14, 1976).

7. Interview with Tim Wirth.

8. "Congress Report," *National Journal*.

9. Draft of Speech to New Members Caucus, and Transcript, Carl Albert Papers, University of Oklahoma, Box 21 (January 16, 1976).

10. "Aged Aid Rise Approval Seen: Democratic Freshmen Meet with Chairmen," *Washington Post*, January 18, 1976.

11. Mary Russell, "Hill Freshmen Will Discuss '76 Priorities," *Washington Post*, January 16, 1976.

12. Cornell's fellow priest, Robert Drinan, a Massachusetts Jesuit, voted against the Hyde amendment, arguing that government should not be involved in what was a moral and medical decision.

13. "Desegregation and the Public Schools," *New York Times*, September 13, 2013.

14. *Congressional Quarterly* 32 (July 6, 1974). Several of these same liberals had similarly opposed efforts to desegregate housing in the 1960s because of constituent pressures.

15. *Congressional Quarterly* 34, no. 5 (January 31, 1976).

16. National security decision memorandum 64 (June 4, 1970), in Box 6, folder "Panama Canal Treaty Negotiations: April 17, 1976" of the White House Special Files Unit Files, the Gerald R. Ford Presidential Library, http://www.fordlibrary museum.gov/library/document/0010/6283042.pdf.

17. National security decision memorandum 302 (August 18, 1975), White House Special Files Unit Files, Gerald R. Ford Presidential Library.

18. Rosenfeld, "Panama Canal Negotiations." Of course, Alaska had been sold to the United States in 1867, whereas the canal was subject to a lease agreement.

19. Supporters of the Snyder amendment against negotiating away the canal included Krebs, Levitas, Russo, Fithian, Evans, Baucus, D'Amours, Hughes, Ambro, Zeferetti, Neal, Hefner, Mottl, English, and Marilyn Lloyd (TN).

20. Henry Kissinger, National Security Council, Meeting on the Panama Canal, Oval Office (July 23, 1975), located in Box 2, folder: "NSC Meeting, 7/23/1975" of the National Security Adviser's NSC Meeting File, Gerald R. Ford Presidential Library.

21. The vote was 197–203 against accepting the Senate language. No votes included Patterson, Jim Lloyd (CA), Russo, Levitas, Fithian, Evans, Hubbard, Spellman, Blanchard, Hughes, Zeferetti, Neal, Mottl, Risenhoover, English, Derrick, Holland Jenrette, Marilyn Lloyd, and Ambro.

22. Andy Karron, "Hard Days for OSHA," *Harvard Crimson*, April 16, 1976.

23. Among those supporting the small business carve-out were Wirth, Dodd, and Moffett from Connecticut; Carr, Pattison, and Nowak from upstate New York; Florio and Hughes from New Jersey; Sharp, Evans, and Fithian from Indiana; and Krebs, Patterson, and Hannaford from California.

24. Switchers included Hannaford, Dodd, Moffett, Blouin, Florio, Pattison, and Cornell.

25. Viscusi, "Impact of Occupational Safety and Health Regulation," 118.

26. Magnum et al., *Union Resilience in Troubled Times*, 74.

27. *Congressional Quarterly* 34, no. 29 (July 19, 1976).

28. *Congressional Quarterly* 30, no. 32 (August 8, 1975).

29. Nay votes included southerners Krueger, Marilyn Lloyd, Derrick, Hubbard, Holland, and Levitas, as well as Harkin, Krebs, and Pattison.

30. Interview with Larry Pressler.

31. Memorandum from Max Friedersdorf to Jack Marsh, Bob Hartman and Dick Cheney, Gerald Ford Papers (November 21, 1975), Gerald R. Ford Presidential Library; also see subsequent references in http://www.fordlibrarymuseum .gov/library/document/0067/1562867.pdf.

32. "One Labor Bill," *New York Times*, November 22, 1975.

33. *Congressional Quarterly* 33, no. 29 (July 19, 1975): 1532.

34. Interview with Fred Feinstein.

35. Interview with Larry Pressler; Roof, *American Labor, Congress, and the Welfare State, 1935-2010*.

36. "Rep. Burton Held Likely to Seek House Leader's Position," *New York Times*, February 22, 1978.

37. Interviews with Marty Russo and Frank Moore.

38. The discrepancy could be enormous: 4 cents per 1000 cubic feet in the interstate market versus $2 for the same amount within a state.

39. Interview with Bob Krueger. Krueger also referred to the maintenance of controls as "the instant and cowardly way" and asserted that "we are being betrayed" if Congress retained a regulated price.

40. The Senate had passed a natural gas deregulation bill in 1975. Shapiro, *Last Great Senate*, 104.

41. *Congressional Quarterly* 34, no. 6 (February 7, 1976).

42. Keith, *Eckhardt*, 274.

43. The OCS bill would not be signed into law until September 18, 1978, although the House passed a bill as early as July 21, 1976.

44. In January 1976, Congress overrode the FY1976 Labor-HEW bill by a 310–113 margin in the House, including 49 Republicans, and by a 70–24 vote in the Senate.

45. *Congressional Quarterly* 34, no. 40 (October 2, 1976).

46. *Congressional Quarterly* 33, no. 41 (October 11, 1975).

47. *Congressional Quarterly* 34, no. 43 (October 23, 1976).

48. "Conservatives' Success Rate Improved," *Congressional Quarterly* 34, no. 43 (October 23, 1976): 3099. While an improvement, the 58 percent success rate for the Conservative Coalition was still below its pre-1974 low rate of 60 percent.

CHAPTER 8. THE REPUBLICAN REFORMERS

1. Republicans refer to their members as a "conference" rather than the "caucus" terminology used by House Democrats.

2. Smith, *Call to Order*, 34.

3. The 80th Congress (1947-1949) and the 83rd (1953-1955) were controlled by Republicans, the only four years of GOP majorities between 1933 and 1995.

4. Rhodes, *Futile System*, 80.

5. For the role of Republicans in the effort to pass the Civil Rights Act, see Risen, *Bill of the Century*.

6. *Congressional Reform Bill Dies in Rules Committee*, *Congressional Quarterly Almanac*, 1968, 24th ed. (Washington, DC, 1969).

7. Kabaservice, *Rule and Ruin*, 259.

8. This was the second successful effort by House Republicans to purge their leadership. In 1958, after Democrats scored large gains in the off-year election, Republican House members had deposed Minority Leader Joe Martin of Massachusetts, who also had been the only Republican Speaker since 1932.

9. Wolfensberger, *Congress and the People*, 93.

10. Rumsfeld headed the Office of Economic Opportunity.

11. Rhodes, *Futile System*, 81.

12. "Republican Study Group: Right Wing Power," *Congressional Quarterly* 36, no. 26 (June 26, 1976): 1636.

13. "Southern Republicans: Little Hope This Year," *Congressional Quarterly* 34, no. 43 (October 26, 1974): 2959.

14. Frank Starr, "A Fight in the House GOP Caucus," *Chicago Tribune*, December 9, 1974.

15. Dan Balz, "Praise the Lord and Pass the Resolution, *Chicago Tribune*, March 14, 1971.

16. Ibid.

17. The vote was 89–81.

18. Interview with Donald Wolfensberger.

19. Interview with Lou Frey.

20. NCEC press release November 11, 1974, John A. Lawrence Papers, Library of Congress, Manuscript Division.

21. "A Year Older and Wiser, Freshmen Reassess Their Role," *National Journal* 8, no. 7 (February 14, 1976).

22. Interview with Larry Pressler.

23. "The House: New Faces and New Strains," *Time*, November 18, 1974.

24. Interview with Gary Myers.

25. Peter Whoriskey, "Congress Gets Richer as Average American Loses," *Washington Post*, December 26, 2011.

26. Bruce Lambert, "Millicent Fenwick, 82, Dies: Gave Character to Congress," *New York Times*, September 17, 1992. Fenwick served as the model for the Lacey Davenport character in the long-running *Doonesbury* cartoon strip.

27. "House Freshmen Enliven the Capitol Singles Scene," *People*, February 24, 1975.

28. Schapiro, *Millicent Fenwick*, 149.

29. Ibid., 159.

30. Jeffords, *Independent Man*, 131.

31. Alan Clem, "The Case of the Upstart Republican," in Clem, *Making of Congressmen*, 133–135.

32. Interview with Larry Pressler; Clem, *Making of Congressmen*, 149.

33. *Congressional Quarterly* 32, no. 47 (November 23, 1974).

34. *Congressional Quarterly* 33, no. 4 (January 25, 1975): 225.

35. *Time*, June 16, 1962.

36. Interview with Bill Pitts.

37. Malbin, "Congress Report," 1881–1886; Nathanson "Caucus vs. the Barons," 7.

38. Connelly and Pitney, *Congress' Permanent Minority?*, 5.

39. Interview with Matt McHugh.

40. Frances Lee discusses why collaboration runs contrary to political self-interest when the control of Congress is at stake. See *Insecure Majorities*, passim.

41. Ratings of selected Republican reform Class members (May 1976).

	ADA	COPE	CoC	Am Conserv Union
Fenwick	58	55	67	52
Gradison	21	15	86	85
Jeffords	68	50	47	54
Pressler	58	57	53	58
Gary Myers	42	43	76	64

42. Lee, *Insecure Majorities*.

43. Jean White, *Washington Post*, January 29, 1975.

44. Interview with Bill Pitts.

45. Loen was fired by Ford during a White House staff meeting for his behavior toward Pressler.

46. For a thorough discussion of the decreased role of moderates in the Republican Party, see Kabaservice, *Rule and Ruin*.

47. *Congressional Quarterly* 33, no. 29 (July 19, 1975; April 4, 1975): 1342.

48. Daniel Rapoport, "The House Is Troubled," *Washington Post*, June 22, 1975.

49. William Greider and Barry Sussman, "A Difference in Style but Not Ideas: Despite Image, New House Members Remarkably Orthodox," *Washington Post*, June 30, 1975.

50. "Conservatives Organize to Change Congress," *Congressional Quarterly* 34, no. 43 (October 23, 1976): 3027.

51. Clyde Haberman, "Phyllis Schlafly's Lasting Legacy in Defeating the E.R.A.," *New York Times*, September 11, 2016.

52. Zelizer, "This Is Reagan's Party."

53. Pamphlet, Douglas Dibbert Papers (NCEC? September 1975), private collection.

54. "Conservatives Organize to Change Congress," *Congressional Quarterly* 33, no. 43 (October 23, 1976): 3027.

55. Ibid.

56. Ibid. Gerald Ford shared a flippant opinion of his rival. "The simple political fact is that he cannot defeat any candidates the Democrats put up," a press release from Ford's campaign declared. "Reagan's constituency is much too narrow, even within the Republican Party." From his exile in San Clemente, Richard Nixon agreed that Reagan was a "lightweight and not someone to be considered seriously." Zelizer, "This Is Reagan's Party."

57. *Congressional Quarterly* 33, no. 25 (June 12, 1976): 1635.

58. Fenwick unsuccessfully fought against including the provision opposing abortion.

59. Rhodes, *Futile System*, 80.

60. *Congressional Quarterly* 34, no. 19 (May 8, 1976): 1079.

61. *Congressional Quarterly* 34, no. 24 (June 12, 1976): 1634.

62. Lee, *Insecure Majorities*, passim. The Gingrich model was paralleled by the successful "New Direction: Six for '06" platform developed by Democrats in 2006 under the leadership of Rep. Nancy Pelosi (D-CA).

63. David Murray, "GOP in Congress Sets Own Sails for '76," *Pittsburgh Press*, September 29, 1976.

64. *Congressional Quarterly* 34, no. 26 (June 26, 1976): 1637.

65. *Congressional Quarterly* 34, no. 34 (August 21, 1976). *CQ* noted the "enormous leads" Carter held in the South and border states (2247).

66. *Congressional Quarterly Almanac*, 94th Congress, 2nd session, 1976, 32nd ed. (Washington, DC, 1977), 823.

67. "House GOP: Its Survival May Be at Stake," *Congressional Quarterly* 34, no. 26 (June 26, 1976): 1638.

68. Rhodes, *Futile System*, 80; also, regarding the Senate, see Nelson W. Polsby, "Goodbye to the Inner Club," in Polsby, *Congressional Behavior*, 105.

69. Connelly and Pitney, *Congress' Permanent Minority?*, 13.

70. *Congressional Quarterly* 34, no. 25 (June 12, 1976): 1635; Connelly and Pitney, *Congress' Permanent Minority?*, 5.

71. Fenwick ran unsuccessfully in 1982 at the age of 72. She later served as ambassador to the Food and Agriculture Organization of the United Nations, a newly created position located in Rome. Jeffords also ran in 1988, successfully, in Vermont, and switched to the Democratic Party in 2001, turning control over to the Democrats.

72. Steven V. Roberts, "House GOP Freshmen Are Speaking Up on Party Issues," *New York Times*, October 29, 1979; Mary Russell, "Hill Chairmen Return to Meet with Freshmen," *Washington Post*, January 9, 1975. The influx over the next decade of more confrontational freshmen, unwilling to accept the inevitability of minority status grew. By 1993, only 16 of the 176 Republicans in the House had been members prior to 1977.

73. Roberts, "House GOP Freshmen Are Speaking Up on Party Issues."

74. Ibid.

CHAPTER 9. REVOLUTION OR SKIRMISH?

1. See, for example, Remini, *House*, which gives scant mention to any other aspect of the Class's impact on the House. *Congressional Quarterly* mistakenly concluded, "The rigid seniority system was in shambles." "Congress and Government," *Congressional Quarterly Almanac*, 1975, 31st ed. (Washington, DC, 1976), 695–698.

2. Mieczkowski, *Gerald Ford and the Challenges of the 1970s*, 64, 70.

3. Granat, "Class of 1974."

4. *Congressional Quarterly* 34, no. 28 (May 8, 1976): 28.

5. Daniel Rapoport, "The House Is Troubled," *Washington Post*, June 22, 1975.

6. Norman, "1975," 31.

7. David Rosenbaum, "The Framers Would Not Recognize Congress," *New York Times*, May 2, 1976.

8. David Broder, "The Fading Promise of the 94th," *Washington Post*, August 10, 1975.

9. David Broder, "Why Congress Is Floundering," *Washington Post*, August 13, 1975.

10. Ibid.

11. Rapoport, "House Is Troubled."

12. Tom Wicker, "Democrats in Disarray," *New York Times*, June 15, 1975.

13. Mary Russell, "The 'Most Frustrating' Year for Albert," *Washington Post*, October 26, 1975.

14. "They Look After Themselves," *Boulder Daily Camera*, January 29, 1975. Wirth fired back, asserting, "My first duty is to look after the interests of all the people of the District, regardless of politics" and pointed to the "significant procedural reform" already achieved. "Our prime mission is not, as you suggest, to look after ourselves." But sensitive to the criticism, he agreed any pay raise should be done forthrightly and not be hidden, and he pledged to take no pay raise during the recession. *Boulder Daily Camera*, March 14, 1975.

15. Rapoport, "House Is Troubled."

16. Naughton, "Lost Innocence of Congressman AuCoin."

17. *Congressional Quarterly Almanac*, 94th Congress, 2nd Session, 1976, 32nd ed. (Washington, DC, 1976), 3.

18. *Congressional Quarterly* 34, no. 35 (August 30, 1976): 1865.

19. Naughton, "Lost Innocence of Congressman AuCoin."

20. Conlon, "Putting the 94th in Perspective."

21. *Congressional Quarterly* 34, no. 40 (October 2, 1976). Overrides included bills on school nutrition and childcare.

22. Norman, "1975," 31. Of course, having succeeded to the presidency in his unprecedented manner, there were no antecedents for Ford's second year.

23. *Congressional Quarterly* 34, no. 31 (August 2, 1976).

24. Correspondence from William Hughes to John Lawrence, July 17, 2015, John A. Lawrence Papers, Library of Congress, Manuscript Division.

25. E-mail from Andrew Maguire to John Lawrence, July 27, 2015, John A. Lawrence Papers, Library of Congress, Manuscript Division.

26. "Freshmen in the House: A Sobering Six Months," *Congressional Quarterly* 33, no. 31 (August 2, 1975).

27. Loomis and Fishel, "New Members in a Changing Congress," 81–94; Asher, "Learning of Legislative Norms," 499–513.

28. Mary Russell, "Freshman Feel Frustration," *Washington Post*, October 27, 1975.

29. Loomis and Barnett, "Thinking about My Generation." Relaxed rules meant more opportunities for the freshmen to offer such amendments. Between the 91st and the 94th Congresses, the mean number of amendments offered to bills tripled. Between 1955–1956 and 1975–1976, the total number of recorded votes taken on floor amendments rose from 55 to 372. Sinclair, *Legislators, Leaders, and Lawmaking*, 41.

30. *Congressional Quarterly* 34, nos. 35 and 38 (August 28, 1976; September 18, 1976).

31. "After a Year, Rep. Sharp Sees Congress' Big Need as Planning," *Washington Post*, December 26, 1975.

32. "Freshmen in the House," *Congressional Quarterly*, 1676.

33. Naughton, "Lost Innocence of Congressman AuCoin."

34. *Congressional Quarterly* 34 (April 5, 1976): 694; "Freshmen House Democrats: Strong on Unity," *Congressional Quarterly* 34 (January 31, 1976).

35. "Freshmen House Democrats Kept Liberal Voting Record Intact during 1976," *Congressional Quarterly* 34, no. 47 (November 20, 1976). Santini voted with the coalition 51 percent of the time.

36. *Congressional Quarterly* 34, no. 4 (January 24, 1976); *Congressional Quarterly* 34 (April 9, 1976). Among non-freshmen, support for the Conservative Coalition remained the same in 1975 and 1976, at 36 percent (*Congressional Quarterly* 34 [April 9, 1976]). Also see Lublin, *Paradox of Representation*, 69.

37. "The New House Democrats: Loyal And Liberal," *Congressional Quarterly* 33, no. 31 (August 2, 1975): 1678ff.; Interview with John Jenrette.

38. Interview with John Jenrette.

39. *Congressional Quarterly* 33, no. 31 (August 2, 1975).

40. Voting statistics drawn from *Congressional Quarterly* 34, no. 43 (October 23, 1976).

41. "Conservative Coalition," *Congressional Quarterly* 34 (January 24, 1976).

42. The pro/con percentages of these members on Conservative Coalition votes in 1976 were Jim Lloyd 43/58, Russo 34/64, Sharp 42/64, Bedell 35/72, Fithian 44/51, Krueger 62/23, Levitas 67/38, Derrick 64/31, Holland 51/28, Jenrette 70/34. Still, it should be noted that while liberals occasionally voted for issues scored favorably by conservative groups, particularly over spending questions, only a handful of Democrats outside the most conservative districts received ratings above 20 percent from the American Conservative Union and the Chamber of Commerce.

43. *Congressional Quarterly* 34, no. 51 (December 18, 1976): 3364.

44. Quoted in Julian Zelizer, "Learn from the Watergate Babies," *CNN Commentary*, February 10, 2014.

45. The new chairs, in addition to Tom Foley, Mel Price, and Henry Reuss, who replaced those ousted in 1975, and Al Ullman and Frank Thompson, who replaced Mills and Hays, respectively, the new chairs for the 95th Congress included Clement Zablocki (Foreign Affairs), Mo Udall (Interior and Insular Affairs), Ray Roberts (Public Works and Transportation), James Delaney (Rules), and Neal Smith (Small Business).

46. Tim Wirth, Remarks at the "Conference on Corporate Priorities" (November 12, 1975), John A. Lawrence Papers, Library of Congress, Manuscript Division.

47. Clem, *Making of Congressmen*, 184.

48. Interview with Matt McHugh; e-mail from Bill Hughes.

49. "Freshmen in the House," *Congressional Quarterly*.

50. *Congressional Quarterly* 34, no. 31 (August 2, 1976).

51. Ibid., 1676.

52. *Congressional Quarterly* 33, no. 3 (January 18, 1975).

53. Russell, "Freshman Feel Frustration."

54. Ibid.

55. "If he had lied to the Committee," Russo told *Washington Post* reporter Bob Woodward, "I would vote against him, but I don't think he lied." In an explanation to constituents, Russo declared, "I felt there was no evidence . . . to convince me that there was wrongdoing on President Ford's part or that we should

reopen this matter." Details of the conversations among Ford, White House chief of staff Gen. Alexander Haig, and others are in Bob Woodward, "Closing the Chapter on Watergate Wasn't Done Lightly," *Washington Post*, December 28, 2006. Woodward refused to believe Russo was so naïve he had received nothing for the no vote and tried to prove that Russo was close to Ford by producing a White House photo of the two together at a reception. Russo told his chief of staff, "I'm done. Woodward's going to kick my ass and say I made a deal." Russo tells his version of the vote in an op-ed in "Russo Explains Pardon Probe," *Sun Standard* (Chicago), n.d., 1976.

56. Interview with Marty Russo. Years later, encountering Ford while golfing, Russo explained that his vote had prevented an impeachment inquiry and complained that the former president had subsequently campaigned against him. A grateful Ford promised, "I'll never be in your district ever again," and the two became fast friends.

57. Lineberry, Sinclair, Dodd, and Sager, "Case of the Wrangling Professors," 206.

58. Interview with Mike Blouin.

59. *Congressional Quarterly* 32, no. 31 (July 31, 1976). Levitas's plan, a response to Ford's heavy-handed veto, was defeated in the House after being criticized as unconstitutional.

60. Interview with Jerry Patterson.

61. Interview with Andrew Maguire.

62. The appointees were Hughes, Dodd, Russo, Zeferetti, and Miller, who was appointed after Burton complained about the absence of a California Democrat. The OCS bill would not be signed into law until September 18, 1978, although the House passed a bill as early as July 21, 1976.

63. Richard L. Lyons, "Hill Freshmen Seek Strength," *Washington Post*, July 15, 1975.

64. William Greider and Barry Sussman, "A Difference in Style but Not Ideas: Despite Image, New House Members Remarkably Orthodox," *Washington Post*, June 30, 1975.

65. Lyons, "Hill Freshmen Seek Strength."

66. "Six Month Review," *Congressional Quarterly* 33, no. 31 (May 2, 1975): 1677.

67. David E. Rosenbaum, "Two-Year Ford-Congress Struggle Viewed as a Draw by Both Sides," *New York Times*, October 3, 1976.

68. "Freshmen House Democrats Kept Liberal Voting Record Intact during 1976," *Congressional Quarterly* 34, no. 47 (November 20, 1976).

69. Conlon, "Putting the 94th in Perspective."

CHAPTER 10. BEFORE YOU CAN SAVE THE WORLD, SAVE YOUR SEAT

1. "Freshmen Concerned about Re-election," *Congressional Quarterly* 34, no. 31 (August 2, 1976).

2. *Billings Gazette*, March 28, April 2, May 10, 1974.

3. Interview with Don Bonker.

4. Interview with John Gregory, former staff to Rep. Derrick.

5. Mary Russell, "Freshman Class Is Running Scared," *Washington Post*, January 12, 1976.

6. Interview with Marcia Hale.

7. Denny, "Whatever Happened to Toby Moffett."

8. Interview with Dave Evans. Others in the group included Floyd Fithian, Tim Wirth, and Les AuCoin.

9. Fithian to Albert and O'Neill, Carl Albert Papers, University of Oklahoma, Box 5 Correspondence (June 13, 1975).

10. Daniel Rapoport, "The House Is Troubled," *Washington Post*, June 22, 1975.

11. David Broder, "The Fading Promise of the 94th," *Washington Post*, August 10, 1975.

12. Only a few of the freshmen Republicans, including David Emery, Gary Myers, and Charles Grassley, were viewed as potentially vulnerable because of the of the likely Democratic strength in the presidential race in their states.

13. Michel Malbin, "A Learning Experience for Freshmen," *New York Times*, August 24, 1975.

14. Rapoport "House Is Troubled."

15. "Fall Election: House Republican Gains Likely to Be Modest" *Congressional Quarterly* 34, no. 27 (July 3, 1976). Among freshmen seats thought to be potentially at risk were Bedell, Tsongas, Lundine, AuCoin, Moffett, Dodd, and Howe.

16. Christopher Lydon, "Democrats: Big Field of Dark Horses for 1976," *New York Times*, November 10, 1974; *Congressional Quarterly* 34, no. 10 (March 4, 1976): 512.

17. Others in toss-up seats included Meyner, Russo, McHugh, Jim Lloyd, Bob Edgar; and Harkin and Blouin in Iowa; Allan Howe in Utah; and Tim Lee Hall of Illinois.

18. Russell, "Freshman Class Is Running Scared."

19. *Congressional Quarterly* 34 (April 1976).

20. Haley had earlier served eight months in prison after being convicted of involuntary manslaughter. A 1944 fire at the Ringling Brothers, Barnum & Bailey Circus, where Haley served as president, had killed 169 people. Coincidentally, Haley was replaced in Congress by Andy Ireland, who later became a lobbyist for Ringling Brothers. Ireland was elected as a Democrat but switched to the Republican Party in his fifth term, tracking the shift of many southern Democratic seats in the 1980s.

21. Interview with Dave Evans.

22. At Patman's funeral, the long elegy describing his passing ignored his removal as chairman of the Banking Committee the prior year. Stanley, "Death of Wright Patman."

23. In addition, Senate Majority Leader Mike Mansfield of Montana and Republican Leader Hugh Scott of Pennsylvania both stepped down.

24. Ehrenhalt, *United States of Ambition*, 239.

25. "Congress Report: A Year Older and Wiser, Freshmen Reassess Their Role," *National Journal* 8, no. 7 (February 14, 1976). Other freshmen, including Hubbard, Derrick, and Simon, pledged their continued support.

26. Mary Russell, "The 'Most Frustrating' Year for Albert," *Washington Post*, October 26, 1975.

27. Albert, *Little Giant*, 368; Morton Mintz, "The Speaker: Carl Albert to Retire This Year," *Washington Post*, June 6, 1976.

28. Interview with Joel Jankowsky; Interview with Charles Johnson.

29. Waldman, "Majority Party Leadership in the House of Representatives"; Sundquist, *Decline and Resurgence of Congress*, 398.

30. Don Bonker to Carl Albert, Carl Albert Papers, University of Oklahoma, Box 4 Correspondence (June 16, 1975).

31. Naughton, "Lost Innocence of Congressman AuCoin."

32. Interview with Thomas Downey.

33. Parker and Dull, "Weaponization of Congressional Oversight," 50.

34. Interview with Henry Waxman.

35. "Russo Explains Pardon Probe," *Sun Standard* (Chicago), n.d., 1976.

36. "Westlands Investigation," Miller newsletter, March 1978, John A. Lawrence Papers, Library of Congress, Manuscript Division.

37. Interview with Elliott Levitas.

38. Obey, *Raising Hell for Justice*, 124.

39. "Freshmen Concerned about Re-election," *Congressional Quarterly*, 1677.

40. AuCoin was annoyed when two senators added unrelated flood control provisions and the bill was vetoed by President Ford.

41. *Congressional Quarterly Almanac* (1975).

42. Interview with Matt McHugh.

43. Interview with Bob Krueger.

44. Interview with Les AuCoin. He cringingly recalled Tip O'Neill repeatedly referring to "Viet*ma*mese" during one interview; "Freshmen in the House: A Sobering Six Months," *Congressional Quarterly* 33, no. 31 (August 2, 1975).

45. "Congress Report," *National Journal*.

46. Russell, "Freshmen Class Is Running Scared."

47. *Congressional Quarterly* 34, no. 46 (November 13, 1976), 3159; Steven V. Roberts, "The Life of a 'Watergate Baby,'" *New York Times*, May 13, 1986.

48. Roberts, "Life of a 'Watergate Baby.'"

49. Interview with Marty Russo.

50. Interview with Phil Sharp.

51. Interviews with John Gregory and Marcia Hale, former staff to Rep. Butler Derrick.

52. "Freshmen in the House," *Congressional Quarterly*, 1676.

53. Interview with John Jenrette.

54. Interview with Willie Blacklow.

55. Interview with Thomas Downey. When the committee leaders refused to conduct a hearing on the issue, Downey held his own, and more than 50 Class members showed up to support him.

56. Steven Roberts, "Working Profile: The Life of a 'Watergate Baby'; Philip Sharp," *New York Times*, May 23, 1986.

57. Interview with Donald Wolfensberger.

58. Richard Madden, "House Democrats Battle to Keep Seats Won in 1974," *New York Times*, April 4, 1976; "Congress Report," *National Journal*; "Freshmen Concerned about Re-election," *Congressional Quarterly*. William Greider and Myra McPherson, "Casework-District Relations Pay Off: Honk When the Election Is Over; Why the Voters Are Turned Off," *Washington Post*, October 31, 1976.

59. "Freshmen's Frustrations," *Baltimore Sun*, July 15, 1975.

60. Broder, "Fading Promise of the 94th."

61. David Broder, "Why Congress Is Floundering," *Washington Post*, August 13, 1975.

62. Interview with Thomas Downey.

63. E-mail from Andrew Maguire to John Lawrence, July 25, 2015, John A. Lawrence Papers, Library of Congress, Manuscript Division.

64. Granat, "Class of 1974"; Interviews with Andrew Maguire and Mike Blouin.

65. *Congressional Quarterly Almanac*, 94th Congress, 2nd session, 33 (1976): 823.

66. *Congressional Quarterly* 34, no. 52 (December 25, 1976).

67. *Congressional Quarterly* 34, no. 45 (November 6, 1976).

68. *Congressional Quarterly* 34, no. 46 (November 13, 1976): 3160.

69. Interview with Frank Moore. Carter ignored O'Neill's advice and met with the new members.

70. *Congressional Quarterly* 34, no. 36 (September 4, 1976).

71. *New York Times*, April 11, 1992, 24.

72. Wirth, "Diary of a Dropout."

73. Interview with Tom Harkin.

74. Fourteen of the top-ranked 32 were from the 1974 Class. None of them were southerners. Les Francis, "Analysis of Support for the Administration in the House of Representatives," Memo to the President (May 5, 1978), John A. Lawrence Papers, Library of Congress, Manuscript Division.

75. Mary Russell, "New House Democrats Called More Restrained," *Washington Post*, December 2, 1976.

76. Ibid.

77. "Election Issue," *Congressional Quarterly* 34, no. 45 (November 5, 1976).

78. Richard Lyons, "Hill Freshman Being Widely Briefed," *Washington Post*, December 6, 1976.

79. Edward C. Burks, "Toby Moffett: Washington Outsider Settles In," *New York Times*, February 26, 1978.

80. Russell, "New House Democrats Called More Restrained." Among this new Class were many who would later rise to prominent positions within the federal government, including White House chief of staff and CIA director Panetta, Secretary of Agriculture Dan Glickman, Vice Presidents Dan Quayle and Al Gore, Senators Barbara Mikulski, Bill Armstrong, and Paul Trible, Budget Director David Stockman, Democratic whip David Bonior, and Democratic leader Dick Gephardt. Two 1976 freshmen, Gore and Gephardt, became credible presidential aspirants.

81. Lyons, "Hill Freshman Being Widely Briefed."

82. Interview with John Jenrette.

CHAPTER 11. CODA FOR REFORM

1. "DSG Adopts Proposals to Overhaul House Procedures," *Congressional Quarterly* 34, no. 40 (October 2, 1976).

2. *Congressional Quarterly* 34, no. 48 (November 27, 1976).

3. Democratic Organizing Caucus (January 15, 1976), Democratic Caucus Papers, Library of Congress, Manuscript Division. Some favored raising the number to 44. Efforts during the 93rd Congress to raise the number to 40 or even 33 had also failed. Smith, *Call to Order*, 36.

4. Obey noted that the vast majority of the roll call votes were decided by overwhelmingly favorable margins, demonstrating that the roll call was employed as delaying and obstructionist device.

5. Democratic Organizing Caucus (January 15, 1976), 366.

6. Ibid., 359.

7. Noting the competing proposals for a threshold of 20, 33, 44, Tom Downey, sarcastically suggested that the caucus "compute each Member's age and let that be the number of votes that would be required" for a vote on that member's amendments so that younger legislators would need fewer votes to secure a recorded tally.

8. Democratic Organizing Caucus (January 15, 1976), 25.

9. *Congressional Quarterly* 34, no. 11 (March 13, 1976).

10. Ibid.

11. *Congressional Quarterly* 34 (June 4, 1976).

12. Interview with Fred Wertheimer. For some reason, Burton often referred to Foley as "Steven," and he told people that he was careful to keep him "very close to me."

13. John Jacobs, *Rage for Justice*, 244.

14. Review of *House Out of Order*, *Commentary Magazine*, December 1, 1965.

15. Interview with David Cohen.

16. Interview with Don Wolfensberger.

17. Review of *House Out of Order*, *Commentary Magazine*.

18. Obey, *Raising Hell for Justice*, 228. Bolling's books were *House Out of Order* (1965) and *Power in the House* (1968).

19. Obey, *Raising Hell for Justice*, 228. Interviews with Abner Mikva, Tom Harkin, and David Obey; Champagne, *Austin-Boston Connection*.

20. *Congressional Quarterly* 34 June 4, 1976); *Congressional Quarterly* 34 (October 2, 1976).

21. Michael Green, "Phillip Burton: Political Genius," *San Francisco Examiner*, April 11, 2014. Interview with Fred Feinstein.

22. Leary, "Phillip Burton of the Caucus," 38.

23. Interview with Josiah Beeman, Association for Diplomatic Studies and Training Foreign Affairs Oral History Project, Interviewed by Charles Stuart Kennedy, Josiah Beeman Papers, Library of Congress (May 14, 2001), online.

24. Robinson, *You're in Your Mother's Arms*, 237.

25. Michael Harris, "Phillip Burton—a 'Fighting Liberal' Who Usually Won," *San Francisco Chronicle*, April 11, 1984.

26. *Los Angeles Times*, April 11, 1983.

27. Leary, "Phillip Burton of the Caucus," 264.

28. Interview with Bill Brodhead.

29. John Jacobs, *Rage for Justice*, 310.

30. Michael Green, "Phillip Burton: Political Genius," *San Francisco Examiner*, April 11, 2014.

31. Beeman Papers, Library of Congress; Robinson, *You're in Your Mother's Arms*, 258; John Jacobs, *Rage for Justice*, 238; Interview with Abner Mikva.

32. E-mail from Tim Wirth to John Lawrence, June 22, 2017, John A. Lawrence Papers, Library of Congress, Manuscript Division.

33. Sisk, *Congressional Record*, 200. McFall testified before the Ethics Committee but was reprimanded by the House in 1978 for taking an illegal contribution from Park, and he lost his reelection campaign later that year. Coming shortly after Watergate, the Korean bribery scandal established the frame for most future Washington scandals, for which the suffix "-gate" was affixed.

34. Roland Evans and Robert Novak, "The Wright Consequences," *Washington Post*, December 10, 1976.

35. John Jacobs, *Rage for Justice*, 311.

36. Letter from Jim Wright to John Lawrence, September 24, 2014, John A. Lawrence Papers, Library of Congress, Manuscript Division.

37. West, "Wright Stuff."

38. Letter from Jim Wright to John Lawrence (emphasis included by Speaker Wright), John A. Lawrence Papers, Library of Congress, Manuscript Division. Speaker Carl Albert took the reverse position on the two bills, voting *against* the 1957 law but *for* the 1964 act.

39. Ibid.

40. Steven V. Roberts, "The Life of a 'Watergate Baby,'" *New York Times*, May 13, 1986.

41. Champagne, *Austin-Boston Connection*, 224.

42. "House Leadership Race: Wide Open Contest," *Congressional Quarterly* 34, no. 40 (October 2, 1976).

43. John Jacobs, *Rage for Justice*, 310.

44. Letter from Speaker Wright.

45. *Congressional Quarterly* 34, no. 25 (June 12, 1976).

46. *Congressional Quarterly* 33, no. 28 (August 2, 1975).

47. *Congressional Quarterly* 33, no. 28 (August 2, 1975): 1676.

48. E-mail from Ben Palumbo to John Lawrence, May 8, 2015, John A. Lawrence Papers, Library of Congress, Manuscript Division; Interview with Ben Palumbo; "Wright Is Elected House Majority Leader," *Washington Post*, December 1976.

49. Kaufman, *Carter Years*, 360; e-mail from Bill Hughes to John Lawrence, June 19, 2017, John A. Lawrence Papers, Library of Congress, Manuscript Division.

50. Interview with William Cable. Bill Hughes, a moderate, said he voted for Burton despite some reservations; Interview with Bill Hughes; Interview with Ben Palumbo.

51. Champagne, *Austin-Boston Connection*, 226; Interviews with Abner Mikva, Norm Mineta, Bill Brodhead.

52. Interview with Mark Gersh.

53. Evans and Novak, "Wright Consequences."

54. Mary Russell, "Burton's Defeat as Majority Leader Laid to Aggressiveness, Over-Ambition," *Washington Post*, December 8, 1976.

55. "Wright Is Elected House Majority Leader," *Washington Post*.

56. Ibid.

57. "O'Neill Is Speaker: Rep. Wright of Texas Wins Majority Post," *New York Times*, December 7, 1976.

58. "Last of the Red Hot Liberals," *Newsweek*, April 25, 1983.

59. E-mail from Tim Wirth, June 22, 2017.

60. Keith, *Eckhardt*, 248.

61. The whip became an elective position in 1986.

62. Robinson, *You're in Your Mother's Arms*,

63. "Wright Is Elected House Majority Leader," *Washington Post*; Interview with Ben Palumbo.

64. E-mail from Tim Wirth, June 22, 2017.

65. "Rep. Burton Held Likely to Seek House Leader's Position," *New York Times*, February 22, 1978.

66. Democratic Organizing Caucus minutes (December 4, 1978), Democratic Caucus Papers, Library of Congress, Manuscript Division, 43.

67. Smith, *Call to Order*, 45. The irrepressible Bob Bauman called the expanded use of restricted rules that constrained Republican mischief making "the most serious and scandalous blow struck against democratic procedures in the House to date."

68. West, "Wright Stuff"; Evans and Novak, "Wright Consequences."

69. Evans and Novak, "Wright Consequences."

70. Ibid.

71. "Summary of Recommendation of the Commission on Administrative Review" (unpublished manuscript, September 19, 1977), private collection.

72. *Washington Post*, October 11, 1977.

73. The Republican conference supported the reduction in subcommittees, but it was rejected by the majority Democrats whose members stood to lose valued chairmanships. Interestingly, in 1977, the Senate did reduce the number of committees by 23 percent and cut back the number of subcommittees by one-third. This reform, which task force chairman Adlai Stevenson called "incremental idealism," also ensured younger senators appointment to two major committees and an expanded choices of subcommittees.

74. Polsby, *How Congress Evolves*, 133.

75. Democratic Organizing Caucus notes (December 7, 1978), Democratic Caucus Papers, Library of Congress, Manuscript Division, 11.

76. Democratic Organizing Caucus minutes (December 5, 1978), 84.

77. Ibid., 86.

78. Ibid., 62–64.

79. Ibid., 77–79. The chair ruled the amendment passed, but Stratton objected, noting the absence of a quorum of 50 percent of caucus members.

CHAPTER 12. REFORM AND THE RISE OF POLARIZATION

1. John F. Bibby ed., *Congress Off the Record: The Candid Analyses of Seven Members*, AEI Studies 383 (1983): 23–24.

2. Tim Wirth, Speech to the Conference on Corporate Priorities (November 12, 1975), private collection.

3. Rohde, *Parties and Leaders in the Postreform House*, 15.

4. *New York Times*, April 11, 1992; Interview with Tim Wirth.

5. Lee, *Insecure Majorities*, 198.

6. Wirth, "Diary of a Dropout."

7. Daniel Rapoport, "The House Is Troubled," *Washington Post*, June 22, 1975.

8. Mieczkowski, *Gerald Ford and the Challenges of the 1970s*, 64.

9. James Naughton, "Watergate: Effect Five Years Later," *New York Times*, June 16, 1977. Zelizer, *On Capitol Hill*, 263.

10. Naughton, "Watergate."

11. Kristol, "Post Watergate Morality." For a more contemporary discussion of the unintended consequences of transparency mandates, see Cain, *Democracy More or Less*.

12. Naughton, "Watergate." Ironically, Cranston himself would become ensnared in scandal in 1991 for his association with savings and loan executive Charles Keating and was reprimanded by the Senate, ending his long career.

13. *Congressional Quarterly* 34 (January 24, 1976).

14. Bach and Smith, *Managing Uncertainty in the House of Representatives*, 102, 108.

15. Democratic Organizing Caucus (January 13, 1975), Democratic Caucus Papers, Library of Congress, Manuscript Division, 436.

16. Naughton, "Watergate."

17. Wolfensberger, *Congress and the People*, 98.

18. *Congressional Quarterly Weekly* 34, no. 12 (March 20, 1976). "O'Neill reassessed the impact a few years after television coverage began, asserting the only discernible impact among his male colleagues had been their increased tendency to show up on the floor in 'blue shirts, red ties and stickem on their hair.'" Cook, "House Members as Newsmakers," 217.

19. *Congress and Mass Communications*, 104.

20. House Report 94-539 recommended that all legislative and House-Senate conference committees open their hearings to broadcast coverage, among other reforms.

21. Following a major confrontation between Speaker O'Neill and Republicans, whom he accused of misleading viewers, the broadcasting channel C-SPAN in the mid-1980s added a message beneath the coverage of special orders noting that the House had concluded its legislative business for the day.

22. Stephen Frantzich and John Sullivan, *The C-SPAN Revolution* (University of Oklahoma Press, 1996), quoted in Gentzkow, Shapiro, and Taddy, "Measuring Polarization in High-Dimensional Data."

23. *Congressional Quarterly* reported in January 1975 that 184 of 215 Democrats polled, and 91 of 114 Republicans, favored open meetings. "Open Committee

Trend in House and Senate," *Congressional Quarterly* 33 no. 2 (January 11, 1975); *Congressional Quarterly* 34, no. 4 (January 24, 1976).

24. Interview with Bill Brodhead.

25. Interviews with David Obey, Bill Hughes, and Leo Zeferetti.

26. *Congressional Quarterly Almanac*, 94th Congress, 2nd session, 1976, 34th ed. (Washington, DC, 1977).

27. Interview with Donald Wolfensberger.

28. Democratic Organizing Caucus (December 5, 1978).

29. Bach and Smith, *Managing Uncertainty in the House of Representatives*, 89, 135.

30. See Robert Bauman, "Majority Tyranny in the House," in Rousselot and Schulze, *View from the Capitol Dome*; Smith, *Call to Order*, 34.

31. *Congressional Quarterly* 33 (August 2, 1975): 1676.

32. Interview with John LaFalce.

33. Interview with Matt McHugh.

34. Edwards, *Parties versus the People*, 114.

35. Ornstein, "Causes and Consequences of Congressional Change."

36. O'Neill, *Man of the House*, 283; Ehrenhalt, *United States of Ambition*, 239.

37. Ornstein, "Causes and Consequences of Congressional Change."

38. *Congressional Quarterly Almanac*, 95th Congress, 1978, 34th ed. (Washington, DC, 1979).

39. Lawrence Dodd and Bruce Oppenheimer, "The House in Transition: Change and Consolidation," in Dodd and Oppenheimer, *Congress Reconsidered*; quoted in Rohde, *Parties and Leaders in the Postreform House*, 12.

40. Bach and Smith, *Managing Uncertainty in the House of Representatives*, 59.

41. Interview with Bob Carr.

42. John Yang, "In Wake of Watergate, Reformers Charged Hill: But Class of '74 Now Draws Some Fire," *Washington Post*, June 15, 1992; Ted Vaden, "Subcommittee Reforms, *Congressional Quarterly* 33 (January 5, 1975).

43. E-mail from Andrew Maguire (April 25, 2014).

44. Interview with Henry Waxman.

45. *Congressional Quarterly Almanac*, 95th Congress, 1978, 34th ed. (Washington, DC, 1979).

46. Norman Ornstein, "Causes and Consequences of Congressional Change."

47. Yang, "In Wake of Watergate, Reformers Charged Hill"

48. Parker and Dull, "Weaponization of Congressional Oversight," 58.

49. Ibid., 61. Similarly, during periods of unified government, as during the first six years of the George W. Bush administration of the first two years of Barack Obama's term, the pace of oversight slumped noticeably. With the election of Donald Trump in 2016, policy oversight by the Republican Congress dropped significantly compared to the inquiries during Obama's last six years in office, although investigators in both the House and Senate opened examinations early in 2017 of Russian hacking of the presidential election and potential collusion with Russians by Trump campaign officials.

50. Kevin Kosar, "So . . . This Is Nixon's Fault?," *Politico*, October 24, 2015.

51. Ibid.

52. Interview with Bill Pitts.

53. Obey remarks, Symposium, "Order in the House? Conflict, Order and Reform: The 94th and 114th Congresses" (Washington, DC, 2015).

54. See *Congressional Quarterly* coverage of Supreme Court decisions on campaign finance, especially 34, no. 2 (January 10, 20, 1976). The court ruled the congressional appointments to a regulatory agency to violate the separation of powers restrictions in the Constitution.

55. *Congressional Quarterly* 34, no. 16 (April 17, 1976); Anne Groer, "Bob Sikes, a Power in Congress for Decades, Dies," *Florida Sentinel-Bulletin*, September 29, 1994.

56. Bibby, *Congress Off the Record*, 24.

57. Waxman, *Waxman Report*, 223.

58. Interview with Bill Gradison.

59. Interview with Bob Krueger.

60. Interview with Ray LaHood.

61. Interview with Don Bonker.

62. Interview with George Miller.

63. Interviews with Mike Blouin and Jim Free.

64. Interview with John Gregory.

65. Interview with Mark Gersh.

66. Connelly and Pitney, *Congress' Permanent Minority?* The authors echoed the analysis of incoming House Speaker, Newt Gingrich, who had observed that under the GOP leadership he had challenged and would soon replace, "there are more rewards for being a good minority legislator then there are for trying to become a majority legislator" (5).

67. Interviews with John Gregory and Marcia Hale.

68. *Congressional Quarterly* 34 (January 24, 1976).

69. Herman Kahn quoted in "Post-Industrial Politics: A Guide to 1976," *Congressional Quarterly* 33, no. 46 (November 1975): 2475.

70. Smith, *Call to Order*, 15–36; Bach and Smith, *Managing Uncertainty in the House of Representatives*, 102.

71. Interview with Pat Schroeder.

72. Perlstein, "Exclusive."

73. Bibby, *Congress Off the Record*, 29.

74. Bass and DeVries, *Transformation of Southern Politics*, 29; Interview with Bill Pitts.

75. Interview with Marcia Hale.

76. Richard L. Lyons, "Speaker, Activists Confer: Albert Lauds. Suggestions; Tensions Ease," *Washington Post*, June 19, 1975.

77. *Congressional Quarterly* 34, no. 29 (July 19, 1976).

78. Obey, *Raising Hell for Justice*, 229.

79. "Republican Study Group: Right-Wing Power," *Congressional Quarterly* 34 (June 26, 1976): 1636.

80. Connelly and Pitney, *Congress' Permanent Minority?*, 23–29.

81. Interview with Martha Keys.

82. Bibby, *Congress Off the Record*, 29.

83. Chris Sautter, "Newt's Rise Began in Indiana's Bloody 8th," *Howey Politics Indiana*, November 21, 2011, http://howeypolitics.com.

84. This account was corroborated by two participants in the meeting, both of whom asked that their names not be associated with its disclosure.

85. Barry, *Ambition and the Power*, 68; Edwards, *Parties versus the People*, 99.

86. Kabaservice, *Rule and Ruin*, 368.

87. Connelly and Pitney, *Congress' Permanent Minority?*, 81.

88. Interview with Bill Pitts.

89. Interview with Ray LaHood.

90. Susan Baer, "A Man of Ambition, Drive and the Times," Washington Bureau *Baltimore Sun*, November 20, 1994.

91. Ironically, when Pressler did seek a Senate seat in 1978, Dolan and other conservative activists from NCPAC mailed postcards to party activists denouncing his apostasy for aligning with Democrats on key votes and for helping to override Ford's vetoes.

92. Interview with Bill Pitts.

93. Connelly and Pitney, *Congress' Permanent Minority?*,79.

94. Interviews with Tom Harkin, Don Bonker, and Jim Florio; Baer, "Man of Ambition, Drive and the Times." The escalation in the use of epithets preceded Gingrich, however. As early as 1976, Class member Richard Ottinger had castigated Bob Bauman's floor remarks as "racist," leading the Maryland conservative to call the New Yorker a "pipsqueak," remarks later removed from the official House record. *Congressional Quarterly* 34, no. 18 (May 1, 1976); Baer, "Man of Ambition, Drive and the Times."

95. Obey, *Raising Hell for Justice*, 275–276.

96. Adam Iscoe, "Interview: Congressman George Miller," *Daily Californian*, October 23, 2015.

97. Loomis, *New American Politician*, 227.

98. Ehrenhalt, *United States of Ambition*, 224.

99. Interview with Les AuCoin.

CONCLUSION

1. The only chairman not from the Class was Ways and Means' Charlie Rangel (NY), who had ousted a scandal-plagued Democrat in a primary in 1970 and who, ironically, would lose his chairmanship in 2010 after accusations of improper conduct and censorship by the House.

2. "Watergate Babies Take Power," *Congressional Quarterly* 53 (September 2, 1995).

3. Ryan Grim, "Watergate Babies, Now Fully Grown, Dominating Health Care Endgame," *Huffington Post*, March 18, 2010.

4. Loomis and Barnett, "Thinking about My Generation," 501.

5. Only Sen. Charles Grassley (R-IA) remained in continuous service after 2014.

6. Class members who had moved to the Senate included Tim Wirth, Charles Grassley, Paul Simon, Jim Jeffords, Bob Kasten, and Larry Pressler, as well as Harkin and Dodd.

7. Mary Russell, "New House Democrats Called More Restrained, *Washington Post*, December 2, 1976; Interview with Bob Carr.

8. Quoted in John Jacobs, *Rage for Justice*, 258.

9. Edward C. Burks, "New Guard on Capitol Hill: Three Musketeers in Washington," *New York Times*, July 9, 1978.

10. Parker and Dull, "Weaponization of Congressional Oversight," 58; Bach and Smith, *Managing Uncertainty in the House of Representatives*, 13; Sundquist, *Decline and Resurgence of Congress*, 8.

11. Interview with Bill Brodhead.

12. *Congressional Quarterly* 34, no. 36 (September 4, 1976).

13. Interview with Matthew McHugh.

14. "The Old Order Changing in 94th Congress," *Morning Record* (Connecticut), February 5, 1975.

15. William Greider and Barry Sussman, "A Difference in Style but Not Ideas: Despite Image, New House Members Remarkably Orthodox," *Washington Post*, June 30, 1975; Granat, "Class of 1974."

16. See, for example, Bach and Smith, *Managing Uncertainty in the House of Representatives*, 5, 12–13.

17. O'Neill, *Man of the House*, 283.

18. Shapiro, *Last Great Senate*, 17. For an analysis of the counterproductive impacts of congressional reform, see Turley, "How American Politics Went Insane."

19. Interview with Donnald Anderson.

20. See Zelizer, *On Capitol Hill*, 263; Perlstein, *The Invisible Bridge*, passim.

21. Democratic Organizing Caucus (December 5, 1978), Democratic Caucus Papers, Library of Congress, Manuscript Division, 84.

22. Sinclair, *Legislators, Leaders, and Lawmaking*, 48.

23. Parker and Dull, "Weaponization of Congressional Oversight."

24. Turley, "How American Politics Went Insane," *Atlantic* (May/June 2016).

25. Quoted in MacNeil and Baker, *American Senate*, 132. Cannon served in the Ford White House and as chief of staff to Senate Majority Leader Howard Baker.

26. See Barbara Sinclair, "Congressional Reform," chapter 35 in Zelizer, *American Congress*, 625.

27. Waxman, *Waxman Report*, 62.

28. Bill Hughes e-mail to John Lawrence, July 15, 2015, John A. Lawrence Papers, Library of Congress, Manuscript Division.

29. Poll of voters in Wisconsin by the Peter Hart Organization, quoted in Shapiro, *Last Great Senate*, 302.

30. Interview with Bill Gradison.

31. Shapiro, *Last Great Senate*, 369.

32. Ibid., 366.

33. "Watergate Babies Take Power," *Congressional Quarterly*; Phillips, *Post-conservative America*, 60.

34. Polsby, *How Congress Evolves*, 133, 135.

35. Granat, "Class of 1974," 498–505.

36. "Freshmen's Frustrations," *Baltimore Sun*, July 15, 1975.

37. "Quitting Was Right, Rep. Gary Myers Says," *Washington Observer-Reporter*, November 20, 1978.

38. Kenneth J. Cooper, "Voluntary House Retirements Reach 54 as McHugh Departs," *Washington Post*, May 5, 1992.

39. Interview with Carr; Granat, "Class of 1974."

40. Naughton, "Lost Innocence of Congressman AuCoin."

41. "Freshmen in the House: A Sobering Six Months," *Congressional Quarterly* 33, no. 31 (August 2, 1975).

42. Interview with Elliott Levitas; Loomis and Barnett, "Thinking about My Generation," 507.

43. Naughton, "Lost Innocence of Congressman AuCoin."

44. Edward C. Burks, "Toby Moffett: Washington Outsider Settles In," *New York Times*, February 26, 1978.

45. Democratic Organizing Caucus notes (December 4, 1978), Democratic Caucus Papers, Library of Congress, Manuscript Division.

BIBLIOGRAPHY

E. Scott Adler. *Why Congressional Reforms Fail: Reelection and the House Committee System.* University of Chicago Press, 2002.

Carl Albert. *Little Giant: The Life and Times of Speaker Carl Albert.* University of Oklahoma Press, 1999.

Clio Andris, David Lee, Marcus J. Hamilton, Mauro Martino, Christian E. Gunning, and John Armistead Selden. "The Rise of Partisanship and Super-Cooperators in the U.S. House of Representatives." *PLoS* (April 21, 2015), online.

Herbert B. Asher. "The Learning of Legislative Norms." *American Political Science Review* 67 (June 1973).

Stanley Bach and Steven S. Smith. *Managing Uncertainty in the House of Representatives, Adaptation and Innovation in Special Rules.* Brookings Institution, 1988.

John M. Barry. *The Ambition and the Power: The Fall of Jim Wright; A True Story of Washington.* Viking, 1989.

Jack Bass and Walter De Vries. *The Transformation of Southern Politics: Social Change and Political Consequence since 1945.* University of Georgia Press, 1995.

Thomas E. Behuniak. "The Seizure and Recovery of the S.S. *Mayaguez*: A Legal Analysis of United States Claims." *Military Law Review*, no. 82 (Fall 1978).

Stanley Berard. *Southern Democrats in the U.S. House of Representatives.* University of Oklahoma Press, 2001.

Merle Black and Earle Black. *The Rise of Southern Republicans.* Belknap Press of Harvard University Press, 2003.

Richard Bolling. "Congress and Its Committee System." *Annals of the American Academy of Political and Social Science* 411 (Winter 1974): 1–14.

———. *House Out of Order.* Dutton, 1965.

———. *Power in the House: A History of the Leadership of the House of Representatives.* Dutton, 1968.

———. "What the New Congress Needs Most: Concerning Choice of Chairmanships." *Harper's Magazine*, January 1967.

Hugh Bone. *Party Committees and National Politics.* University of Washington Press, 1958.

Bruce Cain. *Democracy More or Less: America's Political Reform Quandary.* Cambridge University Press, 2015.

James Cannon. *Time and Chance: Gerald Ford's Appointment with History.* University of Michigan Press, 1998.

Anthony Champagne. *The Austin-Boston Connection: Five Decades of House Democratic Leadership.* Texas A&M Press, 2009.

Joseph S. Clark. *Congress: The Sapless Branch.* Harper & Row, 1964.

Thurston Clarke. *Ask Not: The Inauguration of John F. Kennedy and the Speech That Changed America.* Holt, 2004.

Alan L. Clem. *The Making of Congressmen: Seven Campaigns of 1974.* Duxbury Press, 1976.

Andrew Cockburn. *Rumsfeld: His Rise, Fall, and Catastrophic Legacy.* Scribner, 2007.

Congress and Mass Communications: An Institutional Perspective. Joint Committee on Congressional Operations, 1974.

Congressional Research Service for the U.S. Senate Committee on Rules and Administration. *The Evolving Congress.* December 2014.

Richard Conlon. "Putting the 94th in Perspective." *Harvard Political Review,* Winter 1976.

William F. Connelly Jr. and John J. Pitney Jr. *Congress' Permanent Minority? Republicans in the U.S. House.* Rowman and Littlefield, 1994.

Timothy E. Cook. "House Members as Newsmakers: The Effects of Televising Congress." *Legislative Studies Quarterly* 11, no. 2 (May 1986): 203–226.

Tom DeFrank. "Gerald Ford's Pardon of Nixon Doomed His Political Future: But It Cemented His Legacy." *National Journal,* September 7, 2014.

Jeffrey Denny. "Whatever Happened to Toby Moffett?" *Common Cause Magazine* 18, no. 4 (Winter 1992).

Drew DeSilver. "The Polarized Congress of Today Has Its Roots in the 1970s." Pew Research, June 12, 2014.

Lawrence Dodd and Bruce Oppenheimer. *Congress Reconsidered.* CQ Press, 1981.

Mickey Edwards. *The Parties versus the People: Howe to Turn Republicans and Democrats into Americans.* Yale University Press, 2013.

Alan Ehrenhalt. *The United States of Ambition: Politicians, Power, and the Pursuit of Office.* Times Books, 1991.

Richard Fenno. *Congress at the Grassroots: Representational Change in the South, 1970–1998.* University of North Carolina Press, 2000.

James S. Fleming. *Window on Congress: A Congressional Biography of Barber B. Conable Jr.* University of Rochester Press, 2004.

George Galloway. *The Legislative Process in Congress.* Thomas Y. Crowell, 1953.

Matthew Gentzkow, Jesse M. Shapiro, and Matt Taddy. "Measuring Polarization in High-Dimensional Data: Method and Application to Congressional Speech." NBER Working Paper No. 22423. July 2016.

Diane Granat. "The Class of 1974: Whatever Happened to the Watergate Babies?" *Congressional Quarterly,* March 3, 1984, 498–505.

Stephen Haeberle. "The Institutionalization of the Subcommittee in the United States House of Representatives." *Journal of Politics* 40, no. 4 (November, 1978).

Billy Hathorn. "The Changing Politics of Race: Congressman Albert William Watson and the South Carolina Republican Party, 1965–1970." *South Carolina Historical Magazine,* October 1988.

Elizabeth Holtzman. *Who Said It Would Be Easy? One Woman's Life in the Political Arena.* Arcade, 1996.

John Jacobs. *A Rage for Justice: The Passion and Politics of Phillip Burton.* University of California Press, 1997.

Meg Jacobs. *Panic at the Pump: The Energy Crisis and the Transformation of American Politics in the 1970s.* Hill and Wang, 2016.

James M. Jeffords. *An Independent Man: Adventures of a Public Servant.* Simon and Schuster, 2003.

Geoffrey Kabaservice. *Rule and Ruin: The Downfall of Moderation and the Destruction of the Republican Party; From Eisenhower to the Tea Party.* Oxford University Press, 2013.

Burton Ira Kaufman. *The Carter Years.* Infobase, 2009.

Gary Keith. *Eckhardt: There Once Was a Congressman from Texas.* University of Texas Press, 2007.

Alexander Lamis. *The Two-Party South.* Oxford University Press, 1990.

Mary Ellen Leary. "Phillip Burton of the Caucus: 'I Aim to Open Up the System.'" *Nation*, January 18, 1975.

Frances E. Lee. *Insecure Majorities: Congress and the Perpetual Campaign.* University of Chicago Press, 2016.

Robert Lineberry, John Sinclair, Lawrence Dodd, and Alan Sager. "The Case of the Wrangling Professors, the Twenty-First District of Texas." In *The Making of Congressmen: Seven Campaigns of 1974*, ed. Alan L. Clem. Wadsworth Press, 1976.

Burdett Loomis. *New American Politician: Ambition, Entrepreneurship, and the Changing Face of Political Life.* Basic Books, 1988.

Burdett Loomis and Timothy J. Barnett. "Thinking about My Generation: The Impact of Large Congressional Cohorts." *Forum* (2014): 499–517.

Burnett Loomis and Jeff Fishel. "New Members in a Changing Congress." *Congressional Studies* 9 (Spring 1981).

David E. Lowe. "The Bolling Committee and the Politics of Reorganization." *Capitol Studies* 6 (Spring 1978): 39–61.

David Lublin. *The Paradox of Representation: Racial Gerrymandering and Minority Interests in Congress.* Princeton University Press, 1997.

———. *The Republican South: Democratization and Partisan Change.* Princeton University Press, 2004.

Neil MacNeil and Richard A. Baker. *The American Senate: An Insider's History.* Oxford University Press, 2013.

Garth L. Magnum et al. *Union Resilience in Troubled Times: The Story of the Operating Engineers.* Routledge, 1994.

Michael Malbin. "Congress Report: New Democratic Procedures Affect Distribution of Power." *National Journal* 6, no. 50 (December 12, 1974).

Yanek Mieczkowski. *Gerald Ford and the Challenges of the 1970s.* University of Kentucky Press, 2005.

Iric Nathanson. "The Caucus vs. the Barons." *Nation*, January 11, 1975.

James Naughton. "The Lost Innocence of Congressman AuCoin." *New York Times Magazine*, August 31, 1975.

Jane Norman. "1975: Watergate and Vietnam Cast a Pall." *Congressional Quarterly* 73 (September 14, 2015).

David Obey. *Raising Hell for Justice: The Washington Battles of a Heartland Progressive*. University of Wisconsin Press, 2007.

Thomas O'Neill with William Novak. *Man of the House: The Life and Political Memoirs of Speaker Tip O'Neill*. Random House, 1987.

Norman Ornstein. "Causes and Consequences of Congressional Change: Subcommittee Reforms in the House of Representatives 1970–1975." Manuscript in possession of the author; later published in *Congress in Change: Evolution and Reform*, ed. Norman Ornstein. Praeger, 1975.

———. *Congress in Change: Evolution and Reform*. Praeger, 1975.

David C. W. Parker and Matthew Dull. "The Weaponization of Congressional Oversight: The Politics of the Watchful Eye 1947–2010." In *Politics to the Extreme: American Political Institutions in the Twenty-First Century*, ed. Scott Frisch and Sean Kelly. Palgrave, 2013.

Rick Perlstein. "Exclusive: Lee Atwater's Infamous 1981 Interview on the Southern Strategy." *Nation*, November 13, 2012.

———. *The Invisible Bridge: The Fall of Nixon and the Rise of Reagan*. Simon and Schuster, 2015.

Kevin Phillips. *Post-Conservative America: People, Politics, and Ideology in a Time of Crisis*. Random House, 1982.

Nelson W. Polsby, ed. *Congressional Behavior*. Random House, 1971.

———. *How Congress Evolves: Social Bases of Institutional Change*. Oxford University Press, 2004.

Larry Ramey and Daniel Haley. *Tackling Giants: The Life Story of Berkley Bedell*. National Foundation of Alternative Medicine, 2005.

Daniel Rapoport. *Inside the House: An Irreverent Guided Tour through the House of Representatives, from the Days of Adam Clayton Powell to Those of Peter Rodino*. Follette, 1975.

Robert V. Remini. *The House: The History of the House of Representatives*. HarperCollins, 2006.

Leo Rennert. "Phillip Burton and the Children's Crusade." *California Journal*, February 1975.

John Rhodes. *The Futile System: How to Unchain Congress and Make the System Work Again*. EPM, 1976.

Don Riegle. *O Congress*. Doubleday, 1972.

Clay Risen. *The Bill of the Century: The Epic Battle for the Civil Rights Act*. Bloomsbury, 2014.

Judith Robinson. *You're in Your Mother's Arms: The Life and Legacy of Congressman Phil Burton*. Self-published, October 1994.

David Rohde. "Committee Reform in the House of Representatives and the Subcommittee Bill of Rights." *Annals of the American Academy of Political Science* 411 (January 1974).

———. *Parties and Leaders in the Postreform House*. University of Chicago Press, 1991.

Tracy Roof. *American Labor, Congress, and the Welfare State, 1935–2010.* Johns Hopkins University Press, 2011.

Stephen Rosenfeld. "The Panama Canal Negotiations: A Close-Run Thing." *Foreign Affairs* (October 1975).

John Rousselot and Richard Schulze. *View from the Capitol Dome: Looking Right.* Caroline House, 1980.

Amy Schapiro. *Millicent Fenwick: Her Way.* Rutgers University Press, 2003.

Judy Schneider, Christopher David, and Betsy Palmer for the Congressional Research Service. *Reorganization of the House of Representatives.* October 20, 2003.

William Schneider. "JFK's Children: The Class of 1974." *Atlantic*, March 1989.

Wayne Shannon. "Revolt in Washington: The South in Congress." In *The Changing Politics of the South*, ed. William C. Havard. Louisiana State University Press, 1972.

Ira Shapiro. *The Last Great Senate: Courage and Statesmanship in Times of Crisis.* Public Affairs, 2012.

Robert Sherrill. "Breaking Up Big Oil." *New York Times Magazine*, October 3, 1976.

Patricia Schroeder. *24 Years of House Work . . . and the Place Is Still a Mess: My Life in Politics.* Andrews McMeel, 1998.

Barbara Sinclair. *Legislators, Leaders, and Lawmaking: The U.S. House of Representatives in the Postreform Era.* Johns Hopkins University Press, 1998.

Bernie Sisk. *A Congressional Record: The Memoir of Bernie Sisk.* Panorama West, 1980.

Griffin Smith Jr. "Off with Their Heads." *Texas Monthly*, March 1975.

Steven S. Smith. *Call to Order: Floor Politics in the House and Senate.* Brookings Institution, 1989.

Mark Stanley. "The Death of Wright Patman: Mourning the End of an Era." *East Texas Historical Journal* 42, no. 1 (2004).

Arthur G. Stevens Jr., Arthur H. Miller, and Thomas E. Mann. "Mobilization of Liberal Strength in the House, 1955–1970: The Democratic Study Group." *American Political Science Review* 68, no. 2 (June 1974).

Matt Stoller. "How Democrats Killed Their Populist Soul." *Atlantic*, October 2016.

James L. Sundquist. *The Decline and Resurgence of Congress.* Brookings Institution, 2002.

William Tabb. "The Real Ford Strategy." *Nation*, March 22, 1975.

Sam Tanenhaus. "The Power of Congress." *New Yorker*, January 19, 2015, 70.

Jonathan Turley. "How American Politics Went Insane." *Atlantic*, May–June 2016.

United States Association of Former Members of Congress and the University of Maryland College of Behavioral and Social Sciences. *Order in the House? Conflict, Order and Reform: The 94th and 114th Congress.* 2016. Report of a symposium held in the U.S. Capitol on September 17, 2015. http://www.go.umd.edu/orderinthehousedc.

Eric Uslander. "The Decline of Comity in Congress." Paper presented at the Midwest Political Science Association meeting, April 1987.

Eric Uslander and Margaret Conway. "The Responsible Congressional Electorate: Watergate, the Economy and Vote Choice in 1974." *American Political Science Review* 79 (September 1985).

Kirk Victor. "New Kids on the Block." *National Journal*, October 31, 1987, 2626.

W. Kip Viscusi. "The Impact of Occupational Safety and Health Regulation." *Bell Journal of Economics* 10, no. 1 (Spring 1979).

Jerry Voorhis. *Confessions of a Congressman*. Doubleday, 1947.

Sidney Waldman. "Majority Party Leadership in the House of Representatives." *Political Science Quarterly* 95 (Fall 1980): 373–393.

Henry A. Waxman. *The Waxman Report: How Congress Really Works*. Twelve, 2010.

Paul West. "The Wright Stuff." *New Republic*, October 14, 1985.

Timothy E. Wirth. Address to the "Conference on Corporate Priorities." November 12, 1975, unpublished.

———. "Diary of a Dropout." *New York Times Magazine*, August 9, 1992.

Donald Wolfensberger. *Congress and the People: Deliberative Democracy on Trial*. Woodrow Wilson Center Press / Johns Hopkins University Press, 2001.

Julian Zelizer. *The American Congress: The Building of Democracy*. Houghton Mifflin Harcourt, 2004.

———. *The Fierce Urgency of Now: Lyndon Johnson, Congress, and the Battle for the Great Society*. Penguin, 2015.

———. *On Capitol Hill: The Struggle to Reform Congress and Its Consequences, 1948–2000*. Cambridge University Press, 2006.

———. *Taxing America: Wilbur D. Mills, Congress, and the State, 1945–1975*. Cambridge University Press, 1998.

———. "This Is Reagan's Party." *Atlantic*, February 3, 2016.

———. When Liberals Were Organized." *American Prospect*, Winter 2015.

INTERVIEWS

MEMBERS OF THE CLASS OF 1974

Les AuCoin

Berkley Bedell

James Blanchard

Mike Blouin

Don Bonker

Bill Brodhead

Bob Carr

Thomas Downey

Glenn English

Dave Evans

Jim Florio

Bill Goodling

Bill Gradison

Tom Harkin

Carroll Hubbard

Bill Hughes

John Jenrette

Martha Keys

John Krebs

Bob Krueger

John LaFalce

Elliott Levitas

Andrew Maguire

Matt McHugh

Abner Mikva
George Miller
Norm Mineta
Toby Moffett
Gary Myers
Steve Neal
Rick Nolan
Jim Oberstar

Richard Ottinger
Jerry Patterson
Larry Pressler
Marty Russo
Phil Sharp
Henry Waxman
Tim Wirth
Leo Zeferetti

OTHER MEMBERS

John Burton
Lou Frey
Elizabeth Holtzman
Ray LaHood

David Obey
Don Riegle
Patricia Schroeder
Jim Wright

CONGRESSIONAL AND WHITE HOUSE STAFF AND OTHERS

Donnald Anderson
Willie Blacklow
William Cable
David Cohen
Douglas Dibbert
Fred Feinstein
Les Francis
Jim Free
Mark Gersh
John Gregory

Marcia Hale
Joel Jankowsky
Charles Johnson
Frank Moore
Ben Palumbo
Bill Pitts
Donald Skinner
Fred Wertheimer
Don Wolfensberger

INDEX

The term *gallery* indicates an unpaginated figure follows page 146.